Social Policy

Social Policy

A Conceptual and Theoretical Introduction

edited by

Michael Lavalette and Alan Pratt

SAGE Publications
London • Thousand Oaks • New Delhi

computer programs. In this regard, the statistical manuals accompanying various computational software are often as useful as, if not more useful than, those traditional statistics texts.

In terms of selecting proper test procedures for your research questions, measurement level is usually the first consideration. Generally speaking, the X^2 procedure is suitable for testing nominal-nominal or nominal-ordinal associations. Of course, higher level variables can also use this test with appropriate categorization. The F procedure is suited for dealing with associations involving at least one interval variable. As for the ordinal-ordinal association, although Z or t test of the measures of association is recommended, researchers have a tendency to take it to the interval-interval level and use the F test instead. You should prepare a rationale or justification when you follow this practice, however. A general statement is: "...various statistical methods are more or less robust to distortions that could arise from smooth monotone transformations; in other words, there are cases where it makes little difference whether we treat a measurement as ordinal or interval" (Sarle, 1996). This conclusion, however, does not apply to the difference between nominal level and interval level. In SPSS, X^2 is given in the CROSSTABS procedure, along with other forms of test of significance suited at the nominal level. The F test can be found in such procedures as REGRESSION, CORRELATION, and ONEWAY analysis of variance. T-TEST remains a separate and useful procedure although some statisticians do not think this is necessary given the availability of the more general and powerful F procedure. Similar to the F test, the t procedure requires interval level, though group membership is a categorical (nominal) factor. The relationship between a t-test and an F test may be presented as $t^2 = F$, where t has k degrees of freedom while F has k and 1.

The second criterion has to do with the requirement of normal distribution of the variables in the population, although the central limit theorem in statistical theory guarantees a normal sampling distribution for the statistics to be examined in some cases. Basic statistical texts typically do not explain why this is the case. But you should protect yourself from serious violation of such assumptions. Generally speaking, there are two kinds of statistical tests with regard to this requirement. A test with the normality assumption is called a parametric procedure; a test without the normality assumption is called a nonparametric procedure. A parametric test usually requires the interval level, and is considered more powerful or accurate. A nonparametric procedure, on the other hand, is distribution-free and safer to use. The F and t tests are parametric procedures,

First published 1997
Reprinted 1998

 SAGE Publications Ltd
6 Bonhill Street
London EC2A 4PU

SAGE Publications Inc
2455 Teller Road
Thousand Oaks, California 91320

SAGE Publications India Pvt Ltd
32, M-Block Market
Greater Kailash – I
New Delhi 110 048

British Library Cataloguing in Publication data

A catalogue record for this book is available from the British
Library

ISBN 0 8039 7532 5
ISBN 0 8039 7533 3 (pbk)

Library of Congress catalog record available

Typeset by Photoprint, Torquay, Devon
Printed in Great Britain at the University Press, Cambridge

Contents

Contributors

Yasmin Ali, Senior Lecturer in Race and Ethnic Studies, University of Central Lancashire.

Tony Fagan, Lecturer in Social Policy, Edge Hill University College.

Kevin Kearns, Senior Lecturer in Social Policy, University of Central Lancashire.

Michael Lavalette, Lecturer in Social Policy, University of Liverpool.

Phil Lee, Head of Department of Applied Social Sciences, Edge Hill University College.

Andros Loizou, Senior Lecturer in Philosophy, University of Central Lancashire.

Gerry Mooney, Senior Lecturer in Sociology and Social Policy, University of Paisley.

Tony Novak, Lecturer in Social Policy, University of Liverpool.

Laura Penketh, Lecturer in Social Policy, University of Central Lancashire.

Alan Pratt, Principal Lecturer in Social Policy, University of Central Lancashire.

Angelia R. Wilson, Lecturer in Social Policy, University of Manchester.

Mike Wilson, Head of Urban Policy Studies, Edge Hill University College.

Kath Woodward, Staff Tutor in Sociology, Open University.

Acknowledgements

Many people have helped in the preparation of this book, not least the contributors, who have responded with promptness and good grace to our requests to meet deadlines. Our especial thanks to Karen Phillips at Sage, who has been a constant source of good advice and encouragement. And finally thanks to our respective families, who have, as usual, been a tremendous support.

Michael Lavalette
Alan Pratt

May 1996

1

Introduction

Michael Lavalette and Alan Pratt

Most university teachers spend some time at the beginning of first-year undergraduate courses explaining to students something about the nature of the subject(s) they are studying. This usually involves a brief foray into the origins, traditions, methods and scope of the discipline in the hope that students will, at an early stage, acquire some sense of direction, some location in the intellectual universe. For students and teachers of Social Policy this is a particularly difficult problem for a variety of reasons, despite the fact that since the end of the Second World War, Social Policy has become a well-established subject at most British universities. Yet, to follow a degree course in Social Policy is, for most students, something of a shot in the dark. Social Policy does not formally appear on the school curriculum although an increasing number of students will have come across it in one guise or another on some BTEC programmes or on 'access' courses designed to prepare students from 'non-traditional' points of entry for the rigours of higher education. It is also true that issues of Social Policy are covered at schools and colleges in subjects like History, Sociology, Politics and Economics. The consequence is that many, perhaps most, students are to some extent unclear as to what the subject is about. Clearly, students need to know the nature of the beast they are faced with and the skills they will need to develop in order to engage successfully and enjoyably with a demanding and exciting discipline of enormous relevance to their everyday lives as citizens, parents, workers and consumers. The simple aim of this textbook is to outline and introduce what we believe to be the conceptual and analytical tools essential to the consummation of this objective.

In this first chapter we start by trying to define Social Policy as a subject. Then, in the rest of the book, we proceed with a critical exposition of some key theoretical approaches to both of these dimensions of social policy as well as a number of the most important issues currently being debated. Our hope is that by the end of the book, students will be more aware of the contested nature of social policy debates and recognize the need to examine carefully *all* positions and statements on social welfare issues, no matter how painful the experience might be.

What is Social Policy?

Richard Titmuss, who, more than any other academic and teacher, made the subject of Social Policy an accepted and 'respectable' academic discipline, wrote somewhat wearily of 'this tiresome business of defining social policy' (Titmuss, 1974: 28), and it is difficult not to sympathize with him.

One approach would be to follow the example of a multitude of books over the years and quote the opinions of the good and the great of the subject. Indeed, Titmuss himself adopted this policy on a number of occasions and it is a method adopted by David Gil (1973) in his now classic text, *Unravelling Social Policy*. Although Gil's analysis is some 20 years old, it can be argued that it remains one of the most authoritative and rigorous in the entire literature. He devotes considerable time to a review of then existing definitions of social policy as discipline and practice and, in the end, rejects them all as being too limited; even Titmuss himself, though afforded due recognition for his sophistication and breadth, is regarded as being too narrow. For Gil, the major focal concern of social policy is the analysis of access to life-enhancing and life-sustaining resources and, as such, even foreign policy could legitimately be included within its domain. In contrast, Titmuss's observation seems rather narrow: basically,

> we are concerned with the study of a range of social needs and the functioning, in conditions of scarcity, of human organisation, traditionally called social services or social welfare systems, to meet those needs. This complex area of social life lies outside or on the fringes of the so-called free market, the mechanisms of price and tests of profitability. (Titmuss, 1976: 20)

Whatever its shortcomings for Gil, Titmuss's approach takes us to the heart of the matter and, in so doing, raises other problems which are as intractable as the definition of social policy itself and just as relevant. In essence, Titmuss is concerned with the allocation of a limited range of resources to meet a range of social needs. In reality, although there have been variations between countries, these social needs are for health care, housing, education, income maintenance during periods of interruption or cessation of earnings, and that multiplicity of dependencies which in Britain are the concern of the personal social services. The market's role in meeting these needs should, according to Titmuss and the entire intellectual and political tradition he did so much to shape, be minimal. Consumption of these erstwhile commodities is far too important to be left to command over resources in markets. At this point it should be noted that there is no practical reason precluding the allocation of health care and the rest through unfettered private markets. An allocation of these experiences could be secured in this way, and classical liberals in the past together with their neo-liberal counterparts today make exactly this point. The crux is whether such an allocation would be successful in meeting the population's needs.

Once again we are driven into the realm of definition. What constitutes need? Can anyone ever define need objectively? Is there a generally agreed definition of social need or must it be as open-ended as the definitions of

social policy itself? Thus we move from concept to concept, from definitional problem to definitional problem and there is no easy way out, except
perhaps to say, as the classical and neo-liberals do, that the only 'things'
whose allocation falls properly within the realm of public policy, and thus
outside the market, are defence and law and order, the classical functions of
the night-watchman state. Otherwise, when we speak of social problems and
social needs we are merely giving voice to our own particular prejudices,
values and opinions. Such opinions may be more or less well informed and
clearly or ill articulated, but if we move beyond the harsh and rigid logic of
public goods theory we are left with little other than personal preference and
tradition.

The tradition that the allocation of the experiences identified above *is*, in
part at least, the proper responsibility of government is well established
throughout the industrial world, and rather than languish in a fog of relative
values or be directed by the remorseless logic of perfect markets (which
probably don't exist anyway), it might be both productive and sensible to
proceed from this reality and to take it as a 'given' in our analysis. For a
variety of reasons, in a variety of methods, and with varying degrees of
success all countries, to a greater or lesser extent, modify the operation of
market forces in the allocation of health, housing, education, income
maintenance and the personal social services. One of the continuing fascinations of Social Policy as a subject is the way in which debate about the
propriety of state intervention itself and the relative merits of particular
strategies and tactics of intervention has changed and developed over the
years. Significant advances in conceptual and theoretical sophistication have
been made over the last 50 years (many of them covered in this book) as the
subject has grown and matured but the objects of analysis remain much as
Titmuss discussed them almost 30 years ago. Thus:

1   The analysis and description of policy formation and its consequences,
    intended and unintended.
2   The study of structure, function, organisation, planning and administrative
    processes of institutions and agencies, historical and comparative.
3   The study of social needs and of problems of access to, utilisation, and
    patterns of outcome of services, transactions and transfers.
4   The analysis of the nature, attributes and distribution of social costs and
    diswelfares.
5   The analysis of distributive and allocative patterns in command-over-
    resources-through-time and the particular impact of the social services.
6   The study of the roles and functions of elected representatives, professional
    workers, administrators and interest groups in the operation and performance
    of social welfare institutions.
7   The study of the social rights of the citizen as contributor, participant and user
    of social services.
8   The study of the role of government (local and central) as an allocator of
    values and of rights to social property as expressed through social and
    administrative law and other rule-making channels. (Titmuss, 1976: 22–3)

Titmuss was, of course, as aware as anyone of the significance of occupational and fiscal welfare – indeed he pioneered their study (Titmuss, 1962) –

but the long quotation above is limited to the extent that it omits three areas of concern. First, there is no mention of the role of the market. To Titmuss and his colleagues market failure was both an historic fact and an article of faith. He shared with Myrdal (1972) the conviction that the long, post-war progress of the social democratic welfare state was an immutable reality. Although the occasional tactical retreat might be necessary at times of transient political crisis, the strategic conquest of the market was secure. The history of industrial capitalism had demonstrated the market's unsuitability as an allocative agency for those resources essential to the experience of a full and complete life. Any possibility that a return to the market might be seriously advocated was minimal. Organizations like the Institute of Economic Affairs, founded in 1957, which canvassed such ideas were regarded as amusing, marginal irritants with nothing serious or substantial to contribute to the intellectual and political debate.

Second, there is a failure to recognize that social policies can be instruments of social control. Inherent to this Fabian complacency (although specifically rejected by Titmuss) was the idea that social policy would always tend to be beneficial, humanitarian and progressive; that in a world changed forever by the intellectual revolution personified by Keynes and Beveridge discussions about the future of the welfare state would focus on points of administrative and technical detail rather than the institutional model of welfare itself. It was left to the theorists of the Marxist left and the neo-liberal right to point out the control and oppression of individuals and families present in relatively undemocratic and unaccountable welfare structures. The Fabian tradition of social administration, organized by and delivered to a relatively powerless population, was always susceptible to charges of paternalism. Authority and power did not rest with the citizen but with the bureaucracy which operated at several removes from those who received education, health care, housing and so on. It also became clear that much of this provision was structured on lines of class, 'race' and gender. The terrain of social policy was an area of contention and struggle. On an altogether different plain, confirmation that social policy could be actually destructive and evil was to be found in the very recent example of Nazi Germany where the torture and murder and mass destruction of millions of Jews, homosexuals, Gypsies, and the physically and mentally impaired was accomplished in the name of a clearly conceptualized and articulated social policy.

Finally, social policies are intimately bound to the societies in which they develop and reflect the priorities of those systems. Social democratic thinkers like Titmuss found this relatively unproblematic as we now lived in welfare societies where meeting the basic needs of the majority was paramount. But for other traditions in social theory this is not the case. For Marxists social policies exist within capitalist socio-economic systems and for neo-liberals within free-market economies. In both these paradigms social policies are inherently problematic, reflecting, on the one hand, the contradictions of class divided societies and, on the other, the futility involved in attempts to control the free play of market forces.

Social Policy or Social Policies?

One of the most useful questions that we can ask of social provision is whether it represents a social policy in the singular or simply a collection of ill-related social programmes. For us, to speak of 'a social policy' implies that a government or political party has a clear vision of what constitutes the good society. Whatever characteristics this good society might possess each of the programmes in the discrete areas of health, education, housing, economics, taxation and so on has to be structured in such a way that they enable the consummation of the overall vision. Without such a vision as an organizing totality there is the probability that social provision will proceed through a series of incremental adjustments. Policy will happen by accident rather than be created through directed, political will. We have already suggested that the Third Reich possessed a social policy, and we can point to periods in British history when a similar sense of clarity and purposiveness has existed. Thus, the 1834 Poor Law Report together with the Poor Law Amendment Act it inspired were designed primarily to create a 'free', national labour market through the implementation of a harsh, deterrent system of poor relief based on the principles of less eligibility and the workhouse test. In this way British industrialization was supposed to proceed unhindered by the sentimentality and relative generosity of the 'Old' Poor Law.

The long break-up of the post-1834 Poor Law was finally and officially concluded by the National Assistance Act in 1948 which in its turn was a manifestation of the liberal, collectivist social policy encapsulated by the Beveridge Report in 1942. Beveridge's initial brief was to examine, and suggest reforms to, the chaotic and complex collection of income maintenance schemes in existence at the beginning of the 1940s. By introducing his three 'Assumptions' of a national health service, a system of children's or family allowances, and full employment he transformed his task into what became the project which created the Keynesian-Beveridgean Welfare State, which in its turn was challenged by the Thatcherite project whose neo-liberal foundations represent an attempt to resurrect the economic and social philosophy of 1834.

From this perspective social policy can be seen as an intensely political project and, as such, an immensely important arena in which competing ideologies can clash. Consequently, politics matter a great deal and political activity is afforded no little significance in the policy-making process in particular and the shaping of social policy in general (Ringen, 1986). In this regard it is important for students to bear in mind as they read this book that the one thing which unites the various contributors is their rejection of the primacy afforded to the market as an institution of resource allocation by the government and, increasingly, by the Labour Party. The authors occupy a

whereas X^2 is a nonparametric test. Nonparametric procedures have gained popularity in social science research where large sample size often compensates for its weakness in statistical power. Parametric procedures also remain widely used since many of them are quite robust (i.e., not very sensitive to the violation of the normality assumption). As a principle, however, you should check the distributions of your variables before you use a parametric procedure. In other words, such assumptions are an integral part of your hypothesis testing. The problem is, this often means looking only at the sample you have. Statistical texts emphasize the necessity of transforming your data if the distribution is nonnormal, though the distribution of your sample and the distribution of the population are obviously not one thing. Here the concern is actually not the sampling distribution but a sample distribution. It is good for you, however, to practice some of the data transformation techniques as most people prefer.

In addition to the two major requirements mentioned above, the F procedure used for comparing group means also requires that the variances of the different groups are equal. The t procedure can deal with unequal variances but gives different sets of results (the F procedure can be used here to compare the variances). At the interval or ratio level, the linearity of the relationship also makes a great difference. F test based on γ is a test of linear association, whereas the same test based on E^2 is a test of general, nonlinear association. Comparing the two quantities will form a diagnostic test of linearity of the association, though it may be easier just to let the computer produce a scatter plot for a visual examination.

When we consider multivariate analysis, the number of variables to be included both as dependent variables and independent variables will be another decisive factor in selecting appropriate testing procedures. We will further discuss this in the following section.

Test of significance has become a predominant concern in quantitative social science research. It is so highly stressed that the examination of the size of the effect, or the magnitude of the parameter or association itself, is often overlooked. We should, however, treat the results of a significance test with care and put both aspects of quantitative research in place. As a matter of fact, test of significance has very limited use because it only deals with the null hypothesis. Inferential statistics may further be handicapped by the complication of the sampling process. Test procedures developed for a simple random sample (SRS) are hard to modify to address all potential practical problems. The adjustment of standard errors seldom gets beyond some simple weighting scheme for

variety of left-of-centre positions and, it should be noted, disagree with one another at least as much as they do with the main thrust of Conservative social policy. Given that one of our major objectives is for students to understand the contested nature of the ideas and concepts dealt with in this book, it is probably an advantage that it is a multi-authored text. Whatever our personal opinions about the merits of the examples of social policy referred to above, that they represent a unified and purposive intent cannot be in much doubt. They enable us to see social policy as a manifestation of political economy in the sense that Hutton uses the term: 'It has economics and the economy at its heart, but attempts to link them to the wider operation of the social and political system' (1995: xi).

Implications for Studying the Subject and the Organization of this Book

From the little that has been said so far about the domain of social policy as activity and practice it will be clear that as students of social policy you are presented with a challenging and exciting task and that you need a variety of intellectual tools and approaches if you are to accomplish that task. As an academic discipline, Social Policy is concerned with the critical analysis of social provision in the public, private, occupational, voluntary and informal sectors; that is, with a comparative, historical and theoretical examination of health care, education, housing, social security, the personal social services and other related activities in what was commonly called the 'welfare state'. As a subject it has clear and close connections of methodology and substance with the other social sciences, although possibly its most distinguishing characteristics are its eclecticism and its normativeness. Social Policy has always been concerned with a wide field of activities and, at its best, it has managed to operate in a distinctively integrative fashion. It has never been as restricted to relatively narrow and discrete boundaries in the way that some other subjects have. Although Social Policy may still lack the variety of theoretical refinements that distinguish cognate subjects such as Economics, Politics and Sociology (a feature not nearly so marked as formerly), this characteristic is balanced by its capacity for selecting, developing and deploying existing theory in the examination of a significant area of human activity, social provision. This is its eclectic strength.

Our belief is that important dimensions of any analysis of social welfare are that it be comparative, historical and theoretical. Each of these dimensions is demanding in itself and together they can only begin to be achieved through the entirety of an undergraduate course. Obviously, even to attempt such a project within the pages of a single introductory volume would be impossible. All we do in mentioning these characteristics is to indicate what we believe to be essential requirements of a sophisticated and comprehensive approach to the subject. This book is simply intended to make a contribution to this end, although it is also fair to suggest that the theoretical perspectives discussed in these pages, as well as the problems and issues of policy they treat, are likely to be relevant to the investigation of Social Policy in any society.

This belief underpins the structure of the present text. The book is divided into three sections: theoretical perspectives; radical critiques; and issues and debates. In the first section we outline competing interpretations of the social world based on the perspectives of social democracy, neo-liberalism and Marxism, and attempt to ascertain where social welfare fits into these broad paradigms. These theoretical traditions cover the political spectrum and emphasize our contention that Social Policy is an inherently political activity where decisions about the extent, nature and form of welfare provision are intimately connected to our political values and judgements regarding what we perceive to be 'right' and what we think it is possible to achieve. At heart these competing perspectives diverge over whether they think we should structure modern societies to meet human needs (Marxism), whether we should free individuals to pursue their own wants through market mechanisms (neo-liberalism), or whether we should try to combine elements of both of the above via the workings of a 'social market' (social democracy). Whatever conclusion we come to, each of these traditions has something important and interesting to say about Social Policy and welfarism and as a result it is important for you to engage with each of them.

In Part 2 we move on to look at some radical critiques of welfare provision. Here we have grouped together a number of perspectives which emphasize the range of inequalities which Social Policy often fails to acknowledge. We start with the feminist critique of welfare (Chapter 5) which looks at the way in which welfare practices and social policies make assumptions about the role of women in society and, both consciously and unconsciously, reinforce women's oppression. We then proceed to analyse the way in which social policies also make assumptions about notions of 'race' and hence act in an institutionally racist way (Chapter 6), and about our sexuality and the institutional discrimination that takes place against gays and lesbians (Chapter 7). The analysis of each of these forms of oppression has grown out of and developed from the political movements for the liberation of women, blacks and lesbians and gays. These political movements are often referred to as the 'New Social Movements' (NSMs) and hence we conclude this section by including a more reflective chapter on NSMs and social welfare where we include a discussion of the political strategies of the NSMs and the implications this has for the developing new NSMs to obtain freedom from oppression for the disabled community, for example. Finally, it is worth emphasizing that in each of these chapters we will address the writings of authors whose main concerns are to raise the women's perspective, the black perspective or the lesbian and gay perspective but who will very often do so in combination with some of the ideas of social democrats or Marxists or neo-liberals which we address in Part 1.

Finally, in Part 3 we move on to look at a number of issues and debates within Social Policy. Again in this section the ideas and debates being discussed build on, refine, apply or take issue with the various perspectives and critiques covered in the first two parts. Here we look at a range of issues which continue to inform debates within the subject (such as what we mean by contested concepts like social justice and citizenship), look at issues traditionally at the core of the subject (such as poverty), discuss the form of welfare provision (universal versus selective provision), and conclude with a review of recent changes of welfare provision in Britain (the development of quasi-markets and alterations to the state's role as the main provider of welfare). There are undoubtedly important issues which have been left out due to restrictions of space, but it is our contention that the debates included here will always have a resonance for students of the subject.

In each chapter, in order to aid reflection and understanding, the authors have included a range of activities for you to carry out. Sometimes these are simply questions which can be answered from the text itself but on other occasions you are asked to carry out tasks of a more practical nature drawing on experience and practice in the outside world. We offer this book in the belief that the sooner you begin to engage with theoretical debate, the more profound will be your understanding and the more enjoyable and successful will be your endeavours.

Part 1

THEORETICAL PERSPECTIVES

In this first part we introduce the three paradigms which have traditionally structured discourse in the social sciences in general and social welfare studies in particular: social democracy, neo-liberalism and Marxism. These traditions all focus primarily on the broad and general features of social life and attempt to provide holistic interpretations of the social world and historical developments based on the utilization of universally applicable categorizations (such as concepts like equality, justice, freedom and class). As such they are not primarily concerned with the specifics of social policy or developments in welfare provision but, nevertheless, each includes social welfare (its cause, developments and consequences) within its remit.

In Chapter 2 Kevin Kearns explores the social democratic tradition of theorizing state welfare. The chapter begins with a brief introduction to some of the problems associated with attempts at 'theorizing' collective social provision and then moves on to an account of the ways in which social democratic theorists 'make sense' of the historical emergence and the contemporary role of the welfare state. The emphasis of the chapter is on the significance of 'social democracy' as a theory with both analytical plausibility and persuasive normative claims. It concludes with the suggestion that, after a period in the wilderness, social democracy may well be a re-emerging force in contemporary debates about the role of the state as an organizer and provider of welfare services.

In Chapter 3 Alan Pratt examines those aspects of neo-liberal theory which have made such an important contribution to the explanatory power of New Right ideology in general. After a discussion of the behavioural assumptions on which neo-liberal theory is predicated, he focuses on the claims of the free market as an allocative institution and the nature of politics in a mass democracy, and goes on to consider those characteristics which provide much of the clarity and edge of the entire perspective.

Finally, in Chapter 4 Michael Lavalette introduces Marx and the Marxist critique of welfare. Perhaps more than any other perspective Marxism produces most student apprehension. The concepts, terminology, ideas and language used by Marxists are 'new' to students and sometimes the language used by many academic Marxists is unnecessarily complex. Nevertheless Marxism remains a crucially important tradition

with which students need to engage. Thus the chapter begins by introducing the central concepts used within Marxist writing before proceeding
to outline what Marxists identify as the conflicting and contradictory
roles performed by social policy and welfare in modern capitalist
societies.

2

Social Democratic Perspectives on the Welfare State

Kevin Kearns

In common with the other contributions to this part of the book, the present chapter is concerned to explore one of the major 'perspectives' or 'theories' through which the welfare state can be 'explained' or 'analysed'. As you will have gathered from the Introduction to Part 1 of the book, the very ideas of 'theory', 'explanation' and 'analysis' can themselves create difficulties and you will probably need to bear these in mind in the course of your work on this chapter. On the other hand, you are likely to be on familiar ground with this particular tradition of theory. This may appear surprising, particularly if you consider yourself a total stranger to theorizing about society, let alone theorizing about the welfare state. This familiarity, however, stems from the fact that many of the ideas and concepts at the core of social democratic thinking form the foundations of what might be called our dominant political culture – that is, the ideas, values and beliefs that shape and inform our everyday thinking about politics and society. Thus they are a part of our common experiences and they reflect prevailing assumptions about how society is, and should be, organized. Indeed, for most of us for most of the time they represent sound common sense rather than a 'theory' of state and society. As we shall see, this does not mean that social democracy leaves no room for political disagreement; but it does mean that the tradition itself imposes limits on the range of legitimate controversy. Those positions that go beyond it are invariably labelled 'extreme', 'irrational', 'dangerous' or often all three. It is important to remember, therefore, that the social democratic perspective is one, though only one, of a range of theoretical approaches to understanding state welfare systems. It is also crucial to recall that the very familiarity of its concepts should make us particularly careful to scrutinize its claims; what may appear to be little more than accepted truth should, perhaps, be treated with even greater self-conscious scepticism than ideas that clearly fly in the face of conventional wisdom.

Following this introduction the next section will seek to highlight some central concepts or 'core ideas' of the social democratic perspective, while the following two sections will provide what might usefully be called the 'storyline' of the social democratic account of the emergence of the welfare state in the context of the British historical experience. In the course of this you will be reminded of some of the significant forces and processes associated with the expansion of state welfare. In the section beginning on page 14 the focus will alter from providing an *analytical* account of the emergence of the welfare state from a social democratic perspective, to a consideration of the *normative* case for a social democratic welfare state. In other words, we shall examine the claim that state welfare provision organized on social democratic principles is superior to the alternatives – two of the most important of which are examined in Chapters 3 and 4. The chapter will conclude with a consideration of the continuing relevance of social democratic thought to the issues of state welfare in the late 1990s, followed by a brief conclusion which seeks to draw the themes of the topic together.

Social Democratic Perspectives on State Welfare

The social democratic perspective on state welfare offers us an explanation of the emergence of the modern welfare state and its current role and function that contains at its core a relatively small number of concepts. These, once grasped, unlock much of the apparent complexity of this tradition. These concepts are not unique to social democracy – indeed they are to be found in alternative theoretical approaches – but they are used within this perspective in ways that are significantly different from those of rival theories. It might be helpful to identify at least the most important of these 'core' concepts at this stage of the argument.

The State

In common with all theories of the welfare state the 'state' itself is at the heart of social democratic perspectives. The state, which can be broadly defined as the institutions within which public power is located, and through which public power is exercised, is, to social democratic theorists, a positive force within modern societies and one that has a unique potential for benevolence. This does not mean that social democratic theorists believe that all states are good or that all governments place the best interests of their citizens at the top of the political agenda (such a view would clearly fly in the face of a mass of historical and contemporary evidence of how actual states behave), but it does reveal that within this tradition of thought the state is perceived as potentially positive; capable of enhancing the welfare of all. As you will gather from Chapter 3, this contrasts starkly with the suspicion amounting to hostility with which classical liberal theorists perceive the state, or the view that the state represents the particular interests of the dominant groups within society which is central to Marxist thought (see Chapter 4).

Individual Liberty

Social democratic theory shares with classical liberalism a commitment to individual liberty as that idea has been developed from the seventeenth century onward. Classical liberals and social democrats conceive human beings as possessing certain 'rights' which derive from 'nature' or from 'God' or from a moral preference for treating people as if they possess these 'fundamental rights' even if the origins of the rights are difficult to establish. To the liberal and to the social democrat the ultimate foundation of these rights is located in the unique capacity of human beings to reason and therefore to exercise choice. It follows from this that individuals should be free to think their own thoughts, read what they wish to read, express their views freely without fear, worship as they wish, associate with others for social or political purposes and acquire and dispose of their own property. In the memorable words of a writer who both historically and intellectually stands on the bridge between classical liberalism and social democracy, 'Whatever crushes individuality is despotism, by whatever name it may be called' (Mill, 1972: 121). It is important, if social democracy is to be understood, to acknowledge both its foundations in classical liberal ideas and its continuing relationship to them. We shall return to the theme of the state and the individual a little later.

Democracy

With this final core concept we begin to see a gap emerging between classical liberalism and social democracy. Classical liberal thinkers are in essence 'instrumental democrats', they tolerate the paraphernalia of elections and representative parliaments if – and only if – these appear to offer a surer protection for individual liberty than any of the alternative possible constitutional arrangements. However, this is an entirely pragmatic stance, often recalled in the reminder that some of the world's most tyrannical regimes have secured power through systems of representative democracy and subsequently attempted to legitimize their excesses by claiming to be expressing the will of the people. To classical liberals democracy is very much on trial: its value lasts only as long as its capacity to protect those individual liberties that are central to the liberal credo (see generally Chapter 3). Social democratic theorists, on the other hand, embrace democracy as not simply one form of government, but that form of government which by its nature enhances and 'completes' liberty itself. Thus democracy is no mere instrument for protecting our 'human rights'; it is, in essence, a human right in its own terms, and therefore of equal value with the others.

The starting point for our analysis of social democratic ideas about the welfare state is thus the recognition that it is a *normative* theory which seeks to combine individual liberty and democracy in a purposive and positive state. Social democratic theorists do not believe that an active state need pose a threat to liberty; on the contrary, they subscribe to the view that it is only through the activity of the state that 'liberty' can be extended to the largest possible number of people. However, to return to an earlier point, social democratic theories of state welfare are *analytical* as well as *normative* in that they attempt to explain how the welfare state has emerged historically and reveal its role and purpose in contemporary society. To make sense of this we shall need to look briefly at the historical development of state social welfare in its modern form.

Activity 2.1

- What part do the ideas of 'natural rights' or 'human rights' play in social democratic theory?
- How do social democratic theorists view the potential of the state?

The Emergence and Growth of Welfarism

What might be called the 'storyline' of the modern welfare state can be understood in social democratic terms as the gradual and progressive emergence of a socially reforming state. This reforming impulse was, of course, no mere accident; it arose from a complex set of forces and circumstances, all of which played their part in propelling the state into social provision, and to understand this development the outline at least of these forces and processes needs to be grasped. Important as the changes in what we shall call the material or 'real' world were, there were also developments in the realm of ideas; people began to think differently about issues such as poverty, child labour, urban conditions, unemployment and so on and as a consequence began to demand changes in 'social conditions'. This second point is important for an understanding of social democratic theory; its supporters seek to explain social change not merely in terms of developments within the economy and society but also in the way people think about the society they inhabit and seek to achieve change as a result. Theories that emphasize the role of 'ideas' in history are often referred to as 'idealist' theories. This is not because they are 'visionary' or 'romantic' in their objectives but because they stress the importance of ideas as independent forces that play a part in shaping historical developments.

In the following brief subsections you are invited to look at some of the more significant of these historical forces, processes and ideas.

Industrialization

The development of Britain over the period from the eighteenth century onwards from a predominantly rural and agricultural society to an overwhelmingly urban and industrial one is a transformation of such proportions that it is almost impossible to grasp. Economic and social historians continue to examine and debate the relative influence of factors such as the growth of population; improvements in agricultural productivity; the related phenomena of capital surpluses available for investment; the existence of a liberal political system which emphasized property rights and market mechanisms of exchange – and thus provided the opportunity for profit; a legal system which recognized and enforced contractual obligations but did not burden individuals with heavy responsibilities towards those with whom they may have other social relationships, such as employees, tenants, wives and children and so on. The central point for our present purposes is that the process of industrialization led to profound changes in patterns of social life both within families and within the wider society. It also created living and working conditions particularly in the new urban industrial towns that are often now summed up in the name of Charles Dickens, who exposed them in fiction with perhaps greater effect than that achieved by the reports of official bodies or the royal commissions of the day; few of us are unaware of what is conveyed by the adjective 'Dickensian'. The impact of industrialization on living standards may still be the subject of dispute among economic historians, but there is no doubt that it was accompanied by poverty, squalor, high rates of morbidity, mortality, widespread structural unemployment and a range of other 'social problems' that could not be tackled on anything like an adequate scale by the existing systems of poor relief and voluntary philanthropy.

To social democratic theorists industrialization created the social conditions that required a collective response at the level of society as a whole – that is, through state activity. The forces and processes that provoked this collective response are the subject of the next part of this chapter.

The Expansion of Democracy

In the 96 years between the passing of the Parliamentary Reform Act of 1832 and the Representation of the People Act of 1928 the proportion of the adult population with a vote in parliamentary elections increased from under 2 per cent to almost 100 per cent. Progress over this period was certainly not even; indeed women were excluded until the eighty-sixth year of the period – and even then they were not granted the franchise on the same terms as men; nevertheless, there is some descriptive value in referring to the nineteenth and early twentieth centuries as the 'age of democracy'. In terms of the 'story' of state welfare as seen from the perspective of social democracy this 'democratization of politics' was of profound significance. This was so first of all because it resulted in the growth of mass political parties which had increasingly to seek popular support in order to secure office – that is, electoral competition became the norm; and secondly because it stimulated political debate and political activity among ever-widening sections of society – fuelled by the growth of the popular press. Politicians from the middle of the nineteenth century onwards could no

disproportionate stratified sampling. Descriptive analysis, on the other hand, may greatly enrich the meaning of the results and provide more detailed understanding about the data sets. The results of descriptive analysis are in fact the basis of test of significance. In the case of a relational analysis, what counts is the magnitude of the association between variables (the effect size). A test of significance is also based on the variance of the focal variable for any given allowable error and confidence level when the sample statistic is used to represent the population parameter. However, the test of significance is also affected by sample size. In a sense, an overstatement of the role of the test of significance is nothing but playing up the effect of the sample size.

Finally, it should be stressed that randomization is a prerequisite condition for applying statistical inference. Although you can argue that "nonrandom" does not necessarily mean "nonrepresentative" in a broad sense, it is through randomization that probability laws apply and inferential statistics stands. In research practice, tests of significance are widely used to analyze nonrandom data, and some argue that significance at least points to the presence of a relatively considerable effect. However, why should anyone prefer this approach to the direct calculation of sample statistics including measures of association? The real danger is that it may cover up some serious abuses of the kind of test of significance. Another potential problem is that researchers tend to equate their success with the "passing" of some specific statistical tests. This, in the long run, will have a sad consequence for the social and behavioral sciences as people ignore the implications of those negative results or "failures." Social and personal histories testify that we move forward in large part by trial and error, or by learning from failures as well as successes. But due to the scientific community's preoccupation with the "successful" test results, the interests of individual researchers are all too much driven by the significance levels. Many have to get around the problem of uncertainty by making up those hypotheses that are almost guaranteed for a successful "pass." This, in the worst case, may even lead to the faking of test results. Scientific discovery, however, is filled with and is by nature a challenge to uncertainty. Statistical tests are charged with the tasks of both validation and falsification, while the relationship between the two cannot be understood simply in terms of the passing or failing of a particular test. The integrity of social and behavioral sciences depends heavily on a thorough epistemological understanding of the research process. Only on such a basis would the significance of a "successful" test not be overstated and that of a "failure" not be neglected.

longer achieve office by either privilege or corruption or both; a mass
electorate and the secret ballot meant that they must now seek the support of
large sections of the least advantaged groups within society.

The Emergence of the Working Class

As a consequence of industrialization and parallel to the expansion of
democracy, the nineteenth century witnessed the development of a 'working
class' in Britain. The relative weight of the social forces that stimulated this
development and the nature of the working class that emerged (as well as the
nature of the class structure) remain, like much else in this period, the
subject of controversy among social and economic historians and social
theorists. It is enough for our purpose to note that industrialization, and
urbanization together with a gradual but definite movement towards the
'freeing' of social and political activity from legislative control, stimulated
both the growth of working-class collective activity and the development of
forms of class consciousness. There is considerable historical controversy
regarding the extent to which the new working class was a single, identifiable, self-conscious force; and the degree to which it was structured and
organized; there is little doubt that within it there was rivalry and indeed
conflict and that sections of workers never became part of this 'movement'
in any real sense. What is clear, however, is that this formative period
nurtured a class system which reflected a certain coincidence of interest
between those involved in wage labour and that this had an impact on the
politics and ultimately the state policies of the time. Thus 'working-class'
politics both through trade unions and later the Labour Party became a major
force in the democratic process.

Voluntarism

One of the most striking features of the period we are considering is the
degree to which the initiative in responding to the social conditions of the
time came from what we would now call the voluntary sector. This was the
age of the heroines and heroes of social reform who both campaigned for
changes in the law and who worked to improve the lives of those most
affected by the social consequences of capitalist industrialization. Even for
those of us with little historical knowledge the names of Lord Shaftesbury,
Florence Nightingale and William Wilberforce resonate with the ideas of
charity and good works, as do the names of organizations which remain
active in social welfare today but were founded during this formative period,
such as Barnardos, the Church of England Children's Society, the Peabody
Housing Association and many more. In 1869 an attempt was made to bring
much of this activity under the canopy of a single federal structure known as
the Charity Organisations Society with the aim of ensuring that voluntary
effort was well organized and directed towards the needs of the new

industrial society and to ensure that effort was channelled specifically to supporting those members of the working class most deserving of help.

As important – indeed perhaps even more important for the long-term development of state welfare activity – was the tradition of self-help and working-class organizational welfare which was a growing feature of the period. In contrast to the 'middle-class philanthropy' of the large charities this was typified by a form of mutual insurance of one kind or another by which members of organizations or communities sought mutual support. It ranged from the friendly societies and large-scale trade union funds on the one hand to the street or community burial clubs on the other. Thus the pattern of social welfare within this voluntary tradition was complex and multi-layered – and set the scene from within which state welfare was to emerge and to a considerable degree set the agenda of the debate about the relative role of the state and the voluntary sector – a debate which continues in our own time.

State Welfare

During this formative period, the role of the state as a possible force for ameliorating the harsh consequences of industrialization and rapid social change was minimal. The Poor Law was certainly 'reformed' in 1834 by the Poor Law Amendment Act of that year, but not in a direction that would enhance what we would now consider to be humanitarian values, but rather in favour of a reassertion of the classical liberal notion of a minimal state and the disciplines of the market – particularly the labour market. The concept of 'less eligibility' (namely, that the conditions of those who received state help through the Poor Law must be harsher or 'less eligible' than the poorest of those in the lowest paid work) and the notion of the 'workhouse test' (that is, that living conditions in the public workhouses must be poor enough to discourage all but the most desperate from entering them) were eloquent restatements of a fundamental commitment to restricting the state's role to the very minimum for preventing absolute starvation – and even then in only a restricted set of circumstances. By the middle of the century it was still voluntarism that dominated social provision – the role of the state was both minimal and grudging.

Activity 2.2

- What connections can you see between the emergence of the 'working class' and what is referred to in this section as 'the expansion of democracy'?
- What were the guiding principles of state intervention in welfare under the 1834 Poor Law Amendment Act?

From Minimal State Welfare to the Welfare State

From within the perspective of social democracy the transition from a situation in which the state was a reluctant, indeed grudging, provider of minimal welfare to one in which the state became a welfare state, accepting the primary responsibility for the general well-being of its citizens, is a consequence of the effect of these forces and processes working on each other. Thus social democratic theorists suggest that once the working class began to secure the vote, particularly after the electoral reforms of 1867 which extended the franchise to urban working-class men, it became apparent to politicians that in order to gain office they would need to offer social reform to those whose vote they sought to secure. It is no accident – so this argument goes – that within three years the Education Act of 1870 witnessed the state's most significant step into direct education provision and just over a decade later school attendance was made compulsory. Improvement in the conditions of the towns was advanced by the introduction of public health and housing legislation – aimed in the latter case at dealing with the problems of slum dwellings – and improvements were made in personal health provision by the humanizing of the poor law infirmaries which, in time, led to their transition to local authority hospitals. This process of 'democratization' continued into the present century and reached something of a crescendo with the so called 'Great Liberal Reforms' of the 1906 to 1911 period. These saw the introduction of limited systems of health and unemployment insurance, further extension of education provision, a nascent old-age pension scheme, legislation to protect children and the development of a system of labour exchanges to encourage the more fluid movement of labour and the easing of unemployment. Such developments – it is plausibly suggested – are most convincingly explained in terms of the political rivalry between the Liberal Party, seeking to retain its pre-eminent position as one of the two major political parties in Britain, finding itself compelled to offer reform by a relatively new but expanding Labour Party which had been formed by the trade unions in conjunction with a number of socialist organizations such as the Fabian Society and the Independent Labour Party. This new party threatened to replace the Liberals as the main opposition to the Conservative Party. Thus the Liberals were forced into providing state welfare on an unprecedented scale in an effort to retain their electoral position. In this sense, what we can surely call the beginning of the modern welfare state was secured by 'democratic pressure.'

Much the same analysis is offered to explain the next great tranche of social reform, which occurred in the years around the end of the Second World War. Between 1944 and 1948 the state accepted responsibility for securing high and stable levels of employment; for organizing a comprehensive system of social insurance and social assistance to protect citizens from the risk of poverty; for providing a comprehensive health service free at the point of use allocated on the sole criterion of need; for organizing improved education provision with secondary education for all and improvements in housing provision and in the general standards of social amenity. In the rather dramatic language of the Beveridge Report of 1942 the state was committed to slaying the five giants that stood in the path of social progress, namely, 'want', 'disease', 'ignorance', 'squalor' and 'idleness'. In social democratic theory the reason for these developments is not difficult to find; it was in the demands of the electorate that had just been through the first total war in British history which was fought by people at home as well as by those in the theatres of conflict and during the course of which the nation had shown itself capable of immense effort in order to secure victory over the Axis powers. Those who had made common cause for the war effort now demanded the fruits of their sacrifice which was expressed in growing public demand for social reform and which was transmitted into a landslide Labour victory in the general election of 1945 – despite the popularity of the war hero Churchill who led the Conservatives.

These post-war reforms were significant, however, in another sense. They not only reflected what has come to be seen as something of a high watermark in the history of social democracy in Britain, but they also represent the first systematic attempt to apply the work of social democratic theorists to the solution of social problems. John Maynard Keynes through an analysis of the modern capitalist economy, particularly in his book *The General Theory of Employment, Interest and Money* (1936), had demonstrated that modern governments need not stand by helplessly in the face of economic recession and rising unemployment. Keynes argued that managing the level of demand in the economy by control of the money supply, by manipulation of taxation and by adjusting the level of public expenditure would enable governments to pursue full employment as a policy objective. Beveridge similarly argued that poverty was not an inevitable consequence of the economic cycles associated with industrial capitalism. His ideas for a social insurance scheme which would guarantee protection from poverty for virtually all citizens – which, in his own words, would give them 'freedom from want' – became a legitimate objective for the modern state to undertake.

Debates surrounding the continuing relevance of Keynes and Beveridge to the role of the modern state are still alive and flourishing. It is interesting in this connection to note that within the space of one month in 1996 a national broadsheet newspaper devoted four pages of its review section to an analysis of Keynesian ideas and devoted part of its front page to a photograph of Beveridge together with quotations from his 1942 report, *Social Insurance and Allied Services* (*The Guardian*, 8 May 1996). The central point here is that both Keynes and Beveridge were liberal thinkers; they were both committed to the preservation of liberal capitalism. They both believed that this could only be achieved through the purposive actions of a benign and positive state which could balance the reasonable aspirations of its citizens for economic and social security, while preserving the economic dynamism of market capitalism and the traditional freedoms associated with classical liberalism. It is, perhaps, no exaggeration to claim that Keynes and Beveridge are the central theoreticians of modern social democracy.

The story continues to the present. The continual shifts in the direction and details of social policies in Britain, whether it be the steady expansion of the frontiers of state welfare during the 1950s and 1960s, or the shift to retrenchment followed by attempts at fundamental reconstruction in the 1980s and 1990s, once again reflect the choices made within the democratic political process. Whatever the policy preferences of the individual, it is the will of the people expressed through the channels of representative government that is the ultimate determinant of the overall direction of state welfare. In broad terms we get the welfare state that we want, which may or not for any individual be the welfare state that he or she desires.

This account is, of course, rather schematic in that it ignores the details of the historical events which led to the social reforms identified. Similarly, it is painted with a broad brush and thus neglects important issues such as the degree to which it can be said that within a 'first past the post' system of representation such as that in Britain in which the legislative process is dominated by the executive (government of the day) democracy in any real sense operates. It might also be suggested that the very idea that governments implement the wishes of the electorate is fundamentally to misunderstand the nature of power in liberal democratic societies. It might also be suggested that other factors have at least as much influence on the decisions about welfare made by governments: the need to ensure that the economy is competitive; the desire to ensure that social protest does not reach a point at which the stability of the entire politico-economic system is put at risk; the need to make sure that the governing elites retain their position of power and privilege. It would, of course, be impracticable to explore these and other reservations here. The point to note is that from a social democratic perspective the nature of social provision in any liberal society is to a considerable degree a reflection of the social choices that are made by the electorate through the institutions of representative government.

As we noted in the introduction to this section, social democracy, in common with other social theories, has a *normative* as well as an *analytical* dimension; that is, the social democratic tradition also addresses the moral issues of state welfare and it is to these that we shall turn. Before doing so, however, it is worth remembering that the analytical and the normative may not always be separable. In this instance we shall see that the normative theories and theorists present a view of how we should organize our society in order to achieve the social goals they consider appropriate. These views become part of the political process and thus influence political debate and the ways electoral choices are made by individual voters or the way debates are developed within political parties. Clearly, the relationship between 'ideas' and political activity is complex and difficult to unravel in specific instances.

Activity 2.3

- Identify the major periods of social reform that have occurred during the twentieth century.
- How might a social democratic theorist explain these developments?
- What do you understand by the claim that social democracy is an 'idealist' theory?

Social Democracy, the Normative Theory

Social democracy as a normative theory of social welfare can appear somewhat hard pressed; it is challenged on the one hand by the full-blooded force of Marxism with its compelling analysis of the human condition and its clarion call to transformative change as the only way to assuage the inevitable iniquities of exploitative capitalism (see Chapter 4). It is pressed on the other hand by an assertive classical liberalism which warns in terrifying terms of the risk to fundamental freedoms and consequently to the very essence of our humanity by the growth of a state machine that will reduce us to a new slavery (see Chapter 3). In the competition of ideas social democracy looks pale; from the perspective of both its rivals it appears as at best an insipid compromise with the forces of evil, or at worst a betrayal of fundamental truth – of which each, of course, claims to be custodian. The argument in this final section of the chapter will be that such a characterization is not merely a distortion but a caricature; that social democracy is a distinct tradition, not merely a compromise of the others, and that it retains its vitality and its potential for innovation and creativity to a degree lacking in its rivals.

The New Liberty

As we saw earlier, classical liberal theory places at centre stage the idea of individual liberty; understood as the maximum possible personal choice over one's life and property – a necessary implication of which, it is argued, is minimal interference by others and particularly by the state. Social democratic theorists share this starting point but move on from it to a definition of liberty that is historically more realistic and a good deal more socially relevant. By the final third of the last century thinkers such as T.H. Green were arguing that this classical conception of freedom was too narrow. While writing from within the classical liberal tradition Green recognized that human beings are essentially social and that their rights and liberties do not exist outside society but are derived from within their social relationships. The consequence of this is that there is a collective responsibility to ensure that all members of society have access to the opportunities necessary to exercise their fundamental rights. To T.H. Green the 'common good' (his way of expressing this idea) is not an alternative to individual liberty; it is a necessary pre-condition for it. In short, Green recognized a collective responsibility to secure individual liberty. These ideas, developed in the works of non-Marxist socialists and what might be called liberal reformers, such as Hobhouse and Hobson, were translated into a theory of the state which emphasized its potential as a positive and reforming force capable of extending liberty, not merely restricting it. Ideas of a positive state led on in turn to the idea of positive liberty which contrasted with the negative 'freedom from' conception of classical liberalism. From now on this second concept of liberty, with its emphasis on the need for positive intervention to ensure that citizens were able to exercise freedom, became a major intellectual force in political discourse and justified the calls by the Fabians and others for state intervention in matters of social welfare.

Positive Equality

If social democracy as a normative theory recasts the classical liberal conception of liberty, it also attempts a similar reconstruction of one of the central moral commitments of socialist thought – 'equality'. It is, of course, true that classical liberal theorists were and remain concerned with 'equality', but within that tradition equality is limited to the rather formal 'equalities', such as equality before the law, equal civil and political rights and, perhaps, 'equality of opportunity' in the sense that barriers to personal advancement should be removed – that is, the equal right to become unequal.

Socialist theorists – both Marxist and non-Marxist – condemn this notion of equality as a sham; both in the sense that it is simply a justification for maintaining the *status quo* of power and economic inequality characteristic of capitalism, and because it supports an ideology which deludes the mass of the population into accepting its own exploitation in the belief that everyone has the opportunity to move up the social and economic hierarchy. In essence socialists argue that unless the so-called equalities of liberal theory are underpinned with real equalities of income, wealth, status, power and so on; unless the criteria of distribution move from what people can secure in the market to what they need to be able to live fulfilled lives, then the 'equality' of liberal morality is hollow. The necessary implication of this approach is social change on a transformative scale – in substance, social revolution. Novel mechanisms for the production, distribution and exchange of wealth would need to be created and the ownership of capital would have to be 'socialized' in the sense that it would be placed at the disposal of the community as a whole – through the mechanisms of a state system which reflected a new morality.

Social democratic theorists reject both conceptions of 'equality'. They reject the liberal conception on the socialist grounds that it lacks substance and consequently denies to the majority of individuals the necessary social and economic pre-conditions for the exercise of real liberty and choice. They reject the socialist conception on the liberal grounds that the nature and degree of the collective action that would need to be taken to achieve its goals would create tyranny. Thus 'equality' requires to be recast in a way which will provide a moral basis for liberty while providing a justification for the positive state action needed to secure the concrete conditions that make liberty capable of realization for all.

The work of two social democratic theorists – though both may well have wished to reject the label – captures the essence of this recasting. R.H. Tawney's seminal work *Equality* (1931) was published at the height of the struggle for ideological supremacy in British politics. C.A.R. Crosland's *The Future of Socialism* (1956) appeared at a moment in post-war British history when it seemed that traditional socialist thought had ceased to be relevant to the needs of society and had ceased to find favour with the electorate. It would be impossible to reveal the richness of the contribution that these works have made to the debate about the issues considered in this chapter, or the impact they have had on later thinkers in such a limited space as this text affords; nevertheless, it is important to attempt to grasp something of the core of their approach. The ideas that informed these works remain those that are at the heart of the contemporary social democratic approach to state welfare.

To both Tawney and Crosland 'equality' is itself a desirable social goal towards which the political and social forces of society should legitimately be directed. Equality is desirable both in the sense of civil and political rights as these are understood by classical liberal theorists and in the substantive terms of economic and social rights as they are advocated within socialist thought. Although writing from different philosophical positions – Tawney from within the Christian socialist tradition and Crosland from a secular socialist 'revisionism' which attempted to provide an agenda for Labour Party electoral success in a period during which traditional socialist arguments seemed less appealing – both stressed the requirement that the state should secure through mechanisms of intervention a much greater degree of social and economic equality than could be achieved through the mechanisms of markets. Both writers stressed the moral case for equality based on the common humanity of human beings but they also emphasized the political and economic benefits to a society from policies, especially social policies, underpinned by the concept of equality. Thus they would argue that access to education for all will result in the more effective use of the available talent which is beneficial for society as a whole as well as enhancing the life-chances of the individual; health-care provision distributed on the basis of need not only ensures better health for individuals but also increases the economic efficiency of the community as a whole; a more equal distribution of income not only helps to protect individuals and families from poverty and insecurity but supports the economy by sustaining the level of demand and thus levels of employment.

These, and other thinkers within this tradition, are not arguing for equality in some absolute sense; their case is rather that it is the task of the state to mitigate those gross inequalities that flow from birth, inherited wealth or the accumulated advantage of economic power. These essentially 'unearned' inequalities cannot be justified socially or economically and consequently the state via progressive taxation and redistribution must seek, as the major purpose of public policy, to redress them.

This argument about equality goes further, however; it recognizes that economic inequality necessarily leads to and is reinforced by political inequality. Social democratic theorists supported by the findings of much contemporary social science recognize that the claim made for modern electoral democracy – that is, that political power is equally distributed even if economic power is not (often summed up in the quip that the chairman of ICI like the rest of us has only one vote at elections) is a fallacy. The reality is that inequality is multi-dimensional; it constitutes a pattern of interlocking and self-reinforcing privileges or disabilities, and as a result its effect cannot be significantly reduced by development in one area alone, such as the extension of electoral democracy.

In this section we have suggested that the 'core' ideas of social democracy are 'liberty' and 'equality' and that these are defined within this tradition in particular ways. In the concluding sections the implications of these ideas for current debates about public welfare policy will be pursued.

Activity 2.4

- How would you explain in your own words the ideas that are referred to in this section as the 'new liberty'?
- In what senses do social democratic theorists consider 'equality' to be a necessary condition for liberty? Do you find these arguments convincing?
- In what ways is the distinction drawn in the introduction to this section between 'normative' and 'analytical' theorizing helpful when considering the ideas discussed here?

Social Democracy and the Welfare State in the 1990s

The 'Death' of Social Democracy

It will be apparent from a number of the chapters in this book, but particularly, perhaps, from Chapter 3, that the period from the mid-1970s to the early 1990s was one in which the ideas associated with social democratic theory such as 'positive liberty', 'social and political equality' and 'state intervention' have been in retreat. The social democracy of the post-war era, we were told, stood exposed as a failure; it not only damaged the economy by creating high levels of public expenditure on social welfare with the inevitable consequence of high levels of personal taxation, which in turn destroyed incentives – the engine of successful capitalism – but also generated inflation, thus destroying international competitiveness. It also created a dependency culture among the growing army of those people on social benefits, who therefore became consigned to poverty as a consequence of the very policies that had been developed to alleviate it. In summary, the productive efficiency of the economy was damaged and the moral fibre of the nation largely destroyed by a succession of increasingly expensive and cumulatively disastrous attempts to sustain the economy and use the welfare state as a mechanism of redistribution. This felony was compounded by allowing the democratic processes of the British constitution to be subverted by the development of *corporatist* decision-making bodies such as the National Economic Development Office which placed political power in the hands of industrial pressure groups, particularly the trade unions – who used it to pursue their sectional interests at the expense of the public interest in general. The 'winter of discontent' in 1978/79 is often cited as the nightmare consequence of these developments; the sick lay uncared for, the dead lay unburied and the public infrastructure appeared on the point of collapse. It was only by returning to classical liberalism as the basis of public policy that these seismic faults in the social and political terrain could be corrected. Thus the late 1970s was not seen merely as another period of intense political debate in which the substance of policy was decided but rather as a fundamental turning point in which the nature of the state itself was being redefined. Thus it is important in this context not to see this period simply in terms of party political rivalry between the Labour Party espousing social democracy and state intervention and the Conservatives providing a focus for a return to a classical liberal stance. Though there is some truth in this characterization of the period, it is a gross oversimplification. In reality, the late 1970s witnessed a shift in the political culture that appeared to many commentators to be as profound as that towards the interventionist state described in the section on social democratic perspectives on state welfare (page 14). At the party political level the Conservatives retained within their ranks a strong strand of collectivist sentiment, while the leadership of the Labour Party displayed clear signs of a loss of faith in the party's collectivist heritage – particularly its belief that the economy could be 'managed' in order to secure high and consistent levels of employment. More significantly, however, the sequence of Conservative electoral victories during the late 1980s and early 1990s on platforms that were essentially anti-collectivist seemed to confirm that the social democratic agenda had been defeated in favour of a return to classical liberalism.

The Resurgence of Social Democratic Theorizing

Any attempt to offer a full analysis of social and economic policy in Britain over the last two decades would take us far beyond the confines of this chapter. Nevertheless, few would disagree that within limits attempts have

Causal modeling and multivariate analysis

Scientific research emphasizes the discovery and validation of the interrelationship, especially causal relations, among variables. Social and behavioral science researchers usually have a causal reasoning in mind, although their ability of causation may be very limited. The kind of causal modeling with various kinds of visual aids, such as diagrams and flow charts, provides an effective guide to the conduct of complex research analysis involving more than two variables.

A univariate analysis does not address the question of what facts determine the behavior of a variable. A bivariate analysis enters the field of relation but cannot answer the question of causation. Traditionally scientists have used these kinds of elementary analysis to determine causal relations based on structural means such as the experimental design. More refined techniques are needed, however, to accommodate the advancement in causal modeling, as embodied in the experimental design but even more importantly in a nonexperimental setting. Multivariate analysis, therefore, has become more and more popular in social and behavioral science research.

In real terms, a bivariate relational model is almost surely an oversimplified representation of the reality of social life. As we take into account more variables by a more comprehensive causal modeling, our understanding of the behavior of the variables involved becomes more accurate. The introduction of more variables, or the progression from bivariate analysis to multivariate analysis, involves the very important idea of statistical control. This also gives rise to such concepts as different orders of correlation and different dimensions of a data set constituted by large numbers of variables and cases. This, however, does not mean that the more variables included in a model, the more desirable the design. The criterion is not simply the delicacy of the analytic model either. As always, we need to strike a balance between accuracy and simplicity in analytical modeling. And the key is to find out the most important facts contributing to the distribution of a focal variable or the relationship among a set of such variables via both theoretical and empirical means. In real terms, the goal of multivariate procedures is to reduce the complexity of data while keeping as much as possible of the original information. The use of a bivariate model, which represents the extreme reduction of data, must be guided by the results of multivariate analysis. The problem is, people start learning statistics from univariate and bivariate analyses, and few social science researchers arrive at a mastery of the multivariate procedures. This is as likely to cause the abuse of bivariate analysis as the

been made to implement policy that is reflective of an anti-collectivist political philosophy. This can be seen in industrial relations policy and the deregulation of finance capital; in the successive waves of 'privatizations' of public utilities; in the 'contractualization' in a variety of forms of central areas of public welfare provision; in the restructuring of services such as health and education in an attempt to subject them to the disciplines of the market; and in a stream of social security initiatives aimed at reducing the state's role in pensions provision; in financial support during periods of illness, unemployment, disability or caring responsibilities; and in the systematic movement towards a more 'targeted' approach to social security provision. The ultimate aim of these policies is to hold and even reduce expenditure on social security – the biggest single item of government expenditure.

Without entering the debate about the appropriateness of these policies or the strategies of implementation, it would seem to be the case that they have not been an unqualified success. The average performance of the British economy did not significantly improve during this period; public expenditure continued to rise dramatically, unemployment increased and remained stubbornly high throughout the 1980s and early 1990s (recent reductions largely reflecting the creation of part-time, low-paid 'flexible' working opportunities) and the number of people in poverty – by almost any reasonable measure – is at its highest for over a generation, while inequality of income is wider than at any time since the 1880s.

Important as these measurable indices of failure are, there is clearly less tangible, though none the less significant, evidence of political and social distress. Economic insecurity has spread widely from those at the margins of the labour market to those who until relatively recently felt themselves safe within it. Thus the professionals, the middle managers, the traditional 'white-collar' workers and the skilled craftspeople, in both the 'public' and 'private' sectors, have all felt the blast of change and witnessed their security diminish. Added to this, large numbers – particularly older, younger and unskilled workers – have virtually lost any meaningful link with employment, as the industries or jobs in which they might have expected to secure work have disappeared. This is significant not merely in economic terms but also in terms of the social fabric of society and the self-identity of those affected. As if all this was not enough there is clear evidence that the fear of crime is at an all-time high; family breakdown is at record levels and racist attitudes and behaviour remain a scar on the lives of many individuals and communities. (For a fuller discussion of all this see Hutton, 1995.)

To attempt to lay the blame for these apparent failures entirely at the door of individual governments or to explain them purely as a result of the changes in state direction that occurred from the late 1970s onwards would be a nonsense. Nevertheless, the apparent failure of what appears to many as a sustained attempt to implement classical liberal policies has helped to breathe life into the intellectual tradition of social democratic theory. Consequently, it is probably no exaggeration to claim that this tradition is once again on the march, and that its adherents no longer feel that they have lost the intellectual initiative, and that they therefore need to adopt a defensive posture.

Although something of an oversimplification, it may be helpful to consider the resurgence as consisting of two interrelated strands: the political and what, for want of a better word, we might call the intellectual. This is neither to suggest that politicians lack intellect nor that those who consider these issues outside the framework of party politics are in some way above the heat and dust of 'real world' issues – it is merely a device to identify some useful strands of the debate.

There seems little doubt that in the political arena the mantle of social democracy has been adopted by 'New' Labour. Under the leadership of Tony Blair the party now seems set on establishing itself as the exponent of policies that clearly reflect social democratic credentials. Thus the emphasis on 'fair' taxation, which, by implication, must involve some measure of redistribution, investment in industry and training, and the policy goal of high and sustained levels of employment are clearly social democratic in substance. At a special conference in April 1995 clause IV of the party's 1918 constitution with its commitment to securing 'for workers by hand or by brain the full fruits of their industry and the most equitable distribution thereof that may be possible upon the basis of the common ownership of the means of production distribution and exchange' was replaced with a new clause IV which reflects the social democratic concerns of economic growth, full employment and equality of opportunity within the context of an essentially capitalist society. The following extract from the new clause IV may help to make the point:

1   The Labour Party is a democratic socialist party. It believes that by the strength of our common endeavour, we achieve more than we achieve alone so as to create for each of us the means to realise our true potential and for all of us a community in which power, wealth and opportunity are in the hands of the many not the few, where the rights we enjoy reflect the duties we owe, and where we live together, freely, in a spirit of solidarity, tolerance and respect.

2   To these ends we work for:
    – a dynamic economy serving the public interest, in which the enterprise of the market and the rigour of competition are joined with the forces of partnership and co-operation to produce the wealth the nation needs and the opportunity for all to work and prosper, with a thriving private sector and high quality public services, where those undertakings essential to the common good are either owned by the public or accountable to them.

This event has been hailed by some and condemned by others as the point at which the Labour Party finally abandoned socialism and became a social democratic party.

Further evidence of the political revival of social democracy can be found in the Report of the Commission on Social Justice published in 1994. Although not a Labour Party policy document, much less an election manifesto, it attempts an exposition of a policy stance on key policy areas such as industry and investment, training, taxation and social welfare provision that will inform the leadership of the Labour Party whether in opposition or in government. It may also influence wider political debate as we approach the next century. A single extract from the report may help to convey something of its flavour:

> In the UK today, economic inequality makes us all poorer, out-of-date social attitudes deny too many people the chance to develop their talents. . . . The cure is not easy or quick, but it is available. Our standard of living and quality of life depend on new opportunities to earn, learn, save and own; on the security provided by an intelligent welfare state which is designed to help people manage economic and social change; and on the responsibility we owe each other to build strong families and strong communities. (Commission on Social Justice, 1994: 23–4)

The Labour Party itself has attempted to develop new approaches to the issues surrounding the social democratic agenda. The one that has provoked the most interest and which is often seen as 'Labour's big idea' is that of *stakeholding* or the creation of a 'stakeholding society'. To cynics this may appear little more than a politician's slogan; to politicians it may be a useful shell into which any convenient policy can be poured; but to those who believe that social democracy as a set of principles has a great deal of life left in it, stakeholding offers the most recent attempt to put into operation some of these principles. How this idea should be translated into specific policies remains the stuff of immediate controversy. Thus suggestions range from the idea of worker/shareholders with real influence in the affairs of their company to ambitious visions of direct democracy in the running of local services. The important point to note here is not the differences between rival accounts of how stakeholding might work in practice, but the extent to which the concept of stakeholding represents a new and useful addition to *normative* social democratic theory.

The intellectual strand of the revival is characterized by the work of academics and serious journalists who have sought to analyse the weaknesses as they see them of the policy stances of the last two decades and emphasize the possibilities of a more interventionist role for the state. David Marquand and Will Hutton have been among the most creative writers within this strand. The Report of the independent Commission on Wealth Creation and Social Cohesion in a Free Society, published in 1995, reflects much of this academic work; again, a quotation from its introduction may help reveal something of revived social democratic thinking:

> It is no longer a matter of course that wealth creation and social cohesion can be combined with liberal democratic institutions. Some believe that a sacrifice in freedom – a new kind of authoritarianism – is needed if we want both prosperity and community. . . . We do not share such gloom, nor do we accept the implied polarization of values. Achieving growth, cohesion and liberty at the same time may be difficult; it may even mean squaring the circle which of course cannot be perfectly realized; but we can get close to the aim. (Dahrendorf et al., 1995: ii)

In their differing ways and with important differences of emphasis they – and others – stress that the beliefs which found favour in the 1940s, at the centre of which were the twin assumptions that Keynes's analysis of capitalist economies was essentially correct and that it was possible and necessary for the state to intervene by adjusting the aggregate level of demand to secure 'full' employment, and that the Beveridge/Butler/Bevan model of the welfare state was not only morally desirable but also politically and socially necessary.

It is important not to misunderstand this 'resurgence' of social democratic theory; it is not a simple return to the policies of the 1940s – indeed, if you read for yourself the practical policy recommendations advanced by contemporary writers you will quickly gather that this is no nostalgic yearning for a bygone age. The central point about social democratic theory is that it represents a set of principles, not a specific policy agenda. This agenda changes as society develops but the principles remain.

Activity 2.5

- Why do you think social democracy lost its appeal during the 1970s?
- Why is there a resurgence of the ideas and values of social democracy?
- Why do we attempt to distinguish between the principles of social democracy and its policy agenda?

Conclusion

This has been a high-altitude flight over a complex terrain. Like all such flights, the best one can hope for is a view of the broad contours below; although the mountain tops and the valleys may be clear enough, very little detail of the landscape is visible. However, it may be the case that the ground underneath is of sufficient interest to tempt some of the passengers to take a closer look and even to explore some of the area on foot.

To pursue this analogy just a little further you may find it helpful to take a summary of the flight plan with you so that any ground-level exploration will be a little easier.

1 Social democratic theory is one of a number of attempts to theorize the nature and role of the welfare state. In common with other social theories it attempts to offer abstract models through which we understand the working of the 'real' social world of which we are a part.

2 Social democratic theorists understand the emergence of state welfare over the last two centuries or so in terms of the response of the state to a range of economic, political and social processes – particularly industrialization, democratization and the formation of the class system.

3 Much emphasis is laid within this tradition on the role of voluntary provision and 'self-help'. Much of the initiative for state intervention came from what we now refer to as the voluntary sector.

4   The major social reforms of the twentieth century, particularly those of
    1906–11 and 1944–51, were largely the consequence of growing popular
    demand and the need of those at the apex of the political system to retain
    the support of the electorate.
5   The period from the mid-1970s to the early 1990s was characterized by
    a loss of faith in social democratic approaches to public policy in general
    and social policy in particular. This was a period in which policy was
    directed towards disengaging the state from active social intervention in
    both economy and society.
6   The apparent failure of classical liberalism appears to have led to a
    resurgence of social democracy both within the political system and
    among theorists. These principles are being applied to the new social and
    economic situation of the 1990s.
7   Social democracy remains a live force both in the theory and practice of
    state welfare.

3

Neo-liberalism and Social Policy

Alan Pratt

An earlier chapter has examined the positive contribution of Liberal collectivism to the growth of the British welfare state. The purpose of this chapter is to consider the other major strand in liberal theory, that of possessive individualism, and its part in the rise of that set of ideas and values generally grouped together as the 'New Right'. Thus it is *not* an account of the full range of 'New Right' ideas, and consequently says nothing (except in passing) of neo-conservatism's espousal of monogamous sexual relations and the 'traditional' two-parent family nor of its hostility to abortion, easier divorce laws and same-sex relationships, all of which have found a sympathetic home in the Republican Party in the United States and, to a lesser extent, in the British Conservative Party. (For a discussion of many of these issues, see Chapters 5 and 7.)

Instead, it attempts a synthesis of the economic and political theories, and the behavioural assumptions on which they rest, which have played such an important role in the sustained attack upon institutionalized welfare provision in Britain and the rest of the western industrial world. Although Britain will be the heart of our analysis it must be remembered that the ideas and theories we will be considering have had a resonance even in Sweden, that quintessential social democracy committed to the socialization of consumption.

This analysis is located in the changed economic circumstances of the early 1970s which saw successive western governments fail to maintain the full employment and economic growth which together provided the underpinnings for the construction of post-1945 welfare states. It discusses the key individual components of the whole intellectual system, such as rationality, the supremacy of the market as an allocative mechanism, public choice theory, the public burden theory of welfare, government overload, and the superior morality of individual responsibility and self-reliance over the 'culture of dependency'. After considering the consistency and coherence of these ideas the chapter concludes with an assessment of the extent to which this ideology has succeeded in creating a momentum towards a convergence of welfare systems based on a residualist model of state welfare and a larger role for voluntarism, the private market and occupational welfare.

The Context

> [c]onsensus policies became increasingly inappropriate to Britain's evolving needs. They had to be either reformed or replaced. In the mid-1970s, they were, of course, to be replaced – ironically, by policies which closely resembled the very ones which had been perceived to fail in the 1930s. (Lowe, 1990: 182)

This extract from Lowe's essay on the historiography of the post-war consensus provides us with the basis of our agenda, which is about tracing and explaining the replacement of one intellectual paradigm by another. Although significant, if unplanned, progress had been made in British social provision during the inter-war period, it was chronic, involuntary unemployment that was the dominant problem of economic and social policy. It dwarfed every other aspect of domestic politics and, notwithstanding the work of revisionist historians of the period, unemployment remains as the single most potent image and memory of the age. The then dominant neo-classicism failed to provide any solutions and only slowly did a coherent and rigorous non-Marxist alternative emerge, and even then it took the transforming experience of total war to force even the smallest break in Treasury orthodoxy.

At the heart of social democracy was Keynes's critique of a central assumption of neo-classical economic theory, that full employment was a general case. In *The General Theory of Employment, Interest and Money* (1936), Keynes demonstrated that equilibrium could exist at a less than full employment level of output and, because the system was in equilibrium, unless exogenous intervention occurred chronic, involuntary unemployment would persist. If governments had the desire to reduce unemployment they now, thanks to Keynes, had the tools to do the job. Whatever its equivocations and failings, the 1944 White Paper on employment policy seemed to promise that henceforth public policy would be very different. The commitment it contained to 'a high and stable level of employment' can be seen as the most important single event of the reconstruction of the welfare state achieved by successive governments in the 1940s. Among other things it met the most important of the three 'Assumptions' on which Beveridge executed his plans for social insurance and allied services. (The other two, of course, were the creation of a National Health Service and the introduction of a system of children's or family allowances.)

Just as the 1944 commitment to full employment symbolized the dawn of a new collectivist age with an active, interventionist government at its heart, so the abandonment of full employment, and the economic theories which had contributed to its creation, by Callaghan and Healey after 1976 can be seen as the harbinger of a new–old world, a world shaped and informed by exactly those theories which Keynes had apparently de-throned some 40 years before. In a very real sense the world had come full circle. Hayek, perhaps the twentieth century's most articulate and important classical liberal voice, emerged from relative obscurity and became the single most important intellectual influence on the Conservative government which took office in 1979. Hayek's influence was particularly significant on that government's most creative thinker, Sir Keith Joseph. The ability of ideas by themselves to effect significant changes in the strategic dispositions of public policy is necessarily limited by the objective realities of economic and social structures. Hence Kavanagh's recollection of John Stuart Mill's observation that 'ideas must conspire with circumstances if they are to be successful' (Kavanagh, 1990: 64).

The Collapse of Consensus

That the circumstances alluded to by Kavanagh altered in the 1970s seems unquestionable, and in a relatively short period a paradigm shift occurred. Moreover, there is general agreement about the nature of those changed circumstances. One of the most important achievements of international economic policy after 1945 was the creation of an ordered pattern of relationships between trading nations based primarily on the system of fixed exchange rates that emerged from the Bretton Woods Conference. Co-operative and relatively free trade governed by institutions and structures such as the World Bank and GATT, designed to prevent the competitive devaluations and economic autarky that compounded the depression of the 1930s, was seen as the best hope for humankind. However, this ordered world system could not cope with the instabilities generated by the fiscal demands of American governments engaged in a war in South-east Asia and a domestic war on poverty. The Smithsonian Agreement of December 1971 failed to contain the pressure and in 1973 a new system of floating exchange rates was introduced.

If, to these important institutional arrangements, we add the reality of major technological change, an explosion in commodity prices (especially of oil) and the ending of the long post-war boom, the sudden collapse of the Keynesian system becomes understandable. As a consequence, a crisis in state authority developed throughout the western industrial world and the search began for a 'new' analysis and for policy prescriptions more in tune with this new world order. Britain, as the weakest of the world's major capitalist economies, experienced this crisis probably earlier and more intensely than anywhere else. The failure of the corporatist attempts at modernization in the 1960s meant that 'the existing policy regime was severely discredited by the dramatic worsening of performance on unemployment, inflation, economic growth and the balance of trade' (Gamble, 1987: 192).

Neo-liberal Theory: the Substance

Although there are differences in emphasis and approach reflecting the predilections of individual writers, neo-liberal theory in general offers a coherent and consistent explanation of the way the world works and ought to work. Departures from the ideal can be quickly remedied if the old verities are reasserted and the 'proper' relationships re-established between government and economy, between state and individual, between state and civil society, and between individuals themselves. Drawing especially on economics, politics and philosophy, a powerful theoretical synthesis has been forged, one whose influence in the last 20 years has been immense across the whole range of industrial economies, offering a sense of direction and purpose in a world whose economic foundations have been transformed by revolutionary changes in technology and trading relationships. This section offers a synopsis of these ideas.

Assumptions

Although detailed aspects of neo-liberal theory can be intellectually complex the totality is relatively clear and simple, resting as it does on a very particular set of assumptions about human behaviour and institutions. Of these assumptions the most important are *methodological individualism, rationality*, and the *supremacy of the free market*.

Methodological individualism asserts that 'all phenomena are reducible to individual behaviour; organic entities such as "society" or the "state" are comprehensible only in terms of the activities of their constitutive individuals' (King, 1987: 94). In Margaret Thatcher's memorable phrase, there is no such thing as society. Free individuals go about their business within the general framework of the 'rule of law', knowing wherein their best interests lie, pursuing pleasure rather than pain. Embodied in contractual exchanges these individual pursuits produce a set of collective outcomes, which by themselves are neither good nor bad. They simply are. Others may take a moral position on these outcomes but methodological individualism would suggest that such positions are irrelevant. They belong to another realm.

The individual pursuit of self-interest only makes sense if individuals act rationally. So important is this assumption that without it the whole edifice of neo-liberal thought would be endangered. For, if individuals do not always behave in a rational fashion in all circumstances, what should we conclude about the nature of the outcomes of such behaviour? In this universe rationality is understood as the pursuit of perfectly informed self-interest. Any other kind of behaviour is inconceivable.

The perfect arena in which rational, self-interested, perfectly informed individuals should meet is the market. Markets as institutions are good; perfect markets are perfect. Markets are about exchange, and for neo-liberals exchange relationships are supreme, far outweighing the claims of other kinds of relationship such as political transactions. Although sometimes mistakenly understood as being a synonym for capitalism, markets long predate the capitalist mode of production. They have existed since the first act of trade took place. They make trade possible and are the best institutional setting for the generation of wealth. Given these assumptions we can now move on to a consideration of the major elements of neo-liberal thought.

Economics

The Market   In essence, neo-liberal theory hardly differs from the classical political economy developed by Adam Smith, David Ricado and their disciples in the late eighteenth and early nineteenth centuries. At its heart is a belief that the market is the best institution yet created by human agency for the conduct of economic activity. Individuals bring their preferences to markets and the aggregate weight of consumer preference can compel suppliers of all kinds of commodities to comply with consumers' demands. Failure to comply will guarantee the failure of any company foolish enough to behave in such a way. Given freedom of entry into the market, other potential suppliers are always available who will recognize the fact of consumer sovereignty. These characteristics make markets efficient, sensitive and speedy signalling mechanisms, doing spontaneously that which is impossible for the planning structures of command economies. Modern industrial societies are such vast and complex entities that the idea of government taking responsibility for the myriad decisions necessarily involved in the allocation of resources is foolish. It is beyond the capacity of governments to do what markets do. Hayek (1944) derided the whole concept of government planning, and argued that any and every attempt to replace the market with a system of politically administered decision-making was bound to end in tyranny and disaster. The recent collapse of the economies of the former Soviet bloc, the enormous changes that have taken place in the economy of the People's Republic of China and the retreat of managed economies everywhere all testify to this. Capitalism has triumphed, and free market capitalism in particular.

In markets decision-making is delegated to the lowest possible level, that of the individual consumer and firm, and this decentralization of decision-making not only renders unnecessary the complex and overstaffed public bureaucracies of non-market economies (at a great saving in public expenditure) but also produces outcomes which are autonomous, spontaneous and, because they represent the choices of free, perfectly informed and rational individuals, valid. In markets freedom of choice is guaranteed and respected; not to respect it would result in loss of profit and potential bankruptcy. As Marquand notes, 'in the market-liberal ideal, free men, freely exchanging goods and services without intervention by the state, maximize the general interest by pursuing their own interests' (Marquand, 1987: 66). For neo-liberals the question is not so much what goods be allocated through the market but what goods can the state, and the state alone, provide. It is concerned with the nature of *public goods*. If we can clearly establish the identity of truly public goods then it must follow, given the superiority of the market as an institution for the allocation of resources, that all other goods can, and should, be provided through the market. Although there are differences of emphasis in the work of individual neo-liberal theorists, the general outlines of agreement are clear. Typical of them is Seldon, who

abuse of multivariate analysis. Those who are only used to bivariate procedures should realize the potential problem of overreduction and/or incorrect selection of the focal variable.

Semi-multivariate analysis

Before we deal with the "real" multivariate techniques, let us stay with the bivariate focus while taking into account the role of other variables in an attempt to explicate the idea of statistical control. The situation can be called "semi-multivariate analysis," which in formal statistical terminology is called "elaboration."

The purpose of "elaboration" is to analyze the relationship between two variables (usually a dependent variable and an independent variable) under a controlled situation. The type and degree of statistical control depends on the kind and number of other variables (called control variables) included. Elaboration itself does not indicate whether or not the relationship is causal; it is up to the researcher to give the results appropriate interpretation.

The idea underlying statistical control is that the relationship between two variables measured and tested in a bivariate analysis could be "spurious," or caused by some other variables that are not included in such analysis. This hypothesis can be tested by taking into consideration the other variables that are deemed to be most responsible for the potentially spurious relationship between the two focal variables. When a control variable is made constant in a part of the sample for all the values of the two focal variables, we can examine if the relationship between the two focal variables has to do with the control variable. The logic is that if the said relationship disappears or weakens after controlling for the other variable(s), then the relationship is totally or to a certain degree spurious. If the relationship stays unchanged after controlling for the other variable(s), then it is probably true or nonspurious (note: it is only "probably true" because there may be still other variables that need to be taken into consideration).

For nominal or categorical data, statistical control can be carried out via the partial or sub-table approach. That is, to divide the sample into different groups according to the different values of the control variable. The sub-tables can easily be obtained by using multiple BY's in the CROSSTABS procedure of SPSS: CROSSTABS (dependent variable) BY (independent variable) BY (control variable). More control variables can be introduced by using more BY's. Since

argues that public goods have characteristics that distinguish them from other goods. Public goods are

1   supplied collectively rather than separately to individuals or small groups;
2   provided by general agreement to pay jointly, 'that is, they require voluntary collective arrangements to coerce one another and also individuals who do not want the services at all but who cannot help benefiting from them' (Seldon, 1977: 17);
3   non-rival in the sense that until full capacity is reached they can be used by more and more people at no additional cost;
4   for Seldon though, 'the essential characteristic of public goods is that they cannot be refused to people who refuse to pay, and who would otherwise have a "free" ride if they were not required to pay. Public goods, to be provided at all, cannot therefore be produced in response to individual specification in the market: they must be financed collectively by the method known as taxation' (Seldon, 1977: 18–19).

Given the validity of the criteria advanced by Seldon, is it possible to establish a list of functions which only the state can perform? Through the application of the 'free rider' principle Seldon identifies the commodities and services which can properly be described as public goods. It is not a lengthy list, and comprises defence, a system of law and order, protection against contagious disease, and what he describes as 'a not obvious but important one: the production of knowledge and information' (Seldon, 1977: 19). Street lighting, lighthouses and externality problems such as pollution, together with provision to protect children and the mentally infirm, are sometimes added to extend the list slightly.

The expansion of the state's role to include the provision of services other than true public goods is the hallmark of what has been termed the 'interventionist state' (Hall, 1984). This expansion, which normally includes education, health care, housing, a variety of income maintenance programmes and the personal social services, has led to a very substantial increase in public expenditure's share of national income in all OECD countries in the twentieth century but especially since the end of the Second World War. The implications of this rising trend of expenditure for public finances, and for the efficiency of the market economies within which this expansion has been located, is a particular concern for neo-liberal political economy.

The Problem of Public Expenditure   In 1979 the first public expenditure statement of the incoming Conservative government asserted that 'excessive' public expenditure lay at the root of Britain's economic problems. In this it was no different from its predecessor led by Edward Heath in 1970, which came to power armed with exactly the same economic philosophy as that which later became known as 'Thatcherism'. The manifestos on which the Conservatives fought the 1970 and 1979 general elections share the same economic analysis and advocate the same prescriptions for recovery, with the exception that in 1970 monetarism had not yet become politically fashionable (it never became very popular among economists at British universities who, by a substantial majority, remained broadly Keynesian in disposition).

Public expenditure is invariably seen as a major problem, a real and present threat to economic efficiency. Hence the popularity of the public burden theory of welfare with all neo-liberal theorists. As governments moved further and further away from their proper concern with the provision of public goods and took on responsibilities that ought to have remained with individuals in markets they inevitably found themselves engaged in a competitive conflict with the private, productive sector of the economy for available scarce resources. In this conflict there could be only one winner. Governments could offer a guaranteed return on the loans they sought from the financial markets; the private sector could not. The public sector was also in competition for skilled and educated labour, and even though it could not always match the salaries available in the private sector, both job security and guaranteed, inflation-proof pensions could always sugar that particular pill. In brief, wealth-creating activity in the traded goods sector was 'crowded out' (Bacon and Eltis, 1976). If this process was allowed to continue, negative sum welfare-efficiency interactions were a certainty (Geiger, 1979). In other words, the productive ability of the economy would be compromised by the public sector's excessive demands. Taxation and government expenditure are regarded as burdens having to be borne by commerce and industry in the private sector, the only real source of genuine wealth creation.

The expansive and expensive welfare regimes of social democracy place a great strain on governments' revenue-raising capacity. Impelled by the insatiable demands of greedy electorates and self-interested bureaucrats intent only on empire-building, governments have to tax and borrow more and more. The level of direct taxation is of particular concern to neo-liberal economists. If personal and company taxation is too high at the margin incentives will be damaged. Why should employees work harder and take on more responsibility if they know that the net advantage to them of the marginal pound they earn is going to be significantly reduced by the government's depredations? In neo-liberal theory there is the certainty that high marginal rates of income tax and high rates of corporation tax reduce work incentives and discourage risk-taking. The end result is bound to be an economy in which productivity declines, output is reduced, and innovation and investment are both discouraged. Negative-sum welfare efficiency interactions are the norm. In order to reverse this debilitating decline it is essential that governments reduce the rates of these direct taxes on individuals and companies. Incentives would then be restored and augmented, and risk-taking and investment both encouraged. As a consequence, output and real incomes would both increase and Britain's long, relative decline halted.

For neo-liberals the dismal reality of a high-tax, low-growth economy is compounded by the consequences of a benefit–earnings ratio skewed in favour of benefits. It has been argued that one of the avoidable causes of the currently high levels of unemployment is that people in receipt of benefit will not consider taking one of the large number of low-paid jobs that are available because the wages such employment would generate are not noticeably higher than benefit income levels and would not compensate them for the effort, time and energy they would have to expend in the labour market. Being rational, they will tend to prefer the leisure of unemployment to the demands of work. The neo-liberal solution to this dilemma is not to increase earnings through measures such as a minimum wage (this would only add to the costs of employers, especially small companies, in what are usually very competitive sectors of the economy and create more unemployment) but to reduce benefits and make them more difficult to claim (Minford, 1987). The labour market implications of income maintenance programmes have always been a critical concern for all types and forms of political economy, but for the neo-liberal this concern is definitive.

The Labour Market   Labour is a commodity like any other and therefore susceptible to market operations. The larger market contains a market for labour, and that market can be cleared if the price of labour – that is, its wages – is determined by the normal market forces of demand and supply. If the market is left to its own devices and not distorted by government intervention (through the provision of a minimum wage and the operation of wages councils) and the activities of powerful trade unions equipped with significant legal immunities, the tendency would be towards little or no involuntary unemployment. There would always be frictional and structural unemployment of course; these are the desirable and natural features of any dynamic market economy as people change jobs and employers in their search for better wages and conditions and as old industries decline and new ones emerge in response to new technologies and changing tastes. If involuntary unemployment does exist it is because of 'artificial' rigidities in the labour market occasioned by the behaviour of organized labour. Therefore, for the neo-liberal, the battle against unemployment should be dominated by an assault on the bargaining power of trade unions and their privileged position in law. This would assist the necessary progress back towards a 'natural' rate of unemployment in a deregulated and flexible labour market. Any other approach is doomed to failure in the long run. Keynesian inspired attempts to force unemployment below its natural, market-determined rate might secure some temporary success but in the long run there would be greater inflation as governments resorted to deficit financing and pump-priming to stimulate aggregate demand, and ultimately higher unemployment. As Hayek put it, 'unemployment has been made inevitable by past inflation; it has merely been *postponed* by accelerating inflation' (quoted in Marquand, 1987: 86).

Inflation   The suppression and control of inflation is the key policy objective of neo-liberal economics. Secure it and a multitude of benefits will flow. Regular, sustainable increments to economic growth, low unemployment, rising disposable real income, and even improvements in the quality of justifiable public services can only be secured if inflation is conquered. If this means temporary hardship and suffering for some, as the toxin of Keynesianism is expelled, it is a necessary experience. As Norman Lamont said, unemployment is a price worth paying.

The precise nature of the alleged relationship between excessive public expenditure and inflation has varied over time. All that neo-liberals are sure of is that there *is* a causal relationship. If governments cannot raise all the revenue they need to fund their welfare commitments from taxation and charges then they have to resort to borrowing. If the public sector borrowing requirement (PSBR) is high and/or rising as a percentage of GNP, the government may be forced to raise interest rates to induce the finance markets to take up the stocks and bonds on offer. A general increase in the cost of borrowing will have potentially serious implications for business activity as costs increase, and for the politically sensitive housing market as well. If market conditions permit manufacturers will be tempted to pass on their higher costs to customers in the form of higher prices. If market conditions are depressed it will not be as easy to increase prices and business operations may have to be scaled down. Either way the news is bad. Similarly, an increase in housing costs could lead to potentially inflationary wage claims as workers seek to make good this implicit cut in their real incomes.

If governments are unable to meet their borrowing requirements in this way they have the option of resorting to a form of borrowing which can be used by the banking system to expand its credit base and thus increase the supply of money in the economy. For economists such as Friedman the most significant long-term cause of inflation is an expansion of the money supply beyond that dictated by market-led economic activity. After a time lag of around two years an increase in money supply generated by avoidable government borrowing will lead to an increase in the general price level: there is a mechanistic, causal link between money supply and the price level.

In their earlier years the governments led by Margaret Thatcher were particularly enamoured of Friedman's version of monetarism, an attachment which manifested itself in the adoption of a Medium Term Financial Strategy (MTFS), which incorporated clear, fixed targets for monetary growth, targets which were in line with expectations of growth rates in the real economy. While monetary aggregates are clearly an important feature of any economic theory, and have always been recognized as such, for neo-liberal economists they are critical. However, this aspect of neo-liberal economics in many ways has proved to be the most disappointing feature of the theory as a whole. There was much discussion, and no general agreement, about what constituted a proper definition of M (the money supply) in monetarists' equations, and in the real world of economic policy it proved very difficult to control any definition of M at all. Eventually the MTFS was abandoned and with it went one of the central planks of monetarist theory.

Despite this failure the control of inflation remains the key objective of neo-liberal economic theory. Inflation, as measured by the Retail Price Index, is at its lowest level for over 30 years and only a fraction of the peaks reached in the 1970s. There is even a suggestion that inflationary pressures have been squeezed out of the system completely. British inflation still remains at the top end of the range for nations within the European Union and, as we have noted, it is very unlikely that the government will relax its stance.

Activity 3.1

- In what ways do neo-liberals' behavioural assumptions affect their views on the economy?

Neo-liberalism: Aspects of Political Philosophy

> When properly presented, their arguments strike at the heart of the normative assumptions of the post-war welfare state. (Plant, 1990: 7)

Inevitably, the value premises of neo-liberalism are determined by its assumptions. Methodological individualism, rationality and a preference for the free market are as important here as they are in its economics. Indeed, economics and philosophy are part of the seamless web that is neo-liberal political economy. Plant's analysis of the normative content of neo-liberalism provides a perceptive and coherent framework which we can use to develop a relatively complete synthesis of neo-liberalism's values and preferences (Plant, 1990).

Liberty

For Hayek liberty was the supreme value, far outweighing any other, be it democracy or social justice or fraternity. The great tragedy of modern European civilization was the gradual retreat from the understanding of liberty developed by British liberals from Locke onwards in face of the advance of the German tradition of an authoritarian, interventionist state possessed of a belief in its right to shape the economic and social destiny of its citizens. It posited a belief in the existence of a discernible 'national' interest which could be pursued and achieved through a range of specific programmes and instruments. For the classical and neo-liberal, 'market relationships are freer, more spontaneous, in a strange way more authentic than political relationships: market power does not exist, while the state is, by definition, the realm of power and domination' (Marquand, 1987: 67).

Hayek argues that after 1870 the tide turned against liberalism; increasingly, planning and regulation became the new lodestones, deployed in the interest of a chimerical equality and social justice. Possibly Hayek chose 1870 because it marked the triumph of Prussia in its war with France and the consequent emergence of a new, unified German state under Prussian leadership and with Prussian traditions (Hayek, 1944). As an émigré Austrian intellectual Hayek was well qualified to point out the dangers of authoritarian collectivism, especially in conditions of mass unemployment, and its attendant social tensions. His passion for liberty and suspicion of democracy are characteristics present in a great deal of neo-liberal writing, and, as we shall see later, they are characteristics which present neo-liberal theorists with some very real dilemmas. Hayek, though, had no doubts; liberty should triumph in every contest.

Since the emergence of liberal collectivist thought in the last quarter of the nineteenth century in the work of Green, Hobson, Hobhouse and Ritchie, there has been an assumption about the relationship between liberty and welfare. Liberal collectivists moved beyond the formal, procedural notions of liberty central to classical liberalism such as those attached to civil, political and legal rights, and asserted a *positive* as opposed to *negative* concept of liberty. In the twentieth century the idea has become associated with the notion of an *equal worth of liberty* (Plant, 1985). Thus, liberty is inextricably bound up with access to those resources and experiences essential to the living of a full and civilized life, like education, health, housing, and a guaranteed income, in fact those resources whose distribution is perhaps the most important feature of modern welfare states. To paraphrase Tawney (1931), the pauper and the prince are both formally free to dine at the Ritz. In reality, of course, one can and the other cannot because, in markets, access is determined by command over resources. If we substitute education, health, housing and a guaranteed income for dinner at the Ritz, then the conclusions are obvious. Just as war is too important to be left to the generals so is access to the formative experiences of modern life too important to be left to the market. Hayek recognized the significance of linking the freedom to act with the ability to act. It provided a powerful basis for arguing that vertical redistribution of resources should be sought, because to do so would increase the worth of liberty enjoyed by those at the bottom end of the initial, market-determined distribution of income by enhancing their ability to act. This switch from a negative to a positive concept of liberty within the liberal tradition was a significant factor in the growth of the interventionist state in late-nineteenth-century Britain with the consequent movement from the free-market, minimal-state ideal of classical liberalism.

Neo-liberals reject the idea of positive liberty, liberty as power and opportunity, and reaffirm their commitment to the older interpretation. Their position has nowhere been better expressed than in the following statement: 'Liberty is liberty, not something else. And the slave is a slave: you do not set him free by feeding him' (Joseph and Sumption, 1979, quoted in Pope et al., 1986: 221). Negative liberty therefore is the only valid approach. Liberty means the absence of coercion and market outcomes are unforeseen. They are not the consequence of a deliberate political judgement made by those with the authority and power to determine such outcomes. The free market cannot restrict or otherwise impinge on liberty. Market outcomes are the consequence of individual choices made by rational beings with the intent of maximizing individual satisfaction. These individual decisions in markets become powerful aggregates whose signals cannot be ignored by suppliers. The results may mean that some people get more than others, that there is inequality, but there is no compulsion involved; no political authority has intervened. As Hayek has observed, individuals are still free to try to improve their position by any means open to them provided that such actions are legal, do not coerce others, and that all such actions are governed by the overarching 'rule of law' providing transparent, known and generally understood procedures. Life may be unfair, some may be luckier than others, talents and resources may be unequally distributed, there may be suffering, but in market economies people are always free to try again using whatever abilities and energy they possess.

Social Justice

The positive liberty of liberal collectivism demands a rigorous, clearly articulated and generally accepted concept of social justice to serve as the criterion through which resources can be allocated by non-market mechanisms. If market forces are to be modified or dispensed with, the least that is needed is a valid basis on which to intervene. Neo-liberals reject the possibility of such a notion. Hayek was contemptuous of every attempt to develop an operational concept of social justice and dismissed them as self-indulgent posturing (Hayek, 1944). Because market outcomes are unintended they cannot be unjust since social injustice can only be caused by intentional acts. Consequently, 'the moral demands of social justice evaporate' (Plant, 1990: 11). Social justice as a concept lacks specificity. There are many possible criteria of social justice (need, merit, desert and so on), but in a free society there can be no general agreement about which criterion should be used as the operational basis of resource allocation. Therefore,

1   because of the absence of agreed criteria allocation through non-market methods will be arbitrary and discretionary. 'This will mean that at the very heart of the public policy of a welfare state will lie the arbitrary and discretionary power of welfare bureaucrats and experts charged with the impossible task of distributing resources according to intrinsically unspecific criteria' (Plant, 1990: 11).
2   Because of the absence of known and agreed criteria there will be selfish and destructive competition by interest groups for resources. It is the relative power of interest groups that will be significant in the allocation of scarce resources. The powerful will inevitably win.

For all these reasons illusory ideas about social justice should be abandoned and the market liberated from government intervention. If a welfare state had to remain in place then it should be a residual one providing a minimum safety net for those who were not able to compete or operate in the market.

Consistent libertarians such as Nozick would, of course, dispense with any kind of welfare state (Nozick, 1974).

Rights

The idea that people possess welfare rights as a constitutive element of citizenship is essential to the liberal collectivist/social democratic view of the welfare state (Marshall, 1950 and Chapter 10 of this book). In contrast, neo-liberals totally reject the idea of social or welfare rights. They see a clear and fundamental distinction between the civil and political rights at the core of classical liberalism and the more recent claim of alleged rights to welfare. These traditional rights which liberals have asserted for centuries all imply negative duties of forbearance rather than the commitment of resources to substantiate them. The reality of scarce resources implies a limit to the exercise of rights which demand that resources are made available to fulfil them. The resource implications of recognizing that citizens have rights to a certain amount of health care, education, income and so on are immense. On the other hand, civil rights are categorical and absolute. To claim that people have rights to welfare demands that we have a view of needs, and the probability is that such views will tend to be open-ended with clear consequences for governments trying to decide between the validity of a range of competing claims on resources. There is certain to be intense interest group competition for these resources, and opportunity cost means that meeting one group's claim will lead to the neglect of some other group. The lack of agreed criteria to distinguish between these claims must lead to anger and frustration, and possibly to the erosion of faith in the political institutions of liberal democracy.

Poverty

Neo-liberals adopt an absolute concept of poverty rather than a relative one. Given this, their belief is that there is very little, if any, poverty in late twentieth-century Britain (Joseph and Sumption, 1979). A free market economy, liberated from the debilitating effects of government intervention, an institutional welfare state and the burden of high taxes is much the best mechanism for helping the poor; more precisely, of helping the poor to help themselves. Market economies do generate inequalities; in fact the existence of inequalities is a significant part of the motive force of market economies; but they are far more successful than any other form of economic system for the generation of wealth and jobs. The greater productive power of market economies will do more than anything else to improve the real living standards of the poor; not least through the 'trickle-down effect' and the greater demand for labour. Poor people need the opportunity to work their way out of poverty and to break free from the culture of dependency which disfigures their humanity.

Culture and Values

If the poor are to be weaned away from welfare dependency and reintro-
duced to the world of enterprise, risk and work it is essential that the role of
the free market is expanded and the values of the enterprise culture
proselytized. Neo-liberals believe that poverty is not caused by a dysfunctional economic system, nor by a dysfunctional social system. Poverty is
culturally determined through the values, mores, attitudes and lack of
aspirations transmitted across generations. Ergo, if the policy objective is to
improve the conditions of the poor, then the behaviour of the poor themselves must be changed (see Chapter 12). Welfare dependency saps initiative, enterprise, autonomy and the sense of being responsible for one's own
destiny. If we remove the resources that encourage dependency and restructure social policy so that people are moved off welfare and prepared instead
for the world of work, then we can begin that process of cultural transformation essential to a real attack on poverty – real because it treats the causes
and not the symptoms. Such a change might result in some initial discomfort
but the prize of an economically dynamic and remoralized society is one
worth securing.

Public Choice Theory: the Apotheosis of the Rational Egoist

It has been argued that both the novelty and the real cutting edge of neo-
liberalism is to be found not in its economic theory, which, as we have seen,
is not new anyway, but in its view of politics. The promises of Keynesian
social democracy were based on the belief that government was inherently
benign and inherently competent. 'The real originality and power of present
day neo-liberalism lie in its attempt to turn that central presupposition on its
head' (Marquand, 1987: 75).

The economic consequences of late-twentieth-century liberal democracies
are determined by the nature of political activity in these societies, the major
features of which are the existence of competitive party politics, mass
electorates and well-entrenched, well-organized interest groups. In this
situation, market failure (a reason for government intervention in the first
place) is less likely than government failure. Although neo-liberalism is not
a monolithic creed it can be understood as a cluster of related ideas and
attitudes which share the same underlying theme of 'overload'. The system
cannot cope with the excessive demands generated by the politics of
Keynesian social democracy. As governments provide more, electorates
demand more. In consequence, governments overreach themselves.

'The result was a paradox. Big government turned out to be ineffective
government. The more it tried to do, the more it failed. The more it failed,
the more it lost authority. The more authority it lost, the more it failed'
(Marquand, 1987: 73). Public choice theory is a microcosm of neo-liberal
political economy, resting in a particularly intense way on the same
behavioural assumptions. In King's words: 'The emphasis is on the micro-

economic assumptions of actors (egoism, self-interest) and context (a perfect political "market"), with utility maximisation and rational action by the parties also assumed' (1987: 100).

Downs's (1957) central assumption was that political parties develop policy objectives in order to win elections rather than to consummate some vision of the public good. They are reactive rather than proactive.

Given the assumption of rational self-interest the sceptic can be forgiven for asking why individuals can safely be left to express their own wishes in the economic market-place but not in the political one. Surely, what is good for the consumer is also good for the voter? They are, after all, the same people, and rationality is a general assumption. The neo-liberal response is that there is a fundamental difference between the economic and political markets. In the former, consumers are constrained by an awareness of their own resource limitations; therefore they can be relied on to act with caution. In the latter, voters are under no such inhibition since in democracies majority opinion will prevail. Voters do not directly pay as individuals for the policies they 'buy' (vote for). Even if a voter prefers cheaper policies to expensive ones, she or he will have to pay her or his share of the expensive policies, if that is what voters want. Marquand illustrates the problem well with his restaurant analogy:

> He is like a skinflint, dining in an expensive restaurant with a party of friends, who have agreed to share the bill equally between them. However tight-fisted he may be, it is not rational for him to order the cheapest items on the menu. If he does, he will probably end by subsidizing his fellow diners. It makes more sense for him to opt for the caviar and champagne. (1987: 76)

This destructive pursuit of self-interest by individuals as voters creates a dilemma for public choice theorists. Liberty is the prime value and the free market is the institution most likely to protect economic freedom. Similarly, democratic politics, based on universal adult suffrage, is in one sense synonymous with liberty. We choose our rulers in free elections and, if they fail to please us, we can remove them. However, the selfish, if rational, behaviour of individuals as voters is an important cause of the system overload observable in all liberal democracies. How then can people be prevented from damaging or destroying that institution, the free market economy, wherein they can find the best opportunity of fulfilling themselves as individuals and which is also the best guarantor of that liberty which is the supreme political value?

In public choice theory bureaucrats cannot be expected to lay a restraining hand on the excesses of democratic politics. After all, they share the same behavioural characteristics of all the other actors in the drama, voters, parties and interest groups. The idealized norm, characteristic of received wisdom, of the disinterested, objective public servant, impervious to any shred of self-interest, is a fiction. Bureaucrats are just like the rest of us; greedy, vain, ambitious, and keen to follow their own interests. Occasionally those interests might coincide with the public good (if such a thing exists) but the

the cases in the same group will have the same value on the control variable, this will provide a control for analyzing the relationship between the two focal variables within each group. The interpretation of the findings will depend on your research purpose and the type of results. There are basically two types of results:

(1) The results for the partial table analyses are largely the same. In such cases, the interpretative logic mentioned above can be used to explain the results. The control variable has no impact on the relationship between the two focal variables if all the partial table analyses render the same results as the original relationship. The control variable has an impact on the relationship between the two focal variables if all the partial table analyses render weaker results than the original relationship. Depending on the purpose of research, the control variable can be regarded either as an antecedent variable in a causal model, or as an intervening variable in a causal link model. There is a special situation when the control variable strengthens rather than weakens or eliminates the relationship between the two focal variables. If this is the case, then the control variable is called a suppressor variable and the study a suppression analysis. If the sign of the relationship is reversed, then it is called a distortion analysis and the control variable a distorter variable. Suppression and distortion are uncommon, but they are possible.

(2) The results for the partial table analyses are not the same. In such a case, the control variable can be regarded as a conditional variable, which does not prove to be simply reinforcing or undercutting the focal relationship under study but to specify different conditions under which the relationship will be different. The analysis can be called a conditional analysis or specification model. A conditional analysis may also discover some suppressors or distorters of the focal relationship.

In both types of study, additional analysis may be conducted on the relationship between the control variable and each focal (dependent or independent) variable to enrich your analysis and research report.

Elaboration is an important direction for researchers to increase the depth of thinking by moving beyond the simple bivariate analysis. The introduction of appropriate control variables, however, poses a challenge to your practical knowledge, theoretical understanding, and research insights. Here creativity is highly valued, and the trial and error strategy is especially important.

bureaucrat is more likely to judge success by the size of the departmental budget and the number of people on the payroll.

Many neo-liberal writers have proposed a series of institutional changes which would transform the nature of political life in liberal democracies. These include constitutional amendments to enforce a balanced budget and the establishment of an independent commission to control the money supply. Not unexpectedly, Hayek has made the most radical suggestions with his scheme for limiting the suffrage to those over the age of 45 and excluding civil servants, old-age pensioners and the unemployed. The legislature elected through this process of less than universal suffrage would have its members in place for 15 years and would content itself with laying down general rules for the conduct of business. Administration would be left to a subordinate assembly whose decisions would only be binding if they conformed to the general rules of the legislature. As Marquand goes on to note, if 'the source of the problem is democracy, how can it be solved democratically?' (1987: 81).

Activity 3.2

After reading the last two sections:

- What services do you think a neo-liberal would argue should be the state's responsibility?
- What, in their view, should be the responsibility of the individual?
- How do they justify these allocations?

From Idea to Practice: the Role of 'Think Tanks'

Ideas may provide penetrating insights into the nature of economic and social reality, but they also need effective transmission mechanisms to ease their progress from university departments to public policy initiative. Politicians need to be captured, bureaucracies permeated. One of the most significant features of the political landscape in the last 20 years has been the proliferation of neo-liberal 'think tanks', impelled not just by a desire to proselytize but also by a determination to destroy the social democratic/ liberal collectivist paradigm. Of the major liberal democracies perhaps only Germany has been free from their influence, an influence which has become paramount in the politics of Australia, Britain, Canada and the United States of America (see, for example, King, 1987; Kavanagh, 1990; Self, 1993).

Equipped with substantial financial backing from big business they have succeeded in creating networks of formal and informal contacts linking intellectuals, the media, bureaucrats and politicians. In so doing they have been equally successful in changing the policy agenda in many countries. Their ability to do this has been facilitated by the failure of the left to create similar structures. In Britain, for example, the Institute for Public Policy Research, so active in the proceedings of the Commission on Social Justice, was founded only in 1988, by which time the neo-liberal critique was already well established and successful in shifting the policy terrain to the right.

Although the British think tanks all share a profound distaste for the interventionist state, they have favourite individual themes. Thus, the Institute of Economic Affairs (IEA), founded in 1957, initially provided an organizational base and publishing house for bringing the individualist, free-market ideas of Hayek and Friedman to a wider audience. Later on the IEA publicized the public-choice theorists such as Niskanen and Buchanan. The Adam Smith Institute, created in 1977, is libertarian on social and political issues and is particularly associated with the policy of privatization of public sector industries and services. A relatively recent suggestion calls for the privatization of all education for children aged under 5, whose parents would be given vouchers to purchase places in private nurseries (*The Observer*, 8 January 1995). The Social Affairs Unit, set up in 1980 by Digby Anderson and his associates, shares the same philosophical assumptions as the IEA and from the outset has applied this analysis to the public provision of social welfare. In Anderson's words, 'just as it [the IEA] attacked a sclerotic consensus in economics, we wanted to do something similar on social policy' (Kavanagh, 1990: 85). The remaining important body, the Centre for Policy Studies, was formed in 1974 by Margaret Thatcher and Sir Keith Joseph with the specific intent of pushing the Conservative Party towards a free-market, individualist line after what they regarded as the disastrous betrayals of the Heath government, of which, it should be remembered, they were both leading figures.

The ideas and programmes advocated by these organizations have informed every single area of economic and social policy in Britain since 1979 and have helped to shift the centre-left to a much more pro-market, low-tax position. Does anyone seriously expect any Labour government of the near future to reverse this general trend?

Neo-liberalism: Summary and Concluding Assessment

How are we to assess the success or failure of the neo-liberal critique of the Keynesian-Beveridgean welfare state? To do this we need to form some judgement of the approach in its own terms, of how successful it has been in achieving its general and particular objectives.

A good place to begin is by asking the question, has there been a paradigm shift? Do intellectuals, politicians, policy-makers and the public in general now view the world in a different way than they did 20 years ago? The evidence would suggest that the answer must be a qualified 'yes', although the extent to which this change is a consequence of structural imperatives such as economic globalization, and the continuing revolution in technology or the superiority of neo-liberal theory itself in explaining the significance and meaning of these structural changes must remain to some extent a matter of personal choice. As evidence of this sea change we can point to the acceptance by left-of-centre political parties of the market as an allocative instrument with much to recommend it, indeed in many cases as one to be preferred over non-market mechanisms. To some extent this change has taken place everywhere but is perhaps most obvious in France and Spain, and latterly in Australia, New Zealand and in Britain where under the leadership of Tony Blair, 'New Labour' has become a social democratic rather than a socialist party (see Chapter 2). So significant has been this transformation that some political scientists have felt it appropriate to talk in terms of the 'Thatcherization of the Labour Party'. In this view the Labour Party is attempting to present itself as the party of low and fair taxation; of being opposed to any significant increase in public expenditure as a share of GNP; of accepting the creation of quasi-markets in health, education and the personal social services (see Chapter 13); and of being opposed to the return of the privatized utilities into public ownership. Free maintenance grants in higher education are to be abolished and repaid through the imposition of a higher national insurance contribution payable over 20 years. Even Child Benefit, created by the last Labour government in 1975, is apparently not sacrosanct, and is itself being reviewed by the party in its search for a more effective (that is, better targeted) utilization of scarce public resources (see Chapter 11).

At a general theoretical level, then, neo-liberalism seems to have been successful in changing the nature of mainstream political debate and in recasting the ways in which we think about the respective responsibilities of the individual and the state. We turn now to a brief assessment of neo-liberal ideas in two of the most important substantive areas of policy concern, the economy and the welfare state.

In order to address this second general issue it is perhaps appropriate to consider a statement made in 1979 when the first of Mrs Thatcher's governments, in its first public expenditure white paper, asserted that excessive public spending lay at the heart of Britain's economic problems, and expressed its determination to reduce state spending. That public expenditure takes up the same share of GNP now as it did in 1979 is not so much a consequence of neo-liberal theory as an indication of the demands generated by an ageing population and the extra social security expenditure caused by consistently high levels of unemployment.

As with public expenditure so with taxation. Although there has been a significant reduction in levels of *direct* taxation with a basic rate of 23 per cent and a highest rate of 40 per cent, this reduction has been matched by a significant increase in *indirect* taxes such as VAT and the duties levied on petrol, tobacco and alcoholic drinks. Taxation as a proportion of GNP is now about 1 per cent higher than it was in 1979, but the structure of that taxation, the balance between direct and indirect taxes, has altered profoundly, a development which reflects the importance of low rates of direct taxes in neo-liberal theory.

The significant overall increase in unemployment we have noted previously has been accompanied by the creation of a flexible, deregulated labour market, one in which casual and part-time employment have become widespread (see Chapter 12). Industrial relations in this labour market have been transformed by a series of eight employment Acts whose collective impact has been to reduce trade unions to their weakest position since before the First World War. These changes to the labour market and the reform of industrial relations are a direct consequence of the application of neo-liberal theory.

All of these changes were intended to improve the overall performance of the British economy compared with the years of Keynesian ascendancy. While productivity per worker has increased sharply, this has been achieved by approximately the same level of output being produced by a much smaller workforce. Annualized growth rates since 1979 are smaller than the average for the previous 35 years; investment in manufacturing industry is barely at the level it reached in 1979 and the balance of payments remains in chronic disequilibrium. Neo-liberal theory then has failed to reverse the long relative decline of the British economy, and, as we have seen in Chapter 2, one of the results of this has been a revival of social democratic theory with its very different views on the proper relationship between state and economy.

Thirdly, in the arena of social policy, although the institutions of the welfare state (in the shape of the NHS, education free at the point of use, a social security system, personal social services and a much reduced social housing sector) remain intact, there have been great changes in the nature of the policy instruments used to deliver public social provision. Neo-liberal theory, particularly in its themes of markets and choice, has been the major motive force in securing these changes. These have been considered in some detail in the third section of this chapter and are discussed further in Chapter 13.

We began these conclusions by suggesting that at the intellectual level there has indeed been a paradigm shift and that neo-liberal ideas now dominate in policy discussion. We have also noted that there are signs that neo-liberalism's dominance is now beginning to be challenged in a serious and sustained way. By focusing on what he believes are the consequence of years of sustained neo-liberalism, on the 'palpable insecurity running through almost every layer of society in Britain about jobs and the chronic risk to a civilised standard of life that unemployment threatens for almost all of us', Gray (1994) has developed a sustained critique of neo-liberalism from a liberal, communitarian perspective. There is a profound irony in the fact that Gray, himself a firm believer in 'the dynamism of market institutions', should have become one of the most articulate and impassioned critics of a set of ideas whose *raison d'être* is the liberation of individuals through markets.

4

Marx and the Marxist Critique of Welfare

Michael Lavalette

Karl Marx died in 1883 and his lifelong friend and confidant, Friedrich Engels, died in 1895, more than 50 years before the creation of what is commonly known as the British 'welfare state'. Together, the writings of Marx and Engels cover a vast intellectual area that includes, among other things, writings on philosophy, economics, history, sociology, politics, art and mathematics but they wrote little on social policy. Despite these facts, however, the power, breadth and endurance of Marx's ideas are such that no textbook purporting to analyse social policy would be complete without a discussion of Marx, Engels and their subsequent followers. Marxism is relevant to the study of social policy because it provides a comprehensive theory of society and as such, according to Mishra, it offers 'an explanation of the nature of welfare and its development in . . . [various] . . . societies' (1977: 61).

In what follows we shall first try to illuminate the essence of Marx's ideas, his approach and method, his analysis of capitalism and the centrality of the concept of social class to his theory of society. For Marx, modern society is ridden with antagonistic class divisions and these shape and affect all our lives in innumerable ways – including the shape and form of social welfare delivery. After laying the ground and analysing his basic ideas we will turn to focus on their relevance to the study of social policy and welfare. We start by looking at what was distinctive about Marx's method of analysing social life.

Marx's Method

Marx's starting point is radically different from that of the various writers identified in Chapters 2 and 3. His method is known as *historical materialism*, and it rejects the pessimistic notion that humans are essentially selfish and greedy individualists. Marxists would reject these as peculiarly 'modern' values and would in turn point to earlier times and different cultures where co-operation, and not competition, was the norm and the basis for social living. Rather than starting with 'abstract individuals' entering into contracts with one another to form a society, Marx begins with the concept of *material production* and the assertion that humans are producers, labouring animals. In one of his earlier works, when writing with Engels, he asserts:

> Men can be distinguished from animals by consciousness, by religion or anything else you like. They themselves begin to distinguish themselves from animals as soon as they begin to *produce* their means of subsistence, a step which is conditioned by their physical organisation. By producing their means of subsistence men are indirectly producing their actual material life. (1846: 31; emphasis in original)

To labour, to be productive and creative, is what distinguishes humans from other animals and this activity is a fundamental feature of human nature (Geras, 1983). Further, Marx asserts that labouring, working collectively with tools and machines on natural resources, *is the source of all wealth*. Goods are only valuable and have a 'worth' because people have worked on them and turned them into useful and exchangeable items. Without such labour they would remain in their natural state. As a result production is viewed as a *social activity*.

Finally, two points are crucial for Marx. First, humans have the potential consciously to reflect on the way they work and gradually improve and refine their methods, techniques and tools of production (what Marx called the forces of production). In general terms there has been a gradual improvement in the technology of production throughout history: great advances in technology occurred in the Middle Ages and even the Dark Ages long before the Industrial Revolution of the eighteenth and nineteenth centuries. Such improvements increase the quantity and quality of the product of human labour, cutting the amount of time required to produce subsistence levels (*necessary labour*) and increasing the amount of time devoted to producing surplus (*surplus labour*). All of which means that it is possible for human societies to produce more than is required for the immediate subsistence needs of its population: to produce a 'surplus'.

Secondly, production can be organized in a number of different ways. According to Marx, a number of distinct ways of organizing the productive life of the community (*modes of production*) have existed. Each of these has involved different relationships between the people in society (*social relations of production*), has involved people working with various implements, tools and natural resources (*means of production*) and in a production process that has entailed the utilization of these different tools by labour with specific techniques, ideas, concepts and/or knowledge about production (*the forces of production*) to meet society's goals.

What makes the human animal distinct from other creatures, then, is the combination of the following factors:

1 the requirement to work with others to meet their long-term survival needs;
2 the ability to utilize complex tools;
3 the ability to reflect on production techniques and improve and refine the methods of production;
4 their ability to adapt their environment and master nature, and

5   the ability to produce and store more goods than are required for direct
    consumption and survival.

For Marx, then, the key feature of any human society is how it produces the
food, clothing, shelter and other basic needs that allow people to survive.
Marx termed the production of these goods 'the first historical act', but
emphasized that this is an act that must be fulfilled on a daily basis if
individuals, and society generally, are to survive. The important point for
Marx is that the way in which society is structured to meet our basic needs,
the way in which production is organized, can and does vary historically.
*Thus Marxism is the empirical study of societies, which places the organiza-
tion of the* **production process** *at the centre of its analysis.*
   But Marxism is more than this. As we have noted, within Marxism there
is a recognition that humans are conscious animals who can reflect on their
techniques of production, expand the forces of production, and produce
more than their minimum survival needs. The key issue, then, becomes what
happens to the *surplus product* (the extra goods and services provided by the
surplus labour)? For Marx, in the majority of societies the surplus is taken
by a small minority for their own ends and uses at the expense of the needs
of the vast majority. The minority, or dominant class, has, as a result, been
able to lead a more or less leisured existence while the majority have had to
work to support themselves and the dominant class. In each mode of
production, it is the dominant class's control over the conditions of production that has been central to the formation of the *exploitative relationships* on which society is based. These relationships are embedded within
the political, legal, social and economic structure of each society or mode of
production. As the Marxist historian G.E.M. de Ste Croix notes: 'the most
significant distinguishing feature of each . . . mode of production . . . is not
so much *how the bulk of the labour production is done*, as *how the dominant
political classes*, controlling the conditions of production, *ensure the extraction of the surplus* which makes their own leisured existence possible'
(1981: 52; emphasis in original). It is, then, one's location, with regard to the
exploitative relationships, that defines one's social class. But 'class', for
Marx, is essentially a *relationship*, it refers to the group of people within
society who have an identifiable position within the entire system of social
production, defined above all else, according to de Ste Croix: 'to their
relationship (primarily in terms of the degree of ownership or control) to the
conditions of production (that is to say, the means and labour of production)
and to other classes' (1981: 43).
   Within any society, these exploitative relationships force the majority of
the population (*the direct producers*) to work for the benefit of the minority.
The direct producers will not only give up most of their output, their surplus,
but will now be 'alienated' from their product. Although labour is the
'essence of man', an essential part of human nature, in class societies the
direct producers lose control over both the labour process and the output, the
product of their labour. This means that the direct producer feels his or her

labouring activity to be a burden, undertaken for the benefit of someone else in conditions determined by them. In the ensuing struggle for survival, other 'direct producers' will, on occasion, be viewed as competitors, rather than co-operative allies, though in other circumstances political, social and/or economic events may lead to united activity by the direct producers in defence of shared interests against the dominant class and their representatives. As a consequence, class societies are deeply alienating: they stop us fulfilling our potential, separate us from the product of our labour and divide us from others when we are naturally social animals (cf. Waddington, 1974).

Finally, Marx's perspective is one that looks at the *'social totality'*. That means that each mode of production is shaped by, not just economic relationships, but social relationships in their widest sense. It incorporates an understanding that each mode of production will involve relationships between the rulers and the ruled, producers and non-producers, men and women, old and young, and that some modes of production will incorporate other divisions between peoples (for example, dividing the world's population into discrete 'races' and the practices of racism which result from this are a specific feature of the capitalist era (cf. Miles, 1984; Callinicos, 1993). The notion of social totality also emphasizes the fact that, for example, societal institutions and practices (such as welfare provision and social policies) are intimately connected with and shaped by the dominant mode of production within society. Thus within each mode of production specific ideas, social institutions and social practices will be created and re-created and each of these elements will in turn affect the primary economic relationships. In this sense, the criticism that Marxism is a form of 'economic reductionism', that it reduces all phenomena, practices, perspectives, attitudes and views to economic criteria, is misplaced. For Marxists, political, social, cultural and ideological events should be studied as elements within society and as having a dramatic effect on social life. But for Marxists these events take place within a context: the contradictions and conflicts created by social production and the class divisions and relationships created by this process.

To conclude this section we will draw out and emphasize some of the key conclusions of Marx's general methodology. *First, the starting point for analysing any society is how production is organized.* However, this is more than a mere economic perspective. Marx assumed that interwoven with any economic relations of production were a set of political, ideological, social and cultural practices. Marxism, therefore, is an analysis which views societies as 'integrated wholes'. It therefore analyses the 'totality of social relations and practices' that occur within each mode of production. *Secondly, generally, history has witnessed a gradual expansion of the forces of production and human productive potential.* This has meant that it has been possible to fulfil more than minimal survival requirements, but under conditions of class society such potential has been severely restricted. *Thirdly, class societies are, by their very nature, conflictual.* In each society the dominant class is able to utilize its control over the productive life of the community to exploit the direct producers and extract surplus from them. The direct producers resist this process wherever possible using a variety of means large and small, overt and hidden, individual and collective. As Gough notes:

> classes then are groups in antagonistic relation to the means of production [defined in terms of the dominant class's ownership or control over these: ML]. One class is the exploiter, the other the exploited. Corresponding to these classes are specific class interests which inevitably result in class conflict as a ubiquitous feature of all exploitative societies. (1979: 19)

Fourthly, the form of exploitation changes historically in each mode of production. As Mayer notes:

> In slave systems surplus labor is extracted through direct coercion of the slave, in feudal economies by a combination of coercion and ideology, and in capitalist economies by the labor market. . . . Under slavery surplus labor is appropriated as a quantity of labor: the slave is compelled to perform a certain amount of labor for the master's benefit. Under feudalism surplus labor is appropriated as a useful product (e.g. grain or vegetables): the local lord takes a share of what the serf has produced. Under capitalism surplus labor is appropriated through the sale of labor power: the capitalist buys labor power for less than she can produce using that labor power. (1994: 59)

Finally, each mode of production contains political, social and economic contradictions and conflicts. These lead to social disharmony, class conflict and the possibility of revolutionary change which will establish a new mode of production. The move from antiquity to feudalism and from feudalism to capitalism represents the successful outcome of such revolutionary configurations.

Activity 4.1

- What are the major differences of approach between Marx and the writers and theories developed in Chapters 2 and 3?

Marx's Critique of Capitalism

We now have the basic 'tools' or concepts developed by Marx to explain the social world and so will focus on how these concepts are applied to the study of the modern world. Marx spent the major part of his intellectual life trying to analyse capitalism, its operation, contradictions and conflicts. In developing Marx's critique of capitalism it will be useful initially to reiterate two points. First, for Marx the basis of every society is the labour process, humans co-operating in order to make use of the forces of nature and hence meeting their needs with, as a result, the material necessities of life being produced by human labour. But labour is of limited use without appropriate tools, whether they are simple wooden ploughs or complex computer-aided machines: without such tools even the most highly skilled worker will be unable to produce the goods necessary for physical survival. The distinguishing feature of capitalist society is that the necessary tools and the natural resources on which they work are privately owned: the means of production are owned and controlled by the dominant class, known within capitalism as the bourgeoisie.

Secondly, whereas the product of human labour must meet some human need (what Marx called its *use-value*), under capitalism the products of labour take the form of *commodities* and are produced in order to be exchanged. Thus, under capitalism, goods have a use-value and an *exchange-value*. As Callinicos points out, however, use-values and exchange-values are very different from each other. 'Air is something of almost infinite use-value to human beings since without it we would die, yet it has no exchange-value . . . Diamonds, on the other hand, are of comparatively little use, but have a very high exchange-value' (1983: 106).

While a use-value has to meet a specific human need – if you are hungry a pen or a typewriter is no good – the exchange-value of a commodity is simply the amount it will exchange for other commodities. Exchange-values reflect what commodities have in common rather than their specific qualities, and what they have in common, Marx argued, was labour: a car costs more than a television because there is more labour embodied in it (whether it is the labour of the workers employed on the production line making the car or the television or the 'dead labour' of previous generations of workers present in the machines and tools themselves, because these too are the product of human labour).

Capitalist societies are characterized by what Marx termed 'generalized commodity production'. That is, capitalism is a system where the products of labour are made in order to be exchanged on the market: goods are produced in order to be sold. The complex and specialized division of labour that capitalism produces means that no producer is able to survive on the output of his or her own production alone. Instead, they must sell their own products and in turn purchase the products of others. Producers, therefore, are interdependent. But commodities must be sold in order to realize their value, and this means that unsold commodities become a wasted resource. Further, whether commodities will sell is something that can only be discovered after they have been manufactured. In this sense production, in capitalist societies, is always a risk-taking exercise.

The obvious question to pose is, 'Where do profits come from?' Marx rejects any perspective which suggests that profits can be created in the selling process. Although 'supply and demand' will affect the price of goods, they will, nevertheless, fluctuate around their 'true value' (the embodiment of the socially necessary labour power worked in them). So profits (or more widely surplus value) are created in the process of

select the courses that are most relevant to those career possibilities.

There is a tendency for some students who are frustrated with their quantitative research skills to declare that qualitative methods are the only or major ones that they are interested in or going to use. Therefore, they would definitely not like to waste time studying the awful mathematical language and the boring computer software. It might be true that you are not going to become a "quantitative person;" yet it may be false that you will do or feel very well without some quantitative capability. Many quantitative researchers also try to equip themselves with qualitative understanding since they know that the quantitative and the qualitative aspects actually cannot be separated in a real research process. A coping strategy of denial and avoidance in school will likely bring regret to you later. In real terms, most graduate students in the behavioral and social studies are required to take certain quantitative courses including basic statistics. It is to your advantage to fulfill such requirements with confidence, interest, and extra energy if needed.

No matter what courses you are taking, or even without taking any courses, you will often find yourself reading some texts, reference books, monographs, and journal articles. The process of reading gives people very different feelings and learning results. To some students, it is the most boring thing in their life; and the best they can do is to manage to fulfill the course requirements and get some passing grades (some may be more ambitious than this; yet the subject interesting them is a better grade, ideally an A, not something else). Who cares about what is right and what is wrong in the reading? Some others, however, do care about what is being said in the book. They try to identify each point the work contains and know what all the rest is about. They try to analyze and understand what the author is attempting to say, and they hold a critical view about it. The book may have included too much "trash," or the entire article could be outdated. They do not believe all that is found in the book, but every point they get would provide some stimulation to their own thought. Some would even start reading as an author planning and writing his own work, and with such an approach they have a sharp eye, immediately seeing what is relevant to their interest and what is not. Some others would read as a professor preparing for teaching, and thus realize they have a responsibility to finish their reading in time and get some insights to share with others (their own imagined students and real classmates). Such a practice has nothing to do with bragging or arrogance; it is an effective way to survive and succeed in reading by taking the essentials and discarding the dross. After all, don't forget the saying: "high

Partial correlation

For continuous data at the interval or ratio level, the above sub- or partial table approach is generally not applicable. However, the relationship between two focal variables in a controlled situation can be more conveniently measured by directly calculating the net effect size of the "true" relationship. This is called partial analysis, and in the most popular linear treatment the result is a partial correlation coefficient. This can also be applied to the above causal and causal link analysis models as correlation coefficients are routinely calculated in contingency tables. Semi-multivariate analysis or the elaboration model provides a context for explicating the idea of partial analysis, and this idea will develop into a basis for more complex multivariate models.

In case the application of a control variable completely dismisses a spurious relationship, the measure of a partial correlation coefficient will be zero, i.e., $R_p = 0$. If the control variable does not affect the relationship at all, the partial correlation coefficient shall be the same as the measure (R) obtained without any control, i.e., $R_p = R$. If the control variable contributes only part to the focus relationship, then the net effect size measured by the partial correlation coefficient should be smaller than that obtained without any control, but greater than 0, i.e., $|R| > |R_p| > 0$. This statistic is a comprehensive indication of the impact of other variables. It is more convenient than the sub-tables, especially at the interval and higher levels. Indeed, partial correlation is analogous to multi-way cross tabulation, measuring the relationship between two continuous variables while controlling for other variables. A clear conclusion can be drawn by comparing the partial correlation coefficient and the original correlation coefficient. The partial correlation coefficient is a quantity summarized from the results of all partial tables, which is very comprehensive and helpful. It is also complementary to the conditional analysis in which the results for the partial tables differ considerably from one another.

Depending on the number of control variables introduced, partial correlation coefficients are calculated at different "orders." The correlation between variable X and variable Y controlling for only one variable is called a first-order correlation and is denoted by $\gamma_{xy \cdot 1}$; the correlation between the two variables controlling for two other variables is called a second-order correlation and is denoted by $\gamma_{xy \cdot 12}$; and so on. Accordingly, the correlation between variable X and variable Y without control is called a zero-order correlation and denoted by γ_{xy}. This is actually what we first learned about Pearson's γ and used as-is in the

production. Within capitalist societies exploitation 'is so thoroughly concealed that most people . . . , even the victims of exploitation, do not
recognise it exists' (Mayer, 1994: 59).

Although it *appears* as if capital and labour are equivalents, interdependent of one another (one providing the means of production, the other the
labour to work with machines and tools on natural resources to produce
commodities), the reality is somewhat different. The bourgeoisie's ownership and control of the means of production gives it enormous power to
exploit the labour activity of the vast majority within society who do not
own any means of production and can only survive by selling their labour
power for a wage. However, there is no mechanism forcing the bourgeoisie
to pay wages equivalent to the wealth (or value) created by the labourers
they employ. The form taken by the exploitative relationship creates surplus
value, wealth created by labour but 'belonging to' or under the control of
capital and used to pay rent, rates, various bills, reinvestment costs and
provide profits and dividends.

Out of this list the most important is 'reinvestment costs'. But why should
the bourgeoisie bother with reinvestment? Why do they not simply consume
all the surplus as the dominant classes did in antiquity or under feudalism?
The answer for Marx rests, once again, in the very nature of capitalism.
Although the major class division in society is between the bourgeoisie and
the working class, the bourgeoisie are in fierce competition with one another
to sell their commodities: the capitalist economy is one that is divided into
separate, interdependent and competing producers. Marx termed the bourgeoisie a 'band of warring brothers', competing with one another, trying to
drive one another out of business, but with a common 'brotherly' interest in
suppressing the potential threat posed by the working class.

The competition among capitalists drives the system forward, and in this
sense capitalism is a very dynamic system. This dynamism has two
consequences. First, capitalism is increasingly bringing 'new areas' under its
domain. A system that started in western Europe is now truly global. And
secondly, capitalism is constantly changing 'what' is produced and 'how',
and therefore the 'world of work' and the labour tasks we perform are
subject to constant change: the job of a miner, an engineer, an office worker
or even a lecturer is radically different today from 20 or 30 years ago. The
source of such dynamism is that each 'unit of capital' (whether it is an
individual, a national corporation, a multi-national company or even a state)
must try to produce more goods at a cheaper price than its major competitors. But because the value of commodities is set by the amount of
labour time necessary to produce them, then there are only two ways in
which they can do this: either they must (1) increase the exploitation of their
workforce, and/or (2) reinvest greater sums in machinery and technology
and in constantly 'revolutionizing the forces of production'.

Taking each of these methods we can identify two ways in which the
bourgeoisie can directly increase the rate of exploitation of their workforce.
First they can cut wages. This reduces the amount of time the worker spends

creating value equivalent to his or her wages and increases the amount of time the worker spends creating surplus value. Secondly, the capitalist can try to extend the working day, again ensuring that there is more time devoted to the creation of surplus value. However, both of these have severe limitations. Wages cannot be reduced below subsistence levels, and if the working day is extended too long workers become fatigued and inefficient. Further, both of these practices can produce offensive responses from workers. Thus these are potentially dangerous strategies (though ones that employers still try to pursue whenever possible).

The second way of cheapening goods is by investing in technology. Such investment allows commodities to be produced in a shorter time and in greater number than was the case previously. But this process leads to three problems which can be termed the major economic contradictions of capitalism.

First, the very fact of competition between rival 'units of capital' means that production in general does not take place in a rational and planned manner. Instead, historically, the system has lurched from periods of boom into periods of severe crisis. When 'units of capital' expect a 'reasonable' profit they will invest in factories, machines, raw materials and labour: a boom is under way. But the frenzy of competition has the effect of pushing up the price of the 'scarce resources' (land, raw materials and labour) and thus increases the costs of production. Eventually a point is reached where some firms realize that the costs have risen so much that all their profits have disappeared. The boom now gives way to an investment slump. Harman neatly summarizes what now happens.

> No one wants new factories – construction workers are sacked. No one wants new machines – the machine tool industry goes into crisis. No one wants all the iron and steel that is being produced – the steel industry is suddenly working 'below capacity' and becomes 'unprofitable'. Closures and shutdowns spread from industry to industry, destroying jobs – and with them the ability of workers to buy the goods of other industries. (1993: 49)

Secondly, the boom/slump cycle shows the *inefficiencies* of the market system. The system generates *over-production* (for example, European Union food mountains), when goods are not sold or not even offered on the market. Generally, when boom turns to slump products are left to rot, and resources (including labour) are left idle.

Finally, the competitive pressures to invest in capital and technology create an even greater problem. For Marx, the exploitation process under capitalism creates surplus value, but the pressure to invest in capital and machinery (to keep up with competitors) eats into this. What the capitalist has left after paying these costs Marx terms the *rate of profit*, and this is the central measurement the capitalists themselves will work with. However, as firms get larger and technological advances improve and become more expensive, the *organic composition of capital to labour* will rise (that is, there will be fewer workers, the creators of surplus value, working with larger and more expensive machines). Further, the drive towards innovation (to undercut competitors) means that machines become redundant and are discarded before they are exhausted or have been paid for. The result is that there is a tendency for the general rate of profit to fall. The costs of entering the productive process (to buy the newest machines and factories) are excessive and the surplus value created by the relatively few workers proportionately small. The consequences for capitalism are severe: the result is that each boom gets shorter and more shallow and each slump longer and deeper.

Such crises do not mean that capitalism will inevitably collapse. But in order for recovery to take place the working class must 'pay the price': their living and working conditions must deteriorate dramatically and the rate of exploitation drastically increase. Against these worsening economic conditions, however, there is always the possibility of united activity by the working class to protect their position within society or, to go further and establish a new form of living, what Marx referred to as 'socialism'.

Thus, to summarize:

1   capitalism is a system built on the exploitation of the majority (the working class) by the minority (the bourgeoisie);
2   exploitation is hidden within the production process;
3   Competition between capitalists forces them to:
    (a) constantly try to increase their exploitation of the working class,
    (b) reinvest larger and larger sums into the production process;
4   the capitalist economy is plagued by recurrent booms and slumps. But the tendency of the rate of profit to fall means that the slumps gradually get longer and deeper;
5   recurrent economic crises and class conflict lead inevitably to social and political crises and conflict.

Activity 4.2

● Why is class conflict inevitable in class societies?
● What forms do economic crises take under capitalism?

Class and Capitalism

The competitive drive of capitalism constantly forces 'units of capital' to attack the working class: lowering their wages, lengthening their hours at work and trying to cut back social spending. Class divisions and class conflict are, therefore, central to Marxist analysis, but what do Marxists mean by 'class'? The term 'class' is used in daily discourse. The newspapers, some politicians and many people use the term to describe various aspects of social life: it may be used to refer to types of jobs, lifestyles, the places were we live or, in general terms, our 'life-chances'. However, for Marxists class has a more specific and 'fuller' meaning than that given by many of the more 'commonsense' definitions. As we have noted, for Marxists, one's class position is determined by one's location within the process of production. This means that 'class' is an objective criterion. Whether you describe yourself as working class or not is, at this level, immaterial. The job that you do, and where this is located within society's major antagonistic relationships, will reflect and affect your position within society and this can be determined without reference to your subjective understanding of your class position.

Marx saw capitalism as a historically superior system of labour exploitation (that is, the techniques of production allowed much greater levels of surplus labour to be extracted from the subordinate class than was the case under feudalism or ancient slave societies). Further, capitalism has 'simplified' the class system. Instead of a number of classes, capitalism increasingly becomes dominated by two: the working class and the bourgeoisie. Exploitation has become simplified as well: no longer is it 'confused' with political, ideological and social ties and relations; it is now clearly based on 'brutal' economic exploitation.

Marx, then, could not be clearer. Capitalism is a system dominated by two classes in direct opposition to each other. The bourgeoisie, who own and/or control the means of production but who rely on others to work in their factories and offices to produce goods and create wealth; and the working class, the vast majority, who have no means of supporting themselves except by selling their labour power to the bourgeoisie: to work for a wage. Yet this perspective has been rejected by many academics. They claim that Marx's picture is too simplistic and the social world, and with it the class structure, is more complex than his simple dichotomy suggests. This is based on the claim that for Marxists the 'working class' refers to industrial workers in the productive sphere, but that this group is declining numerically. This is an important issue for Marxists and it is one we will address by looking at the early work of the American Marxist Eric Olin Wright (Wright, 1979) and the British Marxist Alec Callinicos (1987b).

The anti-Marxist case here is based on the perceived distinction between 'productive labour', which directly produces surplus value, and 'unproductive labour', which does not and is therefore a drain on capital. Here productive workers are all those employed in factories and mines directly producing commodities, or involved in transporting them to the point of sale (such as train drivers). Unproductive workers would be all those employed in delivering various services, such as welfare workers, office workers, bus drivers or dust-cart workers. This usage, therefore, gives us a 'narrow' definition of the working class, those involved in productive labour only.

Yet, as Callinicos (1987b) points out, this approach contradicts Marx's usage of the notion of productive labour in his major work, *Capital* (Marx, 1976 [1867]). Here, Marx argues that the increasingly complex division of labour within capitalism makes it difficult to utilize such a rigid distinction between 'productive' and 'unproductive' workers and that all workers involved in the entire process of producing commodities are in reality 'productive'. Thus various office workers' tasks are essential to the process of commodity production, their work is therefore productive labour and, as a result, they are productive workers subordinated to the process of production. Further, there is little evidence to suggest that Marx thought that even on this wider definition only productive workers were part of the working class. As Wright notes: 'both productive and unproductive workers are exploited; both have unpaid labour extracted from them' (1979: 49). Instead of the 'narrow' definition of the working class it is perhaps more appropriate to adopt a 'broad' definition. As Mandel has claimed: 'The defining structural characteristic of the proletariat in Marx's analysis of capitalism is the socio-economic compulsion to sell one's labour power' (in Callinicos, 1987b: 20). Thus the vast majority of wage labourers in offices and welfare institutions are part of the working class – not a white-collar service class – and have similar interests and experiences to those of workers in factories, docks and mines.

But does this mean that anyone who works for a wage is part of the working class? Clearly the answer is an emphatic 'no': wage labour is a necessary, but not in itself a sufficient, condition for determining membership of the working class; the majority of 'top industrialists' earn salaries but this fact alone does not make them part of the working class. Why is this?

Previously we noted that membership of the ruling class rested in those who owned and/or controlled the means of production. This means that members of the bourgeoisie do not need to directly own companies as long as they have effective *control over them*. Thus, the managing directors of, for example, British Gas, NatWest Bank, General Motors and Ford will be salaried 'employees', although they may also have substantial share ownership in the company in which they work as part of their perks of 'employment'. But while they do not individually own the company they work for they nevertheless have a significant degree of control over it, its investment and development plans and, as a result, over the labour of those who work for it. Thus the fact that these individuals earn salaries does not make them part of the working class; on the contrary, they are salaried members of the bourgeoisie.

To explain this phenomenon we must look at developments within the capitalist system over the last 150 years. Over this period there have been two key changes. First, 'units of capital' have increased dramatically in scale and size. As a consequence, companies are often 'owned' (that is, the shares are owned) by a range of financial institutions, individuals and other companies. The result is that many members of the bourgeoisie do not legally own the company or companies that they work for (or at least own them outright) although they do have effective ownership and control over them. Secondly, the concentration and centralization of capital over this period has made it impossible for individual capitalists to have hands-on control over the daily operation of the production process. As a result, a range of tasks has had to be delegated to a layer of middle managers and supervisors. This group is not part of the bourgeoisie but nor is it part of the working class whose labour it directly supervises. The combined effect of these changes has been to make the class system more complicated and introduce a layer of intermediaries between the bourgeoisie and the working class.

Thus, while capitalism remains a system divided by the two dominant classes, the bourgeoisie and the working class, the process of social production in the modern world has also created locations within the production process occupied by strata carrying out specific control functions for capital: controlling investment, production and/or the labour of others. If you like, these strata obtain the confidence of capital to carry out a series of important tasks and functions necessary for the smooth running of modern capitalism. In return they obtain higher levels of rewards (pay and perks) and this places them in a materially advantaged position over the working class. Their relative position of power and privilege rests in their ability to keep the working class in its place. Hence, carrying out these tasks, in combination with the rewards they obtain, sets these strata apart from the working class but it does not make them part of the bourgeoisie. Eric Olin Wright has attempted to locate these groups within the overall system of labour exploitation within capitalism. In his terminology, these groups occupy a 'contradictory class location': at different times and in different situations drawn towards, or pushed away from, the two dominant classes. One final point needs to be emphasized: there is not one contradictory class site but several. Some are closer to the working class than they are to the bourgeoisie (line supervisors), some are closer to, or even merge with, the bourgeoisie and some Wright identifies as being between the working class and the 'petty bourgeoisie' (for example, small shopkeepers, independent farmers). These positions can be depicted in tabular form as shown below.

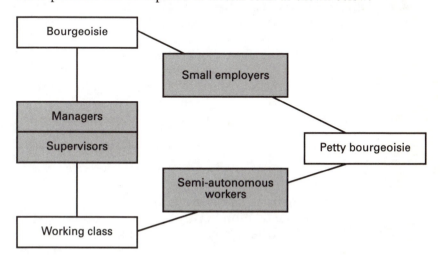

Figure 4.1 *Wright's class locations*
Note: Classes are clear; contradictory locations are shaded
Source: Wright, 1979: 63

The basis of Wright's class differentiation is the concept of control: control over investment and the accumulation process, control over the means of production, and control of labour power. The bourgeoisie have control in each sphere, the working class in none and the petty bourgeoisie control over the first two but not the labour of others: 'Managers, small employers and semi-autonomous workers enjoy varying amounts of control, more than workers but less than the bourgeoisie. Thus, contradictory classes are those who exhibit a mixed pattern of control' (Edgell, 1993: 18).

So, for Wright, workers are 'wage-labourers who also do not control the labour of others within production and do not control the use of their own labour within the labour process' (quoted in Callinicos, 1987b: 27). The bourgeoisie are those who have effective control over the entire process of capital accumulation, while the 'middle class' consists of two groups, those with a contradictory class location between capital and labour and those with a contradictory location between labour and the petty bourgeoisie. The conclusion of this argument is that the vast majority of the population of the 'advanced' economies are part of the working class, the bourgeoisie remain a relatively small proportion of the population, while those occupying 'contradictory locations' account for perhaps 20 per cent of the population (Callinicos, 1987b).

Thus, to summarize:

1 class is the fundamental concept of Marxist social analysis;
2 within capitalist societies the major class division is between the bourgeoisie (who own and/or control the means of production) and the working class (whose only means of survival is to sell their labour power for a wage);
3 as capitalism has advanced over the last 150 years the nature of work and the types and forms of labour have been altered, and as a consequence the composition of the working class has changed;
4 the concentration and centralization of modern capitalism has led to the creation of strata within society who carry out various functions for capitalism, and these groups can be depicted as having a 'contradictory class location';
5 the working class remains, numerically, the largest class within society.

Activity 4.3

- What are the main class divisions in capitalist societies and how does exploitation occur?
- For a Marxist, in what class do you think the following workers would be located: (a) miner; (b) firefighter, (c) bank clerk; (d) small shopkeeper; (e) factory manager (of a medium-sized factory); and (f) bank director?

Capitalism and the State and the Growth of Social Policy

Having identified the basic workings of capitalism and its contradictions, we can turn more directly to the question of social policy. For Marxists, social policy developments take place in the context of capitalist societies. As Jones and Novak have noted:

> throughout the history of capitalism, the existence of some form of 'social' policy has been determined in part by the fact that capitalism as a system of production depends upon a workforce that has neither property nor security. Those who, for whatever reason, are unable to work have nothing to sustain them, and the relief of their necessity, for both obvious political and economic reasons . . . [has been central to social policy development: ML]. . . . In relieving poverty, however, the State has not only assumed part of the responsibility of the maintenance of labour for industry . . . but it has also . . . served to reproduce the conditions and necessity of labour. (1980: 145)

There are two issues which this quotation draws to our attention. First, social policies are policies which are introduced, implemented and organized by 'the state'. Secondly, social policies have developed in response to the problems created by the structure and operation of capitalism in the area of labour reproduction. It will be useful to explore each of these propositions in more detail.

To claim that social policies are 'state policies' may seem rather obvious, but what do we mean by the term 'the state'? The first point to emphasize is that Marxists would reject the narrow liberal perspective which depicts the state as merely the government (made up of the executive and the legislature) and the judiciary. Marxists would argue that the state is much more ubiquitous than most liberals would admit: it includes sections of the civil service and various state administrators, the army and the police (protectors of the existing social order), various local and regional organs of government and a range of *ad hoc*, quasi-autonomous, semi-public bodies. Further, for Marxists, the state is not a neutral entity, equally predisposed to the interests of all individuals and groups within society. They would reject the notion that the state is a separate and independent body which treats and represents all citizens of a nation equally. Thus Marxists reject the notion that 'states' can be separated from 'societies'. The starting point of their analysis is the dominant mode of production, and the state should be viewed as a set of institutions and practices intimately connected with, but subordinate to, that mode of production. For Marxists the state performs a number of roles, but its primary activity is to maintain the conditions for the existence and expansion of capitalism as a socio-economic system. This involves the state in the reproduction of the dominant social relations of production, legitimation of the operation of the capitalist system and the facilitation of the self-expansion of capital. In turn, these may involve the state in:

1 the creation and maintenance of an adequate legal framework to allow business contracts to be maintained and fulfilled;

2   direct economic activity to support its national currency or aid or run
    major manufacturing interests;
3   the amelioration of the worst manifestations of poverty and hardship
    faced by the working class and generated by recurrent economic slumps,
    and
4   the development of social policies to support and discipline particular
    groups within society, partly to legitimate the present form of society
    and partly to control those who may threaten the economic workings of
    society.

Moreover, through the provision of social policies, the state also relieves
individual capitalists of the burden of maintaining and reproducing labour –
doing so in a more rational and efficient manner than would otherwise be the
case. These roles may involve the state in conflict with certain sections of
capital (in the short term) and its activities will be open to alteration and
debate over appropriate strategies. Nevertheless, the parameters of such
debates and strategic decisions are that the state cannot undertake policies
and activities which will undermine the economic and political basis of
capitalist society (of which the state is a part). In other words, the state is
intimately bound up with the socio-economic interests of society and the
'economically' dominant class will also be the 'politically' dominant class.
As Marx and Engels stated in the Commmunist Manifesto, the state is 'but
the executive committee of the *entire* bourgeoisie'. The problem for Marxists, however, has been how to apply this general dictum to the often
complex and contradictory activities of modern state forms. The result has
been a number of competing Marxist perspectives on the state. This is not
the appropriate location for a full discussion of these issues but we can note
seven of the most popular notions within Marxist theorizing, thereby
avoiding oversimplification of this complex issue, and note the variety of
Marxist perspectives.

First, *the relative autonomy of the state*: This terminology was 'popularized' by the French Marxist Louis Althusser. The argument is that the state
(a political entity) is 'relatively' (whatever this may mean) separate from the
capitalist (economic) class. Thus, economic and political interests will not
always be necessarily the same. However, the state will uphold the interests
of the capitalist class in the final instance.

Secondly, *the state in a capitalist society thesis*: This is associated with
the work of Ralph Miliband, who suggests that it is the common social and
cultural background and ideological commitments of state functionaries and
economic actors which produces a shared outlook, a homogeneous class and
thus accounts for the link between economic and political power. The same
form of state organization and institutions could exist (staffed with different
personnel) in a different type of society.

Thirdly, *the state as a 'constituted-divided' entity*: Associated with the
Greek Marxist Nicos Poulantzas, this thesis suggests that the state is
institutionally committed to reproducing the capitalist economic system. But

the state is viewed as being divided on class (and intra-class) lines and is thus an arena of struggle in the same way as the economic sector of society. On this perspective, different groupings of capitalists will try to assert their influence over the operations of the state (thus 'finance' and 'manufacturing' capital may try to ensure that their particular needs and interests are given priority at the expense of others).

Fourthly, *the strategic conception of the state*: This is associated with the 'Analytical Marxist' Adam Przeworski. Primarily concerned with policy outcomes and their *raison d'être*, Przeworski questions whether capitalists have public political power that the state and its various institutions cannot overcome. He questions, then, the very contention that economic and political power are necessarily linked within capitalist societies. It must be questioned, therefore, whether his writings really can be identified as part of the Marxist tradition.

Fifthly, *the state as capital thesis*: This perspective can be traced back to the early works of the Russian Marxist Nicoli Bukharin and more recently with the work of Chris Harman. This thesis notes the increasing role of the state in directly economic affairs, both as organizer and planner as well as direct employer. Further, it emphasizes that 'units of capital' have 'histories' within particular nation states with whom they will identify and look for protection from overseas competition. The economic success of many of the Newly Industrializing Countries (NICs) has been linked to their particular state capitalist form of organization (Harman, 1984, 1991).

Sixthly, *the state as an instrument of social control*: This perspective emphasizes that the majority of the state's activities are geared to the purpose of controlling the activities of the vast majority within society. Squires (1990), for example, would suggest that 'social policies' are in many respects 'anti-social' policies, committed to controlling and disciplining the poor and disadvantaged within society.

Lastly, *the 'capital logic' thesis*: This perspective suggests that the state must have a degree of distance from any particular unit (or units) of capital. This then allows the state to act in the logically best interests of the system as a whole, and it may lead it to act against the short-term interests of particular units of capital. This may, for example, lead the state to incur an economic cost to secure a political goal such as a compliant working class.

It is perhaps worth noting that some of the above perspectives could be combined, but the main point to emphasize is that, no matter the form taken by the state (whether it is liberal-democratic, fascist or state capitalist), it is clearly linked to the economic organization and structure of capitalist societies. This said, however, these perspectives are different and, depending on which one is adopted, it will shape writers' attitudes to government activity and to social policy developments. Thus, the first two positions of Althusser and Miliband open up the possibility that strong social democratic or left-wing parties (perhaps in conjunction with extra-parliamentary sup-port) could use government power to redirect resources substantially in

preceding pages. The calculation of $\gamma_{xy \cdot 1}$ is based on γ_{xy}, γ_{x1}, and γ_{y1}; the calculation of $\gamma_{xy \cdot 2}$ is based on $\gamma_{xy.1}$, $\gamma_{x2.1}$, and $\gamma_{y2.1}$; the calculation of $\gamma_{xy \cdot 3}$ is based on $\gamma_{xy.12}$, $\gamma_{x3.12}$, and $\gamma_{y3.12}$; and so forth. The formulas are a little complex, but you can leave them with the computer statistical software. SPSS can compute partial correlation coefficients up to the order high enough to meet your needs. Partial correlation coefficients range from -1 to 1, which may also be tested for statistical significance via the F procedure.

Sometimes it is helpful to calculate so-called semi-partial correlation. This is also called part correlation. Note here part correlation is not partial correlation. Partial correlation requires total control of the influence of the other variable(s) on the relation between two focal variables, which means the control for both focal variables. But part correlation only controls for the influence of the other variable(s) on one of the two focal variables. In other words, the control applied for calculating part correlation coefficient only removes the linear effect of the controlled variables on X, *or* Y, while partial correlation coefficient removes their linear effect on both X *and* Y. The absolute value of a part correlation coefficient is never greater than its corresponding partial correlation coefficient. This is very important since it suggests that the only influence the other variables might have on Y is a suppressive effect on the role of X in its relation with Y. Part correlation coefficients are mostly used as a middle product for the computation of other statistics and seldom used as an independent type of measure. It should be noted that controlling for X or Y may lead to different results. This is also very important since a particular way of control will give a multivariate model a particular meaning.

In addition to the partial correlation coefficient applicable to interval and ratio variables, we can also calculate partial Gamma (G) for ordinal variables. Similarly, we can also calculate partial Lambda (λ) for nominal variables. Test of significance of partial associations may also be performed at the lower levels by, for example, calculating partial Chi-squares in the log-linear models. The calculation of partial correlation is more frequently seen at higher measurement levels, however, because they allow such refined analyses as multiple regression and path analysis where the use of such measures is necessary or very helpful.

Multiple causation, regression, and correlation

Elaboration is a model where there are only two focal variables (i.e., dependent variable and independent variable) while other variables are all taken as control

favour of the working class. Legislation, and social policies in particular, can be viewed, therefore, as a beneficial gain for workers obtained by 'political' class struggle against the economic capitalist class. The 'state as an instrument of social control' thesis would reject this perspective and instead emphasize the way(s) in which legislation restricts our freedom, makes assumptions about our lives and ways of living and tries to control us.

The second issue that we identified at the start of this section related to 'how' and 'why' social policies have developed in response to the problems generated by capitalism. Social policies and spending on social services and welfare provision are only part of any state's activities which are geared to enabling capitalism to exist and expand. States are actively involved in 'economic' policy (from direct investment in industries to macro-economic planning), 'public' policies (such as providing a transport infrastructure) and 'law and order' strategies aimed at obtaining internal control over their own population. Social policies are linked to each of these but are primarily by means of those activities which are concerned with the reproduction of labour power and the maintenance of non-working groups within society. Thus the development and expansion of 'social policies' and welfare provision has been intimately bound up with the consequences, problems and social conditions created by capitalism. The expansion of capitalism has resulted in large numbers of people living and working in close proximity, and these features have created a number of social problems which have threatened the very existence of the system itself. Yet the development of social welfare has not simply reflected the needs of the system or the bourgeoisie. Rather, social legislation and the creation and activity of welfare institutions reflect the outcome of the interaction of four competing and conflicting pressures. We will look at each of these in turn.

The first pressure could be termed the '*structural needs of the system*'. For capitalism to exist and expand there is a requirement for certain activities to be performed and for certain services to be provided. Capitalism needs relatively fit and healthy workers to work efficiently in the offices and factories; it needs some sort of support mechanism for non-labouring individuals (and this may include basic financial provision); and new workers must be trained in the skills they will utilize while at work. These provisions can either be provided by individual capitalists (or groups of capitalists), be based on some form of 'insurance scheme' with payments being given to private companies to provide these services or they can be provided by the state. An example of state provision can be seen in the development of the education system in Britain, which partially reflects capitalism's need for more educated workers (Simon, 1960).

The following two pressures reflect the impact of individual or collective political activity or 'agency'. Thus the second element is that some policy responses reflect the political activity of certain sections of the bourgeoisie or are the result of intra-class conflict between sections of the bourgeoisie. Historically, there have been considerable intra-class divisions among both the bourgeoisie and the working class over the form welfare provision should take. This can be illustrated by taking the examples of housing and educational provision. With regard to the development of the education system we can locate a number of perspectives. Throughout the nineteenth century many textile owners were hostile to developments because they threatened to deprive them of a cheap source of (child) labour (Lavalette, 1994); other sections of the bourgeoisie saw such developments as being vital if Britain was to maintain its pre-eminent position as the 'workshop of the world' in the face of growing competition from the United States and Germany (Hay, 1975). Within the working-class movement there were sections who demanded and supported educational facilities as a means of educating workers as to their plight, the source of their misery and the possible political solutions to such questions, while at the same time these groups were often hostile to the form and disciplinary nature taken by state schooling (Simon, 1968). Other sections of the working class objected to the loss of earnings and costs of schooling and hence the material hardship that full-time schooling brought with it (Frow and Frow, 1970), while many working-class children objected to the process of schooling *in toto* (Humphries, 1981).

In the area of housing similar divisions can be traced. With regard to intra-class divisions among the bourgeoisie Jones and Novak note that: 'with regard to working class housing . . . 'progressive' sections of the ruling class accuse[d] landlords and builders of superexploitation in the single-minded pursuit of profit regardless of its physical and social consequences' (1980: 150).

The third identifiable pressure is collective working-class activity. The working class itself has on occasion been able to assert collective demands for social welfare legislation either to protect or improve its living conditions. Welfare provision can be identified as part of a 'social wage'; that is, not a direct wage payment paid by an individual capitalist but one which refers to the 'sum of the collective benefits which are transferred to individuals or families in both cash and kind via the state' (Bryson, 1992: 32). In other words, it is services provided by the state which meet or provide certain social needs. As such it can be a necessary part of the working class's living requirements and without it living conditions would be worse and the struggle for basic survival that much harder. In these circumstances it is not surprising that the working class has occasionally fought to obtain or maintain state welfare provision.

Such popular struggles demanding 'welfare' are often devalued or dismissed from histories of social policy. But despite being 'hidden from history' they remain important, as the following three examples emphasize. The first comes from the rent strikes which took place in Clydeside (Glasgow) during the First World War. The move to a war economy meant that there was a rapid expansion of war-related industries in Glasgow. Labour was sucked into the city to work in the shipyards, engineering factories and related industries and as a result there was a severe housing shortage. Landlords now had control of a valuable and scarce resource and put up their rents. The response from sections of the working class in Glasgow was to go on rent strike. These were led and organized by working-class women and quickly gained the support of a wide range of working-class activists and trade unionists. When the strikers were pulled in front of the debtors' courts there was a mass walk-out from many workplaces on Clydeside, the women were released and the government introduced the Rent Restriction Act, which pegged rents to their pre-war level and prohibited landlords from increasing rents for the duration of the war (Melling, 1983). In a similar vein, Harloe (1981) has argued that the introduction of socialized municipal housing in the 1920s was partly a result of the demands of the organized working class for improved and subsidized housing. Two further examples are, first, the campaign to free the Poplar councillors (in London), who went to prison in 1921 rather than set a rate which their constituents could not afford. The councillors were released as a result of the support campaign (Branson, 1979). And second, in the 1930s there was significant agitation against the means test led by the National Unemployed Workers' Movement. The Birkenhead riot (in Merseyside) was successful in obtaining more generous local poor relief and played a central role in the creation of a national response to unemployment generally (cf. Croucher, 1987).

Finally, the capitalist mode of operation is one that depersonalizes and alienates individuals. On occasions social policies have been developed to give the working class the impression that they have a stake and a say in the system. Social policies, therefore, have a role in the *legitimation process* within capitalist societies. As Lord Hailsham said, on the introduction of the post-war British welfare system, 'if you do not give the people reform, they are going to give you revolution' (quoted in Birchill, 1986: 49).

The interaction of these four sources, the structural needs of the system, intra-class divisions, inter-class conflict and the legitimation process, are not always easy to dissect, and generally policies cannot be assigned as easily to any one category as our examples above may suggest. Nevertheless, they each remain important *tendencies* shaping the development of welfare institutions and social policies.

Thus policy developments are the outcome of a complex process of struggle and conflict which takes place within a context: the structural needs and requirements of capitalism and the uncertainties (economic, political and social) created by social life within capitalist society. There are thus two elements to this process, first, the notion of struggle and conflict. At times this can be the 'open' class struggle of strikes, riots and demonstrations (for example, over unemployment in the 1930s or the 'poll tax' in the 1990s) or it may be a local campaign against a hospital opt-out or a demand for more resources from a community or tenants' group. But often the conflict will be less dramatic or overt. It may take place in the 'official public arena' between political parties or sections of the ruling class and it may concern issues which are apparently one stage removed from the concerns of working-class people in society. The second element relates to the context in which policies develop. They have been proposed and discussed in particular political, social and economic settings.

The operation of these two elements means that policy outcomes often take the form of an 'uneasy compromise' either between fractions of the bourgeoisie and/or these and the working-class. Resultant legislation can often be contradictory in its operation and in its impact on the working class. Thus, most welfare institutions and social policies can be seen to reflect, in different measures, elements of both 'care', however loosely and widely this may be defined, and 'control'. Yet any policy developments will, as state policies, reflect the contradictions of capitalist society and the values of the bourgeoisie. Hence all such developments affect and structure our lives. They embody different 'proposed solutions' to any crisis but do so in a way which embodies *ideological commitments*: assumptions about how we live (or should live) our lives (see Chapters 6 and 7, for example), about the causes of poverty and inequality (solutions which blame individuals as opposed to the social structure, for example; see Chapter 12), about the effects of 'choice' in the developing quasi-markets (see Chapter 13) or of 'targeting' on welfare provision (see Chapter 11). Finally, given such 'ideological commitments' it is not surprising that policies become another 'factor of struggle'. Thus the assumptions, inadequacies and/or failures of policies and welfare institutions have often created new crises and struggles and have been part of the process establishing new policy proposals.

Activity 4.4

- What benefits do the working class receive from:
  (a) the NHS;
  (b) education provision;
  (c) social services; and
  (d) the social security system?
- What benefits do the bourgeoisie obtain from the provision of each of the above services?

It will be possible to look at these features in more detail by considering some of the social problems and predicaments created by capitalism and to which social policies are partially addressed. We can do this by identifying four interlinked 'social crisis tendencies' which capitalism inevitably generates. These are issues associated with:

1 the conditions of social existence;
2 the reproduction of labour;
3 technological innovation, the labour process and the division of labour; and
4 the problems of social control, order and harmony.

1 The Conditions of Social Existence

Capitalism brought with it the commodification of labour, industrialization, migration and urbanization. These linked processes meant that, as capitalism developed, there was a growing class of workers who had no means of support but their ability to labour. They were drawn into the rapidly expanding towns and cities to look for work. Housing was scarce, poorly built, overcrowded, expensive, with inadequate (if any) water and sanitation facilities. In these conditions poverty and ill health were the norm. Work, if it could be found, was hard and long, conditions bad and wages pitiful. In order to meet their subsistence needs entire families went out to work. Men, women and children, the old and the young, worked for up to 15 hours a day, but still wages did not provide enough for adequate food and clothing. Further, there was no support for the unemployed, injured, sick, frail, elderly or very young. These circumstances produced a number of severe problems for the working class who had to live in such conditions but it also created problems for the bourgeoisie and capitalism as a system. First, the living conditions forced onto the working class produced ill health and bred disease. But these problems did not only affect the working-class. Although diseases like cholera started in the working-class slums they quickly spread out of the ghettos to the more prosperous parts of the towns and cities. A comparison of the age of death in Manchester and rural Rutland in the mid-nineteenth century emphasizes that geography was almost as important as class in determining the age of death.

Table 4.1   *Average age of death*

Profession	Age in Manchester	Age in Rutland
Gentry and professional classes	38	52
Tradesmen	20	–
Farmers	–	41
Mechanics and labourers	17	38

Source: Rogers, 1993: 8

Not only were the city-dwelling bourgeoisie under direct threat but there was an economic price as well: the early death of persons involved in skilled labour was a waste of an economic resource. Moreover, replacing such skilled labour was not only expensive but it was also a 'risky exercise'. According to Chadwick, the replacements would be 'young, inexperienced, ignorant, credulous, passionate, violent and proportionately dangerous, with a perpetual tendency to moral as well as physical deterioration' (quoted in Rogers, 1993: 8). Thus the basic living conditions and sanitation levels of early capitalism prompted action to improve them.

Secondly, the long hours of work were problematic on three counts. Long working days combined with inadequate nutrition meant that workers were physically exhausted and hence less productive, creating an inefficient use of labour power; the employment of children and women clashed with bourgeois ideological notions of family organization and responsibility, and, finally, such conditions fed the growth of trade unionism and political opposition to industrial capitalism. The combination of these elements promoted the gradual growth of (albeit inadequate) factory and employment legislation (see Lavalette, 1994).

Finally, the lack of adequate support networks for the elderly, sick and unemployed led to concern from some sections of the bourgeoisie over the operation, uneven burden and costs associated with the Poor Laws and promoted the enactment of the Poor Law Amendment Act (1834), which enshrined a national response to poverty, although one based on the concept of 'less eligibility', and had an important role in the creation of a national labour market. The eventual collapse of the New Poor Law in combination with continuing problems of underemployment and unemployment lie at the root of the social security system we have today. As Jones and Novak note:

> The need to do something about social conditions, about unemployment, poverty and disease, was thus set by the recognition that under the need for growing productivity and efficiency, labour was not simply a commodity that could be used up and discarded: that capitalism had both an immediate and long term interest in its healthy maintenance and reproduction. (1980: 147)

Thus the very conditions of existence within capitalist society promoted the development of social policies. The problems of living and existing in capitalist societies today mean that the 'conditions of existence' remain an important factor in social policy developments.

2 The Reproduction of Labour

One central problem in early industrial capitalism was the daily and intergenerational reproduction of labour. There is some evidence that the process of proletarianization in the early to mid-nineteenth century was undermining the existence of the working-class family (Engels, 1845; German, 1989). The long hours of work, combined with shift patterns, meant that in some districts 'family life' was completely disrupted. In these circumstances child-rearing was problematic and domestic labour (cooking, cleaning, personal support) was left inadequately fulfilled. This created problems for both the bourgeoisie and the working class. For the bourgeoisie it threatened the existence of a future workforce: while existing profits could be guaranteed on the basis of the cheap labour of men, women and children (at least to the extent that they can ever be guaranteed given the anarchy of the market system), the creation of surplus value in the future required the existence of a new generation of fit, healthy and disciplined workers. The break-up of family life threatened all of this. From within the working class there were concerns that mass proletarianization was having the effect of 'overstocking the labour market' and hence reducing wages. In these circumstances there were attempts from within both the bourgeoisie and working class to re-establish the family. From the bourgeois perspective this matched their ideological commitment to the family while providing a network that would be responsible for child-rearing, support for the elderly, sick and unemployed and would have a role in maintaining and supporting the existing workforce while socializing future generations of workers (Creighton, 1980, 1985). From the working-class perspective it was suggested that by establishing a 'family wage' (that is, a wage earned by men and large enough to support an entire family) first children and then women could be withdrawn from the labour market. This would protect children from the worst horrors of the factory (Lavalette, 1994) and allow women to engage in domestic labour to support the family. There was then an apparent material reason why such a demand was raised and supported (German, 1989). Here we see a possible convergence of interests around this issue among both the bourgeoisie and the working class. The result was the growth of family-related social policy. These were policies which initially restricted the hours of work and sectors of employment available to children and women, but by the end of the nineteenth century such policies had become much more interventionist, attempting to structure and control working-class family life. Finally, it is worth emphasizing that while such policies were supported by many women as well as men, they represented a significant defeat for women, removing them from the public arena and isolating them within the home. Furthermore, while the 'family wage' demand was ideologically important, it was rarely obtained in practice (Barrett and McIntosh, 1980). Family policy remains, however, a crucially important area within social policy, and one where the conflict between the elements of 'care' and 'control' are most visible. Further, the ideological assumptions regarding the perceived role of women as 'natural carers' is clearly expressed within social policy, such as present-day community care legislation.

3 Technological Innovation, the Labour Process and the Division of Labour

Technological innovation has been a feature of capitalist development. But such innovation brings with it social costs and, as the writer Harry Braverman argued, has been partly shaped and developed by the concern to assert control over the labour process and the workforce. Improvements in technology have a number of consequences within capitalist societies. First, it generally results in job losses as old skills are made redundant. This need not be the case, of course; the technological advances could be utilized to cut the working week on the same rates of pay, but under capitalist structures of organization such strategies are rejected because they are not 'profitable'. Unemployment brings with it social and economic costs which will be borne by many welfare institutions. Secondly, such technological advances can 'deskill' some tasks while changing the skill requirements of others. In general terms, such changes have the effect of cheapening labour. Again this has implications for the reproduction of labour. Thirdly, the outcome of these changes is often a more complex division of labour which can introduce divisions within the working class (these may be based on 'skill', 'race' or gender). Finally, such divisions may be reinforced by various occupational welfare benefits which some 'core' or better organized workers may obtain (Mann, 1992).

Such changes to technology and work organization have also led to debates about appropriate methods of 'skill' training. In particular, there have been demands for a flexible education system able to cope with changing work patterns. The recent rapid expansion of higher education partly reflects the changing composition of the working class and the new skills required to work in the offices and welfare institutions of advanced capitalism. But the state also plays a role in 'employment training' for young and old, whether this is to impart new skills or to encourage workers to accept lower wages in the growing number of 'deskilled' tasks.

Historically, both unemployment and insecurity of employment have had an effect on the creation of the social security system, a system which has been structured as much by considerations of 'controlling' the unemployed as it has by concerns of providing 'relief' from hardship. The existence and operationalization of the division of labour has the effect of institutionalizing divisions within the working class. The consequence is that often social policies

> act on the divisions created by capitalism as a whole. . . . By acting on these divisions, supporting and reflecting them and often creating further subdivisions, social welfare measures have had their greatest success in maintaining and effecting a marked ideological impact. (Jones and Novak, 1980: 162)

4 The Problems of Social Control, Order and Harmony

As has been emphasized, within social policy the 'control' element has been as vital and as central as any element of 'care' policies may contain. For example, although Income Support (IS) in theory provides a 'safety net' against poverty it is increasingly stigmatized and used to discipline groups within society: 16–18-year-olds no longer qualify because they (should) live at home and have access to training schemes; people refusing to take low-paid jobs can lose entitlement because they are deemed no longer to be 'actively seeking work'; and strikers do not receive IS if they are single or if both partners are on strike or are otherwise assumed to be receiving £50 per week in strike pay, whether this is in fact the case or not. The rules and regulations which govern the operation of the DSS or the social services departments, for example, may only directly affect a minority of the population but it is a substantial minority – more than 5 million people were on IS in Britain at the end of 1994 and this figure does not include dependants of claimants (DSS, 1995). Further, such rules, regulations and institutions remain a threat to many more as the problems of poverty and hardship encroach on our lives and economic insecurity becomes a more pervasive threat. In these circumstances such disciplinary activities only need to be applied to a minority within society to have an effect.

Concerns over present and future 'order' have been important in attempts to socialize children within the education system. At times this has been expressed via emphases on rote learning, classroom discipline or the wearing of school uniforms. Thus Cunningham (1990) has held that one of the central arguments promoting universal compulsory education in the 1870s was that it would take working-class children off the streets and solve the 'order' problem created by unemployed working-class youth, while today the National Curriculum clearly expresses government views regarding what is 'legitimate knowledge' (the history of kings and queens, for example) and what is not (the social history of riots, rebellions and revolutions).

Finally, attempts to obtain social harmony have often been constructed via commitments to welfare provision or expansion and, as noted earlier, are part of the legitimation process.

To summarize, we can note the following five points which are central to any Marxist analysis of social policy and its development:

1 Social policies are state policies, but the state is an integral part of the capitalist mode of production, intimately commited to the reproduction of capitalist social relations.
2 Social policies have been, and are, intimately linked with the consequences, problems and social conditions created by capitalism.
3 There are four social crisis tendencies which promote state social policy intervention. These are: (a) the conditions of social existence; (b) the reproduction of labour; (c) technological innovation, the labour process and the division of labour, and (d) the problem of social control, order and harmony.
4 The form taken by policies reflects the outcome of a number of conflictual tendencies that operate within capitalism. These are: (a) the system's 'needs'; (b) intra-class divisions; (c) inter-class divisions; and (d) the need for capitalism and the bourgeoisie to legitimate themselves.
5 Policies develop as a result of conflicts, broadly defined, that occur within particular contexts. Thus social policy developments reflect the interaction of 'structure', 'agency' and the need for 'legitimation'.

Activity 4.5

- What problems, for capitalism, do social policies attempt to solve?
- Why does the working class have an interest in expanding welfare provision, and what contradictions may this bring in capitalist societies?

The Marxist Critique of 'Welfare Regimes'

This section looks at existing Marxist critiques of what may be termed 'welfare regimes'; that is, that amalgam of welfare services, institutions and political commitments to produce different forms of welfare settlements within a range of capitalist societies. Any such critique will involve an acknowledgement of both the state and its social policy developments discussed in the last section. However, prevalent within Marxist writings is not only an acknowledgement of the contradictory constitutive elements to social policy and welfare formation but also a recognition that such developments bring forth their own contradictions for the capitalist system as a whole. We will start by outlining four key points to which Marxists adhere:

Firstly, the term 'welfare state' is generally rejected. This terminology gives the impression either of a concerned post-capitalist socio-economic system or of a separation of economic and political power. For Marxists, no matter the particular form of any welfare regime it remains a part of the capitalist system.

Secondly, the development of welfare regimes has not reduced class inequalities nor has it significantly redistributed resources in favour of the working class. Several studies have emphasized that existing welfare systems essentially redistribute resources horizontally (that is, within the working class) rather than vertically (that is, from bourgeoisie or petty bourgeoisie to the working class) (Gough, 1979).

Thirdly, as we noted in the last section, (a) social policies and welfare systems have developed as a result of the conditions and conflicts inherent in capitalist societies – they reflect structural needs, conflictual outcomes and are part of the legitimation process; (b) the state provides services which would otherwise not be available or provides services on a more rational and/or cheaper basis than would otherwise be the case; but (c) the costs of an expanding welfare system eat into surplus value. Resources spent on 'welfare' cannot be utilized in other directions, such as directly aiding the self-expansion of capital.

Finally, Marxist writers do not suggest that welfare regimes and their associated costs are the cause of generalized economic crisis. Despite the suggestion given in some reviews of Marxist theories of welfare (Mishra, 1984; George and Wilding, 1994), neither O'Connor (1973) nor Gough (1979) gives state welfare spending such a pre-eminent position. The causes of economic crises are located elsewhere for these writers (for O'Connor it is essentially the result of 'over-production' in an era of monopoly capitalism, and for Gough it is the 'distributional struggle' over wages). However, in the midst of such economic crises both writers argue that the welfare system becomes a major contradiction for capitalism: it fulfils certain essential functions and plays a role in socializing and placating workers, but the resources it demands become increasingly more difficult to provide (because the state's revenue is squeezed at times of crisis and such

variables. In other words, there is a clear distinction between an independent variable and a control variable. Multiple causation is a different model. Like the elaboration model, the dependent variable is still there and of focal interest. But unlike elaboration, there is no distinction between independent variables and control variables. All the other variables are considered independent variables (multiple causes), though their mutual impacts among themselves are controlled in certain ways. This is more in line with a "multivariate" analysis.

The simplest multiple causation model is a multiple regression equation containing n independent variables. In such cases, partial analysis can be conducted in exactly the same way as in the elaboration model, though here we will have n partial correlation coefficients with the same order of n-1. Comparing these partial correlation coefficients with one another will help to determine the relative strength of the relationship of each independent variable with the common dependent variable. In SPSS, the n-1 order partial linear correlation is calculated with the REGRESSION procedure, while the CORRELATION procedure will conveniently produce a zero-order correlation matrix.

The special use of the REGRESSION procedure is that it will also produce a set of partial regression coefficients for the regression equation, which can be used to predict the value of the dependent variable based on the values of all the independent variables. Here we should pay attention to the difference between a partial correlation coefficient and a partial regression coefficient. For the effect of an independent variable on the dependent variable, the latter indicates its magnitude while the former shows the relevance of the prediction based on such an effect. An independent variable may have a great impact on the dependent variable (large partial regression coefficient), but the uncertainty in its realization may also be high (small partial correlation coefficient).

A regression equation may take on two different formats: the nonstandardized form $y = a + b_1x_1 + b_2x_2 + ... + b_nx_n$ and the standardized form $Y = \beta_1X_1 + \beta_2X_2 + ... + \beta_nX_n$. The former uses the original units for its variables and therefore the values have actual meanings. However, the predicted values of y will not be exactly the same as those of the actual sample since this is not a deterministic but a probabilistic equation. The standardized equation will lose all the original meanings for the values of its variables, but it will have the advantage of comparability of the regression coefficients in representing the relative effects of the corresponding variables. The standardized β_i is called beta weight. In the simple regression case involving only two variables, $\beta_{yx} = b_{yx}(S_x/S_y)$. Here S_x and S_y are the standard deviation of x and y, respectively.

expenditure is directed at 'non-productive' welfare outlets instead of productive 'economic' ones).

It is these last two points which identify the major contradictions
associated with capitalist welfare regimes. According to O'Connor, the state
must perform two linked roles: accumulation and legitimation. With regard
to the first of these, O'Connor argues that the state undertakes more than
merely creating and supporting a framework for capitalist expansion; it must
become an increasingly active actor in economic life. Thus he notes that the
state attempts to regulate and co-ordinate the economic workings of the
system; and support and direct economic investment and growth to ensure
(or at least attempt to ensure) profitability. Historically, state intervention
arose as a result of the failure of the market system but, according to
O'Connor, while such intervention could be 'successful' in terms of managing economic crises in the short term it could not manage the crises
tendencies of capitalism indefinitely. This was because such strategies failed
to alter the underlying class divisions in society, its economic structure and
organization. Further, the reassertion of economic crises could be made
worse as a result of the state's second role: 'legitimation'. We have already
discussed this concept. According to O'Connor, 'legitimation' refers to those
socio-political activities, performed by the state, which give the appearance
that the capitalist social order is 'just' and 'fair' and by doing so help
maintain social harmony.

As O'Connor notes, it is not always easy to separate the accumulation and
legitimation functions of the state, and the need to fulfil both these functions
has led to a dramatic increase in state activities and expenditure. O'Connor
argues that we can divide the resultant state public spending into two sets of
components: 'social capital' (which is primarily concerned with 'accumulation' and can be further divided into 'social investment' and 'social
consumption') and the 'social expenses of production' (which are overwhelmingly connected to the state's 'legitimation' function). This means we
can identify three types of state expenditure:

First, *social investment*: this expenditure is 'indirectly productive' and
covers services and projects that increase the productivity of labour. For
example, the cheap supply of electricity to industry, spending on roads and
infrastructure and educational spending are all forms of 'social investment'
spending.

Secondly, *social consumption*: again this is 'indirectly productive', and
involves spending on services which will lower the reproduction costs of
labour – for example, Family Credit payments.

Thirdly, *social expenses*: these are completely 'non-productive' but are
necessary for social stability. This includes expenditure on aspects of the
welfare system, such as social security payments, but not national insurance
benefits which have to be earned through work. The aim of this expenditure
is to maintain social harmony.

From our examples we can see that welfare spending falls into all three
categories and indeed O'Connor recognizes that nearly every state agency is

involved in both the functions of accumulation and legitimation and that most state spending is part social investment, part social consumption and part social expense.

O'Connor proceeds to argue that, while the state can fulfil these functions during periods of sustained economic boom (such as occurred in the 1950s and 1960s), in periods of economic downturn it becomes increasingly difficult for the state to meet these requirements. There are several reasons for this. First, in periods of boom, full employment can fulfil the functions of both aiding 'accumulation' and providing 'legitimation'. But in periods of crisis these functions can more easily and openly conflict (the requirement to obtain 'legitimation' may suggest more welfare spending, while 'accumulation' strategies may be based on reducing government expenditure in an attempt to control inflation, for example).

Secondly, throughout the twentieth century there has been a tendency for state activity to increase dramatically in scope (in the social, economic and politico-military fields for example). But while the public sector has expanded, it has rested on the private sector (both commercial and individual) to provide its revenue, primarily via taxation. This has produced a tendency for 'state expenditures to increase more rapidly than the means of financing them' (O'Connor, 1973: 9). Such explanations may be less helpful than simply suggesting that increasing state activity is paid for out of surplus value and such expenditure means that there is less available for directly productive investments both by the state and by capital.

Following from the last point, Gough has noted the expanding costs and scope of welfare. He argues that there are four reasons for the growth in social expenditure. These are first, *rising relative costs* – the social services are labour-intensive and, because there is less possibility of raising productivity to offset higher wages, then there is a tendency for the relative costs of the social services to rise faster than the average. As a result, a higher level of spending is required year on year simply to maintain services at their pre-existing level. Secondly, *population changes* – there has been a growth in the size of the population and also significant changes in its structure. In particular there has been a growth in the 'dependent' population (children and elderly), and these groups tend to be the heaviest users of welfare services. Thirdly, *new and improved services* – there are two elements here: (a) there has been an expansion of welfare services and (b) various technological and/or bureaucratic improvements or rationalizations have provided more services to wider groups. The National Health Service, for example, has been quite successful at expanding its activities and providing, often expensive, life-saving operations. Fourthly, *growing social need* – there are two aspects here: (a) for example, the growth in unemployment since the mid-1970s in Britain has meant that there has been an increasing need for unemployment and social security benefits. But (b) needs, like poverty, are relative to the age and the society in which we live and capitalism is constantly generating new needs. As society becomes more wealthy then the basic requirements for living and taking part in that society (one's basic needs) expand. As a consequence there are demands on welfare to meet these basic needs (although the demands may very well not be met).

The result of these developments, according to O'Connor, has been uncontrolled state expansion and increased costs of government. Further, within the state bureaucracy there are individuals and groups who will tend to pursue their own particular ends, the result of which is the duplication of state activities. As a consequence, these pressures have all been instrumental in producing what O'Connor calls the 'fiscal crisis of the state': the state increasingly spends more than it earns. But, crucially for O'Connor and Gough, any attempt to solve this crisis by reducing state expenditure will (a) affect economic activity, either immediately or in the future; (b) potentially undermine the legitimation process; and (c) possibly provoke a working-class response in defence of such state spending. Thus while the fiscal crisis may be economic in origin, solutions to any such crisis have directly social and political consequences.

The arguments presented by O'Connor and Gough are complex, and both writers utilize substantial data to emphasize the political and economic contradictions of the welfare regimes of modern capitalism. Although we do not have the space to develop their arguments further, the important points to note are as follows:

1   that they recognize the economic, political and social factors driving welfare provision and expansion in capitalist societies; and
2   that such expansion becomes one factor in the general on-going crisis of capitalism, and thus, for the ruling class, one element which must figure in their 'crisis management'.

This does not mean that either of these writers suggests that there will be be an inevitable collapse either of capitalism or of welfare provision. But they do note the contradictions associated with welfare provision in capitalist societies and the struggles that welfare and attempts to restructure welfare provision can produce.

Thus, to summarize, we can note the following:

1   There has been a tendency for state activity to expand and for states to play an increasingly active role in economic, social and political life.
2   There is a tendency for welfare expenditure to increase as a result of (a) rising relative costs, (b) population changes, (c) new and improved services, and (d) growing social needs.
3   The costs of financing increasing state activity comes out of surplus value. Such expenditure can have benefits for capitalism (and can be indirectly productive) but it is also a drain on resources (such expenditure cannot be used in directly productive activities).
4   Such tendencies promote the fiscal crisis of the state.

Activity 4.6

• Why, and in what circumstances, might welfare expenditure produce a 'fiscal crisis' for the state?

Marxism and Welfare: an Assessment and Summary

To summarize, we should note the following eight points which reflect the Marxist critique of welfare provision:

1 Marxism is a critique of capitalism and of class societies generally.
2 The starting point of Marxist analysis is the production process and the social relations this creates.
3 Societies are viewed as 'social totalities' which are: (a) divided by classes with conflicting interests and (b) wracked by internal contradictions which lead to socio-economic and political crises.
4 The two major classes in capitalist society are the bourgeoisie and the working class.
5 Modern societies encapsulate further divisions of oppression, between men and women, black and white, gay and straight, young and old, able-bodied and disabled, and so on. But these divisions are built onto existing class divisions. Thus, for example, not all women share the same class position.
6 Social policies and welfare provision develop in response to the consequences, contradictions and living conditions created by capitalism. In particular, they reflect the influence of four competing and conflicting pressures: (a) the structural needs of the system; (b) capitalism and the bourgeoisie's need to obtain legitimation; (c) the demands of the working class; and (d) intra-class conflict.
7 Social policies reflect the divisions of exploitation and oppression within society (for instance, they reflect assumptions about the role of women and the family in society).
8 The development of welfare regimes reflects the outcome of these competing pressures, but in its wake it brings forth further contradictions which can restrict the process of the 'self-expansion of capital'. Welfare regimes, therefore, are necessary for capitalism but bring major problems which capitalism struggles to solve.

Part 2

RADICAL CRITIQUES

In the following section we introduce a number of 'radical critiques'. By utilizing this terminology we are not suggesting that the approaches which follow are less important or less theoretical than those which were discussed in the last section. Indeed, it is important to stress that the four chapters which follow offer a critique on two levels. First, they question the assumptions of social policy and welfare practices. Welfare institutions and social policies operate in ways which assume things about how we live, or should live, our lives. But by making such assumptions they can have the effect of reinforcing the subordinate position of groups within society. Thus social policies make assumptions about our 'race' and who is 'British', and as a result who is deserving of welfare service support or whose needs should be met; about the correct or appropriate role and activities to be performed by women in society and about the types of families we live in; about legitimate or 'normal' sexual orientations, and about our (dis)abilities and capabilities to perform a range of tasks. But such assumptions are *social constructions*, artificially created by historical processes and should not, therefore, be uncritically accepted or go unchallenged.

The chapters which follow, however, are also radical critiques in a second sense. That is, they are critiques of, and challenges to, those paradigms outlined in the last section. Thus what follows covers a range of theoretical perspectives which have grown up in response to what is often termed the gender, 'race' and sexuality 'blindness' of the traditional theoretical perspectives. In other words, by talking in terms of broad historical structures and periods and utilizing wide, all-embracing concepts like 'class', 'citizenship' or notions of 'abstract individuals', Marxism, social democratic and liberal and neo-liberal paradigms underplay or ignore the role of specific power relations in society which shape the lives of black people, women, gays and lesbians and members of the disabled community.

However, we should also introduce a note of caution. Although the chapters in this Part 2 are critical of the theoretical approaches already discussed, this does not mean that they necessarily reject these paradigms. Some perspectives, like radical feminist or black nationalist theories, may dismiss these approaches as being male-centred or Eurocentric and thus of little relevance to women or black people, but others depict the feminist critique, the anti-racist perspective, the focus on sexuality as necessary elements widening the appeal and areas of concern of the 'traditional' theoretical perspectives. Thus to take feminist writers as an example, we can identify both *socialist feminists*, combining insights from social democratic perspectives, Marxist philosophy and feminist concerns, and *liberal feminists*, who develop traditional social democratic and liberal concerns with equality and justice and apply them to the position of women in society. Thus the aim of these writers is to adjust the priorities and concerns of these traditions (liberal, social democratic, Marxist) to include the previously excluded (women) and their main concerns.

Hence in Chapter 5, Kath Woodward introduces the feminist critique of welfare. She looks at the important role played by early social policy legislation in re-creating the family around the concept of the male breadwinner. She then proceeds to look at the way the welfare state and social policies have developed to de-prioritize the concerns of women and to devalue women as secondary welfare citizens.

In Chapter 6 Laura Penketh and Yasmin Ali look at the assumptions of 'race' and the role of racism in shaping social welfare. They start by challenging us to think about what is meant by terms such as 'race', ethnicity and racism and then apply a committed anti-racist perspective to an analysis of the legislative framework and the operation of social welfare.

Angelia Wilson, in Chapter 7, introduces a number of themes which have been marginalized within social policy for too long. The emphasis on the family within social policy clearly discriminates against those who are perceived to live in inappropriate families or whose lifestyle challenges the moral assumptions of family policy. But institutional heterosexism spreads beyond simply family policy; it is present in a range of social services and is shown in the way that social policy and welfare institutions consciously or unconsciously discriminate against gays and lesbians.

Finally, in Chapter 8, Phil Lee and Tony Fagan, in a more reflective contribution, discuss the role of new social movements in shaping welfare provision and, as a case study, focus on the disability movement.

5

Feminist Critiques of Social Policy

Kath Woodward

This chapter outlines feminist approaches to social policy, starting with some of the shared concerns of feminist critiques and moving on to an exploration of different perspectives within feminism. Feminist critiques are primarily concerned with two themes. First, the ways in which the gendered nature of social practices and institutions has been ignored and gender neutrality assumed within society and social policies, and secondly, on the ways in which issues which are of particular relevance and importance to women have in the past been marginalized or excluded from the welfare agenda. In particular, feminists have drawn attention to the *patriarchal* structure of the welfare state and the different ways in which women and men have been incorporated into the role of citizens (Pateman, 1988).

Particular aspects which have been the focus of feminist critiques are discussed here in order to illustrate the impact of feminism and its different strands. The first of these is the *family*, which has been a major target of state intervention in the implementation of welfare policies and a key concern for feminist research and analysis (Segal, 1987, 1993). Linked to discussion of the family are the issues of domestic violence and sexual abuse, which have become major concerns in recent debates, having been put on the agenda as social, and not individual, problems by feminist activists and researchers with their insistence on listening to the voices of women within families and as survivors (Saraga, 1993). *Citizenship* is addressed as an example of an important concept in discussion of social policy, which feminists have argued is gendered and not universal or gender neutral (see also Chapter 10).

Thus, the main aims of this chapter are to provide an understanding of the major concerns of feminist analyses; to explore some of the differences between these analyses; to show how the different approaches focus on gender difference as a structuring principle in the provision of welfare; to suggest strategies for the analysis of social policy; and, by using the variety of feminist approaches, to develop a critical perspective on other theoretical positions.

Historical Context

As Lewis (1992) argues, one of the key elements underpinning historical changes in welfare provision has been the shifting relationship between women, men, the family and the state. Women have long been the target of state intervention, often where concern with women as mothers was linked with state anxiety about children especially and family life in general. This can be traced back to the intervention of the state in the private arena of the family and notably to the development in European societies from the eighteenth century onwards of policies which were concerned with the body and health in a trend which Foucault called *biopolitics* (Foucault 1987). The idea of state intervention into the family began to be taken for granted, with the notion that women were 'man's salvation, the privileged instrument for civilizing the working class' (Donzelot, 1980).

State intervention has been two-pronged. On the one hand it has been concerned with the regulation of sexual relations and in particular the enforcement of heterosexuality, and on the other it has focused on the 'family' and family-centred legislation, particularly targeting mothers and children. Let us look at each of these in turn.

Enforcing 'Appropriate' Sexual Relations

The two main targets of state policy have been homosexuals and prostitutes, each seen as a danger to the British 'race', motherhood and the population, and with legislation structured by Victorian concerns about purity and pollution. Homosexuality was seen as a social threat, with the potential to affect the birth-rate adversely and to undermine the patriarchal family and, by implication, the hierarchical social order and male authority. Debates about homosexuality in the nineteenth and into the twentieth century related to men, since women were defined as asexual (Weeks, 1977), except as reproducers. The negative public image of the homosexual constructed, for example, by the trials of Oscar Wilde (Weeks, 1977) put pressure on men to marry and have children in order to be seen to be heterosexual, thereby creating a notion of 'normal' sexuality as heterosexual and taking place within the traditional family. This had repercussions for women even if lesbianism was not named in legislation. Lesbians have also been portrayed as a social threat, especially to the 'normal' family. Consequently, although motherhood is seen as women's 'natural' destiny and women are much more likely to be granted custody of their children in divorce cases, even when the woman has committed adultery, the lesbian mother is still less likely to be awarded custody (see Chapter 7).

Explicit and direct attempts were made to categorize and control women's sexuality. This had a moral dimension, where the dichotomy of the 'good' (respectable) woman and the 'bad' (immoral) woman operated. The most obvious instances related to prostitution. The trigger to state intervention was fear about the spread of venereal disease among troops. This was clearly a serious health threat, although anxieties about physical well-being were conflated with those about moral degeneracy. Male sexuality was construed as an imperative which demanded relief. Unlike for the civilian population marriage was not the solution, as in the military population marriage was discouraged because the loyalty of soldiers was to their country and their command. Denied marriage and homosexuality, in theory if not always in practice, the only 'outlet' for men's sexual urges was the prostitute. The Contagious Diseases Acts of 1864, 1866 and 1869 put the entire onus of responsibility and blame for the spread of venereal disease on women (Walkowitz, 1980). Women identified as 'common prostitutes' by the police would then be subject to fortnightly examinations and would be interned in a 'lock hospital' if found to be suffering from venereal disease. There was less emphasis on medical treatment than on moral reform in the lock hospitals, which 'felt obliged to compensate for the chequered reputation of their female patients by stressing efforts at their moral reclamation. As a result, lock hospitals subjected female inmates to a repressive moral regime' (Walkowitz, 1980: 61). The operation of these laws gave the police the right to stop and caution almost any woman, thus allowing in particular for the regulation and control of working-class, single women. Male protection through marriage and the 'respectability' thus afforded became even more pressing for women. Needless to say, the Contagious Diseases Acts had no positive impact on the spread of venereal disease, which actually increased between 1876 and 1882, because men were not inspected, and thus freely carried and spread the disease without any preventive or interventionist action by the state directed at them.

Family Policy

Family policy, including the identification of women as mothers, with its underlying assumptions about what constitutes the 'normal' family – namely, the traditional, patriarchal, heterosexual family form – has been a particular focus of state intervention and welfare provision. The other main focus has been the idea of the *male bread-winner*. The 1834 Poor Law Amendment Act which reasserted the Elizabethan Poor Law was based on a major concern with labour and, in particular, the male worker. Women were on the whole considered to be dependants if they were married and non-workers if they were single. The main aim of legislation was to reduce unemployment and promote industry, the assumption being that much unemployment was voluntary. Men were divided into two categories, able-bodied and non-able-bodied, so that male, and hence family, entitlement to support depended on their capacity for work. Women's position was defined according to their marital status. This produced a three fold categorization, with the first and largest group being married women who were constructed as dependants of their husbands, the bread-winners. The second category included women without a man to support them, seen initially as a homogeneous category (Daly, 1994), to which the state was reluctant to give any support, but later subdivided into the 'deserving' (such as widows) and the 'undeserving' (such as single mothers). Unmarried mothers, who were actually mentioned in the 1834 Report, were themselves to bear sole responsibility for their illegitimate children, although in 1844 it became

Theoretically, you may focus on some of the independent variables and use the regression model for elaboration purposes. It should be noted that the control applied to the calculation of the partial regression coefficients is actually the same as the calculation of the part (not partial) correlation coefficients controlling only for the mutual impacts among the X's (independent variables). Since the coexistence of the effect of other independent variables on the dependent variable is allowed, it may cause some problems in interpreting the regression results. The absolute value of a part correlation coefficient is always equal to or smaller than its corresponding partial correlation coefficient. This suggests that the only influence the other variables might have on Y is a suppressive effect on the role of a specific independent variable X_i in its relation with the dependent variable Y. Especially, the part correlation of two strongly correlated independent variables with the dependent variable will be significantly weakened which, on the other hand, will exaggerate the effect of other independent variables. This situation is called statistical redundancy, or a multicollinearity problem, and will obscure the real relative importance of the independent variables in terms of their partial regression coefficients (not partial correlation coefficients). A multiple linear regression model, therefore, has limits on the kind of variables that can be included.

Generally speaking, you should be careful and selective, excluding those that are not important to the dependent variable or highly correlated with other independent variables. In this regard, control had better also be considered as a prerequisite rather than a pure purpose or consequence of multiple regression analysis. An examination of the correlation matrix of all the candidate variables for a regression model is thus helpful. The stepwise methods in the REGRES-SION procedure is very useful to help get around the statistical redundancy problem and find out the most important variables for inclusion. This process can also be guided by theoretical analysis. However, the regression model will still be limited in its ability to address your theoretical needs.

In addition to the above restriction, the regression model has to deal with a problem called statistical interaction. Regression analysis is normally based on an additivity assumption, that is, the total effect of the independent variables is the sum of their individual effects. Statistical interaction will produce an effect different from the additive effect, which can be called a multiplicativity fact. Such an effect between two independent variables can be dealt with by using their product as a new variable in the equation. This understanding may also be applied to situations other than multiple regression.

possible for them to sue for an affiliation order against the father. In the nineteenth century it was women in this group who were more likely to be sent to the workhouse rather than granted outdoor relief, suggesting something of the contribution of moral discourse to the production of a female identity associated with shame and stigma. Single, childless women comprised the third category, which illustrates a division between women based on marital status that has echoes in British income maintenance to the present day. Such single women were regarded as having a duty to work, especially by 1869–70, when Poor Law administration was reviewed.

The notion of a male bread-winner is closely tied to that of the *family wage*. This idea is bound up with the historical development of the relationship between the family, social production, the modern labour market and industrial production. With the advent of protective legislation such as the Factory Acts of the 1840s, children were excluded from factories and from paid work outside the home. Women were increasingly employed in specifically female sectors of work and married women became less and less likely to be in full-time waged employment, becoming marginalized within the labour market (Barrett and McIntosh, 1980). The financial dependence of carers is implicit in the structure of a society in which responsibility for children and the elderly rests within the family and in which caring for children restricts access to paid work. The family wage assumes women's dependence on men. In the wage bargaining situation it gives men the authority to claim higher wages because of the needs of their dependants. Women do not need outside, paid employment because they have domestic responsibilities and because they are provided for by the male bread-winner; any income they provide is supplementary or 'pin money'. The family wage undercuts arguments for equality of pay and employment opportunities between women and men. Campbell and Charlton are quoted as saying, 'The Labour Movement has managed to combine a commitment to equal pay with a commitment to the family wage' but 'you can't have both' (in Barrett and McIntosh, 1980: 52).

Feminist critiques have not only pointed to the contradictions within the family wage demand, and its incompatibility with demands for equal pay, but they also question the extent to which 'male bread-winners' actually did earn an income sufficient to support a family (Barrett and McIntosh, 1980). Hence, not only did the concept not serve women's interests but neither did it provide the support for working-class families which it purported to do.

Although feminists have adopted different positions on the benefits or otherwise of the family wage it remains a central concept in explanations of social relations, the construction of the modern family and women's place within it. Hartmann argues that the principle behind the family wage, of women's financial dependence on men, and men's rights to women's labour inside the home persists.

> Women's lower wages in the labour market (combined with the need for children to be reared by someone) assure the continued existence of the family as a

necessary income-pooling unit. The family, supported by the family wage thus allows the control of women's labour by men both within and without the family. (Hartmann, 1979: 18–19)

As Lewis (1992) argues, the impact of the family wage, together with the high level of sex segregation in the labour market as a cause of women's low pay, have changed very little over the whole of the twentieth century.

State intervention developed throughout the nineteenth and into the twentieth century. Measures included giving Poor Law guardians the power to remove children from unsuitable, 'bad' mothers (the 1899 Poor Law Act), along with more positive initiatives such as the provision of school meals and campaigns for maternity insurance. Women were also to be educated in the art of mothering (Holdsworth, 1988; Sapsford and Abbott, 1988). The 1918 Maternity and Child Welfare Act which led to the provision of infant, and later ante-natal, clinics aimed to improve the quality of mothering. As Gittins points out, however, help was not given to the mothers themselves through this improvement in state support to children (Gittins, 1985). While trade union pressure led to more protection and security for men at times of illness or unemployment, mothers received virtually no support. The 1911 National Insurance Acts which introduced flat-rate subsistence benefits as of right on the basis of contributions in cases of unemployment, sickness, disability and workplace accidents did not cover married women (Gilbert, 1970), a demonstration of how, in the provision of welfare, women are identified primarily as mothers with little, if any, visible independent existence and identity.

After the end of the Second World War state policy sought to encourage women to leave the workforce and return to the home (Richardson, 1993). The Beveridge Report, although written in 1942 when women were actively participating in the public arena – for example, in the armed forces, in munitions factories and as land workers – assumed that in peacetime women would revert to traditional roles. Thus Beveridge stated: 'in the next thirty years housewives as mothers have vital work to do in ensuring the continuance of the British race' (Beveridge, 1942: para. 117).

Key notions about family life, and women's place within that family, embodied in the Beveridge Report are important in that they set the agenda for British welfare policies and underpin much of what follows. They are mentioned here in order to illustrate that agenda and the implicit assumptions which feminist analysis sought to reveal. Wicks summarizes the assumptions of the Beveridge plan as being:

(a) that marriages are for life ... the legal obligation to maintain persists until death or remarriage;
(b) that sexual activity and childbirth takes place, or at least should take place only within marriage;
(c) that married women normally do no paid work or negligible paid work;
(d) that women not men should do housework and rear children;
(e) that couples who live together with regular sexual relationships and shared expenses are always of the opposite sex. (Wicks, 1991: 93, citing Abel-Smith, 1982)

Beveridge makes quite explicit reference to the domestic, supporting role of women as mothers. Elsewhere, 'women' are subsumed as a category into 'the family', but while such universal categories appear to be gender-neutral, in reality they rest on assumptions regarding women's perceived position within society. Women are defined in familial terms as carers and nurturers, as in the Beveridge Report, or ignored and not mentioned specifically at all, as in discussion of citizenship as a universal category. One of the objectives of feminist research has been to show how

> Women are precisely defined, never general representatives of humanity or all people, but as specifically feminine, and frequently sexual, categories. . . . Being a man is an entitlement not to masculine attributes but to a non-gendered subjectivity. (Black and Coward, 1981: 83)

Activity 5.1

Look back over this section and try to establish (1) what was assumed about women's position in the family, (2) the workplace, (3) the nature of women's sexuality. How have women been defined by state intervention and what sort of divisions characterize women's and men's social positions?

Feminism

One of the distinguishing features of the sexual division of labour and of women's social position has been the division between the public and the private arenas: women have been located within the private arena of the family, home and domesticity and men defined by their public role, especially in relation to the paid work from which women have often been excluded. This section looks specifically at the kind of questions which feminism raises in response to these questions, and suggests some of the conceptual tools which feminists have developed to explain how women's role has been constructed by state interventions.

Feminist perspectives locate gender as a structuring principle of social policy and the provision of welfare. Feminism puts gender first when defining social problems in explaining their causes or exploring appropriate levels of state or voluntary sector intervention. It contains different perspectives from which to address questions of gender, but what unites all feminist approaches is their concern with the question of how social policies affect women *in particular*. Initially, feminism can be seen as highlighting the differences and inequalities between women and men, focusing on the different experience of, for example, a social problem such as poverty. Poverty can be seen as a generic social problem, but feminist research demonstrates the different experience of women and men. For example, the use of the term 'family poverty' obscures gender differences and in particular the 'feminization of poverty' (Millar and Glendinning, 1987).

Feminist research draws attention to the ways in which women and men view household income differently, with women tending to spend their earnings on domestic items and men retaining some income for their own purposes (Payne, 1991). In poor households women are more likely to deny themselves rather than any other family member (Graham, 1987). This illustrates how feminist approaches ask questions about the different experiences of women and men and challenge definitions of social problems, especially the notion of gender-neutral categories.

Another illustration of this is presented by the apparently gender-neutral concept of 'community care', which feminists have shown to be a euphemism for the unpaid work of women for their family members. 'Community care' is, on the whole, care by women (Finch, 1988). Such policies are based on the assumption that there is a gendered distinction between what Dalley has called 'caring for' and 'caring about' (1988). Whereas men are allowed to care about their families – that is, to feel an emotional bond, without having to care for them (that is, to undertake the practical work of caring) – women are expected to show that they care about family members by caring *for* them. Thus it is argued the conflation of 'caring about' and 'caring for' operates to ensure that women will continue to provide unpaid 'community care', with the added constraint of guilt which is experienced by those women who fail to fulfil their 'obligations'.

But feminist critiques are concerned about more than simply exposing the gendered nature of social policies and the definition of social problems with a particular emphasis on women. Feminism also involves some commitment to action to redress the inequalities which empirical enquiry reveals. In the above example of community care, Finch makes a plea for change, and argues, 'Women must have the right not to care and dependent people must have the right not to rely on their relatives' (Finch, 1988: 30). Thus, as well as drawing attention to gender differences and inequalities, through the deconstruction of categories and concepts and through empirical research which emphasizes the need to listen to women's voices and women's accounts of their own experiences, feminism involves a call for change.

Challenging the assumption that it is 'natural' for women to serve and care for others would involve fundamental policy shifts in the provision of care for children, the sick, those with disabilities and the elderly as well as the care of the male workforce within the private arena of the home. It would also necessitate drastic alterations in employment practices. Finally, a further challenge linked to this commitment to action which feminism has presented is a questioning of the traditional orthodoxy of organizations and practices, notably of their hierarchical structures. Feminism has been associated with the collectivist, democratic, non-hierarchical forms of organization of women's groups which reject traditional organizational practices and structures.

Notwithstanding the different approaches and emphases which exist within feminism, there are clearly a number of continuities and shared concerns which include:

1   giving gender a high priority;
2   asking questions about the position of women in particular in relation to
    the definition of social problems and levels of state intervention;
3   listening to women's voices;
4   drawing attention to gender differences and inequalities;
5   having a political dimension which includes strategies for change; and
6   challenging hierarchical forms of organization.

Activity 5.2

● Make a list of tasks generally assumed to be performed by
   men and those generally assumed to be performed by
   women.
● What do you think would happen if it could no longer be
   assumed that women would provide the unpaid care on
   which community care depends?

Feminist Perspectives

Although feminists might agree on the existence of gender inequalities and
seek to highlight women's experience, both empirically in their research
methodology and in deconstructing 'gender neutral' categories, they do not
agree on the causes of gender differences and inequalities, nor on the form
which commitment to change and strategies for effecting change might take.
The search for *explanation* is considered in what follows. This section
outlines some of the differences between perspectives in what has been
called 'second wave' feminism (Rendall, 1985), a category used to describe
developments in the women's movement linking political activity and
feminist theoretical work mainly in Europe and the United States, which
began in the early 1960s. Some of these positions draw on the repertoires of
the 'first wave' feminism of the nineteenth and early twentieth centuries,
especially liberalism, and re-articulate conceptualizations drawn from mainstream – or what Daly (1978) has called 'malestream' – social theory.

Liberal Feminism

'First wave' feminists seized on the language of liberalism and demanded
formal equality and equal rights to citizenship with men. In its campaigns,
liberal feminism has sought to secure equal rights for women within the
public domain, focusing on changing legislation. The concerns of this
approach since the early 1960s have been about equality and civil rights,
with the emphasis on the reform of existing institutions. Explanations of
gender inequalities are located within the systems of social and political

institutions which can be reformed through the actions of individuals. Organizations such as the National Organization of Women in the United States and the Equal Opportunities Commission in the United Kingdom are examples of this strand, with a policy paradigm based on the supposition that, given some reform of social institutions and practices, especially in employment and education, women could attain equality with men.

Socialist/Marxist Feminism

Marxist and socialist feminism has been more important in Britain than in the United States, possibly because of the stronger tradition of class-based politics. This perspective links the position of women to the dominant mode of production, and employs a Marxist analytical framework which presents a critique of *capitalism* (see Chapter 4), along with a feminist critique of *patriarchy*, as a form of power in which adult men oppress women through their authority and domination over everyone else, including boys and younger men (Rowbotham, 1969). Subsequent debates have engaged with the interrelationship between capitalism and patriarchy. This has involved focusing on women's 'dual role': first, their involvement in the reproduction, not only of the workforce, but also of social relations through their role in the private arena as they produce the next generation and care for the current labour force; and secondly, their activities in the public arena as a reserve army of labour, drawn in and out of the labour market to meet shortfalls in the labour supply (Rowbotham, 1974, 1989). This branch of feminism retains the Marxist emphasis on the unequal distribution of economic power, and thus class divisions within capitalist society, as a source of gender inequality, and stresses the interrelationship between public and private spheres of economic relations and those of gender, sexuality and domestic living.

Radical Feminism

Whereas socialist and Marxist feminists stress class relationships and argue for a fusion of class analysis with an understanding of sex inequality, radical feminists argue that it is patriarchal relationships which provide the central division upon which other forms of oppression are based. The term 'sexual politics' (Millett, 1971) was used to describe unequal power relations between women and men, and patriarchy (that is, men's power), was seen as the source of women's oppression whether institutionally or personally. Radical feminism does not prioritize the economic structure and class relations as Marxists do but views the economy as one institution among many through which men exercise control over women. All social institutions, including the family, education, the law, the police and the military, as well as ideologies of romance (and, at the other extreme, representational systems such as pornography), are seen as part of these patriarchal relations.

Some radical feminist positions developed out of what has been called the 'woman-centred' stage of second-wave feminism (Lerner, 1979), which gave priority to female experience as the focus of all study and the source of social and cultural values. Motherhood was a major concern of such approaches (Rich, 1977; Chodorow, 1978). While celebrating motherhood as an essentially female experience, accounts such as Rich's present extensive critiques of motherhood as a social institution under patriarchy which distorts women's experience. In the 1980s and 1990s radical feminist approaches have extended Millett's focus on patriarchy to include heterosexuality as a social institution which oppresses women (Rich, 1980; Jeffreys, 1986), and in both, empirical research and political campaigns and practice have often focused on sexual violence and support for survivors (Kelly, 1988). The women-centred approaches of radical feminists have been important in establishing alternative 'self-help' welfare services outside the confines of the traditional welfare state. An example of this is the women's refuge movement, the establishment of safe homes for women victims of mental and physical abuse by men.

Boundaries between the different feminist approaches have become blurred in the 1980s and 1990s, and other perspectives have developed from the theoretical positions outlined above. Most notably, feminism has had to take on board the critiques of black women, many of whom have challenged the ethnocentricity of what has been seen as a predominantly white women's movement (Lorde, 1984; Aziz, 1992).

These approaches are briefly outlined here in order to indicate some of the differences between feminist positions. The main differences lie in the emphasis which is given to the factors contributing to gender inequality. Arguments which stress economic factors focus on the workplace and include the possibility of shared struggles between women and men, whereas the radical feminist position views men as the source of women's oppression. The liberal position is distinguished by its optimism about reform of the system, even of individuals negotiating their own more egalitarian relationships, without recourse to a revolutionary overthrow of existing social relations. However, all branches of feminism have united in campaigns which derive from liberal discourses such as demands for equal opportunities policies in education and employment, child-care provision and campaigns against sexual violence. All three perspectives give some weight to the social and institutional sources of inequalities between women and men, and each offers some challenge to the imperatives of biological determinism which have often been used to confine women to the private arena of the home and to domestic, caring duties. This discussion also illustrates the close ties between feminist theory and social and political practice. It is through campaigns that feminists have put women and women's concerns on the public agenda, and the explanations which feminists offer for what their research and struggles reveal derive from listening to women's voices.

Activity 5.3

- What do you think are the causes of women's oppression according to

  1 liberal feminists,
  2 Marxist/socialist feminists,
  3 radical feminists?

- What social policy initiatives and wider political solutions do you think each group would promote to secure women's equality?

Feminist Critiques of the Family

As should be clear by now, the family is a key social institution, a major focus of social policy, and of feminist research and analysis. Given the family's pivotal social position it is perhaps not surprising that feminists should see it as the key site for the exercise of male power and authority. As Millett notes, 'Patriarchy's chief institution is the family. It is both a mirror and a connection to the larger society' (1971: 55).

Women's position within the family has often been taken for granted as universal and 'natural' and hence not worthy of investigation (Beechey, 1985). Second-stage feminism has sought to rectify this, and the family has been the focus of many feminist critiques, moving from fierce criticism of the family – notably the patriarchal nuclear family – through powerful celebration of women's role as mothers, to diverse analyses reflecting positions which seek to address differences *between* women as well as those between women and men (Segal, 1993). Feminist critiques of motherhood have ranged from Firestone's demands that women be freed from their biology and 'the tyranny of reproduction and childbearing' (Firestone, 1970: 221) to Adrienne Rich's vision of a time when 'woman (as mother) is the presiding genius of her own body . . . and thinking itself will be transformed' (Rich, 1977: 285–6). What is important for analysis of social policy is the feminist questioning of dominant ideologies of family life and the focus of the patriarchal family as the source of women's oppression.

At the start of second-wave feminism, following the sustained attempt after 1945 to reconstruct and impose the traditional family, with women firmly positioned at its centre (as illustrated by the Beveridge Report), the main concern of feminists was to investigate that familial form, to challenge the view that the family was a safe haven, 'a little world immune from the vulgar cash nexus of modern society' (Barrett and McIntosh, 1985: 28). Friedan (1963) in the United States exposed the experience of the 'problem with no name' and the depression of housewives in the 1950s. Gavron (1966) described the feelings of frustration and isolation of housebound wives in Britain, and attention has been drawn to the despair, and even violence, experienced by women within the family. The alienation and despair experienced by many women within the nuclear family and within marriage was well supported by empirical research – for example, in the United States (Bart, 1971; Bernard, 1973) – and Britain (Oakley, 1974). Evidence was produced by listening to women's voices and by exploring those areas of the private arena, hitherto invisible and unquestioned, such as housework, previously not classified as work (Oakley, 1974).

Feminist research set the context for future methodological and conceptual debates as it fought to expose the gender-specific nature of apparently universal concepts like the family. The research of the early 1970s was concerned with exploring family life, and women's place within it, in order to explain and overcome the existing inequalities between women and men. It meant that the family could no longer be perceived as a homogeneous unit. The research challenged the assumptions of the Beveridge Report and, albeit less explicitly, of social policy initiatives such as community care which assume that the family can be conceptualized as a single unit. The internal organization and functions of the family have to be investigated and the interconnections between the family and the wider social, political and economic context disentangled, exploring the interrelationship between the public and the private arenas.

The aims of many feminists in the early 1970s were to seek gender equality, through, for example, improving the conditions under which women experienced family life, because 'the socialization of housework, paid maternity leave, proper collective childcare, publicly funded, and decent jobs with shorter working hours were the solutions advanced' (Wilson, 1989: 15). This could include more involvement by men in childcare and domestic labour, stressing liberal notions of equality, where women and men should be able to participate in public life and in the labour market as well as being parents and carers.

The later 1970s saw the emphasis shift, with a move within feminism to revalue the female and celebrate uniquely female attributes and qualities, notably women's mothering. Rich makes a distinction between the repressive, patriarchal social institution of motherhood and women's mothering abilities. Dinnerstein and Chodorow explored the psychological effects of the fact that it is women who mother (Dinnerstein, 1976; Chodorow, 1978). Other feminists brought together these notions of a maternal identity, suggesting some universal characteristics of 'maternal thinking' and 'maternal practices' (Ruddick, 1980) and women's separate styles of moral reasoning (Gilligan, 1982). Such approaches have been more popular in the United States than in Britain, although some work using psychoanalytic theory, notably based on the Object Relations School, has informed analysis of the mother–daughter relationship and the work of feminist psychotherapists such as Eichenbaum and Orbach (1982). For other writers this emphasis on motherhood has been seen as reactionary and essentialist in its stress on a biological role and thus as colluding with a traditionalist view of women within the home (Segal, 1987). However, the high priority and recognition given to motherhood have been empowering for women and have served to focus on this aspect of women's experience.

This examination of the two facets of feminism in the 1960s and 1970s shows that it has ranged from critique to celebration of women's maternal role. However, both approaches include the need to explore the diversity of family forms, to challenge the notion that the nuclear family of 1950s ideology was universal and natural, and to argue for a deconstruction of the family as a natural unit and its reconstruction as a social unit (Rapp, 1979). Difference and diversity have increasingly become recognized following the critiques by black and Asian feminists of the ethnocentricity of white feminism's stress on the particular examples of white, middle-class women. Many black women might well have welcomed more leisure time at home freed from the demands of their low-paid work (hooks, 1984) and would not have experienced the boredom of Friedan's housewives. Others sought to secure their fertility rights against enforced sterilization and contraception rather than struggling to obtain rights to abortion on demand as expressed in the demands of the Women's Liberation Movement (Aziz, 1992).

Feminist analyses have also had to engage with the realities of profound demographic and social change in a world whose economics and politics have been transformed since the crises of the 1970s (see, for example, Chapters 3 and 4). In Britain, as elsewhere in Europe, an increasing number of children have been born to unmarried mothers. In 1991 three out of every ten children were born out of marriage. The number of children living with a lone parent doubled between 1979 and 1991, when one in five families was headed by a lone parent. Families are becoming smaller, and the average number of children among married and cohabiting couples in the United Kingdom is 1.9, with many more women choosing not to have a child at all. The OPCS estimates that two in ten women born in 1980 will not have any children. Britain has an ever escalating divorce rate, the highest in Europe, estimated at one in three marriages in 1991, with three-quarters of all divorces instigated by women. More women, including mothers, are participating in the labour market, albeit often in low paid and part-time work. In 1993, 48 per cent of women and 64 per cent of men were in employment in the United Kingdom, with women constituting 44 per cent of the workforce (Social Trends, 1994). All of these factors create a very different pattern of domestic living for women from that represented by the familial ideologies of the 1950s. This changing climate coincided with the Thatcher years in Britain, when social policy involved a retreat from state welfare provision in favour of a market-led system, a retreat which has created difficulties for many women, including the growing numbers of lone parent families, most of which are headed by women, living in poverty (Roll, 1992, and also see Chapter 12). Feminist critiques of the family and social policy over this period have stressed material factors as the major contributors to the problems of single mothers (Campbell, 1987), in contradiction to the rhetoric of New Right politicians who have constructed single motherhood

Multiple regression analysis also has to deal with nonlinearity issues. For the nonlinearity problem, the two approaches mentioned in the case of simple regression are as useful here. These are nonlinear regression (e.g., polynomial regression) and linearization through transformation (e.g., log function). We can use a set of dummy variables to represent an original nonlinear variable. However, one dummy variable in the whole set must be left out as a reference to avoid statistical redundancy. For the gender variable, for instance, you can only include either female (coded 1 or 0) or male (coded 1 or 0) in the equation, but not both. Since dummy variables may make an analysis unnecessarily complicated, researchers tend to consider an ordinal variable as an interval variable, or reduce the number of categories to the minimum if a nominal variable has to be used.

In behavioral and social science research the emphasis of regression analysis is not on prediction using an equation but on the identification of the relative effects of different variables in terms of both magnitudes and probabilities. These effects, reflecting the idea of covariance rather than simply variance, can be generally represented by a summary measure called multiple correlation. The calculation of the multiple correlation coefficient (R) is complicated, yet it is very easy with the use of a computer. The REGRESSION procedure automatically renders the squared multiple correlation coefficient, which is called the coefficient of determination. The coefficient of determination R^2 is an important indicator of the goodness of fit of the regression model, which ranges from 0 to 1 and has a PRE meaning. The quantity $1 - R^2$ is called coefficient of alienation. Since R^2 is also based on the kind of control represented by part correlation rather than partial correlation, it needs to be modified when the number of variables included is large while the size of sample is small. The multiple correlation coefficient can be represented by the zero-order correlation coefficients of the independent variables with the dependent variable being weighted by the standard regression coefficients beta, i.e., $R^2 = \beta_1 \gamma_1 + \beta_2 \gamma_2 + ... + \beta_n \gamma_n$.

As a powerful tool for performing statistical control over variables, regression is not only a fundamental technique in such statistical procedures as path analysis, but also a major means of developing needed scales. Factor analysis that is crucial to multidimensional scaling also has a root in this technique.

Multiple causation involving categorical variables

The regression model requires that all the variables, dependent and independent,

144

within a moral discourse and sought to reinstate the traditional two-parent family. In the words of the Conservative Family Campaign, 'putting father back at the head of the table' (Webster Gardiner, 1986).

Activity 5.4

It would be useful to stop at this point to consider the main features of the feminist critiques of the family which have been discussed here. Which factors do such critiques take into account in analysing the family? What distinguishes feminist critiques?

Violence and the Family

In this section we explore two examples of violence within the family which have been 'rediscovered' in the last 20 years, and consider their implications for social policy.

Domestic Violence

Feminism has contributed to the exposure of domestic violence and has challenged assumptions about the privacy of the home, showing that these assumptions are based on the idea that members of a family have a right to do as they please within that family, and that families should resolve their own problems if any occur and not appeal to outside, public agencies. Feminists have shown that such principles fail to address the unequal rights of different family members, and argue that the family structure reflects and reproduces men's power over women. Empirical investigation indicates that domestic violence committed by men against their female partners accounts for a quarter of all reported acts of violence and that 70 per cent of violence takes place within the home (Pahl, 1985). Feminist research has put this violence on the public agenda and has investigated women's perceptions of their experience.

Feminist explanations of the phenomenon vary, though in general radical feminist explanations see domestic violence as a feature of patriarchy and men's control over women: 'although there are many ways that men as a group maintain women in oppressed social positions, violence is the most overt and effective means of social control' (Yllo and Bograd, 1988). Such feminist approaches and studies of male violence, and especially feminist campaigns including the work of the Women's Aid Federation, have been very important in increasing awareness of gender inequalities, abuse and violence against women which had hitherto been concealed within the private arena of the family and personal relationships (Kelly, 1988). Women's campaigns have led to the establishment of refuges where the victims of violence can escape with their children and receive support and advice, and to increased recognition of the extent of domestic violence against women and the need for intervention – for example, by the police.

Socialist feminism sees domestic violence as resulting from class-related, economic factors, including poverty and material deprivation, which have been identified as significant contributory elements. The poverty which women and children experience is linked to the notion of the male bread-winner and to the construction of women's dependency. The lack of child care, and hence the difficulty experienced by single mothers in participating in the labour market, has ensured women's dependency on the state and on men. The gendered construction of income maintenance produces a system where men's eligibility depends on their labour market characteristics, such as age, invalidity and unemployment, and women's, in contrast, is deter-mined by their marital and family situation. Unless women are single and childless, their access to income maintenance is determined by whether they are seen as having a man who could, or should, support them. Married women were encouraged to rely on derived insurance rights until the late 1970s and were barred from claiming means-tested Supplementary Benefit for the family until the early 1980s. The entitlement of mothers who are not married, or those who are separated or divorced, has been governed by moralistic directives over a period of time extending from the New Poor Law to Beveridge (Daly, 1994). Women's dependence on men or on the state, especially through non-contributory, means-tested provision rather than insurance provision in their own right, has tied women into social and familial relations which have often provided the site of their experience of domestic violence. Feminist perspectives challenge individualistic and psy-chological explanations of domestic violence and locate it within the broader social context.

Child Abuse

The emergence of child abuse as a social problem in the last 20 years has attracted considerable media attention, sometimes leading to moral panics about the breakdown of family life, or perhaps more frequently, the scapegoating of social workers (MacLeod and Saraga, 1988). Feminist research in this area has again challenged existing assumptions about the privacy of the home, the responsibility of individuals, notably mothers, and the idea of 'mother blaming'. Feminists have been concerned to explore the complexity of this phenomenon and to disentangle some of the assumptions about what constitutes child abuse, who is responsible and why it occurs.

In order to address these questions the distinction has been made between *physical* abuse and *sexual* abuse, and empirical research has been conducted which suggests that sexual abuse of children is mainly perpetrated by men, without specific characteristics of age, class or culture. Physical abuse is more frequently committed by women, although it has to be noted that women are much more likely than men to have responsibility for children

(Saraga, 1993). Physical abuse is linked to cases of domestic violence (Finkelhor, 1983) and to class and poverty.

Feminist research raises questions about the definition of child abuse which reflects problems about what is considered normal and what abnormal, what is the boundary between the two, and who decides the location of this boundary. Feminist research has concentrated on the experiences of women and children as survivors of abuse, who had hitherto largely been excluded from research studies. This has raised questions about who should be investigated. Should it be victims or parents (for whom read 'mothers')? The last, and most important question is that of explanation, and it is in this area that the feminist contribution has been most significant. Feminists go beyond describing what happens and, in the case of domestic violence and child sexual abuse, ask questions about why men should seek to exercise power and control over women and children. Feminists do not see this violence as exceptional or deviant masculine behaviour, but rather as an extension of the social construction of male sexuality which is articulated through the language of power and domination (*Feminist Review*, 1988). Even though it can be argued that feminist critiques do not achieve full recognition, they have put domestic violence and child abuse on the public agenda where they have since been acknowledged as social problems. It is no longer possible to dismiss these issues as private concerns or even individual problems, although 'blaming the victim' and 'mother blaming' have not entirely disappeared from explanatory frameworks and interventions.

Activity 5.5

- What behavioural traits would you characterize as

  1 masculine, and
  2 feminine?

- Look at your list and think about which, if any, of these are

  1 biologically based or determined, and
  2 which of them are social constructions.

- Has public policy been responsive to problems stemming from 'masculine identity'?

Gender and Citizenship

This section explores the concept of citizenship upon which the British welfare system is based. In it we widen the debate and examine the concept of citizenship which is accorded a significant role in some theoretical accounts of the welfare state. This section should be read in conjunction with Chapters 2 and 10.

The majority of writing on citizenship does not include the dimension of gender (Marshall, 1950; Mann, 1987; Turner, 1990). A great deal of debate about citizenship has been concerned with social class and draws on the work of T.H. Marshall, with its three components of civil, political and social citizenship (1950, 1975, 1981). Criticisms of Marshall have included discussion of his ethnocentricity and even of his failure to acknowledge the public/private dichotomy (Turner, 1990), but gender as a concept is significantly absent from these critiques. The fact that women did not achieve many of the features of either political or civil citizenship in Britain before 1928 might suggest that women have simply been slower to attain full citizenship status, but that it is still possible. In the liberal view, all that is required is the removal of legislative barriers and overt discrimination. A whole range of other civil rights have been won by women in western nation states: for example, access to education, the right to own property, to terminate a marriage and to professional employment (see Walby, 1988), some before suffrage rights and some in the years afterwards.

Feminist critiques of the second wave have challenged the unified notion of citizenship as a model to which women can aspire on equal terms with men. They locate citizenship within the broader social context and stress the gender differences which a unified concept obscures. Although most theorists include class – and the key debate has been about the relationship between class and citizenship in a capitalist society – the structural factor of *patriarchy* has not been addressed. Feminists argue that 'democratic theorists fail to recognize the *patriarchal* structure of the welfare state; the very different way that women and men have been incorporated as citizens' (Pateman, 1992: 223). The structuring of the public and private spheres is crucial to the position of women and their citizenship status. 'The patriarchal division between public and private is also a sexual division. . . . The public world of universal citizenship is an association of free and equal individuals . . . of men who interact as formally equal citizens' (Pateman, 1992: 226).

Walby argues that the patriarchal institution of the 'male-dominated household is incompatible with full citizenship' (Walby, 1994: 391) and that the solution to the exclusion of women from full citizenship rights is the socialization of women's domestic role, just as other aspects of work in the domestic arena have been socialized – through schools, nurseries and hospitals, for example.

Feminists have shown how social citizenship depends largely on being a paid worker in order to obtain full rights. Women whose primary responsibilities lie with care of children, husbands and the elderly tend not to have access to the higher levels of income generated by occupational pensions. Many women are in part-time employment, and Lister (1990) argues that the demands on women as carers, and their availability for unpaid work, limits their full participation in political citizenship while their financial dependency is an obstacle to civil citizenship. Overall, it is women's domestic and caring duties, part of the institution of patriarchy, which exclude them from full citizenship rights, making clear the gendered nature of the concept of citizenship. However, this also presents a dilemma for feminists. On the one hand it seems that to obtain full civil citizenship rights women should participate in the labour market and abandon the constraints of domestic duties, and on the other that women's caring roles should be recognized and supported. Lister calls for changes 'so as to reflect the value to society as a whole of caring work, whether it be done in private or public sphere' (1990: 464). Do women join the world on men's terms or seek recognition of 'women's work'?

As Pateman (1992) points out, this is a false dichotomy, as is the opposition between men's independence and women's dependence, and it is essential to recognize the interrelationship between the public and private arenas. She argues for the construction of a welfare society instead of a welfare state to accommodate the changes which are taking place in employment and in patterns of domestic living in the late twentieth century. This challenge to mutually exclusive binary oppositions, such as male/female and public/private, upon which much of our understanding of gender has been based, is a feature of recent postmodernist feminist approaches which seek to address and understand difference and diversity.

Activity 5.6

Given the discussion of feminist critiques in this chapter, what challenge can be mounted to the liberal claim that women's achievement of citizenship rights has merely been slower than men's?

Summary and Conclusion

This chapter has mapped out some of the shared concerns of feminist approaches as well as some of the differences between them. It has been argued that it is no longer possible to talk of feminism, but only of 'feminisms' (Crowley and Himmelweit, 1992). However, all feminist approaches include a concern with gender and with asking questions about the position of women in relation to social policy. They go further than this and question the basis of universal categories such as citizenship and equality and of naturalistic concepts like the family, and in deconstructing these conceptualizations reveal their gendered features. Often, as has been shown here, the universal category is largely male and women's exclusion has passed unobserved, until feminism drew attention to this. Feminist theories have developed out of political action and campaigning and are born of the interrelationship between theory and practice.

6

Racism and Social Welfare

Laura Penketh and Yasmin Ali

This chapter will explore the relationship between 'race' and social policy, specifically analysing how racist assumptions and 'race-related' policies have influenced the nature of social services provision for minority ethnic groups. There is considerable evidence to show that minority ethnic communities suffer from racism in a number of fields in modern Britain. Members of minority ethnic communities are more likely to face unemployment and in employment they are over-represented in the worst-paying, least secure and least skilled jobs (Oppenheim, 1990). They are over-represented among the poor in Britain (see Chapter 12), are more likely to suffer physical and verbal abuse, and are portrayed in stereotypical ways in the media (Hall et al., 1978). They also face harrassment from the police and judicial system (Solomos, 1988), and suffer unequal treatment from the full range of welfare institutions (Skellington, 1992).

As well as recognizing these facts, the student of social policy needs to obtain a critical understanding of why such inequalities exist, and why such inequalities are explained in terms of 'race', 'ethnicity' or racism. Thus the first section of the chapter provides a critical analysis of the concepts of 'race', racism and ethnicity. It will demonstrate that these are complex and often misinterpreted concepts which need to be placed in the appropriate political, economic and historical context: in Britain as a capitalist socio-economic system whose history has been shaped by its role in first the slave trade and then imperialism. Both these periods involved Britain in subjugating and oppressing people on the basis of their skin colour and supposed membership of an inferior 'race'.

This will be followed by an exploration of post-war, 'race-related' legislation, focusing on the 1966 Local Government Act and the 1976 Race Relations Act. These two pieces of legislation have particular importance for the legal responsibilities of local authorities in providing services for minority ethnic communities.

The second part of the chapter examines the relationship between 'race' and social services provision. It explores four theoretical perspectives which have, over the years, influenced 'race-related' developments: assimilationist/integrationist; multi-cultural; anti-racist; and New Right perspectives. This analysis will facilitate a critical understanding of how social services provision has been influenced by changing assumptions regarding the position of minority ethnic groups in society. It will also examine how these assumptions have been translated into policy and practice in the areas of education and social work provision.

Definitions

We all carry common-sense notions of 'race' and ethnicity about in our heads. We 'know' to which group we belong, and we can usually assign a racial or ethnic identity to others. Yet as every social scientist understands, common sense is itself a doubtful notion, casual in its perception of history, economical with the facts, and shunning theory.

'Race'

'Race' is the first term to consider. It is written here in inverted commas to indicate that this is a term which we must use with extreme caution. In its pre-modern usage the term 'race' poses few problems. Here it is a synonym for 'nation', as Shakespeare's Richard II suggests when Britain is called 'This island race, this blessed plot'. Sometimes the term is still used in this sense today, but far more familiar at the common-sense level is the 'scientific' use of the term. From the time of Gobineau and other Enlightenment thinkers, and more particularly with the popularization of Darwinian theories of evolution and ideas of social Darwinism, 'race' came to be associated with visible biological differences. Physiological characteristics, such as skin colour, facial features and brain size were all used to distinguish different 'races', and often to rank them in some assumed order of superiority and inferiority.

Biological or scientific racism, as it has come to be known, influenced the development of eugenicist social policies in such countries as Sweden and the United States, as well as the notorious white 'Aryan' supremacism of Nazi Germany which led to the Holocaust.

Eugenicists claim that, according to the scientific laws of heredity, human characteristics are inherited and that policies such as birth control, sterilization and segregation can improve 'race quality' by preventing the fertility of so-called 'degenerates' or inferior human beings. This analysis also incorporates the belief that certain social groups, particularly immigrants, are more likely to exhibit characteristics of deficiency and degeneration. However, following the Second World War scientists and social scientists were asked by the newly established United Nations to examine the question of whether 'racial' difference as expounded by the Nazis had any scientific foundation. They concluded that it had none. More recently, the developing science of genetics has further confirmed this view, with comparative studies of population groups in Northern Europe and West Africa, for example, showing more statistically significant genetic diversity within these population groups than between them. To geneticists, the physiological differences associated with 'race' have no more significance than hair or eye colour.

Psychologists have also been associated with arguments about a scientific foundation for 'racial' difference, their evidence coming not from the study of human genetic make-up, but from the 'empirical' evidence of Intelligence Quotient (IQ) tests. IQ tests have been the subject of much controversy, their content and underlying assumptions criticized as ethnocentric and class-biased. Yet there remain some advocates of IQ testing, particularly in the United States, where the work of conservative sociologist Charles Murray has been used to legitimate cutting back the welfare state and ending affirmative action programmes for racial and ethnic minorities, as well as women (for a discussion of Murray's ideas see Chapter 12).

If there is no scientific basis for the idea of 'race', why does the term continue to be used? The answer is that the notion of 'race' and racial difference has come to be an entrenched part of our culture. It may be socially constructed, but social constructions have consequences that affect real people.

Racism

The term 'racism' is also problematic. It should be distinguished from 'prejudice' and 'discrimination', the first of these meaning irrational attitudes and beliefs held by individuals, and the latter concerning action on the basis of (rational or irrational) beliefs. Visible minorities in society may suffer from the prejudiced beliefs of individuals, and this may result in unfair discrimination, but racism is not merely the sum total of the actions of prejudiced individuals. 'Racism' is a term used to describe and to analyse the process whereby discrimination in favour of or against particular social groups by virtue of their 'race' or ethnic origin is structured and perpetuated. Racism has sometimes been described simplistically as being 'prejudice plus power'. There is some substance to this definition, in the sense that prejudices without powerful social, political and economic reinforcement – for example, against bald people or those without a sense of humour – have no discernible effect upon the life-chances of the groups in question. But the notion of power allied to prejudice implies a psychological motive – a sense of deliberation – in the perpetuation of racial inequality. Undoubtedly there are those who dislike black people, such as members of neo-fascist organizations, but the term 'racism' is best understood as encompassing:

1   the history of colonial and imperialist domination of one section of the world by another;
2   the cultural construction and perpetuation of damaging and inaccurate stereotypes of those who are 'different';
3   the economic interests which benefit from social divisions; and

4   the ways in which factors 1, 2 and 3 above are structured into social institutions with the effect that certain social groups are disadvantaged.

In other words, the effects of history, culture, economics and politics act to ensure that those who are dominant in society are likely to remain in their privileged positions. Sometimes racist societies are institutionalized in ways that overtly discriminate on racial grounds, such as Apartheid South Africa before 1994, or the segregationist Deep South of the United States until the Civil Rights reforms of the 1960s. But more often a society will not set out consciously to discriminate, but through its historical and cultural legacy will have the effect of producing unequal outcomes on 'racial' or ethnic grounds. In Britain, for example, mental health policies and practice based upon white European, middle-class norms of behaviour can result in a system which does not understand that people from other cultural back-grounds may express symptoms of mental health or ill health in different ways. The disproportionate numbers of those of African-Caribbean origin who are diagnosed as schizophrenic, or the under-utilization of mental health services by young South Asian women who have a suicide rate four times higher than that of white women, suggests that we have a system which is out of synchronicity with the realities of a multi-racial society. It is this kind of systemic failure that is described by the term 'racism' in addition to the prejudiced behaviour of individuals.

Therefore, any analysis of racism needs to go beyond the individual and cultural prejudice usually associated with the term, to recognize the structural and institutional nature of racism. Structural analyses see notions of natural inferiority and superiority arising in the conditions of industrial capitalism, and institutional racism describes the systematic discrimination which black people experience in, for example, jobs, housing and education.

Ethnicity

Another term which is important in understanding the question of racism and social policy is 'ethnicity'. This term is sometimes seen as a more 'neutral' or acceptable way of describing difference in society, yet 'ethnicity' is not a synonym for 'race'. Many people in a society like Britain see ethnicity as something that only certain (usually non-white) minorities have. This is a 'minus-one' definition of ethnicity, which assumes that white European culture is the standard or norm, and others deviate from it in a variety of ways. More useful is the notion of ethnicity as encompassing more than one of the following features: a common language, religion, social customs, history and geographical or national origin. In this sense, everyone has an ethnic identity. One form of ethnicity may be the dominant one in a country, and others may be minority ethnicities, but everyone, to some measure, can be defined in this way.

The problem is that people from the majority ethnic group may find it difficult to see themselves as having a shared ethnic identity. They will often be strongly aware of the differences they have (people from Liverpool and from Salisbury may not feel that they have a lot in common). They will be aware of divisions in their 'ethnic group' which encompass gender, disability, sexuality and generational conflict, as well as fundamental class divisions. Yet this knowledge of the limits of 'ethnic' cohesion among the majority does not often lead to an ability to see these limits in the minority ethnic groups.

Paul Gilroy has suggested that too often ethnicity is seen wrongly as a 'fixed cultural essence'(1987). Minority ethnic groups can be attributed a very static ethnic identity in which it is assumed that all members of the group will speak a certain language, have certain dietary habits, religious practices, and marriage and family customs, for example. Some forms of multi-culturalist social policy and practice make these assumptions of uniformity about minority ethnic groups and so may fail to provide services which meet genuine needs. The assumption that all South Asians live in extended families and thus care for all their elderly in the family as a matter of course is one such mistaken but widely believed notion.

It is true that the experience of being a member of a new minority group in society can have the effect of strengthening ethnic identities and some cultural practices, as any look at communities of British expatriates will reveal. Where a new group also experience racism and discrimination, ethnicity may be used as a resource to mobilize people either defensively or to seek access to economic or political influence. Yet any examination of minority ethnic groups in Britain reveals the limits of ethnic identity. Social class, gender, generational and other social divisions cut across ethnic identity for minorities just as much as for the majority.

We should thus make use of the term 'ethnicity' while being fully conscious of its limits. All groups, majority and minority, have an ethnic identity. Ethnicity mediates social experience, but it is neither fixed (all cultures are constantly changing), nor is it invariably at the forefront of the consciousness of minorities. Where ethnicity becomes a resource to mobilize groups, as some Muslims have done around questions of education, it can be a powerful force, but it is difficult to sustain in the absence of a unifying external threat or agreed demand.

One final caution must be sounded about the term 'ethnicity'. Ethnic labels are liable to mutation and change. The religious label 'Muslim' used above was rarely used as an 'ethnic' tag until the Rushdie affair in 1989–90. Where the term 'Bengali' is used in Britain, it usually refers to the predominantly Sylheti Muslim group whose national origins are in Bangladesh, rather than the mainly Hindu population from the Indian state of Bengal. Before 1971 and the war between East and West Pakistan, this group was, in any case, Pakistani. West Indians changed labels to become African-Caribbeans, but the diversity of culture, religion and language on their islands of origin means that the convenient labels we use may obscure as much as they reveal about any particular group.

be measured at the interval level or above. In other words, they should be "continuous" in the sense that their values should include more than a few or a countable number of categories. Nevertheless, in practice we often need to deal with variables measured at lower levels, particularly at the nominal level. These are the variables with limited numbers of values, which may also be obtained through categorization of higher level continuous variables. Multiple causation model can deal with analysis involving both categorical and continuous variables. If all variables are categorical, you can use the sub-table method described in the elaboration model but you must control for various independent variables. The following will consider two different situations of multiple causation involving both categorical and continuous variables, that is, (1) a single categorical dependent variable and multiple continuous independent variables, and (2) a single continuous dependent variable and multiple categorical independent variables.

A single categorical dependent variable and multiple continuous independent variables. When the dependent variable is categorical or measured at the nominal level, the multiple regression model will not be applicable except for its variant logistic regression. This will be discussed later. In such a case, the purpose of analysis may still be to predict the values of the categorical variable based on the values of the continuous independent variables. In order to make the prediction accurate, it makes more sense to first identify the real categories and subsume the sample cases into groups according to their actual values on the categorical variable. The linear combination of the independent variables (similar to the multiple regression equation) can be applied to the groups of cases separately. The results will form several subvariables corresponding to the case groups or categories. For each group or category, the mean of the subvariable can be calculated, which is called the centroid of the independent variables within that group. The purpose of the analysis is to differentiate between the centroids of different groups to the greatest extent, or to maximize the differences among the centroids of the subgroups. This is the principle used to determine the coefficients of a general equation for what is called discriminant analysis. In this type of analysis, the continuous independent variables are called discriminant variables, the equation is essentially a discriminant function, and the coefficients are called discriminant coefficients. The value of the categorical dependent variable is called a discriminant score, which gives a kind of group membership for the sample cases. "Multiple correlation" in such a case is measured by the "discriminating power" of the discriminant function, which can be represented

---

Activity 6.1

- Think of examples of individual prejudice.
- What factors in British history do you think have been of particular importance in shaping 'racial' attitudes?

The Legislative Structure

This section will examine the legislative structure which has informed 'race relations' policy in England and Wales since the 1960s, focusing particularly on the 1966 Local Government Act and the 1976 Race Relations Act. The Scottish framework is slightly different.

The era of post-war migration to Britain from the New Commonwealth lasted from 1948 to the 1960s. Economic and social reconstruction after the war resulted in acute labour shortages which the government at first sought to fill from European sources of migrant labour. Apart from the Irish Republic, which has always supplied the vast majority of migrant workers in Britain, Europe failed to deliver in the necessary quantities, and so Britain looked to the New Commonwealth. West Indian migrants came first, often the most highly skilled and able of their generation. Some sectors of the economy had particular need of their skills, such as London Transport and the newly established National Health Service. In the 1950s Health Minister Enoch Powell went on a recruitment drive to the West Indies. South Asians came a little later, on the whole, entering sections of the labour market which had been abandoned by white workers: at a time of full employment the latter could afford to reject dirty, low-paid or unsocial work, such as permanent night shifts in the declining textile industry.

A combination of factors, including the slow-down in Britain's economy and rising hostility towards migrants, resulted in the Conservative government in 1962 acceding to a campaign by some of their backbenchers and local party associations and passing the 1962 Commonwealth Immigrants Act to limit immigration. Although bitterly opposed by Labour in Opposition, the degree of popular support for the measure caused serious problems for Labour during the 1964 general election (which they won by a very narrow margin), so they reversed their position and not only kept the Act on the statute books, but passed another such Act in 1968 at the time of Enoch Powell's notorious speeches on 'race' matters, and the crisis caused by the expulsion of British passport-holding Asians from Kenya.

Labour sought to 'balance' its new policy on immigration by linking the notion of 'good race relations' with tough immigration control. They did this by passing a series of Race Relations Acts in 1965, 1968 and 1976. The first two Bills were quite timid, and were further diluted in order to pass through Parliament. The 1965 Act outlawed some of the more visible manifestations of the 'colour bar' in cinemas, dance halls and the like, and set up an advisory Race Relations Board. The 1968 Act had been planned as a means of strengthening the 1965 Act, but the crisis of race relations at the time it was due to come before Parliament made this politically difficult. It did establish the Community Relations Commission, but did nothing to outlaw the kind of indirect discrimination which was the major cause of racial inequality. Before looking at the 1976 Act we should look at one other piece of legislation from the 1960s – the 1966 Local Government Act.

The 1966 Local Government Act

The 1966 Local Government Act is notable for Section 11, which to this day remains the major source of funding for projects and services aimed at minority ethnic groups. Initially, the purpose of Section 11 was to offer extra financial assistance to local councils with a high proportion (above 10 per cent) of its inhabitants being of New Commonwealth origin. The funding was used to provide such things as English as a Second Language teaching in schools, translators and bilingual assistants in social services and housing departments, specialist library facilities and other such services. By the late 1970s many councils were eligible for Section 11 funding, but most of them took the cash without necessarily providing all the additional services for which it was nominally intended. Subsequently this abuse has been stopped, and the availability of Section 11 funding has been extended to non-New Commonwealth groups, such as refugees, and it is neither dependent upon the criterion of a fixed figure for the minority ethnic presence, nor upon local government actually being the service provider.

Section 11 funding has been subject to serious criticism. Although councils are obliged to consult with representatives of minority ethnic groups about Section 11 projects, there has been concern that consultative mechanisms are limited and dominated by perhaps unrepresentative people, and that jobs created by Section 11 funding have created a 'second class' of professionals in local government, education and the social services. 'Section 11 workers' sometimes feel themselves to be ghettoized, with little chance of progress through the career structures of which they are nominally part. In some cases, many minority ethnic workers in such areas as social work feel that they have been typecast as Section 11 workers even where they have been employed in the standard way without Section 11 funding. The Home Office, which assesses bids for Section 11 funding, has also been criticized for misdirecting funding by making assumptions about minority ethnic needs which are not in fact justified. Nevertheless, much important work has been made possible by the provision of Section 11 funds, and despite recent changes it has been an important part of the support framework for 'race' and social policy in Britain.

The 1976 Race Relations Act

The 1976 Race Relations Act remains the central plank of 'race relations' policy in Britain, and it is also the most radical piece of 'race relations' legislation in the European Union. Unlike its predecessors, the 1976 Act sought to target such areas as employment, housing, education and the provision of goods and services in a very direct way. Crucially, the Act specified that there were two forms of discrimination, *direct discrimination and indirect discrimination*. Direct refers to intentional and overt discrimination which is easily identifiable. However, indirect discrimination is less easily identifiable. It refers to, for example, unnecessary language requirements for a job as a factory floor sweeper, or height requirements which exclude generally smaller ethnic groups (such as the Chinese). Under the 1976 Act these were deemed illegal unless they could be justified as Genuine Occupational Qualifications (GOQs), such as on grounds of authenticity for an actor, or where a care assistant working with a specific group needed to have a particular language.

Section 71 of the Act gave a large measure of responsibility for enforcing 'race relations' legislation to local government. The Act also established the Commission for Racial Equality as a body empowered to oversee the operation of the Act, to mount investigations, and to assist individuals in bringing cases under the Act to the courts or to industrial tribunals.

The Act does permit Positive Action, but it does not permit Positive Discrimination (what the Americans would call Affirmative Action). Positive Action would include the establishment of a training course specifically for an under-represented ethnic group in a particular field of employment. However, on completing the training successfully they would have to compete on equal terms with other applicants for a 'real job'. It would be illegal to exercise Positive Discrimination and to give a job to someone primarily because they were from an under-represented group. Unlike in the United States, quotas for minorities in education, jobs and so on are illegal, although targets are permissible. The difference is that in setting targets an employer might develop a new strategy for staff recruitment which widens the pool of applicants – for example, by advertising in the minority ethnic press as well as in 'mainstream' publications. Old practices like 'word of mouth' recruitment, whereby entry to a job is effectively controlled by those already doing the work, became, under the 1976 Act, open to charges of indirect discrimination.

The real weakness of the Act is that it is dependent upon an individual coming forward with a case in order to establish a precedent for the law. This can be difficult for individuals who may fear the consequences in the workplace, or the likely impact on their future employment prospects, despite the fact that the Act rules against victimization. Unlike the United States, 'class actions' cannot be brought where many individuals with a similar case pursue it collectively. The Act also does not cover discrimination on the grounds of religion.

The 1976 Race Relations Act is a mirror image of the 1975 Sex Discrimination Act, but latterly it could be argued that more progress has been made in establishing tough anti-sex discrimination precedents. The main reason for this lies in Britain's membership of the European Union.

The Treaty of Rome 1957, which founded the then European Economic Community or 'Common Market', had an explicit commitment to women's equality in it, and the European Commission today has a Commissioner with a responsibility for Equal Opportunities (gender). European law in these areas has to be accepted by the British legal system, with considerable consequences in the 1980s and 1990s. There is no provision, however, for the European Union to deal with racial discrimination. Although the European Parliament has undertaken several enquiries into racism and xenophobia, there is unlikely to be much further action while many European Union countries deny citizenship and other rights to migrants and their families – for example, Germany.

Debates around the problematic nature of 'race-related' concepts and the development of 'race-related' legislation are necessary as a basis for understanding the relationship between 'race' and social services provision. In the next section we will explore this relationship in more detail, building on analyses incorporated in the first part of the chapter.

'Race' and Social Services Provision

This section will analyse the relationship between 'race' and social services provision, focusing specifically on education and the personal social services. It will explore changing theories and assumptions regarding 'race' and culture which have influenced government 'race-relations' legislation, and which in turn have influenced the nature of social services provision which minority ethnic groups receive. It will also incorporate an analysis which demonstrates that ideologies underpinning government welfare legislation are also influential in determining access to educational and personal social services provision.

Before embarking on such an exploration it is necessary to provide a brief social, political and economic contextualization of the position of minority ethnic groups in society, as this impacts on their relationship to the social welfare system, and their projected need for social services provision.

Indicators of poverty demonstrate that minority ethnic groups are more at risk of high unemployment, low pay, shift work and limited social security rights (Oppenheim, 1990; Skellington, 1992; see also Chapters 10 and 12 of this text), and their poverty has been intensified over the past 17 years as a result of Conservative government policies which have resulted in rising unemployment, regressive taxation and an attack on social security benefits. Moreover, black people also face the additional disruption and disadvantage of rising racial harassment and attacks.

The general climate of racism in the country is affected by the policies of successive governments on immigration and nationality, and has a direct bearing on the inequalities which black people experience in relation to social services provision. For example, some black people are refused access to any social services provision as a result of the 1982 British Nationality Act which excludes British overseas citizens (mainly black citizens) from the right to make any claims on the state, and the 1988 Immigration Act extended this 'no recourse to public funds' clause. Thus, although black people's lives are blighted by poverty and discrimination, they often fail to receive social services provision which could respond to this deprivation, as social services institutions themselves tend to reflect and reproduce the racism which is evident in society as a whole. Despite this, the myth persists among the general population that black people receive more than their fair share of social benefits, often at the expense of the more 'deserving' white community.

However, the relationship between minority ethnic groups and social services provision has not been a static one, but has been affected over the years by changing theories and perspectives regarding 'race', racism and culture which have affected practices and procedures within social services institutions. The education and training of social services professionals has also been influenced by these changing perspectives, but their ability to address issues of 'race' and practice in a non-discriminatory way is also affected by government ideologies towards state welfare which have an acute bearing on the basis on which welfare is provided and the resources made available.

Since the 1960s social services institutions have been informed by four different 'race-related' perspectives which have reflected political develop- ments, policies and ideologies. These perspectives differ in terms of their underlying assumptions regarding the position of minority ethnic groups in British society, but are similar in their tendency to 'problematize' issues related to 'race' and social services provision. All four perspectives offer different recommendations regarding the nature of social services provision in relation to the black community, and thus all four have differing implications for black clients/pupils and black staff within educational and social work institutions. The four theoretical perspectives to be explored are:

1   assimilationist/integrationist perspectives;
2   multi-cultural perspectives;
3   anti-racist perspectives; and
4   New Right perspectives.

Assimilationist/Integrationist Perspectives

Assimilationist perspectives have influenced the nature of 'race' and social services provision to varying degrees since the 1960s and continue to exert an influence today. They are based on the belief in the cultural and racial superiority of white society and the associated belief that minority ethnic groups should be absorbed into the indigenous homogeneous culture: minority ethnic groups are expected to adopt the British 'way of life' and not to undermine the social and ideological bases of the dominant white culture.

Integrationist perspectives, in practice, are often conflated with assimilationist perspectives. Integrationists also subscribe to assumptions of cultural superiority, and therefore place the responsibility on minority ethnic communities to learn new customs and ways of behaving in order to be accepted by the indigenous population. However, they also believe that there has to be some attempt on the part of the 'host' community to understand the difficulties faced by minority ethnic groups. Integration was described by Roy Jenkins in 1966 as: 'equal opportunity accompanied by cultural diversity in an atmosphere of mutual tolerance' (quoted in Troyna, 1992: 68).

In terms of educational policies and practices, assimilationist/ integrationist theories led to developments such as the teaching of English alongside a programme of cultural indoctrination and subordination, to the policy of dispersal of minority ethnic pupils to avoid undue concentration of 'immigrants' in schools. Such policies, during the 1960s, were greatly influenced by policies being implemented in the United States of America, and were based on assumptions that too many black pupils in a school would negatively affect the development and progress of white pupils and lead to lower academic standards.

In social work provision assimilationist/integrationist perspectives led to 'colour-blind' approaches to service delivery which are still evident in many social services departments today. This approach is based on the claim that everyone is 'treated the same' and thus everyone is 'treated equally', but no matter how well-meaning such intentions may be, they deny the centrality of racism in the personal and professional lives of minority ethnic groups. It also undermines and de-legitimizes their knowledge and skills and the strengths of their communities. In assuming that there exist values and beliefs to which we all subscribe, assimilationist/integrationist perspectives fail to provide social work provision which is sensitive to the needs of the minority ethnic groups, and minority ethnic social workers are also pressurized into conforming to white middle-class 'norms' in order to avoid pathologization.

Assimilationist/integrationist perspectives are criticized for ignoring structural inequalities and failing to recognize that black people do not possess social, political or economic power in society. They also fail to separate political and economic values and beliefs from values and beliefs based on culture, and advocate social control and conformity to dominant societal values and beliefs. In social services institutions they fail to question or challenge existing institutional practices, procedures and power structures which are often consciously and unconsciously informed by negative and damaging stereotypes of minority ethnic groups. These stereotypes often result in the pathologization of minority ethnic client groups and staff, which result in their over-representation in the 'controlling' elements and under-representation in the more 'caring' elements of welfare provision. For example, in terms of social work provision they are over-represented as clients of probation departments and mental health institutions, yet are under-represented in terms of, for example, domiciliary provision for the elderly or the disabled.

Activity 6.2

- What are the main beliefs and assumptions underlying assimilationist and integrationist perspectives?
- What are the main criticisms of assimilationist and integrationist perspectives?
- How do such perspectives discriminate against minority ethnic groups in educational and social work provision?

Multi-cultural Perspectives

Multi-cultural perspectives are based on the notion that learning about other peoples' cultures will reduce prejudice and discrimination in society (make minority ethnic groups more palatable to the white population), but in contrast to other perspectives explored in this section they cannot be perceived as theoretical perspectives in their own right. Multi-culturalism is more about 'doing' things such as celebrating cultural diversity, within a theoretical framework which is informed by integrationist perspectives.

Multi-culturalists believe that contact with other cultural lifestyles will reduce the ignorance and prejudice of the white population, and multi-culturalism (the 'sari, samosa and steel band syndrome') has been most influential in the field of education. Here the focus is on curriculum change, and the intention is the hope that contact with other cultural lifestyles will reduce the ignorance and prejudice of white pupils. The curriculum is used to emphasize tolerance and respect for other cultures and to point out the achievements of different cultures, as emphasized by Lord Elton:

> We believe that using the curriculum to emphasize the importance of tolerance and respect for other cultures is a . . . productive approach. A variety of subjects can be used to point out the achievements of different cultures. Where possible these achievements should be linked to cultures represented in this school. (1989: 110)

Although multi-cultural perspectives have been most influential in education, they are also used to varying degrees to inform social work practices, where again the belief is that cultural awareness will lead to more sensitive and informed social work provision.

In terms of education, critics feel it is a fallacy to expect educational underachievement to disappear automatically as language and cultural differences are overcome. The Institute of Race Relations speaks disparagingly of multi-cultural reforms and related policies which 'tinker with educational techniques and methods and leave unaltered the racist fabric of the educational system' (1980: 82).

Case Study 6.1

The shortcomings of the multi-cultural approach were seriously criticized in the Burnage Report, *Murder in the Playground* (MacDonald et al., 1989), chaired by Ian MacDonald, QC.

It was based on an investigation into the murder in 1986 of Ahmed Iqbal Ullah, a 13-year-old British Asian pupil at Burnage High School in Manchester. The report provides a unique anatomy of racist harassment in schools and indicts senior staff of the school (and the local education authority) for its mismanagement of relations between the school and local communities before and after the incident.

John (1990) criticized the multi-cultural approaches at Burnage High School on the basis that practices which encouraged the valuing of other cultures assumed that everything else was unitary and homogeneous. As a result, racist harassment was dislocated from the broader context in which children live and make sense of their lives. Cohen (1987) also believes that the suppression of racism through such policies is likely to generate their appearance in 'a more virulent form 'in other contexts. In other words, decontextualized multi-culturalist policies can feed racism and misunderstanding among sections of the white working class who can view them as preferential treatment for minority ethnic communities.

There are similar criticisms regarding social work practice, education and training which is informed by cultural analyses, leading, for example, to developments designed to inform social work professionals about the family patterns of clients from minority ethnic groups. Critics believe that it is a model which unwittingly reinforces the prejudice of practitioners, narrows their perspectives with cultural stereotypes and 'problematizes' the culture of minority ethnic groups. Multi-cultural initiatives in both educational and social work institutions are also based on limited notions of culture which do not reflect the experiences of minority ethnic individuals and families in relation to issues such as racism, housing and employment. In this respect they reflect many of the problems associated with ethnicity which we identified at the beginning of the chapter in relation to treating minority ethnic cultures as static and unitary entities.

Multi-cultural perspectives along with assimilationist and integrationist perspectives individualize the discrimination that black people experience by focusing on ethnicity and culture rather than on structural factors. As such, they obviate facing questions about control, power and conflict and mask the dynamics of 'race', economics and political power. They are perspectives which fail to explain how and why minority ethnic groups are disadvantaged in relation to dominant groups in society. As Sivanandan states:

there is nothing wrong about learning about other cultures but it must be said that to learn about other cultures is not to learn about the racism of your own . . . unless you are mindful of the racial superiority inculcated in you by 500 years of colonization and slavery you cannot come to cultures objectively. (1991: 41)

Activity 6.3

- What are the main beliefs and assumptions underlying multi-cultural perspectives?
- What are the main criticisms of multi-cultural perspectives?
- How do they discriminate against minority ethnic groups in terms of educational and social work provision?

Anti-racist Perspectives

Anti-racist perspectives constitute a fundamental attack on the ideas described above. In contrast to multi-cultural approaches, they are clear theoretical positions which move away from analyses based on personal and cultural prejudice to analyses which focus on the structural deprivation which minority ethnic groups experience in society, and the institutional nature of racism. As such they are political and challenging to existing conceptions of 'race' and racism, unlike assimilationist, integrationist and multi-cultural perspectives, which are distinctly non-threatening and consensual. However, it is worth noting here that the distinctiveness of anti-racism is often blurred and interpreted as multi-cultural practice.

Anti-racist perspectives became prominent during the 1980s when local government took the lead in responding to the particular needs of the black community. This was largely a result of the 1976 Race Relations Act, which under Section 71 required them to make appropriate arrangements to ensure that their services were carried out with due regard to the need to eliminate unlawful discrimination and to promote equality of opportunity. A combination of other factors was also responsible for the more meaningful responses emanating from a small number of local councils: for example, black political consciousness, increased black involvement in local mainstream political activity, the increasing evidence of racial discrimination and the urban uprisings of 1981 and 1985. These are all factors which Benyon and Solomos (1987) believe concentrated minds and injected a sense of urgency for a while.

Also during the 1980s, there was increasing centralization of government power in relation to local authority finance and administration, which led to the introduction of cash limits, rate-capping, compulsory competitive tendering (CCT) and privatization. These were all power eroding policies which in many authorities led to the dropping of 'race equality' and radical anti-racist policies. CCT was particularly important in this respect as it outlawed 'contract compliance', whereby councils would only award contracts to suppliers of goods and services where they were shown to have, for example, effective equal opportunities policies. The developments of the 1980s were also factors which undermined the ability of local authorities to provide adequate levels of social services provision.

During the 1980s the debate around education was further 'racialized' (made an explicit object of public debate and policy formulation) by the publication of three reports. These were the Rampton Report (DES, 1981), the Swann Report (DES, 1985) and a report entitled *Education for Some* (Eggleston et al., 1986). These three reports are analysed in Case Study 2 and reveal that the latter, *Education for Some*, puts more emphasis on issues relating to anti-racist educational practice by emphasizing processes in schools and in society at large which act as constraining factors. This was in contrast to the Rampton and Swann Reports which tend to focus on inherent 'cultural' characteristics in explaining educational disadvantage.

Anti-racist perspectives link educational and other forms of welfare provision to other forms of inequality and injustice, and assert that the established practices and procedures of social services providers operate to reinforce and perpetuate the racism which minority ethnic groups experience. They focus on institutional factors underpinning attitudes and practices in schools and social work departments, such as black staff representation and the effectiveness of anti-racist policies. Black teachers are seriously under-represented in Britain's schools and are also disproportionately represented on the lowest scales and away from mainstream education (Ranger, 1988). There is also a serious under-representation of black staff in social work departments, especially in positions of seniority.

Anti-racists would also point to the fact that although the majority of local authorities possess formal and explicit equal opportunities and anti-discriminatory policy statements and documents, these have only resulted in minor and patchy successes. As such they have failed to make a significant dent in the level of disadvantage, and in many cases have undermined the serious effects of structural inequalities. As stated earlier, the Burnage Report was highly critical of policies which were drawn up without the involvement of the entire school and the community, and also revealed that the attitudes of some members of teaching staff were damaging in terms of recognizing and dealing with racist attitudes and incidents. For example, one senior teacher commented that there was nothing wrong in using the term 'paki' as it was simply an abbreviation of Pakistani!

Anti-racist perspectives also focus on beliefs around superiority and inferiority which are grounded in institutional processes, procedures and policies and which lead to stereotyping that is inaccurate and damaging. These stereotypes are then used to inform educational and social services provision, most often to the detriment of black pupils and black social work clients. For example, in schools Asian and Afro-Caribbean pupils are subject to negative expectations from teaching staff regarding behaviour and educa-

by its eigenvalue. The DISCRIMINANT procedure in SPSS can perform the calculation of all the key parameters and render the needed results. The value of the discriminant coefficients is their relative importance in determining the difference among different groups of the sample cases. The tasks for a discriminant analysis include: (1) the selection of discriminant variables to construct a most accurate and efficient model; (2) the determination of the discriminant coefficients to best differentiate between different groups of cases; (3) the calculation of the discriminant power; and (4) the derivation of the discriminant score. Generally, if there are m discriminant variables and the dependent variable has k categories, there will be k-1 or m discriminant functions needed depending on whichever number is smaller. These functions will meet the requirement of being mutually orthogonal.

If there are only two categories for the dependent variable, another procedure, i.e., logistic regression, may be preferred. Logistic regression is a direct extension of multiple regression. The methods used in multiple regression are the same as in logistic regression, including the forward and backward selection procedures. A difference between discriminant analysis and logistic regression is that the two have different logics. The former is based on the idea of distinguishing between different centroids, and its calculation has to do with canonical correlation, a concept we will discuss later. The latter involves probabilities, odds ratio, and logarithm of the odds. You are encouraged to use both procedures in the same analysis for a comparison.

A single continuous dependent variable and multiple categorical independent variables. In discussing bivariate analysis, we examined the ONEWAY procedure in SPSS, which is a powerful tool for analyzing the relationship between a continuous dependent variable and a categorical independent variable. When the independent variable has only two categories, there is a famous T-TEST procedure available for more detailed inquiry. If we have more than one categorical independent variable, however, we need to resort to a more general procedure of analysis of variance, commonly called ANOVA. ANOVA is suitable for handling a single continuous dependent variable and multiple independent variables which are all categorical. The one-way and t-test procedures can be regarded as special or simple cases of the general analysis of variance procedure. And in statistical calculations we have $F = t^2$.

The logic of analysis of variance is to compare the variance of the dependent variable in an unrelated situation with its variance in a related situation. The former is an examination of the variance of the dependent variable, which is

Case Study 6.2

The Rampton Report – West Indian Children in our Schools (DES, 1981)

The Rampton Report arose partly as a result of campaigning by several groups, particularly black British parents of Afro-Caribbean descent, who argued that their children were significantly disadvantaged and discriminated against within schools. It was controversial, as it suggested that intentional and unintentional teacher racism affected black pupils' experiences and achievements.

The Swann Report – Education for All (DES, 1985)

The Swann Report emphasized the significance of education in improving the opportunities available to Britain's black minorities, and documented the persistence of ethnic under-achievement in schools, especially amongst Afro-Caribbean males. However, although it attributed this to 'racial disadvantages', it saw these disadvantages as being primarily rooted in black culture and family structures, and portrayed a 'culture of deprivation' in Afro-Caribbean families which led to low achievement and behavioural problems at school.

Education for Some (Eggleston et al., 1986)

This was a Department of Education and Science-financed research project on 'the educational and vocational experiences of 15- to 18-year-old members of minority ethnic groups'. It documented forms of discrimination encountered by black students as well as the determination of young black people to succeed in schools in six Local Education Authorities in the North, the Midlands and Greater London.

tional potential (Wright, 1992), and social workers often justify the under-representation of black clients on the basis that the extended family mainly takes responsibility for social and welfare provision. The under-representation of black staff, pupils and clients then results in a situation where social work continues to operationalize ethnocentric and Eurocentric notions of 'normal' and 'pathological', where black definitions of normality are seldom acknowledged as having any validity.

Activity 6.4

- What are the main beliefs and assumptions underlying anti-racist perspectives?
- How do they help us to understand the racism which permeates educational and social work institutions?
- How are they significantly different from assimilationist, integrationist and multi-cultural approaches?

New Right Perspectives

The New Right has waged a campaign against anti-racism since the early 1980s and has had considerable success in setting the terms of such debates and shaping media coverage. It has also been successful in labelling opponents of its views as 'political' whilst presenting its own arguments as non-political and common-sense. At the same time sections of 'the left' approached anti-racism in a way which played directly into the hands of the New Right and failed to enlist the support of the black population and the wider community. That is, Labour councils increasingly adopted equal opportunities statements and initiatives such as Race Awareness Training, which were introduced and implemented on behalf of the black community rather than involving them. They were developments which were also criticized as being based on the personal and individual pathologization of racism (Sivanandan, 1991).

The New Right has tried to detach the concept of racism from the social arena and relocate it in the realm of personal morality, and in the vocabulary of the New Right the word 'culture' has displaced 'race'. Its analysis is strongly linked to notions of British nationalism and a concept of nation which is exclusionary and fails to embrace the black population. For example Woodrow Wyatt, writing in the *News of the World* (5 March 1989), stated that: 'Newcomers here are welcome. But only if they become genuine Britishers and don't stuff their alien cultures down our throats.'

These were also views reflected by prominent mainstream politicians. For example, in 1978 Margaret Thatcher was interviewed on television, and stated:

> I think people are really rather afraid that this country might be rather swamped by people with a different culture and, you know, the British character has done so much for democracy and law, and done so much throughout the world, that if there is any fear that it might be swamped people are going to be really rather hostile to those coming in.

Norman Tebbitt echoed these sentiments in the 1980s when he challenged the 'British' credentials of minority ethnic populations who did not support the English cricket team.

These views provoke anxieties which have been raised for decades, and which were evoked and legitimized when exploring assimilationist and integrationist theories. Nationality or patriotism is seen as a matter of loyalty to people 'of one's own kind', and the preservation of nationhood is used to justify policies which advocate the forcible assimilation and repatriation of black people. Advocates of such views would deny that they were racist, stating that they were simply defending British culture.

Education has been a vital terrain upon which the New Right has developed its arguments. Individuals such as Ray Honeyford and Caroline Cox, and pressure groups such as the Parental Alliance for Choice in Education (PACE), have fought against comprehensive education and have been particularly vociferous in their criticism of multi-cultural and anti-racist initiatives (the two are, characteristically, never differentiated) in education. They believe them to be unacceptable forms of politicization of the school curriculum and to cause a decline in educational standards. For example, Palmer stated that: 'At the extreme schools could be transformed from centres of learning into instruments of political revolution' (1986: 2).

Their attacks on anti-racist education have been enhanced and given extra weight and credibility by government legislation which has aimed to 'increase parental choice', and which has introduced reforms insisting on broadly Christian forms of worship and the use of standard English. A commitment to British nationalism and British culture was reflected in the 1988 Education Reform Act (not relevant in Scotland), which introduced a national curriculum rooted in a prescriptive model of national culture and national history.

Case Study 6.3

The promotion of such assumptions was demonstrated in 1987 in the Dewsbury Affair:

A group of white parents refused to send their children to a largely Asian school allocated them by Kirklees Local Education Authority, stating that they wanted their children to have an education based on 'British culture'. The 1981 Education Act had given legal backing to 'parental choice' of schools, and in 1988 the case went to the High Court and the parents won their 'right' to send their children to schools of their own choice. They were backed through their campaign by PACE (Parental Alliance for Choice in Education).

Other aspects of the 1988 Act have also had a detrimental effect on black pupils. For example, schools now have to compete for financial resources and the implications are that pupils seen as too troublesome or too expensive will be discriminated against, which will disproportionately impact on black pupils. Local Education Authorities have also lost the power to equalize or balance resources between schools according to the social and educational needs of different pupil groups, which again discriminates against the most educationally disadvantaged sectors of society.

Social work practice has also come under attack from the New Right, even though as a profession it has only just begun to address issues of anti-racism, without, as yet, making any significant impact on social work practices and social work provision. During the late 1980s and the early 1990s, the Central Council for Education and Training in Social Work (CCETSW) instigated a number of developments, informed by black practitioners and students, which were an attempt to incorporate anti-racist perspectives into social work education and training. As a result, there are now requirements within the Diploma in Social Work for courses to address 'race' and racism in a constructive manner.

However, there has been a right-wing backlash against these developments, and increased calls for a return to 'traditional' social work practices and skills. Media coverage has been critical, with CCETSW's anti-racist developments portrayed as doctrinaire and abusive, and CCETSW staff described as fanatics and zealots, obsessed with political correctness.

Activity 6.5

- What are the main assumptions underlying New Right critiques of anti-racist perspectives?
- How do New Right perspectives compare with assimilationist/integrationist or multi-cultural perspectives?

Summary and Conclusion

This chapter has demonstrated that in order to understand the relationship between 'race' and social services we first need a critical awareness of the development of key concepts such as 'race', racism and ethnicity. We also need to analyse critically how such concepts have been socially constructed in relation to historical, political and economic developments.

As well as analysing key concepts we need to understand the role of 'race-related' legislation in determining the responsibilities of local authorities and social services departments in relation to minority ethnic groups. Such an understanding necessitates an analysis of political ideologies which have influenced legislative developments and which have also influenced the development of 'race-related' perspectives (and hence emphasize the importance of the ideas discussed in Chapters 2 to 4).

We have seen that such perspectives change over the years in relation to social and political developments and that they offer different analyses regarding the status of minority ethnic groups in society and the nature of social services provision which they receive.

Although there are differences between assimilationist/integrationist and multi-cultural perspectives, we saw that they are nevertheless based on notions of inferiority and superiority and generally believe that minority ethnic groups should reflect the 'British way of life'. These perspectives fail to recognize the nature of structural and institutional racism which affect the relationship of minority-ethnic groups to social services departments and their representation and treatment as staff and clients.

We also examined how, during the 1980s, anti-racist perspectives began to influence the political agenda. They also began to have some influence on social services provision especially in the area of education and social work. Pressure was put on social services providers to examine their own policies, practices, attitudes and assumptions in relation to anti-racist provision rather than expecting minority ethnic groups to conform to existing institutional practices.

However, anti-racist perspectives were soon under attack from the New Right, especially in relation to education and social work. We have seen that, during the 1990s, the New Right has resurrected assumptions reflected in assimilationist and integrationist perspectives, but in a more virulent form. Their views and assumptions are already undermining anti-racist developments in the area of social services provision, and structural and institutional analyses are once again being marginalized and discredited.

7

Social Policy and Sexuality

Angelia R. Wilson

Is Sexuality a Social Policy Issue?

This chapter may seem an unusual contribution to an introductory text on social policy. While issues of discrimination based on 'race' or gender have become familiar topics for social policy students, traditional social policy texts do not address discrimination based on sexuality or sexual orientation in great detail. Some may even wonder how, or why, sexuality can be influenced by state policies. In the next few pages, then, we will look at a few areas where socio-political discourse – for example, morality and ideology – has led to policies which either discriminate against gay men, lesbians and bisexuals or, implicitly or explicitly, give preferential treatment to heterosexuals.

In this discussion it will be helpful to keep in mind two terms which in the last few years have become a part of discourse on sexuality: 'heterosexism' and 'homophobia'. Heterosexism has been defined as 'the system by which heterosexuality is assumed to be the only acceptable and viable life option' (Blumenfeld and Raymond, 1993: 224). This assumption of heterosexuality as a social norm forces lesbians, gay men and bisexuals to struggle against prejudice within society and to develop a positive sexual identity.

> Though not direct or overt, heterosexism is a form of discrimination. Its subtlety makes it somehow even more insidious because it is harder to define and combat. Heterosexism is discrimination by neglect, omission, and/or distortion, whereas often its more active partner – homophobia – is discrimination by intent and design. (Blumenfeld and Raymond, 1993: 245)

Homophobia, on a personal level, is often violent, taking the form of 'gay bashing' which includes verbal harassment and, in many cases, physical assault. Unfortunately, homophobia extends beyond the personal attack. As we will see below, institutional homophobia dictates codes of behaviour through a system of penalties and rewards that actively discriminates against gay men, lesbians and bisexuals through social, political, business and religious practices that sanction heterosexuality and punish, even criminalize, homosexuality. The beliefs and ideologies that attempt to justify this discrimination we will discuss below. Most are built upon myth or moral positioning and have not withstood persistent examination by biologists,

sociologists, psychologists, or gay and lesbian activists. Nevertheless, heterosexism and homophobia, similar to racism and sexism, are a determining
factor in British social structure and pervasive in the construction of social
policy. An initial connection between sexuality and social policy can be
made by recalling two issues which marked the political agenda of the late
1980s: the government's initial response to the AIDS epidemic/crisis and the
regulation of sex education and family life through local government
policies.

The discovery in the 1980s of a virus which had affected the immune
system, leaving the body defenceless against infections and cancers among
some gay men, quickly became a 'medical justification' for discrimination
against an already stigmatized group. Doctors first referred to the new
disease as the 'Gay Plague', later officially labelling it Gay-Related Immune
Deficiency (GRID). Only after gay activists protested that such a name
perpetuated discrimination and hostility towards only one group affected by
the disease was the name changed to Acquired Immune Deficiency Syndrome (AIDS). Unfortunately, the initial label, supported by 'medical' proof
that gay men were the largest number of sufferers in the West, acted as
vindication for already existing homophobia. At an AIDS conference in
Britain in 1986 the Chief Constable of Manchester, James Anderton,
informed the audience that AIDS was a 'self-inflicted scourge' and that
homosexuals were 'swirling about in a cesspit of their own making' (cited in
Jeffery-Poulter, 1991: 196–7). This insensitivity to those affected by AIDS
and prejudice against homosexuals was reflected on a national level as the
Thatcher government failed to respond to the crisis: not until September of
1985, over four years after the first reported British case, did the Department
of Health commit funds for treatment and counselling (Jeffery-Poulter,
1991: 176–98). One would assume that a disease of this magnitude, known
to be transmitted through blood and some body fluids, would be a high
priority for state action such as mandatory blood screening, information
campaigns and funding for treatment. The delay in this case can easily be
linked to apathy, lack of concern, and disgust towards homosexual
citizens.

Another issue that dominated headlines in the late 1980s also indicated
the level of social prejudice against gay men and lesbians. Interest groups
such as the Responsible Society and Family and Youth Concern were
campaigning for the Department of Education to allow parents to withdraw
children from sex education classes. They, like the later established Conservative Family Campaign (CFC), believed that sex education in schools
led to promiscuity, abortions and homosexuality, all of which they argued
would undermine the nuclear family – the backbone of British society. The
1986 Education Act relocated responsibility for sex education curriculum
from local authorities to school governors in hopes that this would provide
parents with more input in the education of their children. Following a
national uproar over Haringey Council's policy to promote 'positive images'
of lesbians and gay men, a Conservative MP, David Wilshire, introduced an

amendment to the Local Government Bill to prevent councils from 'promoting' of homosexuality or teaching its 'acceptability' as a 'pretended family relationship'. Section 28, as it became known, expressed the belief of these groups that homosexuality was 'unnatural', 'subversive' and 'spread disease'. The CFC insisted that if children were taught that homosexuality was an acceptable option and/or were exposed to positive images such as homosexual teachers, they might become homosexual. Even though gay and lesbian activists were able to mobilize strong opposition to the clause, in March 1988, with the support of Margaret Thatcher, the amendment became law under the Local Government Act of 1988.

Policy Summary Box 7.1

Section 28 of the Local Government Act 1988

Part 1 – A Local Authority shall not:
  (a) Intentionally promote homosexuality or publish material with the intention of promoting homosexuality,
  (b) Promote the teaching in any maintained school of the acceptability of homosexuality as a pretended family relationship.

Part 2 – Nothing in sub-section 1 above shall be taken to prohibit the doing of anything for the purpose of treating or preventing disease.

Given that sex education is determined by individual school governors, and given the clear message from the government to local authorities to avoid promoting homosexuality, it is not surprising that homosexuality and AIDS information are not a part of many sex education programmes. In addition support for social services directed at gay men and lesbians has suffered a serious decline in the late 1980s and early 1990s (see Thomson, 1993 and Cooper, 1994).

After briefly considering these two examples we can now see how social policy can come to reflect prejudices about homosexuality and in doing so can legalize discrimination on the basis of sexuality. Although it has been only recently that issues around sexuality have appeared on the mainstream political agenda, beliefs about the unnaturalness, and sinfulness, of sexual acts between men have a long history in British law. In order to locate current debates in a historical and theoretical framework the following section will consider two questions: Why is sexual orientation a basis for discrimination? Which ideologies justify continued discrimination or which can support social reforms?

Sexual History

The western Christian tradition is the bedrock of condemnation of sexual activity between men found in British law. The stories of Sodom and Gomorrah are understood to warn that such behaviour would lead to the worst of punishment from God. In the Middle Ages the English Ecclesiastical Courts punished those who had committed such immoral practices. Henry VIII in 1533 declared the vice of buggery, with man, woman, or beast, a criminal offence punishable by death. Over 300 years later, in 1861, the death penalty was replaced by a sentence of 10 years to life imprisonment. In 1885 the Criminal Law Amendment Act made all male homosexual acts short of buggery, committed in public or private, illegal. As noted in Chapter 5, the late nineteenth century was marked by the formal recognition of the nuclear family as the paradigm of a stable society. Homosexual acts then were not only understood as a moral abomination but also as a threat to the role of the family, a role which was becoming increasingly important to the success of the capitalist economy. The result of this emphasis on the nuclear family was that the penalties outlined in the 1885 Act became known as a 'blackmailer's charter' because those suspected of homosexual acts were targets for blackmailers who preyed upon fears of public scandal and prosecution. But perhaps the most interesting point about the 1885 Act is the significant shift in language describing homosexual acts as 'gross indecency' rather than limiting the law to only acts of 'buggery'. In other words, not only was buggery a criminal offence but the wording of the law now encompassed any same-sex act between men. So while the criminalization of homosexual acts was a partial response to the need to protect the nuclear family, as Weeks points out, the recognition in law and the well publicized trials such as that resulting in Oscar Wilde's conviction actually began the process of constructing a homosexual 'identity' based on desire for the same sex. According to Weeks, 'law does not create public opinion but it does shape and reinforce it' (1977: 11). This statement not only summarizes the way in which law reflected and reinforced the morality of the late nineteenth century but it equally characterizes the role of law in the late twentieth century.

Weeks suggests that a number of elements came into play in the late 1950s and 1960s which led to a review of laws regulating homosexuality and eventually to significant reforms. The emphasis on the nuclear family unit in the post-war years made it clear that this model of family 'by its nature, must exclude homosexuals except as aberrations' (Weeks, 1977: 157). He points out that at this time homosexuality became known as a 'disease', a 'severe mental sickness which usually requires long analytical psychotherapy', a 'mental disorder', or more generally, a deviation from the norm of bipolarized sex/gender (Weeks, 1977: 157). Probably not unrelated to this emphasis on the family, the post-war years saw a dramatic increase in indictable homosexual offences. For example, those charged with 'gross indecency' rose from 316 in 1938 to 2,322 in 1955 (Weeks, 1977: 158).

During this period the police used *agents provocateurs*, usually in public toilets, to 'catch' homosexuals. Some of those arrested were public figures, including Labour and Tory Members of Parliament as well as actors such as Sir John Gielgud. But it was the trial of Lord Montague and Peter Wildeblood which sparked intense publicity and led those in power to order a review of the laws regulating homosexuality. In 1954 the Home Secretary, Sir David Maxwell-Fyfe, asked the Vice-Chancellor of Reading University, Sir John Wolfenden, to head an enquiry into the issues of homosexuality and prostitution. The final recommendations of the Wolfenden Report encouraged legislation which would decriminalize homosexual acts between men, aged 21 or over, in private. However, members of both Houses believed that the present state of public opinion did not indicate strong approval or toleration of homosexuality (Hyde, 1970: 237). Indeed, it was another ten years before the Wolfenden recommendations were enacted. The 1967 Sexual Offences Act decriminalized homosexual acts in private between consenting men, over 21, who were not members of the armed services.

In essence, this new legislation did not legalize homosexual acts; instead it decriminalized a few of them. For example, the Act did not mention lesbians or sexual acts between women, and consequently it could be assumed that lesbians cannot be prosecuted. However, the failure to mention lesbianism cannot be assumed to indicate legal approval. In addition, the Act only applies to those homosexual acts taking place in private; a hotel room, a friend's home – anywhere a third person could be witness to the activities – is not understood as being 'in private'. Finally, although those participating in homosexual activity while a member of the armed services are no longer subject to criminal prosecution, a ban on homosexuals in the military still exists. If their homosexuality is discovered they will be discharged. Thus the 1967 Sexual Offences Act remains the basis for prosecutions of homosexuals today. Moreover, since the charge of 'gross indecency' outlined in the 1885 Criminal Amendment Act has yet to be repealed, many gay men continue to be prosecuted for public 'sexual acts' such as kissing in the street or having sex in a 'public' place.

The supporters of the 1967 Act hoped that decriminalization would remove this issue from the public agenda. They advised homosexuals that the change in law was not an indication of approval but an 'act of toleration'. The original sponsor of the Bill, Lord Arran, warned that 'any form of ostentatious behaviour now or in the future would, I believe, make the sponsors of the Bill regret that they have done what they have done' (Hyde, 1970: 274). Even the Wolfenden Committee had commented that 'it is important that the limited modification of the law which we propose would not be interpreted as an indication that the law can be indifferent to other forms of homosexual behaviour, or as a general licence to adult homosexuals to behave as they please' (cited in Weeks, 1981: 243). But the late 1960s and early 1970s were not a time for quiet thankfulness and private sex; it was a time of sexual revolution.

represented by a "total sum of squares" (TSS), without consideration of the independent variable(s). In the latter situation, the dependent variable is studied in relation to the different categories of the independent variable(s). For each independent variable, the variance of the dependent variable can be studied first in terms of its variances within the individual categories of the independent variable. The total is called "within-group sum of squares" and is denoted by WSS. This part of the variance of the dependent variable will be smaller than its "total sum of squares," and the amount reduced can be regarded as the role of the independent variable. The reduced amount can be calculated in terms of "between-group sum of squares" (BSS) of the dependent variable (Y) in relation to the categorical independent variable. Basically, BSS is the total squared difference between the group means (M_i) and the grand mean (M) weighted by the number of cases in each group (N_i): $BSS = \sum N_i (M_i - M)^2$. The relationship among the three quantities is: $TSS = \sum (Y - M)^2 = BSS + WSS$. The ratio of BSS to TSS is not exactly but analogous to PRE (proportionate reduction in error), which is the familiar measure of association: $E^2 = BSS/TSS$. The ratio of BSS to WSS leads to the famous test quantity F after taking into consideration of degrees of freedom: $F = (BSS/WSS)[(N-k)/(k-1)]$. Here N is the sample size, k is the number of categories or groups, $WSS = \sum (Y - M_i)^2$.

One-way analysis of variance is only the simplest example. In the more complicated case of two-way or multi-way analysis of variance, cross-tabulation or multiple classification is needed to identify all the groupings of cases so that the total within-group variances and the various between-group variances can be calculated. In the multiple independent variables situation, one more thing to consider is the interaction among the independent variables (interactive sums of squares, or ISS). The general ANOVA procedure, therefore, needs to identify and distinguish among the partial or main effect of each independent variable, the possible interaction effect among the independent variables, and the joint or explained effect of all the independent variables. Here E^2 is still the measure of association in terms of the various effects, and F the test quantity.

It should be noted that in some one-way and very simple multi-way situations, the analysis of variance may be replaced by multiple regression analysis using dummy variables. Therefore, in dealing with the relationship between a single continuous dependent variable and multiple categorical independent variables, you have a choice between the REGRESSION and the ONEWAY or ANOVA procedures.

If your independent variables include not only categorical but also continuous

By the latter part of 1967 the Manchester-based North Western Homosexual Law Reform Committee set up the Esquire Clubs to provide 'social facilities for homosexuals' (Jeffery-Poulter, 1991: 85). Although they had difficulty establishing many clubs, by 1970 the *Gay Guide*, published by Spartacus, the first publicly available magazine catering for gay men, listed 60 gay venues in London and more than 200 throughout the United Kingdom. The next 10 years witnessed the birth of numerous organizations focusing on a variety of aspects of the 'gay community'; for example, the Gay Labour Group, the Gay Christian Movement, the Gay Business Club. But the single most influential event which sparked what became known as the 'gay and lesbian movement' took place on 28 June 1969 in the Stonewall Inn, in Greenwich Village, New York. The police raided the pub on a regular basis arresting those thought to be gay but on that night the customers fought back, taking their protest into the streets. As Rosa Parks, who refused to give up her bus seat to a white person, had set in motion the 1960s protests against racism in the American South, those taking a stand that night inspired others to challenge social prejudice and set in motion the gay and lesbian political movement. By November 1970 the Gay Liberation Movement had spread to Britain. The Gay Liberation Front's message was 'that every person has the right to develop and extend their character and explore their sexuality through relationships with any other human being, without moral, social or political pressure . . . we demand honour, identity and liberation' (GLF pamphlet, in Jeffery-Poulter, 1991: 100–1). Although the words built upon the revolutionary mood which marked many of the new social movements in the late 1960s and early 1970s, the determination to expose social oppression of homosexuals and to eliminate political and social inequalities remains the unifying factor of the gay and lesbian movement in contemporary Britain.

As we noted above, the conservative mood of the 1980s and fears over the AIDS crisis led to a renewal of opposition towards the few accomplishments gay and lesbian activists had secured in the 1970s. Many right-wing groups, along with the government, attempted to reinforce the importance of the nuclear family. The culmination of their views found its way into law in Section 28 of the Local Government Act. While this new regulation on local government affected a number of services provided for lesbians and gay men – for example, counselling lines, sex education, and equal consideration in all areas of policy – it also became a rallying point for gay and lesbian activists who were determined such legislation would never again be considered without an organized opposition. In May 1989 a few well-known artists, such as Sir Ian McKellen and Michael Cashman, experienced activists like Lisa Power and Peter Ashman, as well as ex-Tory MP Matthew Parris, organized a professional lobbying group, Stonewall, to monitor legislation and policy-making and to research areas where gay men and lesbians were discriminated against. Other activists groups such as OutRage! emerged around this time and focused on public challenges, protests and demonstrations in order to heighten media attention about prejudice and to encourage large numbers of gay men, lesbians, bisexuals and transgendered people to join the growing political community registering their complaints about social and political inequalities. This activism-orientated tactic also proved successful for Act-Up, which campaigned for government support for research and treatment of those with HIV and AIDS. The growth of these organizations was certainly due to the 'gay culture' which had developed in the late 1970s and early 1980s, and to the power of the 'Pink Pound' – a phrase which has come to define the economic impact made by some gay men and lesbians with significant disposable incomes. The economic and cultural 'gay and lesbian community' of the late 1980s and early 1990s began to flex their political muscle, and the result has been a political constituency receiving at least marginal respect from all political parties and becoming a substantial force to be reckoned with by businesses. This has been proved in at least two instances. First, early in 1994 Parliament considered changing the age of consent for gay male sex. The age of consent for heterosexual sex is 16, but for gay male sex it remained at 21 according to the 1967 Sexual Offences Act. Gay and lesbian activists were joined by a substantial number of MPs and medical professionals as well as a few sympathetic journalists in campaigning for 'equality', in this case an equal age of consent. The Criminal Justice and Public Order Act 1994 reduced the age of consent for gay men to 18. The campaign can be seen as a success as it was the first time in over 20 years that changes in laws regulating homosexuality had been addressed; or it could simply be a failure to achieve full equality. Another developing success story is the recent financial support Stonewall has received from large corporations. With these new funds they have conducted a number of surveys about discrimination and harassment in the workplace, resulting in an equal opportunities good practice guide which increases awareness about heterosexism and homophobia in employment.

The 1990s has witnessed a slight change in public opinion towards gay and lesbian issues. The Prime Minister John Major met Sir Ian McKellen, one of the founders of Stonewall; efforts by moral conservatives to ensure that gay men and lesbians could not adopt children have been thwarted by gay and lesbian activists, and some members of the government seem far less likely to admit openly their prejudice against gay men and lesbians, particularly in the areas of 'family policy' and employment. By way of a summary, then, we can identify four areas of at least some achievement for the gay and lesbian movement. First, high-profile gay and lesbian activist groups have emerged, which monitor the legislation process for signs of discrimination, and they are able to mobilize a large constituency to secure legal change. Second, as a result of this activism, gay and lesbian issues are consistently on the public agenda. For example, those who want to be seen to endorse equal opportunities often include 'sexual orientation' in the list of categories which will not be a basis for job discrimination. Third, after some government-sponsored education about HIV and AIDS, as well as tremendous efforts on the part of AIDS groups such as Act-Up and the Terrence Higgins Trust, a larger part of the population now realizes that AIDS is not a 'gay plague' and should not be necessarily linked to sexual orientation. Finally, the process of 'coming out of the closet', or publicly identifying oneself as a gay man or lesbian, has enabled many heterosexuals in the society to realize the number of homosexual citizens in Britain: citizens who pay their taxes, citizens who work beside them, live next door, raise children of their own, citizens who are simply not deserving of the discrimination and fear that marks their lives.

Activity 7.1

1   What are heterosexism and homophobia? How do they differ?
2   What have been some of the significant factors shaping the development of gay and lesbian politics over the last 40 years in Britain?

Ideology as Justification

A number of arguments concerning the need to regulate homosexuality can be identified in contemporary socio-political discourse. For the most part these hinge upon different aetiological, or causal, explanations for homosexuality. Generally speaking, there are three explanations most often cited: biological theories, psychoanalytic theories and environmental/behavioural theories. A brief sketch of each will provide a basis for looking at the reasons for and against regulating homosexuality.

Biological Theories

Some recent biological research has claimed that sexuality is determined by one's genetic makeup. Levay's (1993) study of male twins has attempted to locate a section of the brain which links homosexuality with particular genetic characteristics. Most researchers in this field would add that biology is probably not *the* determining factor but that it may work in conjunction with social environment, a point we will consider in more detail below However, the biological explanation has received much attention from both those who support non-discrimination policies and those who do not. On the one hand it is argued that discrimination should not be based on a biologically determined factor, similar to gender or skin colour. On the other hand, those who believe that homosexuality is abnormal or is a disease have welcomed this type of research in hopes that in the future genetic engineering could be used to detect homosexuality and alter the foetus's sexuality or give the parents the option of abortion.

Psychoanalytic Theories

Another explanation for homosexuality is rooted in psychoanalytic theories. Freud's description of the development of sexuality as moving through various stages in which the child learns to reproduce sexual norms locates homosexuality as a type of arrested development, or failure to complete the developmental process. On this and similar analysis, homosexuality was considered a psychological illness which, in most cases, could be cured through therapy. A more feminist understanding of psychoanalysis maintains that strict heterosexuality is the result of rigid sex-role stereotyping so that men are forced by social norms to reject all things socially identified as female while women have a greater capacity for bisexuality because their gender role is not as strict as that of the male. This type of approach recognizes the pervasiveness of gender structure as a social norm without suggesting that alternative interpretations of gender/sex should be seen as abnormal or as a psychological illness. In 1973 the American Psychiatric Association and the American Psychological Association eliminated homosexuality from the list of psychological disorders. However, Freudian theory, or the pop-psychology version, remains an important part of cultural hegemony concerning homosexuality. Therefore, there are those who continue to argue that it is a disease and that what is needed is not laws offering homosexuals legal equality but instead a policy commitment which asserts that they can, and should, be cured through therapy.

Environmental/Behavioural Theories

A third explanation for homosexuality can be found in environmental or behavioural theories. Among the many theories of this kind are probably those most often present in contemporary debate about the cause of homosexuality. These 'common-sense' explanations may be based on one or more of the following: that the person had a pleasurable same-sex experience in childhood or was separated from members of the opposite sex at school; or the familiar notion that people are seduced or recruited into homosexuality and would otherwise have been a 'healthy' heterosexual; or maybe the person has had an 'unpleasant' heterosexual experience and as a result turns to homosexuality; or the suggestion that family relationships are the determining factor – a domineering mother or an absent father. One researcher explains the family relationship in this way: 'The child who becomes homosexual is usually overprotected and preferred by his mother. In other cases he may be under-protected and rejected' (Bieber, quoted in Blumenfeld and Raymond, 1993: 142). While this quote covers all possibilities – both protected and rejected – it is also typical of the unsubstantiated nature of this type of explanation. If environment was the cause of homosexuality, how does one explain siblings who share the same familial environment, some developing as heterosexuals and others as homosexuals? Similar cases can be made against most of these theories. Many who have

had one same-sex experience do not become homosexuals; many homosexuals have not had unpleasant heterosexual experiences, in fact many have
had pleasant heterosexual experiences; and homosexuals come from all
types of families – 'normal' loving heterosexual relationships, unhappy
marriages and single-parent families – just as heterosexuals come from all
types of families – 'normal' heterosexual ones, unhappy ones, single-parent
families, and even from same-sex homosexual couples.

While each of these theories – biological, psychological, environmental/
behavioural – may offer some insight into the development of sexuality, one
thing can be said with certainty: in contemporary western culture the social
and political norm is heterosexuality. Part of the reason for this may lie in a
belief in one or more of the above explanations of sexuality but other
arguments are also heard in socio-political discourse about homosexuality.
Two of these in particular spring from a moral belief about proper sexual
conduct and/or about the state's role in regulating individual action. First,
many believe that homosexuality is a sin, that it is an abnormal expression of
sexual desire and that sexual desire should only be expressed in a heterosexual relationship, preferably one bound by marriage. Those who hold such
a belief may regard the state as the proper authority to restrict such action,
protecting the individual from sin and society as a whole from the effects of
such behaviour. Generally speaking, the main concern here is that if the state
is seen to condone homosexual relationships, more people will either choose
to express this sinful sexual desire or will be recruited into a sinful
homosexual lifestyle, thus threatening the sanctity and/or centrality of the
nuclear family. The belief that decriminalizing homosexual acts, or ending
discrimination against homosexuals, would lead to the breakdown of the
nuclear family and in turn the collapse of British society is often reiterated
by politicians and philosophers, such as Lord Devlin in the 1960s or
Margaret Thatcher in the 1980s.

The other moral-political belief that appears to represent a more favour-
able argument lies in liberalism's conception of the separation of the public
and the private. Liberal political theorists argue that individuals should
decide questions of morality for themselves. Therefore, moral questions
regarding sexuality should be left to the individual and should be generally
free from state regulation. According to this line of thought, then, the
individual who chooses to commit homosexual acts should be able to do so
with little state interference. It would seem this liberalism would support
decriminalization of homosexuality, and generally this is the case. One
difficulty with this 'liberal' reasoning is that it is built upon the assumption
that homosexuality is a choice. Conceived of as a moral choice, it is not
given the same protection from discrimination as other biologically determined identities such as 'race' or sex. If it is not a choice, and the scientific
evidence increasingly suggests that it is a biological given, then those who
may seem sympathetic to decriminalizing homosexual acts will need to go
further, crossing the divide between the public and private, by publicly
arguing against discrimination. Future legislation will need to go beyond

decriminalization and progress towards policies which protect against discrimination and provide equal concern and respect for homosexual citizens. Such changes are far removed from the policy-making found in current British government or from the belief that British society should reaffirm heterosexuality as the norm. The social construction of heterosexuality as the norm, regardless of the justification, has become a generally accepted practice in policy-making. In fact, social policy goes beyond tacitly accepting the heterosexual lifestyle as that of the majority and, as we will see below, leans more towards homophobia or 'compulsory' heterosexuality.

Activity 7.2

'Burning is too good for them. Bury them in a pit and pour on quicklime.' Reader's letter, *Daily Express*, 1987, during the first few months of the AIDS crisis.

'It would mean the decay of society if people adopted the latter attitude [that is, approval of lesbianism].'
Judge in lesbian custody case, 1976 (Rights of Women Lesbian Custody Group, 1984: 121)

'If one has a policy as Ealing Council has, of appointing teachers regardless of sexual orientation, how can the House be surprised at the parents' fears that their children will be put in the hands of perverts, practising homosexuals who are interested in children?'
Greenway, MP for Ealing, House of Commons debate, October 1986 (Cooper, 1994: 118)

'I want what every parent wants for their child; a society where they can grow up free to be who they please and equal with everyone around them.'
Sandi Toksvig, comedian and lesbian mother (*Stonewall*, 1993)

'If we want others to give us respect we must first be willing to give ourselves respect. We must be proud of who we are. And we cannot do that if we hide. We have to make ourselves palpable. Touchable. Real. And then we can show the world what we are all about: happy, intelligent, giving people. We can show our whole strength, our dignity and character. We can show our joy and sorrow, our heartaches and our pain. Then we can just be.'
Martina Navratilova after her final Wimbledon match (reported in *Stonewall*, 1993)

'The positive legal recognition of lesbian and gay sexuality (as opposed to negative criminal-law constructions) promotes feelings of self-worth, citizenship, and community identity.'
(Herman, 1994: 4)

Discuss the above quotations and consider the following questions:

1 Which ideological justifications noted in the previous section might support each position?
2 How – and why – are the 'causes' or aetiological explanations of homosexuality significant in determining different political beliefs about the way in which gay men and lesbians should be treated by the state and society?

Enforced Heterosexuality

In the section above we considered the kinds of arguments which are present in debates about the regulation of homosexuality, and in Activities 7.2 we noted the way in which those arguments become a part of policy debates. Yet another way of understanding this discourse on sexuality emerges in the theoretical writings of Foucault (1978), Plummer (1975), McIntosh (1975) and Weeks (1977, 1986, 1991). Each of these, in their various arguments, maintains that definitions of sexuality, both 'normal' and 'deviant' sexualities, are constructed through social discourse. For example, in his influential text *The History of Sexuality* Foucault (1978) shows how concepts of sexuality have been historically constructed through discourse which establishes heterosexuality as the social norm. And McIntosh (1975) explains that the regulation of sexual behaviour was accompanied by the development of the belief that homosexuality was a *condition* afflicting some citizens.

Therefore the definition and regulation of sexuality in themselves established a homosexual 'identity', stereotyped at first as a medical or psychological disease or as social deviance and later by 'homosexuals' themselves as a defining, somehow innate, factor of individual identity. In other words, where some may believe that desire for the same sex was either a chosen sin, or a failure to develop or to replicate sex/gender norms, these theorists point out that the concepts of sin or normalcy are themselves products of socially constructed definitions; definitions which are reinforced through the power structures of the church, science and, more generally, the structure of modern capitalism. This argument, that sexuality itself is socially constructed and maintained through social policies, can enable us to examine the assumptions within policy for what Adrianne Rich has labelled 'compulsory heterosexuality' (see Rich, 1981).

In other words, what is suggested here is that sexuality is socially constructed and reinforced through social policies which assume and advocate heterosexuality to the extent that other sexualities are not only considered socially deviant but are even discriminated against. This heterosexism has received parliamentary approval through Section 28 where gay and lesbian parents with children are maligned as 'pretended families' and is the motivating factor in adoption laws, custody cases or, more broadly, 'family policy'. The second area of social policy we will consider in this section is that of discrimination in employment. While it could be argued that businesses are responsible for their own employment practices, the law requires that an employer should not discriminate on the ground of 'race' or sex. Such a legal protection from discrimination does not exist for gay or lesbian employees, and as a result sexual orientation alone can be grounds for legal dismissal, unequal pay and harassment at work.

Family Policy and 'Pretended Families'

Section 28 confirmed in legislation the central view of the 1980s Conservative government of gay and lesbian families. In other words, while some homosexual acts may not be considered a criminal offence, gay and lesbian families should know that their place in society is secondary and is not equal to that of heterosexual families. The lack of recognition of gay and lesbian couples serves as the basis for this secondary status. Gay and lesbian couples, because they cannot/ legally marry, are denied the rights listed in Policy Summary Box 7.2.

The rights denied gay and lesbian partners listed in Policy Summary Box 7.2 are only a few of the areas in which gay and lesbian partners are victims of discrimination because their relationship is denied legal recognition. It is, needless to say, difficult to build a family in such an oppressive situation. Nevertheless, gay and lesbian partners continue to struggle with this legal discrimination and to raise children despite the secondary status of their 'pretended family'. This discrimination is primarily due to the mixture of beliefs about the unnaturalness of homosexuality, but it also involves, as noted below, fears about the impact gay or lesbian parents may have upon their children.

There are at least four concerns commonly voiced about children of gay or lesbian parents. First, some psychological 'experts' have advised the courts that a child brought up in a household with two parental figures of the same sex may not develop adequately. The child may not learn the sex-gender roles which are considered normal in society; for example, a male child of lesbian parents may not have access to appropriate male role models. Underpinning this concern are the beliefs that homosexuality is morally wrong and/or that children of homosexuals are more likely to 'become' homosexual themselves. Leaving aside the question discussed above concerning legislating morality, or enforcing heterosexuality as a moral norm, this concern reflects a number of assumptions about the development of sexuality. For example, most gay men and lesbians are the offspring of heterosexual parents, therefore strict gender roles of feminine/

Policy Summary Box 7.2

1 Gay and lesbian partners cannot adopt children as a couple.
2 Non-UK partners cannot permanently live in the United Kingdom as homosexual couples.
3 Inheritance law makes no provision for a gay or lesbian partner if the deceased dies without a will. Therefore the family (excluding the gay or lesbian partner) can take the deceased's property – including property for which the surviving partner cannot provide proof of sole payment – for example, the house, furnishings, etc.
4 A gay or lesbian partner is not considered as 'next of kin' (which 'normally' includes a married heterosexual partner, children, parents, siblings, etc.). So the gay or lesbian partner is denied powers of attorney reserved for the next of kin – for example, in handling of a person's affairs, authorizing operations, etc.
5 State pensions, superannuation schemes and company pensions may all discriminate in death benefit provisions against surviving partners either with regard to lump sum payments or in respect of widow's or widower's benefits such as 'dependant's pensions'.
6 Income tax, capital gains tax and inheritance tax all grant special treatment to married couples.
7 Local authority tenancies and private sector secure tenancies grant the right to succession to the spouse of a married couple. Again such security is denied to the deceased's gay or lesbian partner.

---

mother and masculine/father do not necessarily ensure that a child will be heterosexual. Another assumption, and perhaps the most significant, is that all homosexuals exhibit the stereotypical images of the effeminate gay man and the butch lesbian. Not only is this not always the case, but even in the instances where it is, children are likely to be exposed to more 'normal' or socially acceptable sex/gender roles through friends, relatives and constant media images which reinforce the accepted bipolarized gender roles.

A second concern often cited is that gay parents are more likely to abuse their child sexually. This myth persists even though studies show that 97 per cent of cases of child sexual assault are committed by heterosexual men (study conducted by the American Humane Association, Rights of Women Lesbian Custody Group, 1984: 124).

A third reason given as to why children should not be cared for by gay or lesbian parents is that the child will suffer from being teased or abused by his or her peers. This concern for the child's social environment has been the deciding factor in a number of custody cases for placing the child with a heterosexual parent. Again studies do not necessarily confirm this suspicion. Children who are brought up in a loving home and who are taught to have confidence in themselves tend to be able to interact quite normally with their peers. What this assumption fails to consider is that the very heterosexism and homophobia it fears the child will encounter could be overcome through education about different types of families and more social acceptance of gay and lesbian parents. The situation could be avoided, not by removing the child from his or her natural parent, but by combating social prejudice which causes such teasing.

Finally, a factor in many lesbian custody cases is that homosexuality cannot be combined successfully with motherhood. The sexual identity of the mother is seen to be the defining characteristic of her identity. In one case, for example, the court argued that homosexuality is not 'fortuitous or casual, but rather it dominates and forms the basis for the household into which the children would be brought if the custody were awarded [to the mother]' (Lewin, 1981: 7). Unlike the heterosexual mother, the lesbian mother is unable, it is reasoned, to love and care for the child adequately if she has a partner. While this has been grounds for removing the child from the lesbian mother's custody, it also serves as justification for awarding custody to the lesbian mother only if she limit or end her relationship with her partner or insulate the child from contact with the partner (Lewin, 1981). This reasoning reflects the Freudian understanding of lesbianism as narcissistic or a state of 'arrested development' by equating a lesbian relationship with a juvenile infatuation which renders the adult women unable to care for her own children, as if she is incapable of both loving a child and loving a partner. It also resonates with the myth that all homosexual relationships are unstable and are entered into as casual affairs for sexual fulfilment only. This presumption, most often levelled at gay men, fails to consider the homosexual seeking custody as a reasonable adult who may form a long-term partnership with another, and it fails to take into account the rising divorce rate which characterizes heterosexual relationships.

With these concerns so pervasive in the minds of the legislators and judiciary it is little wonder that social policy in 1990s Britain discourages lesbian and gay parenting. While all would agree that in every case the child's well-being must be of primary concern, the dismissal of the possibility that lesbians and gay men make good parents not only places the sexual orientation of the parent above the child's well-being, but also prevents a number of potential parents from being able to provide a home and care for a child who would otherwise remain in custody of the state. Listed below are just a few policies in relation to custody, adoption and fostering which demonstrate the secondary status of gay and lesbian parents.

variables, you will also need to use the ANCOVA (analysis of covariance) instead of simply the analysis of variance procedure. The idea of a covariate in experimental design is a variable used to adjust the results for differences among subjects caused by a factor not included in the intervention package. Statistically, however, a covariate is a continuous variable whose influence needs to be dealt with separately from the categorical independent variables. There is also another type of analysis called multiple classification analysis (MCA). These are all included in the ANOVA procedure in SPSS, though the burden of specifying pertinent models is left with you, the user of the powerful software.

Multiple causation in the sense of a "genuine" multivariate analysis

So far we have discussed various multivariate analytic procedures. Sometimes, however, you may find that statistical literature refers to multivariate analysis in something other than the above situations. Probably that is correct in the sense that our focus of research has so far involved only one dependent variable. The following will briefly introduce some "genuine" forms of multivariate analysis that involves multiple continuous dependent variables. We will distinguish between two major types: one involves categorical independent variables, and the other involves only continuous independent variables.

Multiple continuous dependent variables and one or more categorical independent variables. A feature of the multiple causation model is that it can deal with more than one dependent variable in addition to multiple independent variables. The procedure dealing with the relationship between multiple continuous dependent variables and multiple categorical independent variables is a direct extension of the ANOVA (analysis of variance) procedure. In SPSS, this is a procedure called MANOVA (multivariate analysis of variance). Here "multivariate" means using several dependent variables concurrently within the same analysis. These dependent variables are limited to continuous variables. It should also be noted that even if there is only one independent variable involved, it is still considered a genuine multivariate analysis as long as there are more than one dependent measure to be analyzed simultaneously. On the other hand, the ANOVA is called univariate analysis of variance even though it may involve multiple independent variables.

MANOVA is one of the most complex and versatile procedures in SPSS. A simple use of this procedure may be understood in terms of multivariate t-tests, specifically using a test quantity called Hotelling's T^2, since we have $F = t^2$ as

Custody

Since the 1973 Guardianship of Minors Act mothers have had the same custody rights as the father, and the courts have generally held that unless there was some really good reason children under 6 years of age should be with their mother. However, when the mother is a lesbian this accepted practice is questioned substantially. If the heterosexual father can provide a suitable home for the child the lesbian mother will most likely lose custody. For example, in one case the courts decided that the damage from possible lesbian influence was 'inestimable' and the child might be 'ashamed and embarrassed by his mother'. Furthermore, it was noted that while the child should *accept* his mother, he should not *approve* of her: 'It would mean the decay of society if people adopted the latter attitude. We definitely cannot have the approval. It would be detrimental, anyone might be influenced if it were approved of.' If the child lived with the father, no one would need to know that his mother was a lesbian and he could 'develop along strong normal masculine lines' (case reported in the *Family Law Journal*, vol. 6, 1976, and discussed in Rights of Women Lesbian Custody Group, 1984: 109–10).

Adoption

Although the Adoption Act of 1976 allows for adoption either by married couple or by a single person, joint applications cannot be made by unmarried couples whether heterosexual or homosexual. If the single person is in a relationship, both persons are usually assessed concerning the child's well-being. However, only one person can become the legal parent. Because gay or lesbian couples cannot be legally married, even if they are approved only one can be considered the legal parent. Therefore adoption as a gay or lesbian couple is simply not allowed. Adoption policy expert Janette Logan notes that 'whilst lesbians and gay men can apply to adopt in their own right (i.e., as single applicants), many local authorities remain reluctant to approve or to use lesbian and gay carers for the fear of the widespread public and media criticism that this evokes . . . despite evidence that children raised by lesbian or gay parents are no more disadvantaged than those raised by heterosexuals' Logan et al., 1996: 17).

Fostering

Generally the same criteria have been applied to fostering cases, and recently there has been a more obvious attempt by the government to eliminate the possibility of a gay man or lesbian fostering a child. In December 1990 the government proposed regulations for fostering services, and paragraph 16 of that document reads: 'the chosen way of life of some adults may mean that they would not be able to provide a suitable environment for the care and nurture of a child. No one has a "right" to be a foster parent. "Equal rights" and "gay rights" policies have no place in fostering services.' Following a campaign against this discrimination led by *Stonewall*, the final version of the regulations released in April 1991 did not include the 'equal rights'/'gay rights' statement. However, the 'lifestyles' sentence remained, and in the shadow of Section 28, local authorities rarely consider applications from gay and lesbian potential foster parents.

In this section we have considered the ways in which 'family policy' as found in section 28 and in the social policies governing adoption, fostering and custody marginalize gay and lesbian families. While the concerns about the well-being of each child obviously must be foremost in every case, the underpinning argument throughout this section of the book has been that social policies should not be based on sexist, racist or heterosexist stereotypes. The state, acting on the basis of compulsory heterosexuality, or institutional homophobia, perpetuates discrimination rather than protecting citizens from prejudice and abuse. As we will see in the section below, by denying such protection the state fails to assure equal rights for all citizens. For example, basic employment rights guaranteed by the Sex Discrimination Act and the Race Relations Act have not yet been secured for those facing discrimination based on sexuality or sexual orientation.

Activity 7.3

1   What is compulsory heterosexuality?
2   In what areas can heterosexism be seen as a factor in social policies relating to 'the family'?

Employment

In this section we will consider discrimination and harassment in employment practices. As noted in the introduction, employment practices may not be directly associated with social policy. However, there is no legislation in place providing protection against discrimination based on sexuality or sexual orientation, and it can be the sole reason for dismissal, harassment or vetting during application or promotion procedures. Even companies with sound equal opportunities guidelines which include sexual orientation often indirectly discriminate against gay or lesbian employees by not considering the employee's partner the same as a heterosexual spouse, particularly in relation to pension schemes or company benefits. For example, in *Stonewall*'s (1995) survey of 2,000 people, *Less Equal than Others*, they found that, of the respondents participating in a pension scheme, only 14 per cent could nominate a partner of either sex as beneficiary, while 27 per cent stipulated that it must be only the spouse (heterosexual married partner). Similarly, of those receiving other benefits – travel expenses, discounts, or special leave and so on – only 18 per cent were available to all couples, with 34 per cent available to heterosexual or married couples. In practice then, and according to current law, gay or lesbian employees do not receive, or have the right to request, equal treatment with heterosexual employees. *Stonewall* found that a significant percentage of gay, lesbian and bisexual employees have faced discrimination or harassment at work. The study showed that 22 per cent knew or suspected that they had been denied a job because they were known to be, or suspected to be, gay or lesbian. A similar number, 23 per cent, knew or suspected that they had been denied promotion based on their sexuality, while 8 per cent had been dismissed or forced to resign their jobs because of their sexual orientation. In total, 48 per cent of the respondents had been harassed at work because they were known or suspected to be gay or lesbian. Generally, the harassment was in the form of jokes or teasing, homophobic abuse or aggressive questioning, but in a significant number of cases it had included threats (14 per cent) or physical violence (5 per cent). Little wonder then that many gay men, lesbians and bisexuals choose to hide their sexuality at work. In fact, as the survey showed, 56 per cent have felt it necessary to hide their sexuality in some jobs, and 33 per cent in all jobs, while 68 per cent hide their sexual orientation from someone, or everyone, at their current job. One person, who is unfortunately representative rather than unique, describes her life in this way: 'I lead a bizarre and stupid double life – out to family, friends and neighbours and firmly in the closet at work' (*Stonewall*, 1993).

Case Study 7.1

The *Stonewall* study reports the real life consequences of discrimination in employment, as the following example illustrates.

'Matthew' had been a senior sales representative for a large multi-national corporation for 12 years when his partner, Paul, was killed in a car accident. After taking time off work for the funeral, he was asked to an interview at the company headquarters where he was asked, 'We see you are single, do you have a girlfriend?' Matthew responded, 'No, I'm gay,' and the interview was immediately brought to a close. Following this incident, he was consistently downgraded until he was stocking shelves. He eventually resigned and took them to an industrial tribunal where the company could not defend its action (*Stonewall*, 1993: 7). Matthew and the few others like him who have challenged such discrimination do so on an individual basis usually with an industrial tribunal, and because there is no legal redress, dismissed or harassed employees are not guaranteed that their claims will even be considered as discrimination.

Activity 7.4

1 What does it mean to have equal rights to employment, to equal pay and to determine one's private family life?
2 Is it the role of the state of ensure equal rights for all citizens or is it to maintain social norms such as hetero-sexuality? Could it do both?

Summary and Conclusion

The introduction to this chapter noted two root causes of discrimination based on sexual orientation, homophobia and heterosexism. Homophobia often stems from the belief that homosexuality is morally, or psychologically, wrong, and therefore should be punished either through individual abuse or institutional criminalization. Heterosexism is the assumption that everyone is heterosexual and that society, or in this case social policy, should be organized accordingly. The result in both cases is discrimination.

Throughout this chapter we have examined the reasons for such discrimination and a few of the ways in which these reasons attempt to justify continued discrimination in social policies, particularly in education, health care, family policy and employment rights. Unfortunately, the limits of this examination do not allow space for recognizing every area of social policy which affects the status of homosexual and bisexual citizens. What should be gleaned from this overview, however, is the extent to which society's fascination with sexuality, and the history of negative interpretations of homosexuality, or sexuality which is not heterosexual, have influenced the construction of social policies relating to sexuality. Furthermore, what should be noted is the way in which such discrimination calls into question what most consider a basic right, equality – in education, health care, employment and the raising of a family.

8

'New' Social Movements and Social Policy: a Case Study of the Disability Movement

Tony Fagan and Phil Lee

Agency and Social Movements in Social Policy

It is now well established that social and consumption policies are the result of continual conflict between pressures 'from above', representing the established interests of those with economic and political power, and various pressures 'from below', often orchestrated by social movements and campaigns (see Gough, 1979; Lee and Raban, 1988; and Ginsburg, 1992). Although the ways in which these diverse pressures combine and their precise policy effects are still subject to much debate, it is clear that the study of social movements – their organization and impact on the policy process and outcomes – should be central to any 'critical' study of welfare.

It is no surprise that some of the more detailed and interesting studies of the role of social movements and their relation to social policy formulation have come from radical scholars, and from the feminist, civil rights, anti-racist and community and welfare rights movements tracing their own origins and development. Piven and Cloward's seminal text, *Poor People's Movements: Why They Succeed, How They Fail* (1977) is one of the older and better-known examples of the former. Their book traces historically the organizational forms of struggle and resistance by various 'poor people's movements in the United States, particularly those of unemployed industrial workers in the 1930s and civil and welfare rights movements in the 1960s.

Both their conclusion that such popular resistance pushed governments into wide-reaching and progressive welfare reforms and their attention to the detailed struggles of these movements was until recently unusual among 'critical' social policy analysts. It was, and is, much more likely, particularly for Marxist commentators on social welfare, to emphasize structural matters to do with the state of economic markets, conveyed usually through 'pressures from above' in the guise of the unseen 'logic' of capital and/or the diktats of industrialists and conservative politicians. Where 'struggle from below' was taken seriously it tended to focus on the industrial class struggle of male workers, and their organized influence on welfare policy and outcomes. More recent radical scholarship, influenced by the concerns raised by marginalized groups such as disabled people as well as feminist and anti-racist theory, now judges the influence of such workers in more complex ways. For, while it is quite clear that the organized British working-class movement played a pivotal role in the demand for such reforms as secondary education and a national health service free at the point of use, it is also equally true that many of their 'pressures' and practices have seriously militated against the interests of women – for example, the defence of the 'family wage' (Barrett and McIntosh, 1980; Cockburn, 1983) – Jewish and black people – such as demands for immigration controls and restrictions on welfare provision (Holmes, 1979; Solomos, 1989) and poor and unemployed people – as through the incorporation of the trade unions (Allen, 1971; Gamble, 1985).

It is simple to argue that welfare policies are some sort of compromise between the needs of capital (pressures from above) and broadly defined working-class struggle (pressures from below), but it is much more difficult for analysts to assess the precise form that particular compromises take and the roles played by various social movements in their emergence. For all their natural sympathy with 'popular' pressures and movements from below, it is only relatively recently – the last decade – that British analysts have taken seriously detailed appreciation of the diverse forces represented (like sensitivity to female and black labour, splits in the interests of the working class between able-bodied and non-able-bodied, young and old, and so on) as well as the actual forms that these real and complex movements have taken. Harrison (1993/94) concluded his studies of the black voluntary housing movement in Britain by arguing that such theories have some way to go to theorize adequately both the nature of struggle by social movements representing marginalized groups and their role in the determination of policy outcomes. His own work, he suggested, had only provided merely 'a few more pieces in what remains a very complex jigsaw puzzle' (Harrison, 1993/94: 33).

The role of pressure groups and movements for change has always been studied in some depth by some 'conventional' social policy analysts and political scientists. These studies have addressed important 'how' questions – how we should define a social movement (as opposed to interest or pressure group, or political party), how social movements mobilize support, organize themselves and so forth – albeit within conceptual frameworks that often neglect wider questions about power and oppression. These approaches can be classified into three separate groups (for an overview, see Diani, 1992).

'Collective Behaviour' Perspectives

The 'collective behaviour' approach conceptualizes social movements as forms of peculiar kinds of collective behaviour. Turner and Killian define a social movement as:

[a] collectivity acting with some continuity to promote or resist a change in the society or organization of which it is a part ... a movement is a group within definite and shifting membership and with a leadership whose position is determined more by informal response of adherents than by formal procedures for legitimizing authority. (1987: 223)

Research Mobilization Theory

The second approach can be termed 'resource mobilization theory'. This defines a social movement by reference to the ideas or beliefs that the group has in common, 'beliefs that', according to McCarthy and Zald, 'represent preferences for changing some elements of the social structure and/or reward distribution of a society' (1977: 1217–18). However, the key to this approach is a concern with the translation of these ideas or beliefs into 'actions' which affect the wider political arena and the social, political, economic and/or cultural conditions which facilitate such actions. Such analyses often trace the origins of groups that have had significant effects on the public policy process. These analysts are also concerned with the dynamics of co-operation and conflict between social movements (Garner and Zald, 1985).

Political process

The third approach, the political process position, concentrates even more sharply on how marginalized and excluded groups can gain access to the formal political system (Tilly, 1978). Tilly defines social movements as:

[a] sustained series of interactions between power holders and persons success-fully claiming to speak on behalf of a constituency lacking formal representation, in the course of which those persons make publicly visible demands for changes in the distribution or exercise of power, and back those demands with public demonstrations of support. (1984: 303)

All three of these positions tend to under-theorize questions about *why* movements emerge, being preoccupied with more immediately empirical questions of *how* they mobilize and gain access to the political system.

A Fourth Approach: New Social Movements Theory

New social movements theory is less concerned with the mechanics of mobilization and influence, and concentrates more on why particular move-ments emerge at particular times, and what this tells us about large-scale structural and cultural transformations. The earliest exponent was Touraine (1977, 1981, 1985), who identifies a new core conflict, one which replaces traditional class struggle, at the centre of which is a battle between technocrats and their diverse adversaries in post-industrial society. He argues that certain new movements have emerged that are struggling against their class adversaries 'for the social control of historicity in a concrete community' (1981: 77), historicity being defined as the 'overall system of meaning which sets dominant rules in a given society' (1981: 81). These concerns with social innovation and new social forces pressing for major social change became, hardly surprisingly, very attractive to 'critical' social theorists in the late seventies, although they had less initial impact on discourse about welfare and social policy, which was still contained largely within a conservative Fabian framework (see Lee and Raban, 1988).

'New' Social Movements?

There have been two crucial 'moments' in theorizing these 'new' social movements (NSMs). The first, born in the late 1970s, largely focuses on and welcomes the large variety of 'alternative' political forces – 'the fragments', as an influential book of the early 1980s described them (Rowbotham et al., 1979) – that developed in the late 1960s. These include the plethora of community action, citizenship and self-help groups that flourished in inner city areas, together with the national and international civil rights, anti-Vietnam War and student action groups. In addition to these, the 1970s witnessed the flowering of environmental, women's, anti-nuclear and peace movements, along with the eventual emergence of New Left-libertarian and 'Green' political parties in many European countries. At the same time divergent sub-cultural lifestyles emerged which celebrated 'alternative' cultural values. These developments were highly critical of the worship of economic growth in advanced capitalist societies and questioned the benefits of continued modernization for both the metropolitan and Third World countries.

Many influential social theorists attempted to explain the rise of these movements and cultural values, and many sections of the European left placed great emphasis on them as crucial components in any future challenge to the dominant political order. Offe (1985) regarded them as negative side effects of technological developments and industrial growth, representing groups which had been marginalized by existing interest group and governmental structures. Hildebrandt and Dalton (1978) constructed an ideal-type contrast between an 'Old' and a 'New' politics, the former being based on materialist priorities, with the latter rejecting such matters and adopting 'post-materialist' ones. Berger et al. (1974) suggested that these movements and their values were the latest manifestation of periodic waves of romantic-ideological reaction to the alienating effects of modern industrial societies, whilst Melluci (1980), alongside Touraine, argued that deep structural transformations were taking place in advanced capitalist societies, forging a major re-alignment between society, the state and economy which in turn created new forms of social cleavage and conflict. Common to the majority of these accounts was an emphasis on the importance of revolt by a 'new educated class' which had been inhibited in its desire for upward mobility by the economic *status quo*.

The late sixties and early seventies experienced an intense degree of accelerated social and cultural change, particularly around questions of identity and lifestyle politics (see Dalton and Kuechler, 1990, for an overview). The urgent questions posed by many of these movements have in various ways entered the consciousness of our contemporary lives. This is not to imply that these disparate groups have in any way achieved their ultimate goals, but their key concerns – women's equality, disarmament, decentralization, 'race' equality, self-help – are now very much the stuff of modern political and social debate.

The second important 'moment' in theorizing these NSMs is the one taking place now in a context considerably different from the optimism that surrounded their initial arrival in the 1960s and 1970s. It is vital to note a number of factors which have contributed to the changing context. First, throughout western Europe during the 1980s there have been considerable 'attacks' on the gains achieved by previous working-class and popular movements, leading undoubtedly to considerable fragmentation of the European working classes by income, status and occupation. Second, there is now much greater attention paid by socialist thinkers to questions of gender, 'race' and other significant divisions within the broadly conceived working-class movement. Third, there has been a significant reappraisal of the very nature of the 'socialist' project by many western European left-wing thinkers since the overthrow of the eastern European regimes claiming to be socialist. Fourth, a number of leftward-leaning academics have begun to develop forms of analysis that suggest we are living through a period of profound social change. Concepts such as post-Fordism (see Burrows and Loader, 1994) and postmodernism (see Williams, 1992; Hewitt, 1993; Taylor-Gooby, 1994) have been used which pick up on the earlier themes developed by Touraine (1981) and others in order to explain developments in the social and economic order and their determining effects on the nature of welfare provision and delivery.

New Times? New Movements?

This has led to considerable and renewed speculation about what is happening to the social order, forms of politics and how radical change can, if at all, take place. The now defunct journal *Marxism Today* set down a useful marker by summarizing these complex changes in a brief phrase – 'New Times'. The editors of an important collection bearing that name appear to be in no doubt that NSMs are central to the 'New Times': 'Another feature of New Times is the proliferation of the sites of antagonism and resistance, and the appearance of new subjects, new social movements, new collective identities – an enlarged sphere for the operation of politics, and new constituencies for change' (Hall and Jacques, 1989: 17).

In many respects therefore there is an optimism that after a decade of setbacks the left can readjust its sights and adapt to a different set of agendas. But are things so considerably different? In relation to NSMs Ginsburg has suggested that in 'some senses there is nothing particularly new about these movements, which are just the latest wave of radical and popular movements which have shaped social policy throughout modern history' (1992: 8/9). But there is much more at stake here than a simple judgement about 'oldness' or 'newness'. It is important to address three questions. First, in what significant ways is the contemporary social order changing and, second, how, if at all, is the nature of class and other forms of interest representation altered by these structural transformations? Third, what role(s) do contemporary social movements – 'new' or otherwise – play in this possibly altered scenario?

An influential British contribution to this discussion has been provided by Lash and Urry (1987). They locate the development of NSMs within changes in the class structure. It is a two-part argument. First, the various globalization strategies of multi-national companies and the responses to these by domestic governments has, since the late 1970s, led to considerable restructuring of labour markets, and subsequently weakened the power of national trade union/labour movements. In particular, the working class is split increasingly into the 'core' skilled sector and the growing peripheral part-time sector. These changes are manifest in a decline in class-based voting (see Duke and Edgell, 1984) and severe disruption of corporatist bargaining arrangements. Second, NSMs are partly a reflection of the growing influence, size and power of what they describe as the 'service class' of administrative, managerial and professional employees. Moreover, they see the concept of postmodern culture, and in particular, its central idea that collective identities are breaking down through their contact with new cultural forms, as an important resource for the NSMs.

Much of this analysis, as with the earlier explanations we examined, concentrates too much on structural factors (changes to the socio-economic system) and overestimates the potential of NSMs to act as agents of progressive social change. All attempts to explain a series of quite divergent movements as a product of one set of, albeit complex, social changes must be questioned. For a start, not all contemporary social movements have progressive outcomes as their goals. Moreover, the interests of the service class cannot be conceptualized in this smooth, uniform manner. Why should this class – experiencing the heightening of credentialism and many aspects of the deskilling processes affecting manual workers – necessarily support these selectively chosen NSMs? It is true that the service class, and the potential political power of the middle class, is growing, but to assume that this alone accounts for these diverse NSMs is to overstate the case. Members of this class are quite likely to, and do, support quite reactionary social movements or ones with no real political significance. Some suggest that certain versions of Green politics for example, with their opposition to the very fact of industrialization, cannot be judged to be progressive in any real sense. Bagguley argues that 'the service class provides a resource, and nothing more, for a whole range of social movements, new, working class, reactionary and otherwise' (1992: 40). We see here again that it is unwise to utilize the social base of a movement to ascertain the interests represented by it. We also need to 'examine the cultural and organizational resources through which collective action is achieved' (Bagguley, 1992: 42). In short,

mentioned earlier. A multivariate t-test can give more accurate results than a set of separate simple t-tests, especially when the dependent variables are correlated with one another. Generally, an F test quantity is used to determine whether there are statistically significant differences between the groups. Just as the ANOVA procedure, MANOVA is designed to test for interactions as well as for main effects. The extension from MANOVA to MANCOVA is also similar to the extension from ANOVA to ANCOVA. Unlike ANOVA and ANCOVA, however, the procedures of MANOVA and MANCOVA will examine all of the dependent variables as well as their differences simultaneously.

Two groups of continuous variables. This situation is another direct extension of the multiple regression model. The main difference is that we have here more than one dependent variable. There is also a difference in purpose. Here the focus is on a measure of association rather than on predicting the values of the dependent variables via regression. For the single dependent variable situation (i.e., the multiple regression model), the comprehensive measure of association is a multiple correlation coefficient. Here, for analyzing multiple dependent variables simultaneously, we have a so-called canonical correlation model. It should be noted that unlike the above MANOVA situation, canonical correlation analysis involves both multiple dependent variables and multiple independent variables. If there is only one independent variable, then multiple correlation rather than canonical correlation analysis will apply. As a symmetrical measure, multiple correlation is a special case of canonical correlation, which does not distinguish between dependent and independent variables. This is another feature that distinguishes canonical correlation analysis (including multiple correlation) from the regression model.

With a scope broader than that of multiple correlation analysis, canonical correlation analysis will result in more than one correlation coefficient (generally denoted by CR_i). A CR_i squared (called a latent root or eigenvalue) is not exactly but analogous to the PRE logic. Canonical correlation analysis is first concerned with establishing the maximum correlation, i.e., CR_{max} between two groups of continuous variables. It will also calculate the correlations in other aspects, and identify the specific variables which contribute considerably to a particular correlation between the two groups.

Put simply, canonical correlation is the maximum correlation between the respective linear combinations of two groups of continuous variables. The idea is to construct two composite variables called canonical variates by standardizing the individual variables in each group and combining them into a linear function.

if we are to comprehend the role of NSMs in social policy, it is necessary to examine a phenomenon vital to developing our understanding of welfare struggles, the politics of advocacy.

Contemporary Welfare and New Social Welfare Movements: the Politics of Advocacy

There has undoubtedly been very rapid social change in the last two decades, to such an extent that it is possible to juxtapose what Taylor-Gooby (1995) has described as an 'old sociology' of nation, nuclear family, capital and class to a 'new sociology' of globalization, individualism and diversity. This is a neat way of providing an overview of the changed intellectual terrain which social theorists must try to negotiate after the major social and political upheavals of the last two decades. Reflecting upon those changes and drawing on some elements of this more recent social theory has produced a complex cocktail of urgent issues facing 'critical' social policy analysts.

First, while it is clear they do not favour private forms of welfare provision, they must recognize that some of the choices facilitated by market forces ought to be incorporated into public provision and that various consumer movements do represent potentially important vehicles for social-ist ideas (Plant, 1988; National Consumer Council, 1991). Second, new alternative forms of citizenship have to be developed and promoted to counter the highly conditional form of 'universal' citizenship established after the Second World War which presumed a white indigenous population of wage-earning (which is to say of working age and able-bodied) males supporting families. As Clarke and Langan have noted, such arrangements dictate the existence of 'a set of dependent populations positioned by age (both young and old), by gender (the anomaly of the married woman), by infirmity and by "race" (the "alien" non-citizen)' (1993: 28). Third, while the fragmentation of class politics may have been exaggerated by some commentators, there has been a significant increase in forms of politics organized around identity (Piven, 1995). These developments are not unrelated to the consumerist and media developments referred to above.

One attempt to overcome these problems can be seen in the the journal *Critical Social Policy* (*CSP*). It took a decision in 1988 to encourage writing that does not marginalize concerns with 'race', disability, gender, age and so on. In other words, it has tried to reflect on these complex social changes by giving a real 'voice' to various marginalized 'identities', while retaining a central concern with structured inequality. Fiona Williams has summarized these issues thus:

> The subject matter of social policy deals with material resources, people's access to income, housing, health care, education, transport, social care. It takes account of inequalities in the distribution of provisions and people's need for them. As such, it differs from many of the post-modernist projects which have unhooked diversity from power and inequality . . . [and] whilst it is important to acknowl-

edge the variety of ways in which identities are constituted, it is also important to recognize how far the structured conditions of people's existence create these forms of diversity. (1992: 208)

Critical social policy analysts have welcomed this concern with diversity, and considerable debate has started about how to reconstruct the universalism that underpinned the post-war social democratic vision of the construction of social policy (see Williams, 1992; Spicker, 1993/4; Thompson and Hoggett, 1996). In particular, there has been major concern with how social policies can be planned to reflect an appropriate balance between guarantees of equality, fairness and impartiality (the old paradigm) with sufficient allowance for diversity (such as ethnic preferences) and difference (for example, recognition of non-heterosexual lifestyles).

Traditionally conceived NSMs are not the only source of recognition that universalism has neglected a wide set of diverse needs and that all these needs cannot be conveniently subsumed under the label of 'class'. In any case, it is important to recognize that, while the literature referred to earlier aspires to define NSMs, as Turner has noted, 'the complexity of the definition of social movement is to some extent a reflection of the complexity of social movements themselves in the context of modern politics' (1986: 90–1). The term itself, therefore, is open to a wide variety of interpretations. Turner suggests that NSMs 'typically adhere to a general social philosophy which embraces a strong interest in environmental politics and conservationism' (1986: 91), though this rather overstates the significance of the environmental aspect and results in an unnecessarily narrow view of NSMs. Shakespeare (1993) argues that the term is itself inadequate in that it obscures the difference between two distinct forms of contemporary political struggle: the value shift implicit in post-materialist movements like some Greens, and the liberation politics of groups representing the deprived and the powerless. He suggests that social movements are often concerned with the relationship between the market and the welfare state, and are about the equitable allocation of material resources. As such, they represent the interests of very old constituencies – the poor and the marginalized. Many of what we might describe as 'new' welfare movements represent the interests of these same constituencies, and, often building on the sentiments of community users' groups of the 1960s and early 1970s, are opposed vigorously to certain forms of what they see as professional control over their lives. These movements pose many questions to professional welfare workers about 'whose side are they on' and challenge quite directly their residual prejudices about old, gay, mentally ill, black and poor people, amongst others (see Taylor, 1993). They are not uniform and take a variety of forms, from credit unions, self-advocacy groups (for example, mental patients' unions, men's and women's health groups), black women's refuge groups, carers' groups, survivors' groups, and so on. These groups all share a basic concern with down-to-earth questions about empowerment, rights, representation and ensuring quality in the services they require (Gibson, 1979), and Croft and Beresford (1992) argue that many of these activists regard themselves as sharing key characteristics, qualities and goals with the NSMs.

The presence and continued intervention of these new welfare movements provoke in a heightened form questions that are central to the development of a critical social policy and the role of NSMs therein. First, and obviously, how do we prevent the incorporation – and therefore possible emasculation – of their demands? Second, the demands made by such groups will be complex and occasionally appear contradictory; for example, groups advocating the rights of schizophrenic patients to live in the community in the 1970s were challenged by groups representing the rights of their carers, and particularly their immediate family (see Sedgewick, 1982). Can these groups speak with one voice? Sedgewick's *Psycho Politics* (1982) on the radical mental health movements of the 1960s and 1970s is an excellent catalogue of the dilemmas facing left-wing politics in relation to one significant welfare issue. Third, they will generate intense debate within themselves about the way to best represent their constituency's interests. How will they resolve these debates? Gilroy's (1987) argument that the very successful campaign by black social workers and their allies for 'same-race' placements was misplaced because it reduced complex debates about culture, 'race' and identity to 'professionalized colour matching' with reactionary implications, is a good case in point. Fourth, how far can movements, often immersed in demands for inclusion, go in developing what Lustiger-Thaler and Shragge (1993) call 'counter-rights' in opposition to those based on property and commodification? Or is the real question, posed by Laclau and Mouffe (1985), whether these new welfare movements are merely demanding an extension to themselves of rights already conceded to other groups? We intend to explore some of these issues by focusing on one movement, that of disabled people.

Activity 8.1

With reference to your local community:

1   What forms of political representation can you identify attempting to intervene in the formulation of social policy?
2   What constituencies do they represent, and how?
3   Can you identify any new social movements?
4   What criteria did you use to define a new social movement?

The Disability Movement: a 'New' Social Movement?

It was noted earlier that the first crucial 'moment' in the theorizing of NSMs came in the 1970s as a result of the intense political activity of the 1960s, and it is in this period that the emergence of disabled people as a coherent political force over the last 20 years or so is rooted. This has been a worldwide phenomenon; since the mid-1970s 'organizations composed entirely of persons with various disabilities – physical, mental and sensory – have sprung up in 100 countries' (Driedger, 1989: 1), but especially in Britain and the United States (Shakespeare, 1993), with the creation of what is referred to in the literature as 'the disability movement'.

Some activist commentators within these organizations strongly identify themselves as part of the NSMs of the 1970s. In this regard Boggs (1986) claims that NSMs have emerged in opposition to ideologies which legitimate the existing power structures, including racism and sexism, and have the counter-hegemonic potential to change them. Oliver and Zarb argue that this also applies to disablism. For them, 'the disability movement has had considerable impact on policy formulation and is beginning to influence service provision in Britain. . . . [I]t will come to have a central role in counter-hegemonic politics and the social transformation upon which this will eventually be based' (1989: 237). Their argument is that only by viewing the disability movement as an NSM can its real potential be understood.

Plainly, they invest NSMs with a political significance that promises much more than traditional party and pressure-group politics. The difficulty here is that, as has been shown, the very concept of NSMs is problematic, and this is compounded by the fact that accounts of disabled people's organizations which deal (albeit briefly) with their history in Britain (for example, Pagel, 1988; Oliver and Zarb, 1989; Oliver, 1990; Barnes, 1992), America (for instance, Pfeiffer, 1993) and internationally (such as Driedger, 1989) locate their origins in the nineteenth century, within the general growth of voluntary groups aimed at helping those who were victimized by the rapid industrialization of the period. Given such a history, what grounds can there be for characterizing the current disability movement as a 'new' social movement? To answer this requires some understanding of the effectiveness of traditional forms of representation.

Pressure Groups, Party Politics and Disabled People

Pressure groups like the Child Poverty Action Group (CPAG), Shelter and the Disablement Income Group (DIG), which were created in the 1960s, aspired to represent the interests of certain constituencies that they perceived were being excluded from sharing in the general prosperity created by the welfare state and the long post-war boom. The rediscovery of poverty (see Abel-Smith and Townsend, 1965) among some social groups, notably older people, one-parent families, and sick and disabled people, was clear evidence that despite the rhetoric of 'full' employment and political democracy, the needs of large numbers of people were not being addressed by the supposedly representative political parties. The development of these pressure groups in response to this is regarded by Townsend as 'a reaction to what was perceived to be the fraudulent character of British democracy' (1986: ii). They carried with them a degree of optimism that, through extensive publicizing of their causes and lobbying of political representatives, they could materially affect the circumstances of the groups they represented, and they continue to do so. However the non-confrontational nature of these strategies coupled with the fact that they are organizations *for* rather than organizations *of* the constituencies they represent, has meant that their relationship with the corporatist British state has limited their success (see Cawson, 1982, for an analysis of the role of pressure groups in the corporatist state). The significance of such pressure groups lies primarily in their ability to maintain a place for their causes on the political agenda and thus sustain a reformist argument rather than in the securing of radical material improvements in measures to meet the needs of their constituencies. DIG, formed in 1965, is a good example of this. After 30 years of campaigning for a national income for disabled people, they can be said to have made progress in that all the major political parties have committed themselves to such a scheme. However, these commitments have been equivocal, and no substantial progress has been made in this direction (Oliver and Zarb, 1989).

In the specific case of disabled people, Oliver and Zarb (1989: 223) show how 'it is unlikely that disabled people can expect the party political process to serve their interests well' since despite their numbers – in Britain, 9 per cent of the 18-plus population (Fry, 1987, cited in Oliver and Zarb, 1989) – they are a diverse, fragmented and often segregated constituency. This is often the direct result of policies and services devised and provided by the state and based on the definition of disability as a problem of the individual, rendering her or him dependent and warranting specialist treatment by medical and other professionals – the medical model of disability (see Barnes, 1991; Morris, 1992, 1993). Indeed Barton (1993) states that this medical model is one of the major influences on both government policy and public perception and practice regarding disabled people, and its tendency towards specialism has created a separatism within the disabled community (Borsay, 1986). Moreover, Fry (in Oliver and Zarb, 1989) found that many disabled people are excluded from the electoral register, and that in any case physical access to the party political process and to information regarding it is often denied them.

Borsay (1986) is just as pessimistic about the potential of traditional pressure group politics in protecting the interests of disabled people. The very diversity and separatism which militates against party representation also means that pressure groups working on behalf of disabled people do so with narrowly defined constituencies and limited aspirations. Many of them have their origins in the voluntary and charitable groups of the nineteenth century; and because they are organizations *for* and not *of* disabled people, they are managed by professional staff to meet their assumptions of what disabled people need rather than the self-expressed needs of disabled people. Their relationship with those they aspire to represent is often paternalistic, even patronizing, and their concern is primarily with the health and welfare rather than the rights of their constituencies. Traditional pressure groups for disabled people are in competition with one another for an adequate share of material resources from both public donations and the state, and since they cannot afford to alienate either, confrontational political action is ruled out because it challenges both the state, and the public's perception of disability. In seeking to meet the needs of 'their' group, charitable organizations inevitably accept and reinforce the medical model by arguing that 'their' disabled people are a 'worthy cause'. As is the case with other marginalized people, pressure groups in their traditional form can only offer small-scale incremental change, and this leads Borsay to the conclusion that, using this route, 'for disabled people . . . the chances of immediate and radical reform of social policies are slim' (1986: 19).

Traditional party and pressure group politics in industrialized countries have tended to ameliorate (but not solve) the fundamental contradictions that inform the class struggle, but in doing so have failed to cater for the diversity of needs subsumed within it. If pressure groups can be seen as a response to the failure of party politics, then NSMs can be seen in their turn as a response to the failure of the pressure groups, and Oliver argues that as such their 'newness' lies in the very fact that they are not rooted in traditional party and single-issue pressure group politics, but 'are consciously engaged in critical evaluation of capitalist society and in the creation of alternative models of social organization at local, national and international levels, as well as trying to reconstruct the world ideologically and to create alternative forms of service provision' (1990: 113).

The self-conscious act of stepping outside the established political system in order to challenge it opens up the possibility of using alternative forms of advocacy, notably confrontational direct action in the form of overt protest, street demonstrations, civil disobedience, public disruption and so on, and Alan Scott (1990) suggests that it is this mass mobilization – or the threat of it – by a group of individuals acting instrumentally from a sense of shared identity that gives NSMs their character and their power.

Activity 8.2

- What do you understand by the medical model of disability?
- Contact organizations of or representing disabled people and examine their publicity material in order to determine whether it reinforces or rejects the medical model.

New Social Movements and Disabled People

Oliver (1990) has no doubt that the disability movement is an NSM and cites four grounds for his opinion. First, following the example set by the civil rights and women's movements of the 1960s and 1970s it has embraced these alternative forms of political action in support of a new campaign, summed up by the march in June 1988 demanding 'Rights not Charity'. Since then disabled people and their supporters have staged highly visible demonstrations against inaccessible transport – Campaign for Accessible Transport (CAT) – an inaccessible environment, the exploitation of disabled people by television companies and charities – Campaign Against Patronage (CAP) – and the poverty which often accompanies impairment (Barnes, 1992). These have included blockades of traffic, which subsequently revealed the inadequacies of the criminal justice system to deal with disabled people, and of television fund-raising shows like Telethon and Children in Need.

An important feature of this changing political stance of the disability movement has been the shift towards self-organization and control by disabled people of the organizations representing their interests. Thus Oliver (1990) argues that the umbrella organization *of* disabled people – the British Council of Organisations of Disabled People (BCODP) – and that *for* disabled people – the Royal Association for Disability and Rehabilitation (RADAR) – have very different relationships to the state and the political system, RADAR receiving by far the lion's share of state funding. Oliver suggests that it is this marginalization of the organizations *of* disabled people that marks it as an NSM.

Second, NSMs, as a consequence of what Touraine (1981) called the 'crisis in industrial culture', offer a critical evaluation of capitalist societies based on the treatment of marginalized groups within their structure. The disability movement does this by highlighting the denial of the citizenship rights of the individual which inevitably arises from policy and practice based on traditional views of disability and disabled people. There is a concern here with more than merely control over material resources and the range and quality of services. In essence, it involves a rejection of the medical model of disability and a demand for its replacement by a social model which recognizes that disability is a condition which is artificially constructed by society, not least through the very organizations and institutions that claim to act on behalf of disabled people. From this perspective, people with a physical, mental or sensory impairment are not disabled by the impairment, but by society's reaction to it, and treatment of them. Disability is not a matter of certain individuals being unable to meet the demands of society, but of the failure of society to recognize its own disabling potential, and to meet the specific needs of people with such impairments (see Barton, 1993). Morris illustrates this very succinctly when she notes that:

> an inability to walk is an impairment, whereas an inability to enter a building because the entrance is up a flight of steps is a disability. An inability to speak is an impairment but an inability to communicate because appropriate technical aids are not made available is a disability. An inability to move one's body is an impairment but an inability to get out of bed because appropriate physical help is not available is a disability. (1993: x)

For Oliver (1990) this very powerful critique of the disabling influence of capitalist society is characteristic of NSMs.

When the drive towards self-help results in alternative service provision such as the Centres for Independent and Integrated Living (CILs), and is combined with the notion of rights to access to those services, which the state cannot satisfy, we have an example of the establishment of the 'counter rights' referred to by Lustiger-Thaler and Shragge (1993). That is to say that NSMs construct a discourse of alternative rights which can only be met by radical change in the existing structure of society and which involve the construction of new political and social institutions.

Third, while he is rightly cautious about overstating his case here, Oliver (1990) argues that the characteristic post-materialism of NSMs can be identified in the disability movement. It is concerned with the quality of life of disabled people, but given the extent of material deprivation among them he, like Bagguley (1992), rejects the sort of analysis provided by Lash and Urry, outlined earlier. Despite its post-materialist aspect, the central concern of the disability movement remains the improvement of the material conditions of life for disabled people.

Finally, Oliver (1990) points to the international nature of the disability movement as characteristic of NSMs – see Driedger (1989) for a full account of the Disabled People's International (DPI). He notes that at its Second World Congress in 1986, DPI defined its objectives and strategies around empowerment, and the collective action of disabled people to achieve collective goals. He cites DPI as stressing the need for direct action outside of established legislative or constitutional procedures in order to effect both political and cultural change. In doing so DPI was not necessarily antagonistic to established organizations *for* disabled people, but 'our own organizations should assert that they were the true and valid voice of disabled people and our needs' (Disabled People's International, 1986: 21, cited in Oliver, 1990: 123).

Clearly, Oliver (1990) presents a convincing argument for accepting the disability movement as an NSM, but this does not invalidate the reservations previously expressed about the usefulness of the concept itself. It merely means that we can legitimately use the disability movement as an example of what the literature refers to as NSMs, and Shakespeare (1993) has what amount to fundamental doubts about the usefulness of the concept, and explores these in the context of the disability movement.

For him, the discourse around NSMs overstates the distinction between previous forces for change, mainly the working-class and socialist movements, and the popular movements of today. For example, while approving of the direct action strategies adopted by the disability movement, he notes that they are reminiscent of the tactics used by the women's suffrage movements in the early twentieth century. They are undoubtedly very effective in that they focus attention on the failings of the state, challenge the public's view of what is appropriate behaviour for disabled people (or women, or old people, and so on), and build a sense of solidarity for the participants, but are they 'new'? Shakespeare (1993) notes that mass action has been a feature of popular protest for centuries, and in the absence of any other effective option, like strike action, is the obvious course for those denied access to the political process. This directly contradicts Oliver's (1990) view that NSMs' 'newness' lies in their recourse to alternative forms of political action, and Shakespeare (1993: 258), like Oliver, proposes that perhaps the key characteristic of their newness is that such action is now taken self-consciously and instrumentally, 'rarely spontaneous, often carefully planned to influence opinion-formers, the media, etc.'.

The concerns of many of the supposed NSMs can be seen to be just as traditional as their methods in that they focus on the material circumstances of their constituents and are about resource allocation and empowerment. Shakespeare (1993) does not deny that some movements are based on post-materialist values and are more concerned with the quality of life, but he says that these are fundamentally different forms of contemporary struggle. Thus, whereas the term 'NSM' might usefully be applied to, for example, environmentalism, it is wholly inadequate to describe the complex processes that are involved in the self-organization of people engaged in liberation politics. For disabled people, the very act of organizing politically is not only a response to the failure of traditional political activity, but also provides the vehicle for the recognition and assertion of their identity, challenges stereotypes of disability and rejects a social structure which victimizes and objectifies them. 'In short, the issue is the development of individualization, through the solidarity that the mass movement brings . . . new social movement theory . . . fails usefully to theorize this process' (Shakespeare, 1993: 263).

The concept of *new* social movements generally, therefore, is open to question, and those who have tried to apply it to the disability movement in particular are in some disagreement as to its relevance. But the central problematic with NSMs theory lies precisely in their key claim to be able to offer a more representative voice to their constituencies than that provided by traditional political parties and pressure groups.

Central to the concept of NSMs is the idea of self-conscious collective action based on the actors' shared definition of themselves, and aimed at political and cultural change (Diani, 1992). This shared definition is what gives a social group its sense of identity, and is crucial to the solidarity that Shakespeare (1993) says provides the vehicle for individual empowerment. The question then becomes, why should NSMs be more effective in this than more traditional organizations? In the case of the disability movement the simple answer would be that organizations *of* disabled people must inevitably be better placed than their forerunners to evaluate and articulate the needs of disabled people; thus they will attract the support of the people they aspire to represent, and the movement will grow organically, giving a sense of identity to powerless individuals and in return becoming more powerful by virtue of that shared identity.

There is a beguiling logic in this, but its simplicity conceals a number of difficulties. In the first place, the term 'disabled people' embraces a large constituency of individuals who, though they may share some consequential experiences – poverty, marginalization, discrimination – will have many more differences. As Barton (1993: 239) tells us, disabled people are not a homogeneous group, and their differences extend not only to their material circumstances and issues of class, race, gender and sexuality, but also to their need for support, including medical attention; their degree of self-awareness and pride; membership of activist organizations; view of the professionals' role in their lives; access to information; and the extent to which they are 'actively compliant in their own learned helplessness'. Yet if the disability movement is to prove an effective force, it is essential that these diverse individuals consciously adopt the identity of 'disabled' with the same vigour and sense of purpose as gay, lesbian, and black people have claimed their identities. This necessarily involves the subordination of individual circumstances to a shared sense of social oppression which Shakespeare (1993: 255) says is 'the most immanent aspect of the experience' of being disabled, and he goes on to demonstrate that the construction of such a collective identity is particularly difficult among disabled people.

Of course none of this invalidates the claim that organizations of disabled people are inherently more appropriate for the representation of disabled people, but it does indicate that that representation may be far from universal, and its adequacy, like that of traditional political parties and pressure groups, can be called into question. This point is not lost on some disabled people's advocates (for example, Barton, 1993; Shakespeare, 1993) who acknowledge that the disability movement is, for now, unrepresentative of the whole constituency of disabled people. This is at least partly because in trying to organize, it faces precisely the same difficulties of a diverse, fragmented and segregated constituency as more traditional organizations, and thus becomes colonized by those who have the ability, opportunity and motivation to become politically active. Thus the movement tends to be dominated by younger, relatively active middle-class people, predominantly (but not exclusively) white and male. Although the movement itself has begun to recognize and address these limitations (Barton, 1993), it is unjustifiably optimistic to believe that organizations of disabled people will be more successful in meeting the needs of women, black, gay or lesbian people just because they are not traditional groups. There has to be a limit to the extent that any organization aspiring to be *representative* can legitimately claim, or even hope, to represent the individuals it sees as its constituency. As has been indicated earlier, this diversity of identities demanding recognition has been welcomed by critical social policy analysts, but whether NSMs can provide the universalism that will liberate voiceless and powerless individuals remains open to debate.

If 'representativeness' can be prejudiced by the diversity of identities *within* NSMs, it is also at risk when those identities transcend their boundaries. The demands of different social movements may have the

standard, high achievement."

The pilot research projects

For the doctoral candidates, their dissertation research is unlikely the first research project they have ever undertaken on their own. Even the undergraduate students in the honors program might have done some sort of independent research in fulfillment of the requirements of certain courses or out of their own interests before the honors thesis. All such activities could be regarded as a sort of pilot project in relation to their thesis/dissertation research.

This, however, does not mean that there is necessarily a connection between your thesis/dissertation and all your prior research activities. In fact, the sooner you realize the importance of such a connection and start building it purposively, the better off you will be in completing your thesis/dissertation. Chances are that you will be required to do something on your own now and then in your early years in school. If you are fortunate enough, you may find yourself with those professors who would not waste your time by requiring you to do erratic and irrelevant things for their courses. Rather, they would encourage you to develop your own interests and prepare for your own future by accumulating a systematic knowledge in an area or certain interrelated areas. The training of your general research skills will be closely tied to the discovery of the substantive areas that interest you. The results, significant or trivial, will lay at least part of the groundwork for your ideas about your future thesis or dissertation project. If you are so well prepared, you may find the pieces of your school work ready for practical use years after your graduation. Therefore, you should never let the opportunity of gaining hands-on experience pass you by.

Perhaps few would doubt the value and effectiveness of the learning-by-doing approach to research. Yet doing something without a purpose will lead to nowhere. If you have no experience with thesis research, it is your mentors' responsibility to guide you through the preparation process. Your effort and careful planning in this aspect, however, is the principal factor leading you toward your success.

The correlation between the two canonical variates will then be calculated as a canonical correlation coefficient. Statistically, these two tasks need be performed simultaneously since the calculation of the correlation is based on the construction of the two canonical variates, whereas the determination of the coefficients (called weights or loadings) of the two linear functions depends on the achievement of the maximum canonical correlation.

A single set of the linear combinations only represents one dimension of the data set. To make full use of the information, we need to examine canonical correlation along other dimensions as well. The second set of linear combinations of the two original groups of variables also aims at achieving the maximum correlation between the two additional canonical variates. Nevertheless, the pursuit is along a different dimension, which requires the resultant canonical variates to be orthogonal to the first set of canonical variates. Likewise, the third set of canonical variates, if needed, should have the maximum correlation and be orthogonal to the prior sets of canonical variates. The number of the canonical variate sets and correlations is determined by the smaller number of the original variables in one of the two groups.

The computation of canonical correlation is a difficult process, which involves even more complicated transformation in order to perform a test of significance (e.g., from CR to Wilks' Lambda, and then to X^2 test). Fortunately, these can now be easily done by using computer software. You should, however, understand the purpose of the analysis and know how to interpret the results. Generally speaking, you will have two major sets of results, that is, canonical loadings (or weights) for combining the original variables into canonical variates, and canonical correlation coefficients as general measures of the association between the two groups of variables. For each set of the canonical variates, the canonical loadings will show the relative importance of each variable to the canonical correlation in this particular dimension.

Canonical correlation is a very useful idea in statistical analysis. It finds wide application especially when combined with the analytic technique of dummy variables. For example, to analyze the relationship between two categorical variables, you can derive a set of dummy variables with the codings of 0 and 1 for each variable, and then calculate the canonical correlation between the two sets of dummy variables. This can be used to supplement other measures of association suitable for the nominal or categorical level. A more practical and important use is associated with discriminant analysis, where the single categorical dependent variable is transformed into a set of dummy variables and

potential for contradictory effects for certain individuals. A good example of this is provided by Jenny Morris, who describes herself as 'a disabled feminist' (1991/92: 22). Although the disability movement recognizes that it is not specifically addressing the needs of women, in this article Morris expresses her anger that feminist research and theory fails to address the needs of disabled (and older) women, and she demonstrates the contradictory messages that result. She cites feminist writers such as Mary McIntosh (1981), Janet Finch (1984), Clare Ungerson (1987) and Gillian Dalley (1988) as rejecting care within the community because of the exploitative assumptions it makes about women's subordinate and caring role in the family. The conclusion of these writers, albeit reluctantly, is that the needs of disabled and older people would be better met in collective residential rather than community provision, and the weight of the women's movement should be thrown into attempts to improve that provision and the conditions surrounding it so that it becomes an acceptable strategy (Morris, 1991/92). Morris condemns this focus on the experiences of carers, and this able-bodied feminism's exclusion of the real life experiences of women who receive care. She argues that disabled activists and older people campaign *against* residential care provision both as individuals and through the disability movement, and therefore this approach inevitably causes some anxiety. Morris is especially scathing of Dalley's dismissal of disabled people's demands as stemming from some sort of 'false consciousness' reflecting the dominant ideology of the family, made by organizations which are not representative of 'dependent people' (cited Morris, 1991/92: 32).

Neither movement, therefore, adequately represents the interests of disabled or older women who receive care, but Morris prioritizes the rights of disabled people 'to live within the community in a non-disabling environment with the kind of personal assistance that we would choose' (1991/92: 39), and suggests that, since this also challenges the form that caring takes, feminists should support the disability movement.

Even if we were to accept that NSMs are more capable of adequately representing their constituencies than traditional pressure groups, there are still obstacles to the successful reflection of their concerns in policy, one of the most significant being the danger of incorporation. A major component of the critique of existing political processes which comes through NSM theory is that the organizations which have attempted to provide a challenge to the political and social *status quo* in the past have become incorporated within the state apparatus. This happens because the state manages its affairs so that popular protest is confined to constitutional means, ensuring evolution, not revolution (see Dunleavy and O'Leary, 1987; Held, 1989). In Britain the specific form in which the state has evolved facilitates this process (see Smith, 1990). Thus incorporation may be a result of capitulation after confrontation, or, more commonly, it is a result of the representative organizations having to rely on the state for resources. As has been shown, this has been the case with traditional organizations for disabled people, which have developed too cosy a relationship with the state, and may serve interests other than those of the people they claim to represent; for example, the maintenance of the social *status quo*, the careers of the staff who work for them, or the ambitions of key individuals seeking kudos or formal honours (Oliver, 1990). Rather than challenging the political and social invisibility of disabled people referred to by, *inter alia*, Brisenden (1986), Bynoe et al. (1991) and Finkelstein (1993), such organizations have colluded in their exclusion.

The modern disability movement is very conscious of the dangers of incorporation, as evidenced by the earlier reference to DPI's objectives and strategies, hence their emphasis on non-constitutional direct political action. Barnes and Oliver state the dilemma facing the disability movement very clearly:

> To get too close to the Government is to risk incorporation and end up carrying out their proposals rather than ours. To move too far away is to risk marginalization and eventual demise. To collaborate too eagerly with the organizations for disabled people risks having our agendas taken over by them, and having them presented both to us and to politicians as theirs. To remain aloof risks appearing unrealistic and/or unreasonable, and denies possible access to much needed resources. (1995: 115)

They note that since 1986 the disability movement's campaign to secure civil rights for disabled people has attracted the support of the traditional organizations run by non-disabled people, but the problematic nature of the relationship between the two sets of organizations is indicated by Barnes and Oliver's observation that many of them 'still support and provide oppressive services such as residential "care", special schools, and day centres' (1995: 111).

Barnes and Oliver were writing after the failure of the private member's Civil Rights (Disabled Persons) Bill in July 1994, and after the government published its proposals for what subsequently became the Disability Discrimination Bill in 1995. They are highly critical of these proposals, and note among other things that 'it sets out to prohibit discrimination against disabled people on the grounds of their [not society's] disability' (1995: 113), and is therefore firmly rooted in the medical rather than social model of disability. In their opinion, the proposals will achieve relatively little at considerable expense.

Although they are rightly anxious about the possibility of incorporation, they do not apparently see the government's response to the civil rights demands of the disability movement as akin to incorporation. The movement may resist, but the government has usurped its ideas, diluted and repackaged them, and presented them as the answer to the movement's challenge. In 1992 the Minister for Disabled People, Nicholas Scott, told the Greater Manchester Coalition of Disabled People (GMCDP) that:

> The Government's principal aims . . . are to enable disabled people to maximize their individual potential, to live independently where possible, to have employment opportunities and to enjoy their leisure time . . . Increasingly, disabled people will demand control of their own lives. Governments, local and national

. . . will need to adjust to this new, demanding, but exciting situation. (Cited in Morris, 1993: 148)

However, in 1994 it was this same Nicholas Scott who was the instrument through whom parliamentary procedure was used to kill the Civil Rights (Disabled Persons) Bill, the thirteenth time that such an attempt has failed since 1982. Barnes and Oliver (1995) see this failure as further evidence of the inadequacy of traditional political institutions, and call on the disability movement to regroup and produce not only a more satisfactory civil rights bill, but also a comprehensive agenda for both political and cultural change, not just in terms of tactics, but also a vision of a transformed society. What they leave unsaid is that the Bill failed despite the actions and optimism of, and public support for, the disability movement. There is thus little evidence in this episode that NSMs can be any more effective in securing real political change than traditional groups.

There has, of course, now been anti-discrimination legislation in the form of the Disability Discrimination Act 1995, and to that extent the direct action strategies of the disability movement can be said to have been successful. Ultimately, however, its success will depend on how effectively the legislation meets the needs of disabled people. Barnes and Oliver (1995) are not optimistic, first because government-initiated attempts to eradicate discrimination against other social groups have not been successful, and second because the sort of institutional discrimination highlighted by the social model of disability requires legislation that stresses civil rights and not just individual needs, and provides a framework for enforcement. This Act offers neither.

The concern with civil rights leads to another interpretation of NSMs which echoes Shakespeare's (1993) claim that they are not really 'new'. Laclau and Mouffe (1985) suggest that they are simply demanding that they be extended the same rights of citizenship as other groups already enjoy.

Disabled People and Citizenship

It must be recognized and stressed at the outset that citizenship is a complex and contentious notion which can be interpreted in a variety of ways (see Chapter 10), but for the purposes of this account we shall follow Turner (1986), and start with T.H. Marshall's model which perceives it as a set of civil, political and social rights which each individual has as entitlements, and which carry with them responsibilities (see Marshall and Bottomore, 1992; also Barbelet, 1988; Roche, 1992). Access to and exercise of these rights and responsibilities affords an individual an identity as a citizen, participating in society, first by contributing to it through such things as working and paying taxes, doing jury duty or voluntary work, voting and being politically active, making charitable donations, and if necessary fighting to preserve it; and second benefiting from society through the protection of the law, the right to political representation, and a share in the national wealth via improved material conditions. Citizenship therefore involves participation in society as a whole (Turner, 1986), and before the status of citizenship can be inferred, an individual has to have access to the means to carry out her or his responsibilities, and to benefit from the associated rights.

Turner states that 'citizenship is defined by various forms of social closure which exclude outsiders and preserve the rights of insiders to the full enjoyment of welfare and other social benefits' (1986: 85). Thus entry to and expansion of citizenship inevitably involves some form of struggle by groups and collectivists representing 'outsiders'. In the nineteenth and early twentieth centuries this was the class struggle waged by the political left in various forms, but now, according to Turner, the 'outsiders' cannot be defined by their class location, and are represented by the NSMs. To this extent debating citizenship as a relationship between class and social inclusion is inadequate.

To illustrate the success of these struggles and the expansion of citizenship rights over time Turner (1986) provides the simple and very effective analogy of a series of circles or waves which spread outwards from a common centre where citizenship is narrowly defined in terms of male property owners. In doing so they throw up anomalies which are in turn accommodated, and as the waves of citizenship spread they eventually embrace the full range of human, and ultimately non-human, entities. According to T.H. Marshall (see Marshall and Bottomore, 1992), there is nothing inevitable about the development of citizenship rights *per se*, but given that they have evolved, he says that they could only have evolved sequentially, and Turner's analogy illustrates this well. Thus the first wave reduced the significance of property ownership as a condition of citizenship, extending rights to certain men, and as it spread it embraced men from all classes; the second wave demoted gender and progressively gave similar formal rights to women; the third wave redefined age and kinship relations, and granted independent rights to children and old people. Each expansion raises fresh questions about the status of excluded groups, posed by their representatives, and those questions currently involve the legal status – and thus the rights – of embryos, animals, invertebrates and inanimate forms of nature. This has given rise to a fourth wave of citizenship, and its perception in this way explains Turner's narrow view of NSMs as typically conservationist and environmentalist.

It is worth making the point that while Turner stresses the inadequacy of a view of citizenship based on class, property, gender and age, and indeed sees them – along with ethnicity – as irrelevant to the continuation of modern capitalism, the issues of ability and disability are not addressed. There can be no doubt that he would agree that citizenship should not be conditional upon some notion of 'able-bodiedness', but this is a good example of the invisibility that the disability movement struggles against. This does not invalidate his analogy, of course, which illustrates both the temporal location of NSMs, and the context of the extension of citizenship rights within which they have arisen. The disability movement fits very neatly into this scenario.

People with physical, mental or sensory impairments have the same *formal* rights of citizenship as other members of society, in that they are not explicitly excluded *because* they have an impairment. Leaving aside the problematic aspects of the concept of citizenship, the difficulty they face, along with other marginalized groups, is in translating those formal rights into *substantive* rights. This is at the core of the disabling process, and while recent attention has been focused on anti-discrimination legislation, at the heart of the disability movement is a demand for fundamental change in social and cultural values – the demand that disability be seen in social rather than medical terms. This is a perfectly legitimate demand, and the need for it becomes clear when requests for equal treatment are publicly reinterpreted as demands for special treatment (see 'Terminological inexactitude', *The Guardian*, 30 November 1994, p. 22). Anti-discrimination legislation may assert the individual right of disabled people to determine the material circumstances in which they live their lives, and punish exclusionary actions, but the experience of other groups suggests that it will do little to enable their participation as full citizens, such is the depth of institutional discrimination against them.

From this perspective, the position of people with impairments can be seen as one of the anomalies which Turner (1986) says are thrown up in the course of extending citizenship, and the disability movement as the NSM which highlights its anomalous position and seeks solutions to it. To the extent that the disability movement has identified a fundamental problem with the citizenship status of disabled people, it can legitimately be called 'new'. The paradox, however, lies in the fact that if we accept Turner's analogy, it, and all other NSMs, can only be seen as the latest manifestation of a very old social movement aimed at securing an equal opportunity for all to participate fully in society through their status as equal citizens.

Activity 8.3

Answer the following key questions:
From what you know of the new social movements you have identified:

1 Do you think they are extending demands for traditional rights, or making more revolutionary claims?
2 What difficulties do these movements face in achieving their aims?
3 To what extent have NSMs identified and put into place strategies to overcome these difficulties?

Part 3

ISSUES AND DEBATES

Any selection of a range of issues deemed to be worthy of inclusion in an undergraduate text of this nature is bound to be arbitrary to some extent. A wide range of candidates for inclusion exists, but in selecting poverty, social justice, citizenship, the universality/selectivity debate and the growth of quasi-markets we believe that we are introducing students to ideas and debates that are challenging, complementary and, in their different ways, reflective of significant questions of continuity and change in social policy. Moreover, albeit in different ways, they are all about access to, and distribution of, scarce resources.

Competing concepts of social justice lie at the heart of the ethical and moral debate about the welfare state. In Chapter 9 Andros Loizou examines some of the ideas deployed in these debates and concentrates on the work of Rawls and Nozick, whose work has informed the social democratic and neo-liberal positions respectively.

Citizenship has become one of the most significant and contested issues in social and political theory and it has already featured prominently in a number of preceding chapters. In Chapter 10 Mike Wilson discusses its evolution and rise to prominence. Marshall's work and the relationship between citizenship and social policy provide the benchmark against which other developments are evaluated. Thatcherism's rejection of the idea of social citizenship alongside the exclusion from full citizenship associated with poverty, unemployment, gender and 'race' form the core of this section, and he provides some additional insights with his discussion of citizenship and the elderly population.

In Chapter 11 Alan Pratt examines the major philosophies of resource allocation which have informed social provision in the last half century. In doing so he discusses a variety of concepts and definitions and considers the respective merits of selectivity and universality as allocative mechanisms in the context of developments in the politics and economics of British society.

In Chapter 12 Tony Novak looks at recent debates over the nature, form, extent and causes of poverty in modern Britain. In particular, he assesses the impact of unemployment and the growth of low-paid work in an economy increasingly characterized by casualization and deregulation. He then proceeds to consider whether the growth in poverty in Britain has led to the creation of an underclass and examines recent debates surrounding this much contested concept.

Finally, in Chapter 13 Gerry Mooney looks at changes to state provision of welfare services under the impact of an increasingly pervasive belief in the supremacy of the free market. This belief in the supremacy of 'natural' markets as allocative institutions has increasingly been accompanied by the growth of quasi-markets and changes in the composition of the mixed economy of welfare. The chapter concludes with an assessment of the possible effects of these changes on service users.

9

Social Justice and Social Policy

Andros Loizou

In this chapter we shall be concerned with social justice, and this will involve looking at a number of interrelated ideas. As well as justice itself, we shall look at equality, rights and liberty. The central questions which guide this chapter are: what makes a particular policy just rather than unjust? What makes a particular distribution of resources (health, education, welfare benefits and so on) just rather than unjust? Underlying these there are such questions as: what exactly is social justice? Must it always entail equality of distribution? Are we clear what we mean when we speak of equality?

These questions – particularly the last two – are philosophical questions. They belong in an area of enquiry known as 'political philosophy' (or sometimes 'social philosophy'). Accordingly, this chapter will be, in effect, an introduction to this area of enquiry, from the particular perspective of these particular questions about social justice. It is not our aim in this chapter to arrive at final, definitive answers to these questions. This is an area of fundamental disagreement and debate, where different answers – opposing answers – are possible, and these opposing answers are contested or defended by means of powerful and convincing arguments in each case. Our aim, rather, is a humbler one: to indicate broadly the kinds of arguments deployed in these debates, and to pursue the analysis of justice, equality, liberty and so on to a sufficient depth to enable the reader to engage in informed consideration of the arguments deployed.

The Role of the Idea of Justice

'That is an unjust policy,' says A. 'Why?' asks B. What answers are open to A? Here are some typical examples of answers to B's question: 'Because it is *unequal*.' 'Because it ignores legitimate basic *needs*.' 'Because it violates X's *rights*.' 'Because it denies Y's *liberty*.' Note the italicized words: *unequal, needs, rights, liberty*. Justice is not, therefore, a simple idea; it must be complex if it depends on these other ideas. If an idea is simple, it has a straightforward definition. Take the idea, or concept, of a triangle. How do we define this concept? 'A triangle is a three-sided plane figure.' Will this do? Not quite:

Figure 9.1 and Figure 9.2 each show a three-sided figure, but neither of them is a triangle. We need to try again for a definition. 'A triangle is a

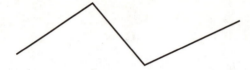

Figure 9.1　*Three-sided figure*

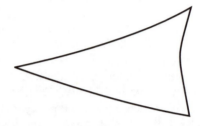

Figure 9.2　*Closed three-sided figure*

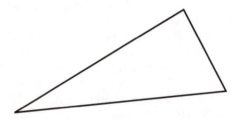

Figure 9.3　*Rectilinear closed three-sided figure*

closed, rectilinear, three-sided figure.' Clearly this is the correct definition. Sometimes there is the additional clause 'and its internal angles add up to 180 degrees', but this is not strictly necessary if you have already defined it as above. It follows logically from the original definition – you can prove it on that basis.

The thing to notice here is that there is one, and only one, definition of 'triangle'. But how about a concept like justice? Consider the following:

1　Justice consists in giving to each what he or she is owed, i.e. what is due to him or her.'
2　'Justice consists in equal treatment of everyone.'
3　'Justice consists in treating everyone as an equal.'

Can you spot the difference between 2 and 3?

4　'Justice consists in respecting equally everyone's liberty.'
5　'Justice consists in respecting equally everyone's fundamental rights.'
6　'Justice consists in giving to each what he/she deserves.'
7　'Justice consists in pursuing those options which promote the greatest happiness of the greatest number of citizens.'

8 'Justice consists in rewarding equal efforts equally.'
9 'Justice consists in taking from each according to his or her ability, and giving to each according to his or her need.'

Activity 9.1

What is your reaction to this explosion of 'definitions'? Do they have anything at all in common? If they don't, what are we to conclude?

If so many 'definitions' of justice are possible, what hope is there of any progress in understanding? Is there no hope at all of finding a common element? Well, between some of them, perhaps; but not all of them. But if we fail to find something in common – anything – how can we say anything meaningful here at all? Doesn't all talk of 'justice' become a mere exercise in subjectivism? At this point it would be useful to say something about the philosophical perspective on these matters, and to begin to engage with the idea of justice from that perspective.

We can begin by asking ourselves, what is the role of the concept of justice? What does it do – whatever definition it has? Look back at the list of 'definitions' of justice given above. Some of them may be close to some others, but mostly it is true to say that they don't have anything in common, taken as a whole. There is not one single element that they all share – there is not a single common feature.

'But they must have a common feature', you may object, 'otherwise how can they all claim to be definitions of one and the same concept, namely justice? The answer to this is that they don't have to have a common feature – but they do have an identical role. There may well be many equally defensible theories or ideals of justice, but what makes them all into theories/ideals *of justice* and not of [say] *equality* is that they all share one and the same role. John Rawls, a contemporary American philosopher who is possibly the most influential contemporary writer on this subject, entitles section 1 of his book *A Theory of Justice* 'The role of justice', and he begins that section as follows:

> Justice is the first virtue of social institutions, as truth is of systems of thought. A theory however elegant or economical must be rejected if it is untrue; likewise laws and institutions no matter how efficient and well-arranged must be rejected if they are unjust. (1972: 3)

Let us reflect on what this means. The important phrase is 'first virtue'. When we are looking at a 'system of thought' or a 'theory', our central concern is: is it true? (Is the theory of evolution by natural selection true? Is the Big Bang theory true?) Analogously, the 'first virtue' of social institutions is not truth but justice. We don't ask: is the social security system in the country X true? We ask: is that social security system just? Both sets of terms – true/untrue, just/unjust – are functioning here as evaluative terms.

canonical correlation is calculated between the set of dummy variables and the set of continuous independent variables. The canonical correlation coefficient (CR) can be used to replace the eigenvalue (λ) of the discriminant function in representing its discriminating power, i.e., CR = $[\lambda/(1+\lambda)]^{1/2}$.

Path analysis

So far we have examined different analytic models that apply to different research situations defined by the number of the variables involved, the mathematical properties of these variables, and the types of their hypothetical role. These are relatively simple models of analysis in terms of the way the variables are connected with one another. In most situations, we have simply divided the variables into two groups: the dependent variables and the independent variables. The realities that the behavioral and social researchers have to deal with, however, are often more complex than this. A variable may have many different relations with other variables. It can be a dependent variable for some related variables but also an independent variable for others. In other words, an analytical model closer to the reality will have to consider a relatively complete causal network as a whole rather than merely focus on a part of it. In statistics, there is a technique suitable for this kind of modeling called path analysis, or analysis of dependence.

Causal modeling in terms of path analysis essentially incorporates the ideas of both elaboration and multiple causation applied to interval or continuous variables. It should be noted that any analytic model is a simplified reflection of the reality, and path analysis is no exception. Since it is a more complex paradigm than any of the previously mentioned models, certain limitations must be clarified to ensure manageability and avoid excessive complication. The causal model, for example, needs to be "recursive," containing only one-way paths of causal effects among all variables, for path analysis to be practical for most applied researchers. Path analysis is based on the idea of structural equations, which are a set of standardized multiple regression equations established according to the structure of the causal model and are dealt with simultaneously. In addition to the limitation of linearity, the model requires the absence of the interaction among variables, or entails the additivity of their effects. The model also requires complete determination of any variable that is influence by other variables (called endogenous variables). To meet this requirement, the role of all other unknown variables must be represented by a

151

When we propose a theory, we are aiming at truth – and so someone else can legitimately pose the evaluative question, is that theory true? Similarly, when we (or our political leaders) create or modify a social security system, we (or they) are aiming at what we (or they) consider to be just – and so someone else can legitimately ask, is this new (or modified) social institution just? The role of the idea of justice is, therefore, to evaluate social institutions. There are, of course, other ways of evaluating them. Are they efficient? Are they popular? But what makes them better or worse as a whole is whether they are just or unjust. That is the point of calling justice 'the first virtue' of social institutions. John Rawls elucidates further the role of justice by means of an important distinction, namely, between the concept of justice and different conceptions of justice. The concept of justice is always the same, whereas there may be many different conceptions of justice in one society. Rawls explains the distinction as follows:

> Men disagree about which principles should define the basic terms of their association. Yet we may still say, despite this disagreement, that they each have a conception of justice. That is, they understand the need for, and they are prepared to affirm, a characteristic set of principles for assigning basic rights and duties and for determining what they take to be the proper distribution of the benefits and burdens of social co-operation. Thus it seems natural to think of the concept of justice as distinct from the various conceptions of justice and as being specified by the role which these different sets of principles, these different conceptions, have in common. Those who hold different conceptions of justice can, then, still agree that institutions are just when no arbitrary distinctions are made between persons in the assigning of basic rights and duties and when the rules determine a proper balance between competing claims to the advantages of social life. Men can agree to this description of just institutions since the notions of an arbitrary distinction and of a proper balance, which are included in the concept of justice, are left open for each to interpret according to the principles of justice that he accepts. These principles single out which similarities and differences among persons are relevant in determining rights and duties and they specify which division of advantages is appropriate. Clearly this distinction between the concept and the various conceptions of justice settles no important questions. It simply helps to identify the role of the principles of social justice. (1972: 5)

What, then, does the concept of justice itself tell us, in addition to telling us about the role of justice? It tells us simply that there are principles by which the rights and duties, benefits and burdens of social co-operation are to be divided, and that these principles operate in a non-arbitrary way. But it does not tell us what these principles are, because this belongs in the area of different conceptions of justice. Each conception of social justice will have its own set of principles on the basis of which the benefits and burdens of social co-operation are to be shared, and each one will operate in a non-arbitrary way on the basis of its own principles.

In the rest of this chapter, we shall accordingly be examining different 'conceptions' of justice in Rawls's sense, and the ways in which they make use of the concepts of liberty, equality, needs, rights and duties. Rawls has his own preferred conception, of course, which he proposes and defends throughout the 600-odd pages of his book, but it is nonetheless only one among other possible conceptions. Most conceptions of social justice have as their basis different understandings of the concepts of liberty and equality and of the relation between them. We shall therefore begin with some remarks on these two concepts in the next section, and then go on to look at different conceptions of social justice in the sections that follow.

Activity 9.2

Before progressing, it may be useful to consider the following two issues:

1 What is your idea of justice?
2 Which, if any, of the institutions of the British welfare state do you think operate on just principles? (a) social work; (b) social security; (c) the NHS; (d) education.

The Politics and the Logic of Liberty and Equality

It was until recently a fact of life, speaking at least for Britain, that the political rhetoric of the two major political parties (Labour and Conservative) proceeded along well-defined, almost ritualized lines, with Labour relying on the rhetoric of equality and the Conservatives on the rhetoric of liberty. The Conservatives typically accused Labour of unnecessary restrictions on liberty in (a) over-regulating the operations of the free market, and (b) dictating that resources freely acquired through the free market should be redistributed via progressive taxation from the earnings of the well-off to provide services, benefits and so on for the poorer sections of the community. And Labour typically accused the Conservatives of hiding behind the rhetoric of liberty to disguise and legitimize policies which favour the rich and allow them to exploit the poor in the labour market.

Two questions arise here. First, how much in these accusations and counter-accusations was truth rather than mere rhetoric? Second, is it necessarily the case that greater liberty is bought at the expense of equality, and conversely that greater equality is bought only at the expense of liberty? Are the two concepts, liberty and equality, truly related in this way? In what follows, we shall pursue the second of these questions and not the first. (A clear answer to the second would be a prerequisite, though not the only prerequisite, to answering the first. And the first is anyway outside the brief of this chapter).

Let us begin with liberty. Is liberty really the enemy of equality? How does liberty work? What is this concept? Does it mean 'freedom for each one to do as he or she likes'? Can you see anything wrong with this view of liberty? Let us consider some examples. (1) I am free to do as I like, you are free to do as you like; I want your car and try to take it, and you attack me. I then retaliate in like measure. And it goes on. (2) I want freedom of speech for myself and my circle of friends and colleagues. In exercise of this freedom, I begin saying damaging things against you and your circle, and you retaliate by saying damaging things against me and mine. And again it goes on. In both cases the struggle goes on until one or the other side gets the upper hand and dominates/represses the other side. All this, under the banner of 'freedom for all'. Clearly something has gone wrong.

What we have here is liberty for some at the expense of others. But true liberty must be freedom for all but not at anyone's expense. It must mean universal freedom. An essential aspect of this must be freedom from coercion by others. But one cannot accept this without accepting the universal obligation to respect the liberty of others; that is, to refrain from coercing them. This is usually supplemented by the clause that the state is the only body which may legitimately coerce the citizen, and then only to enforce the maintenance of liberty thus defined – in other words, it will use its powers only against those who threaten the liberty of their fellow citizens.

The upshot of this is that a universal system of liberty must be an equal system. Some writers, instead of speaking of liberty in general, speak of liberties in the plural, having in mind such liberties as freedom of speech, association, conscience and so on. A system of equal liberty, or liberties, imposes equally on all the strict duty not to violate that liberty (or those liberties). We should note here two points. First, it might seem that liberty as thus defined is restricted, in that everyone's liberty is equally repressed by such a system. But this is, arguably, a mistake, springing from a somewhat negative view of law, which is well epitomized by Jeremy Bentham's statement that every law is an infraction on liberty. This view is negative in that it ignores the fact that, in preventing citizens from coercing one another, law guarantees them the freedom to pursue their own aims and goals without interference. Law thus provides the citizen with a positive good – far from being an 'infraction' on liberty, it secures and enhances it.

The second point – and this is the one which is the more significant for our purposes in this chapter – is that the word 'equal', and therefore the very concept of equality, is central to any definition of liberty. This is something that any notion of liberty – even the most 'libertarian' – is forced to concede. At the heart of liberty, we find some notion of equality. The most extreme libertarian is thus logically constrained, by his or her very own precept, to treat us all as equals. It is therefore a mistake to view equality and liberty as logically opposed to each other. We shall now turn, as promised, to the examination of a number of different conceptions of social justice.

Liberty and Social Justice

In this section, we shall approach social justice via liberty. As will become clear presently, different conceptions of social justice are made possible by different ways of understanding liberty. The difference comes not so much from the definition of liberty itself, but from how widely we extend the category of those factors which count as infringements or constraints on liberty.

Not many would disagree with the statement that liberty cannot exist unless it is equal liberty for all. Most would also agree – anarchists being the exception – that the best way of securing and enhancing a system of equal liberties (freedom of speech, conscience, association, movement and so on) is by means of law, as this is understood, for example, in a liberal democratic state. The law understood in this way protects us from all those constraints which are characteristic of lack of liberty, such as arbitrary arrest, violent attacks, overt pressures to conform to a particular religious or political doctrine, and so forth. So far, it seems clear enough. But how wide is the category of acts, situations, arrangements made by others and such like which defines lack of liberty? Arbitrary restrictions on freedom to associate with others, threats designed to prevent us from speaking freely, attempts to coerce us into accepting a particular political viewpoint – these are all clearly factors which define lack of liberty. But what of extreme poverty, lack of the means to sustain a minimally satisfactory life, and lack of any visible road by which to attain those means? Again, let us suppose that you are not exactly on the poverty line, but that you merely lack the means to take legal action against a rich man who has wronged you and who, unlike you, can afford to hire expensive barristers.

The classical liberal stance on this has been not to count poverty or lack of means among those constraints which define lack of liberty. The only constraints under this heading are those coercive acts deliberately undertaken by particular agents or groups – for example, to coerce us into accepting a particular political doctrine, or to prevent us from speaking freely. Liberals have not, traditionally, included economic constraints under this heading. For economic constraints, they argue, are the result of forces of nature and not human agency. (The operations of 'the market', somewhat like the laws of gravity, are not to be thought of as anything that anyone deliberately does.) In fact, this issue is a bone of contention between liberals and some socialists (including Marxists). Marxists, for example, maintain that economic constraints are the product of an exploiting class, and hence very much the product of human action; therefore poverty and lack of means generally are among those constraints which define lack of liberty. The liberal reply is that this confuses liberty itself with the 'conditions' of liberty, or the 'worth' of liberty, or the 'value' of liberty; or again, that it confuses liberty with equality.

There is a very accessible exposition of the socialist view on this issue by Raymond Plant (1984). Using terms like 'worth of liberty' and 'value of liberty', Plant writes:

> The liberal is interested in equal liberty; socialists are concerned with trying to secure the distribution of resources which will mean that liberty is of roughly equal value to all persons. The worth of liberty to individuals is related to their capacities, opportunities and resources to advance the purposes which they

happen to have. Those with greater income and wealth, fortunate family back-ground, etc. will, on the whole, be able to pursue those things for which we value liberty more effectively than the person who does not enjoy those benefits. It is because we value liberty for all that we are concerned to secure a greater equality in the worth of liberty. (1984: 6)

The difference, then, as regards social justice is this: the traditional liberal, and even more so the libertarian, will see social justice as best served by a conception of liberty which treats issues of relative wealth or poverty – more specifically, economic constraints on one's ability to realize one's aims – as factors which belong to nature rather than to human choice; and the state then has the obligation to its citizens to ensure liberty as thus conceived. This conception of liberty then begins to define the legitimate sphere of government in a characteristically minimalist way, to include whatever is required to guarantee liberty and no more. Redistributive social policies such as welfare benefits provided out of general taxation then become difficult to justify – if they are not exactly illegitimate, they are clearly not obligations of the state.

There is one influential philosopher who has gone even further, to insist that any redistributive social policy is strictly illegitimate. That philosopher is Robert Nozick – a contemporary American and a colleague of John Rawls. Nozick's book *Anarchy, State and Utopia* (1974) contains, among other things, a rival theory of justice to that of Rawls. Nozick calls his theory 'the entitlement theory of justice'. We shall be looking at that theory in the section of this chapter beginning on page 175. In the next section, we shall examine Rawls's theory.

Activity 9.3

1 Make a list of what are, in your opinion, the 'most funda-mental liberties' due to all people.
2 Look at your list and rank them in order of importance.
3 How can we guarantee our own, and others', liberties?

Equality and Social Justice

As we have seen, Rawls distinguishes the concept of justice from the range of possible conceptions of justice. Accordingly, beyond the general claim that justice is 'the first virtue of social institutions' and the ensuing discussion of the role of justice, he needs to propose and defend his own preferred conception of justice. This task occupies the rest of his book.

Rawls's starting point is the idea of the social contract – the idea that all legitimate government is essentially the result of a contract made between citizens, to institute a form of government that enhances and protects their liberties. But Rawls takes 'social contract theory' further than its seventeenth- and eighteenth-century exponents took it:

My aim is to present a conception of justice which generalizes and carries to a higher level of abstraction the familiar theory of the social contract as found, say, in Locke, Rousseau and Kant. In order to do this we are not to think of the original contract as one to enter a particular society or to set up a particular form of government. Rather, the guiding idea is that *the principles of justice for the basic structure of society are the object of the original agreement. They are the principles that free and rational persons concerned to further their own interests would accept in an initial position of equality as defining the fundamental terms of their association.* These principles are to regulate all further agreements; they specify the kinds of social co-operation that can be entered into and the forms of government that can be established. This way of regarding the principles of justice I shall call justice as fairness. (1972: 11; emphasis added)

The task that Rawls sets himself is to decide what principles of justice it would be rational to choose, in accordance with the above (note particularly the italicized sentences). In order to do this, he sets up an imaginary 'social contract' scenario, which he calls 'the Original Position'. Rawls places his imaginary citizens behind what he calls a 'veil of ignorance' which prevents them from knowing (a) their level of wealth and their social position, (b) their psychological make-up and character (for example, whether they are risk-takers, entrepreneurs, leaders, followers and so on) and (c) their full conception of the good (for instance, whether they are religious, liberal humanists, Marxists and so forth). Not knowing any of these facts (a), (b) and (c) about themselves, they will be sure to choose principles of justice which favour neither a particular socio-economic group, nor a particular type of character, nor a particular political or religious outlook. What they do have is rationality, a desire to maximize their own interests (whatever these might be), and a sense of justice. In addition, they have enough knowledge of economics, political science and so on to enable them to make informed judgements about the matter before them; namely, the choice of what principles of justice ought to be unanimously agreed to as defining the basic structure of their society.

In its most general form, the theory prioritizes equality, and this is expressed in what Rawls call 'the general conception' of justice as fairness: 'All social values – liberty and opportunity, income and wealth, and the bases of self-respect – are to be distributed equally unless an unequal distribution of any, or all, of these values is to everyone's advantage' (1972: 62).

Notice that for Rawls it is inequality that calls for justification, not equality. Certain social values cannot be 'traded off' for others, and must remain equal – no one should be asked to sacrifice his or her basic liberties for economic and social gains. This is made clear in Rawls's statement of the two principles of justice which, he claims, would constitute the rational choice and so would be chosen by our contracting parties behind the 'veil of ignorance'. The first principle is: *Each person is to have an equal right to the most extensive total system of equal basic liberties compatible with a similar system of liberty for all.* The second principle has two parts, and it goes: *Social and economic inequalities are to be arranged so that they are both (1) to the greatest benefit of the least advantaged, and (2) attached to offices and positions open to all under conditions of fair equality of opportunity.*

Rawls has a system of priority rules, according to which the second principle only comes into operation within the constraints set by the first, and part (1) of the second principle only comes into operation within constraints set by part (2). The upshot of this is therefore that social and economic inequalities and their permissible levels can only be addressed once the requirements of equal liberty (first principle) and equality of opportunity (part (2) of the second principle) are satisfied, *and in that order*. In other words, citizens should never be required to bargain away their political rights in return for a bigger slice of the economic cake, and neither should they be expected to sacrifice their equal right to be considered for positions and offices which may bring rewards other than the merely socioeconomic, even if it does mean that they benefit economically.

By far the most interesting part of Rawls's theory is part (1) of the second principle: that *social and economic inequalities are to be arranged so that they are to the greatest benefit of the least advantaged*. This is referred to as 'the Difference Principle'. At first sight, it seems illogical: how can inequalities be of *any* benefit to the least advantaged, let alone to their *greatest* benefit?

It is at this point that Rawls's stipulation that the contracting parties behind the veil of ignorance should know something about the economics and politics of the modern liberal democratic state comes into its own.

This is best understood in terms of Fig 9.4. Let *y* represent the level of well-being of a representative person in the least advantaged socio-economic group, and *x* the level of well-being of a person in the most advantaged socio-economic group. What the diagram represents is the increasing levels of well-being of both the extreme socio-economic groups, up to point *D*. Beyond that, the well-being of the most advantaged can only be achieved if

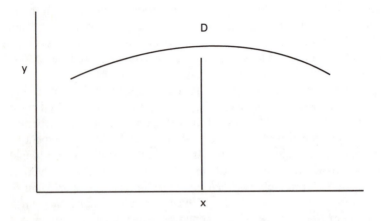

Figure 9.4   *Graph illustrating the difference principle*

the level of well-being of the least advantaged is allowed to fall. This is because the point D represents the point at which the economic system becomes 100 per cent efficient. Beyond this point – that is, to the right of it on the diagram, no one gains unless someone else loses. To the left of that point, the economic system has still not yet reached 100 per cent efficiency.

Point *D* represents the point at which the Difference Principle is realized. This calls for explanation in concrete terms. To the left of this point, the most advantaged are taxed too heavily for them to have any incentive to increase their economic activity. At point *D*, they are taxed less, so that their economic activity is at a level where the least advantaged are better off than at any other point. Beyond this point, to the right of the diagram, they begin to lose out.

To make this clearer, let us ask two questions. First, why not strict equality – that is, everyone getting the same income? Second, why should the most advantaged socio-economic group be prepared to settle for point *D*, if there is greater economic advantage to them to move things to the right of the diagram at the expense of their less favoured fellow citizens? Rawls has an answer to both these questions.

First, it would be rational for the least favoured group to want strict equality *only if they would be better off in absolute terms*. But this, argues Rawls, would not be a realistic scenario, because those whose skills and talents would create opportunities and so forth would have no reason to exercise themselves to their full capacity. For according to Figure 9.4, if the most advantaged group (who would have the aforementioned skills, talents and the means to realize them) were taxed more heavily, the level of well-being of the least advantaged would be lower in absolute terms. So it would be *rational* for the less well favoured to accept the Difference Principle. To find Rawls's answer to the second question, we need to look more deeply into the theory.

We must not forget Rawls's claim that his two principles of justice are what would be chosen in an initial position of equality by all the contracting parties unanimously – and so they would be the rational choice for his imaginary persons in the Original Position, behind the 'veil of ignorance' as specified above. Because they are assumed to be ignorant of their own contingent circumstances (as outlined earlier), they will choose principles of justice from an impartial point of view; that is, only those principles which do not favour one socio-economic group over another. So the contracting parties will see the rationality of (1) ensuring that those who are worst off are better than they would be under any other scheme, and (2) ensuring that those with leadership and entrepreneurial abilities would feel that they could realize their potential and be sufficiently rewarded for it.

We are now in a better position to appreciate Rawls's answer to the second question: why should the most advantaged group settle for the Difference Principle and point *D* on our figure? Why would it be irrational for them to hanker after the greener pastures (for them) that lie to the right of *D*? Rawls's answer invokes another important concept for him; namely, that of 'a Well Ordered Society' (see Rawls 1972: 4–5, 453ff.). A well-ordered society is a society which advances the interests of all its members and is regulated by a public conception of justice; that is, a conception of justice about which there is consensus and agreement between different socio-economic groups. Now clearly the most advantaged socio-economic group could have been better off if they had not chosen Rawls's two principles (particularly the Difference Principle). While it is easy to see how the least advantaged group might be pleased with the outcome of their choice behind the veil of ignorance, has the most advantaged group any reason to be pleased? Rawls's answer is yes – for they know that their greater wealth is not resented, particularly by the least favoured group. For the least favoured group know that they are certainly better off than they would otherwise be, and the most favoured know that they are viewed by the others as deserving their greater wealth. By forgoing what they might have had under (say) a *laissez-faire* system of capitalism, they have the assurance that they are living in a consensual, well-ordered society . But they also know that their sacrifice is not too great; for they are allowed by the Difference Principle to keep a sufficiently large part of the wealth they generate to maintain their productive efforts.

In summary, then, Rawls provides us with a conception of social justice which seeks to strike a balance between a free market situation and a regulated situation. The main idea is that equality is always to be preferred, unless it can be shown that inequality (in whatever respects) is to everyone's advantage. Inequality of liberty is not to everyone's advantage, so equal liberty constitutes the rational choice and is encapsulated in the first principle. What the Difference Principle shows, Rawls claims, is that a certain level of allowable inequality of wealth is to everyone's advantage, and so it is rational to choose the Difference Principle. The Difference Principle can be realized simply by setting general taxation at the right level; enough to ensure maximal benefit to the least advantaged socio-economic group, but not so much that the most advantaged group lose their incentive to lead in the creation of wealth. If we were to sum up the theory in a single phrase, the phrase would be: consensual welfare capitalism.

Rawls's work has generated a vast amount of critical debate (see, for example, Barry, 1972; Daniels, 1975; Wolff, 1977; Sandel, 1982; Pogge, 1989). Among the questions that have been raised are the following: is Rawls's version of the social contract (with his contracting parties in 'the Original Position' and placed behind 'the veil of ignorance') really necessary – couldn't he have defended the two principles of justice without appealing to it? Isn't Rawls's theory flawed because it tries to guarantee equal liberty without at the same time guaranteeing what, earlier, we called 'equal worth of liberty' – despite the claim by Rawls that unequal worth of liberty is compensated for by the operation of the Difference Principle?

Activity 9.4

What do you make of these critical perspectives? Would you have chosen a different set of principles if you were in the Original Position?

The Libertarian Alternative

We turn now to Robert Nozick's strongly libertarian theory of social justice, which Nozick himself calls 'the entitlement theory' and which is propounded and defended in his book *Anarchy, State and Utopia* (1974). Nozick's starting point is a strong notion of individual rights centred on liberty, and the deployment of this notion in support of limited government, or what he calls 'the minimal state'. Anything the state does beyond safeguarding individual liberty is strictly illegitimate. Most notably, it is illegitimate for the state to be concerned with any conception of justice which redistributes wealth – any such redistribution violates the rights of those from whom wealth is taken.

Nozick distinguishes his own 'entitlement' theory from rival theories in two ways: (1) by means of a distinction between patterned and non-patterned principles of justice, and (2) by means of a further distinction, between historical and non-historical principles of justice. Let us take (1) first. Patterned principles of distributive justice would be, for example, 'to each according to their need', 'to each according to their IQ'. Everything having the form 'to each according to their X' is, according to Nozick, a patterned principle of distribution, where X names some 'natural dimension, weighted sum of natural dimensions or lexicographical ordering of natural dimensions' (1974: 156). The point is, for Nozick, that all such principles are aimed at some preferred pattern of distribution that embodies a social value such as equality, need, merit and so on. His own conception, Nozick claims, is unpatterned – he claims not to have a preferred pattern of distribution, but rather to take seriously how the existing distribution came about. This naturally leads us on to (2). Most patterned principles are non-historical, end-state principles, according to Nozick; whereas his own unpatterned principle is historical. It is important to note that it is possible to have patterned historical principles – for example, 'to each according to their moral worthiness [as determined by past actions]'. Nozick's claim to uniqueness lies in the proposition that the Entitlement Theory is an unpatterned historical conception.

For Nozick, the right to liberty is the supreme right, and hence the supreme value; and liberty, he says, is bound to upset patterns. You could only maintain a pattern of distribution by continually intervening to redress the results of individual people's free choices. Suppose we started with some patterned distribution *D1* (an egalitarian distribution, let us assume). Let us

residual variable or error variable, and path analysis requires all residual variables are independent from other variables. Due to these restrictions, the use of path analysis is rather limited, and you must pay special attention to any possible specification error that may be involved.

Path analysis begins with a causal model represented by a diagram consisting of all the variables, influence paths, and arrows showing the directions. In causal modeling language, the variables that influence an endogenous variable are called predetermined variables. Variables that are not influenced by other variables in the model are called exogenous variables. Based on the linearity and additivity assumptions, each endogenous variable can be represented by a linear combination of all its predetermined variables with unknown path coefficients, plus a residual item. This will form a set of "structural equations," and the task is to determine the path coefficients that show the causal effects of the various paths. Assuming all the variables are standardized and all the residual items are independent, these structural equations can be transformed into so-called "normal equations" containing only unknown path coefficients and known correlation coefficients. With a completely recursive causal model, path analysis will have a just-identified model where the path coefficients will be completely determined by an equal number of structural equations.

Path analysis involves complex computation. This tedious process is usually completed by the computer through regression. In real terms, path analysis "is nothing but a repeated application of multiple regression analysis (applied to each variable in succession, with the prior variables as its determiners)" (Van de Geer, 1971, p.86). There are different software packages available for performing this task, including LISREL, EQS, EZ-Path, COSAN, and CALIS. Among these, the statistical program EQS has the merit of simplicity in contrast to the more popular yet more complex package LISREL. EQS is "a simple, consistent, yet technically advanced and accurate approach to structural modeling" (Bentler, 1989). The EQS computer software can deal with a series of regression equations simultaneously and generate an estimated covariance matrix of the hypothesized relationships between the variables contained in the model (Bentler, 1985). The statistical theory underlying this computer program allows for the estimation of parameters and testing of models using traditional multivariate normal theory, but also enables the use of the more general elliptical and arbitrary distribution theories, based on a unified generalized least squares or minimum Chi-square approach (ibid.). In addition to this advantage of generality is its simplicity. Nevertheless, the program has no data-cleaning features such as procedures for

suppose that people are willing to pay to see a famous baseball player in action, and this baseball player contracts with the team management for a certain percentage of the ticket price (say, 10 per cent) to go to him. The baseball player will gain enormously, but those who have paid to see him will be paying (say) £10 rather than £9 per ticket. Their situation is thus not appreciably affected by the extra £1 each is paying to see the player perform. A free choice on the part of thousands of individuals has thus succeeded in changing the distribution from *D1* to something else. If people have chosen to give their money to the baseball player in this way, who, asks Nozick, has the right to take it away? (This example is Nozick's, with some details changed for the sake of simplicity.)

To adopt (and adapt) another of Nozick's examples, imagine we have a socialist society where wage levels are determined by the state and everyone (by and large) is paid the same. Suppose also that Smith decides to work after hours, in time not paid for by the state, in some business of her own devising; and that the business is successful. Suppose others then begin to do likewise, and eventually a wholly private 'after-hours' economy begins to arise. Some individuals might then choose to leave the socialist economy and work wholly in the newly generated private sector. What, we may ask, could stop this development? The only way would be for the state to forbid it. 'The socialist society would have to forbid capitalist acts between consenting adults' (Nozick, 1974: 163). Furthermore, Nozick claims, it would have to exercise its authority continually:

> no end-state principle or distributional patterned principle of justice can be continuously realized without continuous interference with people's lives. Any favoured pattern would be transformed into one unfavoured by the principle, by people choosing to act in various ways; for example by people exchanging goods and services with other people, or giving things to other people, things the transferers are entitled to under the favoured distributional pattern. To maintain a pattern one must either continually interfere to stop people from transferring resources as they wish to, or continually [or periodically] interfere to take from some persons resources that others for some reason chose to transfer to them. (1974: 163)

All this paves the way for the conclusion that paying for welfare benefits out of general taxation, or indeed anything whose rationale is the redistribution of wealth from the well-off to the less well-off, amounts to strict rights violation: the rights of the taxed are being violated. 'Taxation of earnings from labour is on a par with forced labour' (Nozick, 1974: 169]. The only legitimate levying of revenues by taxation is for the purpose of financing the minimal state – the state which guarantees liberty, protects against violence, ensures contracts are enforced, and so on.

So far, Nozick's ideas are very close to those of F.A. Hayek (see Hayek, 1960, and Chapter 3 of this text). In fact Nozick quotes Hayek when he introduces the distinction between patterned and unpatterned principles of justice (Nozick, 1974: 158). What, then, is different about Nozick, and why is he considered so important by political philosophers? It is not his overall conclusions that are novel so much as the sustained argument by which he tries to establish them. Although we cannot go into this in any depth here, there are three features worth mentioning. First, Nozick has an ingenious argument for justifying the minimal state. Second, he has a very strong notion of individual rights, and deploys that notion with great determination in his arguments. Third, the foundations on which he bases historical entitlement to property (for which Nozick uses the term 'holdings') constitute an attempt to state what rights we have over previously unowned goods, natural resources and so on.

The ingenuity of the first lies in the way in which he argues that a minimal state could arise, without violating anyone's rights, from a pre-political society (or 'state of nature') by an invisible hand; that is, without recourse to the notion of a social contract. Whatever moral authority the state has will then derive directly from 'natural rights', namely, those pre-political rights which (according to one tradition of thought) we have by virtue of being human. The minimal state thus justified will be the purest expression of these natural rights and their safeguarding.

We are thus led to the second feature: the notion of individual rights itself. Individual rights determine the framework within which any 'social choices' take place. If we asked each citizen to rank W, X, Y and Z in order of preference, it is not the highest ranked alternative *per se* which will be adopted, but the highest ranked alternative consistent with everyone's individual rights. Hence if they are ranked by a popular vote in the order Z, W, Y and X, and if Z, W and Y would each violate the rights of at least one citizen, then X would be adopted despite its being the least favoured on a straight vote. 'Rights do not determine the position of an alternative or the relative position of two alternatives in a social ordering, they operate upon a social ordering to constrain the choice it can yield' (Nozick, 1974: 166).

Turning now to the third point, there are three principles which go to make up Nozick's Entitlement Theory of justice: the principle of justice in acquisition, the principle of justice in transfer, and the principle of rectification of past injustice. The principle of justice in acquisition determines whether an initial acquisition – namely, an acquisition of something previously unowned, such as a natural resource of some kind – is just. The principle of justice in transfer determines the conditions under which a legitimate first acquisition may be transferred to another owner. Nozick defines the relation between these two principles as follows:

> If the world were wholly just, the following inductive definition would exhaustively cover the principle of justice in holdings.
>
> 1 A person who acquires a holding in accordance with the principle of justice in acquisition is entitled to that holding.
> 2 A person who acquires a holding in accordance with the principle of justice in transfer, from someone else entitled to the holding, is entitled to the holding.
> 3 No one is entitled to a holding except by (repeated) applications of 1 and 2. (1974: 151)

The upshot of this is that if you can trace your ownership through a series of legitimate transfers to a legitimate first acquisition, then your ownership is legitimate. But what if you cannot do so? Nozick has an answer in the form of a third principle: the principle of rectification of past injustice. There are two ways an injustice may have occurred: either the initial acquisition or one or more of the subsequent transfers may have been illegitimate.

There are clearly going to be problems with this. How far back into the dim and distant past do we go in search of the grounds of legitimate ownership? And if we do succeed in getting back to first acquisitions, how do we decide on their legitimacy? Who decides (and don't forget, there is no state authority yet)? What is a legitimate first acquisition in a situation where there are no rules, laws, institutions and so forth? (For further reading on this and other aspects of Nozick's theory, see Paul, 1982.)

Activity 9.5

It is this last part of Nozick's theory that has been viewed with the most scepticism. What problems can you see? (Try to develop any of the points raised in the paragraph above.) Would it be true to say that if (note: if) we could get a clear and acceptable formulation of the principle of justice in acquisition, then Nozick's theory would win over Rawls's theory?

Summary and Conclusion

Let us summarize the journey we have taken in this chapter. We began with the quest for a definition: can 'justice', or 'social justice', be defined? Given that there was no single definition, unlike the case of the definition of a triangle, but a multitude of plausible-sounding definitions, we then explored the role of the idea of social justice as 'the first virtue of social institutions'. In the following section, we came to see how naïve it is to think of liberty and equality as essentially opposed ideas. We then moved on to look at radically different ways of understanding liberty, and the radically different notions of justice that these notions of liberty imply. But by far the largest sections were the last two, dealing respectively with Rawls's and Nozick's theories of justice. Let us end, then, with some final reflections on these two theories.

Rawls's theory of justice has been highly influential, and has at various times been favoured by a number of centre and left-of-centre political groupings (including, in Britain, the Labour Party and the Liberal Democrats). Political groupings to whom it does not appeal include Marxists and libertarians. What most attracts the former political groupings are, it seems, (1) the appeal of the idea of a rational choice between different conceptions of justice, (2) the presumption in favour of equality, unless a particular kind of inequality can be justified in terms of everyone's interests, and yet (3) the ways in which the better elements of a capitalist system are preserved.

Nozick's theory starts from a different basis: the inviolability of the individual right to liberty, with particular emphasis on the right to acquire and transfer property. It is this fundamental right upon which the legitimacy of the state rests – and, in turn, the authority of this (minimal) state extends no further than safeguarding this fundamental right. Taking liberty seriously is, according to Nozick, incompatible with any theories of justice which would seek to impose any pattern of distribution/redistribution of wealth: liberty, says Nozick, upsets patterns (1974: 160). If Nozick is right when he claims that people have rights to ownership prior to state activities or interventions, then any attempt by the state (or any other party) to redistribute what is thus legitimately owned must be illegitimate, and more particularly, the state has no authority whatsoever for engaging in welfare activity. It is thus easy to see how Nozick's theory could be adopted by the libertarian right, including certain elements in the Conservative Party of Britain.

In conclusion, then, we may ask: what are the welfare implications of these two conceptions of justice? Let us begin with Rawls's theory. Clearly, the crucial part of Rawls's theory is the presumption in favour of equality, unless inequality is in the interests of all (and more specifically, the least advantaged), and this presumption is embodied in the Difference Principle. This principle does not prescribe how the transfer of resources so as to benefit the least advantaged is to be achieved. The operation of the Difference Principle would be at the structural level; namely, operating between socio-economic sectors, and not individuals as such. The detail would then be a matter of formally just procedure and administration, in accordance with the general prescription of the Difference Principle. Welfare provision, where necessary within the general context of this redistribution of wealth, would then be simply a matter of detailed administration.

On Nozick's theory, by contrast, the only legitimate expenditure by the state of funds which are got through general taxation is for financing the minimal state (protection of civil liberties, punishment of offenders for crime and so on). Welfare provision, if any, is therefore a matter of the voluntary choice of the provider. If you choose to help the needy, you may do so. No one will stop you. Indeed, many will praise you for it, and recipients will be grateful. But if the state tries to tax you to help the needy, the state thereby violates your rights.

To illustrate these differences further, let us consider some specific implications for social policy. For example, on what basis should medical care be allocated? Nozick would pick on the word 'allocated'. In his words:

> There is no central distribution, no person or group entitled to control all the resources, jointly deciding how they are to be doled out. What each person gets,

he gets from others who give it to him in exchange for something, or as a gift. (1974: 149)

Again, in a passage directed against the thesis that medical care should be allocated on the basis of need, and not the ability to pay, Nozick compares the doctor with the barber. We have no quarrel, he says, with the fact that the barber sells his or her services to those who pay, and withholds them from those who don't. Why, he asks, shouldn't the doctor do the same? The state or 'society', he claims, has no more right to have a monopoly or near-monopoly on distributing the services of doctors than it has in the case of hairdressers. To emphasize his point he takes the example of a gardener and asks whether 'his services' should be 'allocated to those lawns which need him most?' (1974: 234). To *compel* gardeners to work under such strictures would be to exercise part ownership over them, and hence to violate their rights. And the same is therefore true, Nozick argues, for the doctor.

How would this example be treated in Rawls's theory? The basic principle is clearly spelled out by Rawls: 'Social resources must be released to the government so that it can provide for the public good and make the transfer payments necessary in order to satisfy the difference principle' (1972: 278).

The result of this difference in approach from the point of view of health services should be clear. On Nozick's conception of justice, the market should rule entirely, the state intervening only to secure the natural rights of its citizens, whereas on Rawls's theory, the government and its agencies operate according to a principle of redistribution (the Difference Principle) in order to allocate medical resources so as maximally to benefit the least advantaged, as explained earlier in the chapter.

Activity 9.6

How would Nozick and Rawls deal with other areas of social policy – for example, social security, education, social work?

The two conceptions of justice are as far apart as any could be. Clearly, if the idea of welfare provision by the state is to flourish, then some decisive arguments against Nozick's conception of justice must be forthcoming – and note, arguments: not just emotional reactions and rhetorical outbursts. But what would count as arguments, how could there be reasoned debate and not merely ritualized political rhetoric and sloganizing, given these radical differences?

Despite these differences, the two theories do share a common element: the priority of liberty. The role of liberty is clearly visible in the case of Nozick, based as it is on a strong conception of natural rights which goes back at least to Hobbes and Locke. But it is easy to forget, once we get involved in the Difference Principle and its interpretation, that Rawls also prioritizes liberty. The Difference Principle, it will be recalled, comes third in Rawls's 'lexical ordering': first comes the first principle (equal liberty), then comes part two of the second principle (equality of opportunity), and only then does the Difference Principle come into operation, within these two prior constraints. The debate between them, then, comes down in the end to radically different interpretations of liberty (see the section on liberty and justice). Rawls would claim that his own interpretation of liberty is still firmly in the liberal camp, but needs to be added to in order to ensure that it is realizable (hence the Difference Principle). Nozick, on the other hand, will claim that Rawls's additions violate that very liberty which he claims to defend.

10

Citizenship and Welfare

Mike Wilson

Following from our discussion of 'justice' in Chapter 9 we now approach another highly contested concept within social policy: citizenship. Issues and debates around citizenship in a book devoted to analysing social policy lead one towards discussing, not only citizenship, but also welfare and citizenship's relation to it. Yet any discussion of the meaning and contemporary applicability of the concepts of citizenship and welfare – and their relationship to each other – must follow a sapper's procedure in a minefield – extreme caution! Why is this? Much of the answer lies in the highly contestable nature of these concepts. Thus, the Speaker of the House of Commons' Commission on Citizenship located citizenship at the heart of 'modern political struggle' (1990: xv). Later, in an almost throw-away line, the Commission revealed the contingent – even fragile – nature of citizenship, when it declared that 'Citizenship, whatever it means, is a cultural achievement . . . *which can be lost or destroyed* (emphasis added; 1990: xv, see also Steenbergen, 1994: 1). This notion of contestability and contingency dependent on the balance of social, economic and political forces has also been highlighted in various publications (for example, Barbalet, 1988; Turner, 1993; Plant 1988).

What does not appear to be at issue is the merit of citizenship. Like democracy it appears to be an 'OK' word to which people of various political affiliations would subscribe (see Fraser and Gordon, 1994: 90, in Steenbergen, 1994). What the word actually means to these respective affiliations is quite a different matter, however. Nowhere is this more acutely seen than in contemporary Britain. Here, the inherently consumerist approach of the Conservative government's Citizen's Charter (Hill, 1994; Cram and Richardson, 1992), appears to conflict with that of the European Social Chapter, which it has refused to sign on Britain's behalf. The Social Chapter is, of course, one aspect of citizenship as social rights and welfare entitlement to which current anti-consumerist approaches to citizenship are adhering and which are strongly associated with the writings of T.H. Marshall – to which we will turn later.

And yet, no sooner has one sketched out the rough contours of the citizenship battlefield than one is forced to modify them. Thus, while the individualist and consumerist approach to public services is largely followed by contemporary Conservatives, under certain conditions the community is relied upon to deliver specific services – such as community care; or is exhorted to assist public agencies (for example, the police) in the maintenance of law and order, through schemes such as Neighbourhood Watch (Hill, 1994; Mayo, 1994). At the other end of the current party political debate, Labour and its associated supporters have acknowledged the importance of the consumer in the new individualist times (Labour Party, 1989; Hodge, 1991; Smith, 1992; Blair, 1994).

Similar concerns exist with regard to 'welfare'. Welfare is usually thought of – minimally – as measures undertaken to mitigate the excesses of market capitalism (Marshall, 1992). However, despite our familiarity with the term 'welfare state' there is no necessary relationship between welfare and state provision though, especially in the twentieth century, this has tended to be the dominant provision, despite recent government attempts to reduce it (Roche, 1992). Another caveat must be advanced in terms of the liberal and democratic context in which state welfare is usually perceived to be delivered. The examples of Bismarckian Germany and Stalinist Russia show that this context is not a *sine qua non* of state welfare (Roche, 1992).

Moreover, in addition to these issues there are those perceptions which see the welfare state in operation as the opposite of the benevolent complex of institutions originally envisaged. Thus, bureaucratic and insensitive service delivery, disproportionate exploitation by the middle classes or welfare restructuring (which has actually seen welfare entrapping and perpetuating people in poverty rather than liberating them from it) renders problematic the traditional association between welfare and social citizenship (Field, 1981; Le Grand, 1982; Marquand, 1992; Alcock, 1993). Further doubt about the beneficent effects of welfare is provided by the rhetorical hegemony of the 'welfare dependency' phraseology – an echo of the previously popular 'scroungers' and 'spongers' (Golding and Middleton, 1982; Golding, 1986; Alcock, 1993). The Labour Party has not really constructed an effective answer to this and seems to be portraying itself as a party of efficiency as much as a party of compassion. Electoral considerations may well have a role to play here as the bottom 20 per cent of the population, though traditionally more disposed to vote Labour, are less likely to turn out and do so. Much more important are the 70 per cent of the roughly diamond-shaped social structure. This is what Neil Kinnock meant when he suggested that rather than appealing to the 'have-nots' Labour should appeal to the 'have not got quite enoughs' (Lipsey, 1992).

It is to the range of issues associated with these debates that this chapter is devoted. We start by outlining the classical welfare treatment of citizenship encapsulated in the work of T.H. Marshall (in the next section) before addressing the Thatcherite reaction against the concept of 'social citizenship'. We then address what is the pressing issue for theorists of citizenship: whether the growth of poverty and unemployment, combined with 'race' and gender exclusion, undermine the basis for a shared conception of citizenship.

Activity 10.1

Why is the concept of citizenship contestable – and in what ways?

Citizenship and Welfare – T.H. Marshall

If the definitional debates concerning both citizenship and welfare appear to be somewhat complex then it would appear prima facie that the hopes are not high for an understanding of the relationship between citizenship and welfare. On one level this pessimism is misplaced. We have seen that the New Right variant of contemporary Conservatism has a clear, highly negative, view of the relationship between citizenship and welfare. This is, of course, something of a shock to that social democratic consensus of the three decades following the end of the Second World War. Thus, it is not, perhaps, surprising to find one of the seminal authors of that consensus being re-read, re-analysed and, to some extent, reasserted.

T.H. Marshall – and in particular his *Citizenship and Social Class* originally written in 1949 – has re-emerged as a central focus of discussion, as the debates over citizenship have grown in intensity during recent years (Turner, 1993). For Marshall, writing at a time of relative optimism when Rowntree's third social investigation of York had produced the opinion that poverty was effectively conquered in Britain (Alcock, 1993), the impact of welfare was substantial (Marshall, 1992). In effect, the welfare state had, for Marshall, resolved any substantial conflict between free-market capitalism and democracy. The gradual evolution of citizenship through its civil (liberty of the person, freedom of speech) and political (freedom to vote and participate politically) phases of the eighteenth and nineteenth centuries had culminated in the final version of social citizenship, which had now rendered the other versions fully meaningful (Marshall, 1992; cf. Steenbergen, 1994). Thus the institutionalization of the social forms of citizenship in the welfare state had – through measures such as unemployment benefit and health and education provision – achieved a remarkable social settlement. The inherent social inequalities of the class system produced by capitalism would now have their negative impact on individual life chances diminished. Suitably 'tamed', the new form of socialized capitalism would enhance the individual's commitment to the system. Class abatement had now been superseded by class fusion (Marshall, 1992).

Such Marshallian optimism has of course been widely criticized – from Marxists (Ginsburg, 1979; Gough, 1979) for ignoring the realities of class, patriarchal and racist power: and from social democrats (George and Wilding, 1984) for ignoring the realities of the making of social policy and hence the contingent nature of any form of social citizenship. Nevertheless, despite the criticism, there is still a sense of Marshallian legacy in the results of the research for the Speaker's Commission on Citizenship (1990), which maintained that 'the most important rights for the majority of British citizens' are 'social rights – to a minimum standard of living, to medical care, to a job and to education'. For the Commission this demonstrated the survivability of what Dahrendorf had described as an early-twentieth-century belief that 'civil and political rights are not worth an awful lot unless they are backed up by a certain social security which enables people to make use of these rights'.

Activity 10.2

- What is 'social citizenship'?
- To what extent do you think values associated with 'social citizenship' are central to present conceptions of citizens' rights and responsibilities?

The Thatcherite Effect?

Given the strength of this tradition and the considerable survey evidence which has shown that the values of social solidarity – including welfare – have not been undermined by the Thatcherite experiment (Jowell and Airey, 1985; Marquand, 1992), why is it therefore that the impression of the last 15 years appears to be characterized by Thatcher's view that 'there is no such thing as society'? At one level, of course, the answer seems relatively straightforward. The 1980s were years *not* of Thatcherite hegemony but of the crisis of opposition. In other words, the crisis in oppositional politics meant a fragmented parliamentary Opposition which, combined with Britain's insensitive first-past-the-post electoral system, distorted the political mirror of British attitudes. Thus Thatcher entrenched her political power, even though electorally the support for the Conservative Party consistently declined from the high point of 1979. As Marquand has put it, the decade of the 1980s 'is not a story of triumphant Thatcherism; it is a story of enfeebled Labourism. . . . Labour could not translate diffuse and unsystematic sympathy for broadly social democratic values into Labour votes on polling day' (1992: 192–3).

In seeking to explain why this was so, Marquand (1992) goes on to discuss the central theme of this chapter – citizenship. In particular, he focused on the failure of political citizenship and what he saw as the knock-on effects for social citizenship. This is not a new theme. Indeed, in 1985 R.W. Johnson, referring to the 'traditional weaknesses of left leadership in Britain', cited Harold Wilson's 'relegation of such issues as the abolition of public schools, reform of Parliament and the Lords, and . . . failure to deliver . . . more open government' as reflective of 'the left's longer term failure to grasp that in Britain the completion of the democratic revolution must needs

handling missing data, nor is it powerful enough to deal with categorical variables. Since EQS performs better with covariance data, standard deviations need to be provided to transform the correlations into covariances.

A path model reflects a theoretical need and is a complex and structured hypothesis that integrates a number of simple and elementary hypotheses in an organic manner. The explanatory power of the model is indicated by the values of the residual items. The smaller the residual values, the greater the explanatory power of the path model. The total effect of one variable to another variable in the model can be divided into direct effect and indirect effect. The direct effect is represented by the path coefficient directly connecting the two variables. The indirect effect is the product of the path coefficients of all the paths indirectly connecting the two variables. This decomposition of the causal effect is not the same as the decomposition of the correlation coefficient. But it gives a more complete understanding of the role of statistical control as well as the nature of partial correlations. Summing the values of path coefficients between two variables, the grand total will be the slope of a line showing their causal relationship.

If the data come from a random sample, F test may be used to determine whether or not a path coefficient can be inferred to the population, which in turn will determine if the path itself should be kept or not. The standardized path coefficient (p) can be transformed back to the concrete path coefficient (P) by using as a factor the ratio of the variances of the original and the standardized variables.

Generally, path analysis will require all the variables to be measured at the interval level or as continuous variables. Categorical variables may be treated as dummy variables as long as this will not excessively complicate the regression process. Log-linear analysis is another approach to examining the causal relations among categorical variables. For it, much reference material is available.

Intercorrelation

In the above, we discussed semi-multivariate analysis in terms of elaboration via some elementary means of statistical control, and the multiple causation model in light of two major categories, i.e., a single dependent variable and multiple dependent variables. The multiple causation model may also be characterized in another way, i.e., a model involving only interval variables (including regression and canonical correlation), and a model involving interval variables and nominal

precede any hopes of socialist transformation' (Johnson, 1985: 270). Nearly a decade later Will Hutton (1994) re-echoed these themes when, in an article on the relationship of a written constitution to the worker as citizen, he declared that 'without a more entrenched political citizenship, social and economic citizenship . . . does not exist'.

Activity 10.3

Outline the extent to which Britain has failed fully to establish 'political' citizenship, and show how this has affected the establishment of Marshall's 'subsequent' stage of 'social' citizenship.

Legacies of the 1980's – social exclusion, the 'new poor' and the underclass

In many ways these analyses show up another defect of Marshall's analysis. This is the almost Whig-like faith in the linear progression of citizenship, and myopia in relation to the huge political agenda still to be negotiated before adequate underpinning of the conditions of social citizenship can be achieved. One should not be too harsh on Marshall, however. As already indicated, he was – like all political and social theorists – a creature of his time. He could not be expected to foresee the challenge to the immediate post-war welfare provisions, especially when he was writing at the beginning of a decade which had seen the Conservative Party accept the post-war settlement and which was to see welfare expenditure rise at a phenomenal rate during the lifetime of three successive Conservative governments (Judge, 1982).

Similarly, he could not have been expected to foresee the break-up of the old working class and the emergence of new divisions around deprivation during the last two decades of the century. Such divisions were to render inappropriate the post-war welfare consensus on a work- and family-based social security system. Some of these divisions – e.g., female single parents, long-term unemployed, the homeless, minority ethnic communities – together with more 'traditionally' deprived groups – e.g., elderly people and people with disabilities, have been very much the victims of the 'exclusive society' (Lister, 1990). These sections of the population, marginalized by current social and economic trends, have had a recurrent description applied to them: 'the underclass' (see Chapter 12). This description can be a very misleading one. One author has even said it is so misleading as to be in need of redesignation as 'second class-citizens' (Hill, 1994; Steenbergen, 1994). Whatever the description, poverty and the subsequent social and political isolation produces 'a significant erosion of citizenship rights' (Hill, 1994: 4).

Such erosion was not foreseen by Marshall. Somewhat gender-blind in his analysis of citizenship (Bottomore, 1992), he also could not foresee the changing familial structures and restructured labour markets which have contributed to producing the female single-parent household, now one of the central folk-devils of current underclass demonology (Murray, 1994). These particular women have suffered a double blow. First, a continuing exclusion – along with women generally – from a patriarchally dominated labour market has meant continuing economic marginalization (Cram and Richardson, 1992; Adriaansens, 1994). Second, such marginalization is reinforced by a patriarchal income maintenance system which has starkly revealed the inadequacy of the Beveridgean optimism that an essentially male-dominated, full-time, workforce and familial structure would, through a contributory national insurance scheme, largely protect families against any short-term vagaries of the labour market. Moreover, the growth of what was originally intended to be a residual, discretionary, national assistance scheme into the huge income support programme of today has seen many female single parents trapped into – rather than liberated from – continuing poverty by the social security system (Alcock, 1993; Adriaansens, 1994).

Such structural factors – especially exclusion from the labour market – apply to the elderly. Their traditional association with life-cycle poverty is well documented, as is their recent comparative improvement through occupational and state pension schemes (Pampel and Williamson, 1989; Alcock, 1993; Walker, 1993). What gives elderly people their 'newness' in terms of poverty and consequent social exclusion is the emerging demographic time-bomb which will see elderly, non-working people becoming an increasing proportion of the population (Henwood, 1992; Hill, 1993). Correspondingly, the shrinking base of the workforce represents a less numerous source from which to finance the income maintenance and social care of elderly people. When this is combined with the eventual knock-on effects of an elderly population which has not enjoyed the relatively high-paid, full-time and secure working career of some current elderly people, then the prospect of a bleak and even more socially excluded life than is already experienced by elderly people looms large.

Society's reaction to current and possible future exclusion of the elderly from participative citizenship is, in many ways, central to the citizenship debate. For here is a test case of the extent to which market forces can be moderated by community or citizenship-orientated policies. Thus, as Midwinter (1992) points out, 'the empowerment of the elderly is central to a participative and community-based culture'. And yet, the prospect of 'the role of the older person as a participant-citizen' becoming 'familiar and accepted' (Midwinter, 1992) seems farther away than ever. The de-indexing of state pensions from earnings (Walker, 1993: 285), increasing emphasis on private pensions as the answer to the demographic time-bomb of the twenty-first century and increasing erosion of old people's home-based wealth through the privatized costs of residential care all represent a significant threat to the economic base of citizenship (Jones, 1992). Thus for elderly people – especially female elderly people (Groves, 1992) – there is increasing likelihood of social exclusion, if current circumstances persist. What

Marshall called 'full membership of the community' achieved socially through 'the right to a modicum of economic welfare and security . . . the right to share to the full in the social heritage and to live the life of a civilized being according to the standards prevailing in society' (Marshall, 1992: 8) appears to be a cruel mirage for such people. It remains to be seen whether future generations of old people continue the pressure-group tactics that have marked an increasing amount of self-assertion by certain groups of old people (MacQueen, 1993).

Self-assertion has come to characterize the activities of a number of groups from minority ethnic (particularly black and Asian) communities who have suffered, and continue to suffer, not only the exclusions already referred to, but also the consequences of institutionalized racism, as well as the direct aspects of racist activity. It is no surprise, therefore, to find that many of the indicators of poverty – unemployment, poor wages, poor housing and lack of educational achievement – feature disproportionately among the various groups of such people (Alcock, 1993). Whether or not this means, in the words of Harrison, that 'the system operates to their disadvantage . . . primarily because of class bias rather than racial bias' (1983: 387) is a contestable point. However, more than a decade after Harrison's controversial statement that 'institutional racialism is none other than institutional class-ism' (1983: 387), Modood offered some corroboration through his observation that 'Racial discrimination is not a discrete form of disadvantage because many forms of . . . "institutional discrimination" and racial disadvantage are closely related to structural inequalities better understood in terms of class' (1994: 5).

Whether such a perspective owes more to a class-based analysis of discrimination and deprivation or to an analysis which recognizes the complexity of the black 'community' and differences between colour racism and cultural racism is not the subject of debate here. What seems to be less contestable is the fact that the last decade has seen more black representation in community leadership and among politicians (Younge, 1995). Moreover, one recent study – based largely on the Afro-Caribbean 'community' – has found that while 'very few think racism has disappeared', most black people believe that on balance, things have improved in the 'last 10 years' (Younge, 1995). The 'things' referred to in the study highlight, *inter alia*, more sensitive policing, more mixed marriages and a general feeling of 'social ease and confidence' characterized by a perception that 'more doors are open to [black people] than ever before'. And yet the same study, drawing on official Department of Environment statistics, also observes that 'what is interesting about the guarded optimism' is the fact that, using the DOE's own indicators of deprivation – such as employment, mortality rates and overcrowded housing – things have got worse during the last 10 years. Moreover, the increased level of racist attacks (up by 75 per cent) between 1988 and 1992 has affected 'non-white people across the board', though it is admitted that most of this increase in violence is directed against Asians.

'Asians' is of course a generic term which itself hides similar complexities to the catch-all phrase 'black'. Indeed, one contemporary commentator has said that, as an illustration, the 'differences between . . . East African Asians and Bangladeshis are much greater than between Asians and Non-Asians' (Modood, 1994: 2). Thus the cosy stereotypes of an upwardly mobile 'Asian' middle class committed to running its own businesses sits uneasily with statistics showing Pakistanis (29 per cent) and Bangladeshis (32 per cent) experiencing more than three times the 1991 Census national unemployment figure. Such disadvantage is further compounded, for example, by Bangladeshis being grossly over-represented in semi-skilled and unskilled manual work (Modood, 1994). Moreover, not only do such predominantly Muslim communities suffer from some of the worst socio-economic disadvantages and colour racism but also from what Modood calls 'cultural-racism' (1994: 6). He believes this phenomenon is targeted at groups 'perceived to be assertively "different" and not trying to "fit in" ' as perceived 'on the grounds of one's dress, dietary habits, or desire to take leave from work on one's holy days rather than those prescribed by the custom and practice of the majority community' (Modood, 1994: 6). Indeed, it is this self-assertiveness, which Modood calls 'public ethnicity' (the claims that ethnic difference is not first something that needs 'mere' toleration but needs to be publicly acknowledged, resourced and represented), that is a particular focus of the 'backlash' of 'cultural-racism' (Modood, 1994: 2).

Given such hostility, which, Modood maintains, is not matched with anti-discrimination legislation and add to it the 'chronic' under-representation of Muslims in mainstream institutions and fora and the obscuring of Muslim disadvantage through the use of blunt statistical terms such as 'black' or 'Asian', then the plight of nearly half of the United Kingdom's non-white population is – in Modood's view – 'not simply illustrative but urgent' (Modood, 1994: 14). Clearly, for Modood, such a situation demands certain public responses such as 'the urgent extension' of anti-discrimination law to defend all prospective employees regardless of religious background and a new criminal offence of racial violence. And yet, as he himself observes, 'the reality is that those groups who do evidence social mobility (Indians and Chinese) have no special access to state power and have assiduously kept a low political profile'. 'This' he suggests 'should encourage sober reflection on the nature and extent of state intervention in this area' (Modood, 1994: 12). This might, arguably, lead to confusion about the significance of the lack of Muslim representation in 'mainstream institutions and fora' to which he later makes reference. Perhaps, more generously, we might aver that the very issue of role models – whether in politics, media, arts and sport, or trade unions – is very much a double-edged sword.

Thus it might well lead to what Phillips (1995) seems to regard as the illusion rather than the reality of black influence in key decision-making areas. Moreover, the emergent black professional middle class might well distance itself from those still trapped in the inner urban areas, so creating what Howe (1995) has described as the 'fracturing' of black communities. Finally, role models might only seem to reinforce white racist stereotypes of black people – especially in respect of sport (Hill, 1995). The picture of issues around citizenship as they apply to the non-white population in Britain is a complex one. Some communities have assumed a more prominent role whilst some have taken a lower profile – though not necessarily suffering from this in any socio-economic sense. Indeed, some sections of the Asian community might even see security in an increased distancing from the white majoritarian society in desperation at the intolerance they feel they face. The Muslim 'Parliament' and the calls for separate Muslim schools are some examples. Ironically, even these aims nevertheless require some assertion of Modood's 'public ethnicity'. Whether such aims can sit easily with any future moves by a white majoritarian society to develop a more inclusive citizenship will remain a contestable issue as far as one can foresee.

Reactions to Social Exclusion

The issue of whether state action can or should be taken to reintegrate or reinsert such excluded groups has itself been the subject of much controversy (Cannan et al., 1992). For the theorists of the New Right, to attempt such action is dangerous social engineering and liable to lead to a diminution of liberty rather than its enhancement. Thus, apart from securing the basic freedoms – speech, religion, assembly, equality before the law and so on – the state should simply hold the ring. People are thus not physically prevented from making what they will of their lives. Whether or not they succeed has nothing to do with citizenship, which only clouds the clarity of market-based relations between individuals. Thus, in a famous phrase Keith Joseph – one of the leading architects of the New Right – declares that 'poverty is not unfreedom' (Joseph and Sumption, 1979: 47). For the state to interfere in the establishment of spurious social rights would not – for another architect of the New Right, Powell – be an establishment of rights *per se* but would be to elevate human needs into rights (Phillips, 1977). There can never be any defined sense of need to attempt it would be to risk the worst excesses of the old totalitarian Communist systems. Needs are best left to the automatic play of the market. Social casualties – just like bad weather – are unfortunate consequences of a natural system (see Plant, 1984).

Similar suspicion about state involvement with social citizenship – though for very different reasons – are expressed at the other end of the political spectrum. Marxist suspicion of the concept of citizenship as (in practice) implicitly excluding many people, including lone mothers, long-term unemployed people and so on is linked with a view of the welfare state as maintaining and legitimating social divisions such as class and patriarchal and racialized social relations (Ginsburg, 1992; Williams, 1992). This is unsurprising, as the materialist explanation of history shows legal and political superstructures resting on the economic structure. In capitalism this means, in effect, state action biased in favour of the capitalists (George and Wilding, 1985). A similar congruence of views has surrounded the role of voluntarism, as both right and left have sought to develop alternatives to the perceived oppressive and inefficient delivery of welfare services by state bureaucracy. In an attempt to rehabilitate citizenship for its own purposes, a leading spokesperson for the late-Thatcherite agenda sought to portray the 'active citizen' in quasi-Victorian terms. Such a citizen would act from motives which see individual effort as far more reliable than any collectively imposed solutions, springing as it does from altruistic and socially respons-ible motives. Thus, the active citizen was, for Hurd in 1988, a reflection of the mixture of self-help and voluntarism which was, for certain comment-ators, part of the Thatcherite ideology's project to roll back the state through a redefining of individual responsibility to the rest of society, as well as trying to restrict the responsibilities of the state for the fate of individuals (Cram and Richardson, 1992).

The role of voluntarism in this project became, for a while, mixed up with the welfare pluralism debate in the 1980s. Many on the left were associated with this development, as it sought community-based alternatives to tradi-tional state-bureaucratized welfare services. However, early in the 1980s the left became suspicious of welfare pluralism as a 'stalking horse' for the New Right attack on welfare services *per se* (Lawrence, 1983; and cf. Chapter 13). Consequently, the anti-bureaucratic mode of delivery and policy deter-mination in the welfare sphere has tended to be swept up with the debate over the role of new social movements – as we shall see later.

Concentration on the extremes of the political spectrum should not deflect us, however, from consideration of the tremendous struggle by adherents of the liberal collectivist/social democratic consensus, as they sought to resist the onslaught of Thatcherism. Particular resistance has arisen against the view of a citizen as merely an 'economic citizen', whereby citizenship involvement (as exemplified by the consumerist approach of the Citizen's Charter) is measured by redress rather than through rights (Hill, 1994). Such resistance has taken the form of exhortatory statements by leading social democrats to recognize that 'individuals are socially interdependent beings'. (Blair 1994: 4). More substantively, there have been renewed attempts to establish clear philosophical and socially scientific principles of need as the basis of social security policy (Townsend, 1979; Mack and Lansley, 1985). In particular, such writers have sought, in their attempts to eradicate want, to utilize income maintenance policies as a first step towards reintegration of the socially excluded within mainstream society. Such attitudes closely resemble Marshall's views on the need for the opportunity for full participa-tion in society as an indispensable pre-requisite of social citizenship.

However, it can be argued that income maintenance/social security policies are not sufficient by themselves to reintegrate individuals into society. Indeed, in societies where the traditional institutions of social integration – such as the Church and local communities – have been eroded in recent decades, an increase in the level of labour participation may be the most significant integrating factor. Such social participation is increasingly regarded as central to any meaningful sense of citizenship (Adriaansens, 1994). Statements about the necessity of achieving a higher level of labour participation – namely, reducing unemployment and at a rate of remuneration accepted as capable of sustaining citizenship within a traditional industrialized country – remain problematic (Oppenheim, 1990; Low Pay Unit, 1992; Panorama, 1994). Similarly problematic is the ability to act on the recognition – by both politicians and academics – that the manner in which welfare institutions exercise their power is crucial (Marquand, 1992; Blair, 1994); crucial because, as a number of commentators have attested, the experience of citizens' interaction with welfare institutions has often been that of a 'ramshackle . . . remote and high-handed despotism' (Marquand, 1992: 215), which 'only someone who has not actually been on the receiving end of the welfare state would dare call . . . an instance of civil altruism at work' (Ignatieff, 1991: 234). And yet, for Marquand – notwithstanding the various attempts at local socialism throughout the 1980s (Boddy and Fudge, 1984; Lansley et al., 1991) – the 'case for non-statist decentralist participatory forms of public intervention was rarely made, and still more rarely heard' (Marquand, 1992: 216). As indicated, Marquand and others believe that much of the answer lies in Britain's failure to build a powerful and extrenched culture of political citizenship – the indispensable foundation for controlling the institutions of social citizenship. Lacking such a 'civic culture' the British (or at least the English) 'were not, and never had been, citizens of a state, with the rights and duties that go with citizenship, they were subjects of a monarch' (Marquand, 1992: 215). This approach finds echoes in at least one of Turner's (1993) four ideal typical forms of citizenship; that is, the passive, or developed-from-above form.

Activity 10.4

Outline an argument which maintains that a new welfare consensus is vital to the creation of effective citizenship in Britain. What might be the major pillars of such a consensus?

Conclusion: a New Agenda for Citizenship?

Whether such a passive tradition of citizenship can be transformed into a more participative culture, whereby the institutions of social citizenship are made more effectively subject to popular control, remains to be seen. Marquand's practical examples – of 'patients in the doctor's waiting room . . . parents outside the school playground, the crowd waiting to approach the DHSS counter' (1992: 215) receiving what they consider to be satisfactorily

responsive treatment – are left unpursued in terms of detailed operationalization. Moreover, none of the non-statist, decentralized, participatory forms of
public intervention seem to have been considered for application to these
welfare services. Currently the Local Management of Schools provisions of
the 1988 Education Act and the internal market of the health service appear
to be following a privatized, individualistic and consumerist approach to
decentralized authority.

And yet it may be that, as Marquand seems to maintain, a confused
British public blundered into accepting the New Right's view of the whole
project of social citizenship, and adopted exit, the quintessential mechanism
of the market, taking one's custom elsewhere. But Marquand posits the view
that such an approach is only temporary and, in accordance with the
pendulum phenomenon of contemporary society, will swing from the
privatism of the 1980s to a 'tentative and uncertain collectivism', thus
reflecting the reaction of the 1960s and early 1970s to the privatism of the
1950s (Marquand, 1992: 214, 220). One obvious rejoinder immediately
suggests itself: the Conservative Party's victory at the 1992 General Election. New Right market liberalism in the shape of direct/indirect privatization of the railways and the Post Office (an invaluable access point for the
delivery of welfare) is still very much alive and kicking. Moreover, the
continued demonization of welfare recipients – especially female single
parents – continues the strong Poor Law tradition of less eligibility (Ditch,
1992: 38). Nevertheless, the alternative perspectives become ever more
insistent. At a macro level, the European Union (EU) is seen increasingly as
a guarantor of certain aspects of social citizenship not acknowledged by
Britain's Conservative government (Alcock, 1993). At a more micro level
the EU, again, is anxious – through its anti-poverty, and now anti-social
exclusion, programmes – to encourage the socially excluded themselves to
roll back their powerlessness through essentially local participation and
involvement (Cannan et al., 1992).

Parallel to – and occasionally touching on – such developments are the
many issue-based movements/'publics', particularly strong around debates
and action on environmental matters. In one sense this reflects the more
diversified, less homogeneous society than the value-coherent one of Marshall's day (Bottomore, 1992). What has, alternatively, been called the
emergence of a post-Fordist society (Cochrane and Anderson, 1989) has
coincided with increased alienation from the 'official' political system and
more commitment to other forms of non-orthodox citizenship dedicated to
mutual support, help and involvement. As such, the discourse around rights
and obligations, traditionally focused on the state, has become increasingly
refocused on what has been called 'civil society' (for example, Roche, 1992:
40).

Leading activists in such developments are the young, who are at the
forefront of what has variously been called new social movements
(Cochrane and Anderson 1989) and DIY politics (Vidal, 1994; and see
Chapter 8). One charge levelled against this relatively new phenomenon is

that of single issuism (Younge, 1994). But this is not a charge easily accepted by young activists. Thus, for one such activist, 'the gays, road protestors, ravers, animal libbers, the homeless, squatters' are 'all crying for new political values and social justice'. This, she believes, is achieved by 'fighting for each other's causes, making all the links between themselves, between the Third World, and broadening out the debate so it becomes one cause' (Vidal, 1994). This is not just part of 'community resistance to senseless change' or to 'hierarchical power structures dominated by men and decisions made without consultation'. More positively, it is seen as part of a huge growth in 'DIY culture' through which 'people . . . organize themselves in a co-operative way' (Vidal, 1994). Such self-help networks are part of both a local and global phenomenon linked with participants' assertions that the environment cannot be separated from social issues, nor health issues from traffic, nor endangered peoples from the way industrialized nations consume (Vidal, 1994).

These manifestations of loosely linked examples of mutual co-operation are part of what Roche (1992) has called the new phenomenon of duties discourse. This citizenship is defined not by reference to the official 'state' sphere, nor by 'rights' claimed against this sphere. By contrast, its reference points are the mutual expectations of and obligations towards one's fellow participants – not just in one's own immediate group but also in the associate groups and, ripple-like, in wider social movements towards which such groups contribute.

This 'rainbow coalition' may have been derided as utopian (Johnson, 1985), but the motivations remain strong and clearly, in an age of increased alienation from the political system, may yet form an alternative agenda. Such an agenda, as well as forming a coherent value framework for a new style of living for its supporters, may also act as a strong exogenous influence on the mainstream political agenda, as it struggles to develop alternatives to the 'spoon-fed individualism and the need to make money' (Barton, 1994), so characteristic of the last two decades of the twentieth century.

Thus the socially excluded are not necessarily dependent on the state for their re-integration into mainstream society. In many cases some of them are showing that they do not want to be reintegrated but, on the contrary, want to act as a form of pressure group to change mainstream society itself. In any event they are conducting themselves – and their pressure on mainstream society – from a committed self-help and co-operative perspective. The first of these perspectives is, ironically, one of the highly prized social values of the New Right, but for very different reasons. Similarly, criticisms of traditional bureaucratic forms of welfare provision have been voiced for diametrically opposed reasons. Which brings us back to where we started this chapter – citizenship as a contestable concept. Whether New Right individualist consumerism, traditional Tory voluntarism, social democratic, or even new social movement perspectives act as the main driving force of citizenship at any one time remains to be seen.

Hazarding a gaze into the futuristic bowl one can foresee a continued social – if not officially political – erosion of individualist and consumerist approaches to citizenship and its relationship with welfare. What replaces such an approach remains problematic, however, as does welfare's relationship to citizenship. The post-war social democratic consensus has been severely challenged in the last 17 years. The traditional 'cosy' assumptions of citizenship have correspondingly been shaken to their foundations. The consensus has not been totally destroyed, as we have seen. But it clearly cannot simply be reinstated in its old form. A new Marshallian 'coherence' is not yet developed but is the subject of vigorous debate. Much of the new 'official' reforming agenda seems to revolve around the reinvigoration of (mainly) political citizenship through constitutional reform, enhanced regional and local government and a nebulous 'communitarianism'. Whether this provides a sufficient reinvigoration of political citizenship, in the context of political DIY, and whether this will, thereby, lead on to a more substantive underpinning of social citizenship through, for example, popular accountability of welfare and welfarist institutions, remains uncertain.

Activity 10.5

To what extent and in what ways is new thinking on citizenship being shaped by non-traditional political movements?

---

variables (including discriminant analysis, ANOVA, ANCOVA, MANOVA, and MANCOVA). Ordinal variables may be categorized as nominal variables, or simply treated as interval variables depending on how this has been statistically justified.

Path analysis is in a sense a combination of multiple causation with elaboration. We have discussed all these models without specifying the kinds of variables they may deal with in addition to measurement levels. Surely they may be used to analyze the relationships among individual variables or simple facts. Yet they can also deal with composite variables representing complex theoretical constructs or their components/factors. The use of composite measures is based on a twofold purpose: the need for data reduction in empirical analysis and the need for more comprehensive and concise constructs in theory development. In terms of measurement, this is an issue of how to use multi-item measures. Instead of simply lumping all the items or a pool of individual variables together, the notion of dimensionality raises an important theoretical issue regarding the hypothetical latent structure of a broad construct. Methodologically, the methods of grouping individual variables have various applications in exploratory data analysis. In many cases, the grouping of individual variables and the construction of appropriate composite measures is a precondition for using the techniques that have been discussed here.

Intercorrelation is a model different from the multiple causation model and the path model. It does not distinguish between dependent variables and independent variables, and the concern is mainly the reduction of the complexity of data and the clarification of a possible latent structure for the purpose of further analysis. By appropriately subgrouping a large pool of individual items, intercorrelation analysis can be used to explore their relationships more effectively than simple correlations. This technique, sometimes also called multidimensional space analysis, can also address the issue of multidimensionality in measurement. The most frequently used procedures include principal component analysis, factor analysis, and cluster analysis.

It should be noted that the intercorrelation model may be used either to study the relationships among variables (some of them are called stimuli in psychological studies) or to study the relationships among subjects (cases). The former is sometimes called R technique, which is geared to general theory development, and the latter Q technique, which is more important to practical classification. Principal component and factor analyses are usually used as R techniques to subgroup variables, whereas cluster analysis is often used as a Q technique to

154

11

Universalism or Selectivism? The Provision of Services in the Modern Welfare State

Alan Pratt

Once the political decision is taken to remove, wholly or in part, the allocation of a limited range of commodities from the sole ambit of market operations, governments are faced with a new set of problems. If command over income is not to determine the population's access to education, heath care, replacement income and the other goods whose distribution, in one way or another, lies at the heart of most welfare states, then what is? More specifically, what criteria do governments use? Who gets what and why?

This chapter is devoted to an examination of the concepts of universality and selectivity together with hybrids such as positive discrimination. It attempts to establish their precise meaning and their strengths and weaknesses against a range of characteristics (such as cost, effectiveness in meeting ostensible policy objectives, impact on labour market participation, stigmatization and so on). Following this, attention is focused on the historiography of the debate since the reconstruction of the 'welfare state' in the 1940s. Since the early 1950s the debate has often been dormant (though never extinct), has sometimes been dismissed as 'the most misleading of trivial dichotomies', and as a conflict between ideological ghosts (Pinker, 1971). However, what at one level is a technical discussion about how best to allocate scarce resources is also a reflection of a conflict between competing visions of the good society, as evidenced by the periodic outbreak of hostilities between these political economies whenever the long relative decline of the British economy is brought into a clearer focus by, usually, a twin crisis in public finances and the foreign exchange markets.

That these ideas are still at the very heart of the politics of social policy is vividly demonstrated by the activities of the Commission on Social Justice set up in December 1992, almost exactly 50 years after the publication of the Beveridge Report, *Social Insurance and Allied Services*, on the initiative of the late John Smith, then Leader of the Labour Party. Whether the work contained in individual Issue Papers published for the Commission by the Institute for Public Policy Research (for example, Papers 1 and 2, November 1993) and in the Commission's own final report, *Social Justice: Strategies for National Renewal* (1994) is any more successful in resolving these possibly intractable questions remains to be seen, but what cannot be denied is the political controversy it has generated within the Labour Party.

Thus the main aims of this chapter are:

1 to develop a clear understanding of the meaning of universalism and selectivism;
2 to examine protagonists' claims about their respective and relative merits;
3 to become familiar with changes in the academic debate; and
4 to locate these intellectual exchanges in the real world of British economics and politics since the 1940s.

Concepts and Definitions

Given that these contested concepts have periodically generated intense debate and disagreement among and between their respective supporters, it is, perhaps, rather surprising that the literature does not offer many sustained or lengthy attempts to define them with any degree of precision. It may be, of course, that their meaning is so self-evident that any such attempt would be superfluous.

One approach to the problem of definition is to ignore it completely, to say that there can never be any truly universal or selective services because they are differentially used and financed (thus healthy people will not use the NHS, those with no dependent children will not receive Child Benefit or Family Credit, everyone pays a different amount of taxation depending on their income levels and patterns of expenditure). That this approach is a little disingenuous seems not unlikely. Child Benefit is only intended to be received by parent(s) with one or more dependent children. The real question facing government is that once having recognized the extra demands placed on family income by the presence of dependent children, what programme employing what techniques of allocation is best suited to assist the state in the execution of its accepted responsibility of helping families in the critical task of rearing the next generation? By definition, childless families will not receive any benefit designed to deliver assistance to families with dependent children. To argue that because families without dependent children do not receive Child Benefit makes this particular programme selective and not universal is bizarre and almost wilfully neglects the real practical and philosophical issues necessarily attached to questions of the allocation of scarce public resources.

Given the significance of his contribution to the development of the entire discipline of Social Policy we are almost compelled to go to the work of Richard Titmuss for at least the beginnings of enlightenment. Although he was often regarded as the high priest of universalism and as an unswerving critic of selectivity, Titmuss's position was in reality rather more complex, as will become apparent as this chapter unfolds. (For an excellent analysis of the development of Titmuss's work see Reisman, 1977.) For the moment, though, it is enough to consider his understanding of what the terms mean. In one of his most important collections of essays Titmuss (1976) offered a view of universalism which goes beyond a simple definition but which identifies many of the themes central to the debate. Having asserted that *universalism* was the principle embodied in such legislation as the 1944 Education Act, the 1946 National Insurance Acts, the 1945 Family Allowances Act and the 1946 National Health Service Act, he argues that:

> One fundamental historical reason for the adoption of this principle was the aim of making services available and accessible to the whole population in such ways as would not involve users in any humiliating loss of status, dignity or self-respect. There should be no sense of inferiority, pauperism, shame or stigma in the use of a publicly provided service; no attribution that one was being or becoming a 'public burden'. Hence the emphasis on the social rights of all citizens to use or not to use as responsible people the services made available by the community in respect of certain needs which the private market and the family were unable or unwilling to provide universally. If these services were not provided for everybody by everybody they would either not be available at all, or only for those who could afford them, and for others on such terms as would involve the infliction of a sense of inferiority and stigma. (Titmuss, 1976: 129)

In contrast, selectivity, which could mean many different things to most critics of 'welfare statism', denoted an individual means test, some enquiry into resources to identify poor people who should be provided with free services or cash benefits, be excused charges, or pay lower charges (Titmuss, 1976: 115).

Perhaps one of the clearest attempts to define both universalism and selectivity can be found in a brief essay by Collard (1971) in a polemic produced for the Child Poverty Action Group. Collard argues that the criterion of need as the basis of resource allocation should not be income but a range of relatively objective criteria such as the need for medical attention, pregnancy, having dependent children and so on. 'That is to say, there will, for any type of benefit, be a *trigger criterion* which, if satisfied, entitles a person to that benefit regardless of income' (1971: 38; emphasis in original). Selectivists had always argued that this relatively simple needs-based approach represented a waste of resources and that a more efficient, because a more clearly targeted, method ought to be employed. Thus selectivists 'wish to impose a double criterion for free benefits : first a trigger criterion of the objective sort that I have just mentioned and, secondly, *a low income criterion*. Only those people satisfying both criteria actually get the benefit' (Collard, 1971: 38; emphasis in original).

Davies's examination of the school meals service represents a rigorous and powerful investigation into the theory and practice of selectivity, in the course of which he necessarily tests universalists' objections to the residualist model of welfare. We will have good cause to refer to it consistently in much of what follows. Thus it might not seem unreasonable to expect Davies to have offered some definition of the terms in the way that Collard and Titmuss did. That he does not do this is perhaps a reflection of the earlier observation that the meaning of the respective allocative systems is so obvious that one need not waste valuable time in explicating one's position. He contents himself by arguing that

> The essence of the selectivist prescription is that charging should be applied more widely as an instrument of resource allocation in social policy; but that the commodities thus allocated are judged by society to be of a 'merit' character when their recipients are those most vulnerable in markets, so that the consumption of the poor must be safeguarded by the remission of charges. Since the vulnerability of the consumer is due to poverty, it is logical that a means test should be used as the criterion of eligibility for the remission. (Davies, with Reddin, 1978: 7)

Davies's understanding of universalism as a concept, its precise meaning, has to be inferred from his exposition of the case that its promoters have developed over the years. Basically, it is very much the same as Collard's: universal services are available on the basis of a single, trigger criterion.

Activity 11.1

1 How would you define universalism and selectivism?
2 Which of the following do you think the state should provide, (a) universally, (b) selectively, (c) not at all?
   (i) health care, (ii) child benefit, (iii) dental care, (iv) free public transport, (v) access to leisure facilities

---

The Case for Selectivism

On the surface at least, the selectivist argument is both attractive and powerful. In a world whose reality is described and circumscribed by the existence of scarce resources and, in effect, unlimited demands on those resources, it would be sensible, efficient and just to construct public policy in such a way that these scarce resources go to those people who could derive most benefit from their consumption. All that government has to do is to decide on the appropriate volume of resources available, identify those whose needs are greatest and devise service programmes and delivery systems to direct the right benefit to the right people. Common sense and compassion demand no less. In what follows immediately this simple cameo is developed in more detail and in slightly more technical language, but the essence remains the same: it is wrong on every count to treat unequal need equally.

Arguments for selectivity have been set down in many places and on many occasions by the committed, such as Harris (1963, 1965), Seldon and Gray (1967), but one of the most rigorous, coherent and objective expositions of the core of these arguments can be found in Davies's (1978) analysis of the school meals service. For Davies the selectivist position rests on a number of key assumptions which need to be understood before the details of the analysis can be properly evaluated. Thus:

1   The goods and services whose allocation lies at the heart of the modern welfare state, such as health care, income maintenance entitlements, housing, education and what in Britain are called the personal social services, are indistinguishable in character and nature from those goods and services usually distributed through market mechanisms (clothing, consumer durables and so forth). Unlike defence and law and order, they are not truly 'public goods'; that is, there is no 'free rider' principle involved in their allocation and consumption and therefore their distribution through normal market procedures would be entirely appropriate. Moreover, it is probably true to say that these markets should be natural and autonomous, arising out of spontaneous association, rather than the 'quasi-markets' considered in Chapter 13 of this book.

2   The price mechanism within the market is fulfilling its primary task of acting as an efficient signalling device to well informed consumers and suppliers.

3   Demand is not extremely inelastic, so that if the price was at a level not reflecting the true costs of production to society of producing a commodity an inefficient allocation of resources would result.

4   Consumers behave in a rational manner and make rational judgements about costs and benefits. This assumption of rationality is probably the most fundamental of all of the assumptions about human behaviour which lie at the heart of the neo-liberal project, and in this context it is interesting to note the findings of some recent research in the United States which appears to provide solid empirical evidence casting doubt on this centrepiece of neo-classical political economy (Hutton, 1995).

5   Davies offers an interesting addition to the orthodox account of selectivist philosophy when he suggests that 'at the heart of the selectivist argument lies the assumption that consumers face sets of opportunities and incentives which they will seize, in order to make the best of diverse circumstances' (1978: 9). He argues that the implication of this position is that the cultural obstacles to grasping the opportunities referred to above, including the claiming of benefit, are great for only a small minority of the target population. 'It is therefore neither necessary nor right in principle to subordinate the choice of policy instruments to the needs of those whose culture imposes such obstacles' (1978: 9). In fact, since their culture is believed to be a significant feature in their experience of poverty its modification should be a major policy objective.

Armed with these assumptions it is now possible to set down the major features of the selectivist case. Thus:

1   Charging should be used more widely as a technique of resource allocation in the arena of social provision, but once these 'services' come within the ambit of state intervention their distribution should take on the character of 'merit' goods 'when their recipients are those most vulnerable in markets so that the consumption of the poor must be safeguarded by the remission of charges' (Davies, 1978: 7). Since the consumer is

vulnerable because of poverty it is logical that entitlement to 'free' benefits or the remission of charges should be determined by the application of a means test as the eligibility criterion (the secondary criterion in Collard's definition of selectivity noted above).

2   The supply of services made available should reflect the costs to society of making them available and so provide an incentive to potential consumers to behave rationally, thus securing a more efficient allocation of scarce social resources. Charges deter; they are meant to deter.

3   Market operations provide an incentive and an environment within which suppliers have to operate efficiently. They cannot do this when allocations are made through administrative and political processes.

4   The evidence, from opinion surveys, shows that there was no general consensus in favour of universalism. One such survey claimed to show that there were almost twice as many people in favour of selective benefits as of universal benefits (Houghton, 1967).

The Case for Universalism

Universalists approach the question of the distribution of scarce resources from a different perspective than selectivists and use a very different set of concepts and language. Against the claims of efficiency, of cost, of market supremacy and of calculating individuals they counterpose a collectivity in which citizens and their families are often the victims of the rapid change that characterizes modern industrial societies in an increasingly integrated global economy. Economic change creates losers as well as winners, and consequently one of the central problems facing us is the question of where the costs of this 'progress' ultimately lie. The fundamental fact was 'that for many consumers the services used are not essentially benefits or increments to welfare at all; they represent partial compensations for disservices, for social costs and social insecurities which are the product of a rapidly changing industrial-urban society' (Titmuss, 1976: 133).

It was becoming more and more difficult to identify the causal agency or agencies responsible for these diswelfares and so, impossible to seek redress through the courts. Thus we have to consider the potential of universalist and selectivist social services for meeting the problems of 'multiple causality and the diffusion of disservices'. For Titmuss the response was relatively clear: 'Non-discriminating universalist services are in part the consequence of unidentifiable causality. If disservices are wasteful (to use the economists' concept of waste) so welfare *has* to be wasteful' (1976: 133; emphasis added).

Universalists reject each of the assumptions on which the selectivists' case is based, and in so doing necessarily replace them with their own. Thus:

1   The nature of the goods at the heart of social provision is such that their distribution through market mechanisms is inappropriate. Access to, and experience of, health care, education, income maintenance, housing and

so on is so important in determining the nature and quality of everyone's life experiences that allocation cannot be left to command over resources in markets. There is a collective responsibility and a mutual interest in attempting to ensure the guarantee of a certain level of consumption, a level determined by political and administrative judgement. The social services then are properly to be regarded as merit goods.

2   For a variety of psychological and organizational reasons, individuals' ability to claim entitlement to what for them are merit goods is more limited than generally thought. As Titmuss observed, selectivists over-estimated 'the potential of the poor, without help, to understand and manipulate an increasingly ad hoc society' (Titmuss, 1976).

3   The receipt of a means-tested service could be regarded as symbolic of the clash between the social policy ethic (described by Boulding as 'that which is centred in those institutions that create integration and dis-courage alienation' (1967: 7) and the work ethic, a conflict which, according to Davies, means that the ' "evil repute" of the means test is in some circumstances powerful, pervasive and ineradicable' (1978: 11). The receipt of a means-tested service necessarily involves a loss of self-esteem and consequently stigmatization by others 'because it creates a conflict between the work ethic and obtaining benefits which the potential claimant thinks that he (or the dependants for whom he is claiming) needs' (Davies, 1978: 11).

Social cohesion and integration demanded the provision of universal ser-vices, concerns that were imprinted on the minds of those who shaped the reconstruction of the British welfare state in the 1940s, conscious as they were of the systematic degradation represented by administrative devices such as the Household Means Test. Trade-union leadership was even willing to accept the quintessentially regressive poll tax of flat rate National Insurance contributions as the primary funding mechanism of Beveridge's income maintenance proposals if it appeared to guarantee subsistence level benefits without means testing (Pratt, 1988).

Activity 11.2

In what ways do the assumptions on which universalists and selectivists base their arguments differ? How might these differences be reconciled?

From Principle to Practice

Thus far our discussion has been pitched at the level of general principle. It is now time to switch to a consideration of the philosophies in action at programmatic level to see how they fare in practice. What does experience in the real world of policy implementation tell us and what can we learn from it?

Because universal services are made available through the application of a relatively objective trigger criterion (illness or unemployment, or the presence of dependent children in a family), it is not too difficult to set up administrative structures to deliver the appropriate service, be it health care, cash transfers, education or whatever to the relevant target population. All of the evidence suggests that take-up rates are high and administrative costs low. Consequently, opposition to universalism in social provision rests on opinions about financial costs and what is held to be the waste involved in providing services to those who allegedly do not need them. These opinions are necessarily subjective in nature and reflective of political preference and value judgement. Given this, and the fact that British social policy has become increasingly selective in nature, especially, though not exclusively, over the last 17 years, it would seem appropriate to concentrate on selectivism in action. Moreover, it should also be noted that since the foundation of the Institute of Economic Affairs in 1957 the intellectual pace has been set by selectivist theoreticians.

The main elements of a general critique of means-tested social provision have been well established for many years and include a consideration of the following: stigma; take-up rates; administrative costs; the creation of poverty traps and a poverty plateau; and, finally, the impact of economic and social change. It is to each of these that we now turn.

Stigma

Stigma has been well defined as 'a loss of self-respect and personal dignity, a sense of guilt, of shame, of personal fault or failure. It means the sensation of second class citizenship that results from discrimination' (Reisman, 1977: 45).

More than anyone else Titmuss believed that stigma was an inherent characteristic of selective social provision, a characteristic that provided much of the moral case for universalism. To claim means-tested benfits constituted a self-declaration of failure, of inadequacy, of poverty; it represented a demonstration that the claimant was unable to cope in a competitive market economy. Apart from the incalculable psychological damage this inflicts on people, universalists have taken it as an article of faith that the reality of stigma acts as a deterrent to the take-up of welfare entitlements. That take-up rates are low, very low in some cases, is not in doubt, but what is more problematic is the significance of stigma as a factor in this outcome. The evidence is not conclusive (Davies, 1978; Page, 1984).

Take-up Rates

Means-tested benefits have always been characterized by low take-up rates. All of the evidence shows this clearly. Although the proportion of a particular target population claiming particular benefits varies, only rarely does it reach over 50 per cent of those eligible. Governments have always accepted that such benefits will never be claimed by the whole of a relevant group and have budgeted accordingly. When the Family Income Supplement (FIS) was introduced in 1971 the government only made financial provision available for an estimated take-up figure of 85 per cent and committed itself to a very elaborate take-up campaign to achieve even that figure. Take-up campaigns can be successful in raising awareness of the availability of means-tested benefits and, if advertising and other publicity campaigns are intensive and maintained over a long period of time, then take-up rates can be increased.

Such campaigns are expensive, though, and obviously add to administrative and operating costs and so cannot be maintained indefinitely. They demonstrate the prescience of Collard's observation that the marginal cost of raising the efficiency ratio will increase as efficiency rises; that is, it is relatively easy to increase the efficiency ratio from 10 per cent to 20 per cent, but very difficult to raise it from 80 per cent to 90 per cent (Collard, 1971). Governments of all parties have tried to combat this very real problem through initiatives which have sought to simplify what is a highly bureaucratic and complex process of claiming benefit entitlements. Most notable among these initiatives has been the introduction and gradual refinement of what is usually referred to as a *passport system*. In essence, this means that individual claimants, through applying for, and being granted, a particular benefit, automatically secure entitlement to a range of other benefits without having to undergo separate means tests. Such procedures, because they simplify the existing complex generality, do increase overall take-up rates but, ironically, in so doing they run up against what American authors refer to as the 'notch' problem. That is, as more of the potential target population are successful in claiming benefits for which entitlement is usually determined through the application of a secondary, low-income criterion, they face the possibility that as earned income increases their entitlement to benefit is extinguished.

FIS take-up rates never exceeded 50 per cent throughout its existence, and its successor as the main instrument through which the present government has sought to subsidize the low earnings of full-time workers with dependent children, Family Credit, is not claimed by nearly 40 per cent of those with a theoretical entitlement. The average loss of benefit is £22.25 per week, which produces a total under-payment of £200 million. Similarly, more than a million people, some 20 per cent of those entitled to Income Support, do not make a claim, while the figures for the elderly suggest that around 570,000 do not claim. As the final report of the Commission on Social Justice notes, 'means-tested benefits, which cannot prevent poverty, are also remarkably inefficient at relieving it' (Commission on Social Justice, 1994).

Administrative Costs

Notwithstanding the simplification achieved through passport schemes, a social welfare system increasingly characterized by means-testing must mean that individuals seek entitlement to targeted benefits through making individual claims which have to be processed and evaluated as individual claims by the bureaucracy. There is no other way. Evidence from the whole range of selective services has consistently demonstrated that such benefits are inherently more expensive to administer than their universal equivalents. A single current example will suffice to make this point. For every £1 paid in Income Support around 11 pence is spent on administration, while the figures for the Social Fund are quite simply staggering, with 45 pence being incurred for every £1 paid in benefit. In contrast, every £1 in Child Benefit costs two pence to administer and £1 in retirement pension costs just over a penny (Commission on Social Justice, 1994). Whereas a leading selectivist, somewhat defensively perhaps, felt able to dismiss such fears as a minor quibble about mundane administrative costs (Seldon, 1967), Titmuss wrote in scathing terms about the extraordinary and frightening administrative naïvety of such an attitude (Titmuss, 1976). The apparently simple task of identifying the most needy and of delivering appropriate levels of resources to them might not be so simple after all. *Certainly means-tested benefits are expensive to administer.*

Concern about the reality of administrative complexity and expense, together with low take-up rate, has led to a search for a delivery system that could target help precisely and selectively without these associated problems. This search usually focuses on the merits of some scheme of Negative Income Tax (NIT) which would cover the entire population and be used either to raise revenue from taxation or to pay out benefits in a totally integrated taxation/benefits system. A number of such schemes have been advanced over the years and, although there are important differences of detail between them, they all involve looking at the difference between income and the tax threshold appropriate to an individual: if income is below the tax threshold a Negative Income Tax would be used to *pay* an individual whatever percentage of this difference the particular version of NIT allowed for. The majority of such schemes use a 50 per cent payment figure.

Support for this technique has spanned the intellectual and political spectrum, although in general terms support is more likely to come from the right than anywhere else. Indeed, in the late 1960s and early 1970s, some version of NIT was the preferred solution of the Conservative Party to the problem of family poverty. The party's commitment went so far that in 1973 the Conservative government introduced a Green Paper containing proposals for a Tax Credit Scheme (TCS) which, although not purely a Negative Income Tax, had many similarities. Although opposed by the Labour Party and academics such as Townsend and Atkinson, the TCS was welcomed by other left-leaning academics like David Piachaud as being the most radical statement on income maintenance since the Beveridge Report in 1942 and, significantly for our purposes, as representing the end of the selectivity–universality debate. Whatever the merits of Piachaud's claim, the TCS was killed by the incoming Labour government in February 1974, which announced in its stead a system of Child Benefits. The most recent research

subgroup subjects. Since the statistical procedures involved are radically different for component/factor analysis (based on overall variances/covariances) and cluster analysis (based on pairwise comparisons), the latter has a much greater demand on the computer's memory. The results of principal component and factor analyses have important use in multidimensional measurement for scaling subjects, which are distinguished from the Multidimensional Scaling (MDS) technique frequently used for scaling stimuli.

It may be helpful to point out that the difference between cluster analysis and discriminant analysis is that the former aims to identify different group memberships of the subjects based on their attributes (a general set of variables), whereas the latter is aimed at establishing the relative importance of these attributes (independent variables) based the known group memberships (dependent variables) of the subjects.

Cluster analysis. To subgroup subjects based on some key attributes, you must first select the variables to be used as the criteria for cluster formation. Then you need to decide which measure of association to be used in the analysis. The term used here is a measure of distance or similarity between each case or cluster (each case is a cluster of one at the beginning). Instead of using the kinds of measures of association discussed earlier such as γ and G, squared Euclidean distance is frequently used in cluster analysis. There are also other measures of statistical distance, such as the Mahalanobis generalized statistical distance. SPSS will standardize all variables, and use the specified measure to form clusters by combining the two groups that are closest at each step. This will form a hierarchical clustering until all subjects are grouped into one large cluster. The final decision on the number of clusters as well as the level at which to accept the results is a matter of the interpretation of the researcher. It should be based on the needs and purpose of the research.

Principal component(s) and factor analyses. Principal component analysis and factor analysis are different procedures serving different research purposes. The purpose of principal component analysis is more practical, that is, the reduction of data with minimum loss of information. Factor analysis, on the other hand, is more theoretically oriented, aiming at the exploration of a hypothetical latent structure of the data set. Principal component analysis focuses on explaining the total variance of the variables, whereas factor analysis emphasizes explaining the covariance of the variables. Both kinds of analysis have the function of clarifying the dimensionality of the data set, and both have important uses in scale development. SPSS does not have a separate procedure for principal component

into NIT has concluded that it is fraught with a variety of administrative problems which would be very difficult and expensive to resolve. For the foreseeable future, despite the support of the Liberal Democrats, it seems a non-starter (Commission for Social Justice, 1994).

Poverty Traps and Poverty Plateaux

The concept of the rational, income-maximizing individual pursuing pleasure rather than pain is a fundamental of liberal political economy. There is, therefore, some irony to be found in the way that opponents of means testing have used this idea to undermine selective social provision further. Critics of universal benefits have pointed to the alleged disincentive characteristics of the high levels of marginal tax rates generated by the financial demands of quality universal provision, and a reduction of these marginal tax rates, especially of income tax, has been the cornerstone of economic policy since 1979.

As the distributional consequences of the welfare state became clearer, researchers began to take seriously the impact of the overlap between benefits and taxation on people at the bottom of the scale of income distribution. It was quickly demonstrated that a rise in earnings for low-paid workers could, because of increased liability to higher taxation and insurance contributions, together with loss of entitlement to income-related benefits, lead to a marginal tax rate of over 100 per cent – see Lees (1967), Field and Piachaud (1982), Bradshaw and Wakeman (1972) and Meacher (1972). If one assumes that rational economic calculation is not the sole prerogative of the well-to-do and that high marginal tax rates do have disincentive implications for labour market behaviour, then the case for means-tested selectivity is significantly weakened. At the moment around half a million of the poorest people in Britain are, in effect, paying marginal tax rates of 70 per cent or more and living on a very long 'poverty plateau' where families can remain on low incomes for a very long time. It has been claimed that at 1994 benefit and tax rates, a family with two young children and paying a weekly rent of £60 would be scarcely any better off if they earned £10,000 a year than if they claimed Income Support. Their annual earnings would have to rise to £14,000 a year before they were completely free of means-tested benefits (Commission on Social Justice, 1994). There is a real possibility that these arrangements might lead to a significant section of the population becoming permanently dependent on means-tested welfare benefits for the whole or part of their income: *their pauperization is inherent to the system.*

The Impact of Economic and Social Change

Changes in family structure, the labour market and the wider economy have made means testing increasingly complex and irrelevant. Because means-tested benefits are based on an assessment of family income it is rarely worth while for a claimant's partner to enter or remain in the labour market. Married women's labour-market activity is especially sensitive to the benefits system (McLaughlin, 1994). Moreover, as more people live together without marrying, means testing demands increasingly complicated rules which become particularly difficult to enforce in situations where partners sometimes live together and sometimes separately. Means-tested benefits intensify insecurity: they assume stable earnings from employment at a time when the labour market is becoming more and more deregulated and is generating employment income that is insecure and unpredictable. In contrast, a woman who knows that she has a guaranteed right to Child Benefit has a firmer basis on which, for example, she can consider the possibility of leaving a violent partner. Entry into even this insecure labour market becomes less unattractive given the guarantee of at least some income from continuing Child Benefit. This complex, confusing and insecure world is harshest for the most vulnerable and marginal in society. Members of minority ethnic communities are very exposed to the vicissitudes of a system in which, despite some recent improvements (such as the Benefit Agency's introduction of a Code of Practice on discrimination and racial harassment), it is still by no means universal to provide appropriate information for people whose first language is not English (Commission on Social Justice, 1994).

The observations and conclusions of this section are summarized and presented in tabular form below.

Table 11.1 *Universalism and selectivism: a summary of their characteristics*

Characteristic	Universalism	Selectivism
Effectiveness	High/very high take-up rates	Variable (usually low) levels of take-up
Meeting policy objectives	Wasteful of resources (benefits go to those who do not necessarily need them)	Effective use of resources (targeting)
Administrative costs	Low administrative costs	High administrative costs
Public expenditure implications	Relatively demanding of public expenditure	Lessens pressure on public spending
Social costs and social benefits	1 No stigmatization 2 Promotes social integration 3 Egalitarian	1 Considerable stigmatizing propensities 2 Socially divisive 3 Equitable
Labour market implications	Promotes work incentives	High marginal tax rates theoretically damaging to work incentives (the poverty trap)

Activity 11.3

Make a list of those benefits/services which you think are (1) selective, (2) universal. What features do they possess which help you decide which category they belong to?

The Intellectual and Political Context

The allegedly institutional character of the reconstructed welfare state of the 1940s had barely been established when it came under attack from the political right. In 1950 a number of young Conservative MPs, including some, such as Edward Heath, Iain Macleod and Enoch Powell, who were to become leading figures in the party over the next three decades, produced an 'unofficial' statement on Conservative social policy whose title – rather ironically given its general philosophical orientation – incorporated echoes of the party's Disraelian past (Conservative Political Centre, 1950). 'One nation' is important on a number of counts, but for present purposes perhaps its most interesting aspect is its identification of what is perceived to be the crucial difference between the two major parties on social policy. Thus: 'Socialists would give the same benefits to everyone, whether or not the help is needed, and indeed whether or not the country's resources are adequate. We believe that we must first help those in need' (Conservative Political Centre, 1950: 9).

This general observation was developed in more detail in a later pamphlet written by Macleod and Powell in 1952. 'The social services: needs and means' is a sustained critique of the then existing pattern of social provision in Britain. It rejects the argument that the British welfare state was, in fact, universal to any significant degree and argues for a rational and consistent approach to the allocation of resources on a selectivist basis. Given that redistribution was an essential characteristic of social provision, the general presumption had to be that services would be provided on the basis of the evidence of need, otherwise 'the process is a wasteful and purposeless collection and issue of resources, which leaves people in the enjoyment of the same facilities as before, or rather, worse off, to the extent of the waste involved in the administrative process' (Macleod and Powell, 1952, revised by Powell, 1954: 9).

Notwithstanding its internal coherence and intellectual rigour, Macleod and Powell's position failed to find significant support from the party leadership whose 'official' line remained one of public support for the main contours of the post-war settlement. The Conservatives' reluctance to tamper with this settlement after they were returned to power following the 1951 general election not only surprised the now Labour Opposition, which confidently expected them to renege on their conversion to full employment and an expanded welfare state, but was also consistent with the economic prosperity and ideological consensus characteristic of the 1950s and early 1960s (see Lowe, 1990, 1993; Sullivan, 1992).

The 'rediscovery' of poverty during this 'age of affluence' was part of a more general reappraisal of the success of the Keynesian-Beveridgian welfare state in meeting its broad objectives. Titmuss (1962) and Abel-Smith and Townsend (1965) all asked searching questions about the extent to which existing welfare institutions secured a significant amount of vertical income redistribution, and the failures they identified quickly infiltrated the wider political debate. Labour's return to office in 1964 was accompanied by a long and agonized review of its social policy commitments, one which was given a new urgency by the financial crisis leading up to the 1967 devaluation of sterling. As this protracted review went on a number of figures from the centre and right of the party, including Douglas Houghton (1967), then regarded as one of the most authoritative commentators on social security, Ray Gunter (1967), David Owen (1967) and David Marquand (1967) all argued publicly in favour of greater selectivity, while in the Cabinet a similar debate raged. The ostensible Labour/universalist and Conservative/selectivist dichotomy, even if it had never been as clear and simple as political myth would have it, became even more difficult to sustain as the 1960s progressed, and it was within the Labour Party that the shift was most obvious. Significant sections of the party were much more willing to embrace notions of giving most help to those presumed to be in greatest need, especially if acceptable delivery mechanisms could be devised. Houghton's (1967) discussion of a negative income tax is a particularly good example of this.

Perhaps the most significant manifestation of this conflict is provided by the struggle that took place over the shape of family income support policy. A general increase in universal Family Allowances would have been too expensive for a Treasury desperate to keep public expenditure under control while the trade unions, together with some sympathetic MPs, frustrated Jim Callaghan's (then Chancellor of the Exchequer), attempt to 'bounce' the Cabinet into accepting what later, under the next Conservative government, became the Family Income Supplement scheme. The complicated compromise that finally emerged was the 'clawback' mechanism which reduced income-tax allowances in respect of dependent children by an amount exactly sufficient to negate the increase in Family Allowance scale rates. This was the scheme described by Roy Jenkins, Callaghan's successor as Chancellor, as 'a civilized and acceptable' form of selectivity (Pratt, 1976).

Townsend (1972) explains this shift towards selectivity on three grounds – the increasing dominance of economic policy over social policy, a move away from social equality as a national objective, and the degeneration of large-scale planning into piecemeal improvisation – but, whatever the truth of Townsend's analysis, that there was a significant intellectual as well as political change is undeniable. Economic failure, particularly when accompanied by a spectacular crisis on the foreign exchange markets as in 1967, tends to concentrate minds wonderfully. From 1967 onwards a sea-change is evident in the work of left-leaning theoreticians of social policy, and the development of Titmuss's thought provides powerful testimony to this. It shows the most important theorist of the institutional model of the welfare state, one of the key components of which is the availability of high-quality universal services, engaged in a self-conscious attempt at reconciling his commitment to social justice with the reality of scarce resources. His response to these dilemmas was typically creative.

> The challenge that faces us is not the choice between universalist and selective social services. The real challenge resides in the question: what particular infrastructure of universalist services is needed in order to provide a framework of values and opportunity bases within and around which can be developed socially acceptable services aiming to discriminate positively, with the minimum risk of stigma in favour of those whose needs are greatest. (Titmuss, 1976: 135)

This plea by Titmuss for non-stigmatizing positive discrimination must be one of the most quoted pieces in the whole of the academic literature of social policy. It has a profound significance, one which was quickly recognized by Titmuss's neo-liberal equivalent, Arthur Seldon. After sardonically noting Titmuss's earlier, eloquent support for universalism (Titmuss, 1950), Seldon develops a merciless and pointed critique. It merits lengthy quotation.

> The academic advocates of unqualified universalism on principle are in an intellectual dilemma from which they cannot escape except by concession of error. If selectivity is, at last, morally acceptable, there can be no moral reason for insistence on a substructure of wasteful universal benefits. Economic circumstance, intellectual argument and the belated recognition that generalized benefits are inhumane have destroyed the case for universalism. Nor should refuge be taken in attempts to pay lip service to both principles, formerly regarded as moral opposites, now joined in an administrative 'mariage de convenance'. (1967: 50)

His analysis of Titmuss's preference for allocating resources on a group, categorical or territorial basis is prescient, as later research on positive discrimination programmes such as Educational Priority Areas was to demonstrate. Positive discrimination abandoned the moral case for universalism and still failed to help individuals in need. Seldon's judgement could just as easily be applied to Pinker's examination of positive discrimination as a way out of the increasingly barren debate between the ideologies of universalism and selectivism as 'alive in principle, but dead in practice, just as the nineteenth-century struggle between collectivist and individualist doctrines was largely the invention of an intellectual minority' (Pinker, 1971: 108).

The public spending implications of high-quality universal social provision and the problems associated with means-tested selectivity continue to attend the politics of social policy. Perhaps the most important and vivid example of this in the last decade or so came with the publication of a three-volume Green Paper, the *Reform of Social Security* (DHSS, 1985a). Constrained from the outset by the Treasury's 'stipulation that the exercise must not increase social security spending, regardless of whatever unusual need it might identify' (Social Security Consortium, 1986: 3), the review found its solution in the concept of *targeting*, the idea 'that resources must be directed more effectively to areas of greatest need notably low income families with children' (DHSS, 1985b: 2).

We must ask whether targeting, thus defined, obviates any of the problems of traditional forms of selectivity. If targeting as a principle is to deliver extra help to the most needy how is it to be done? What is to be the basis of allocation? Can appropriate policy instruments be derived to translate intent into reality? The evidence of targeting in operation since 1985 would seem to justify a negative response to each of these questions. Means-tested selectivity continues to be the vehicle through which targeting is operationalized. Income Support has replaced Supplementary Benefit and, for the government's constantly reiterated favourite target (the working poor with dependent children), Family Credit has replaced Family Income Supplement and, consequently, means testing remains at the heart of the social security system.

> It represents an attempt to rationalize the present incoherent patchwork of means-tested benefits, while at the same time downgrading child benefit and the national insurance scheme. But the rationalization cannot begin to grapple with the problems endemic to means-testing: low take-up; the poverty trap, complexity. (Social Security Consortium, 1986: 3)

Titmuss's plea for the development of non-stigmatizing positive discrimination has been used by Williams (1992) in her application of postmodernist theory to the analysis of social policy. Postmodernism leads to a distrust of uniformity and universalism, and Williams argues that 'bottom-up' work around gender, race, disability, age and sexuality has exposed 'the "false" universalism of the post-war welfare state – that is, the extent to which social policies have, and continue to be, built on a white, male, able-bodied, heterosexual norm, living within a supportive nuclear family form' (ibid.: 206). She suggests that postmodernism can assist in retrieving the idea of positive discrimination (understood as a form of selectivity), and in developing it through the notion of *diversity* which 'suggests a more subjective and self-determined approach to need' (ibid.: 209). In this way the universality/selectivity debate is taken onto new ground and selectivity is replaced by the idea of diversity, which creates the possibility of 'people articulating their own needs'. For Williams the crucial question is, 'how are we to have welfare provision which is universal in that it meets all people's welfare needs, but also diverse and not uniform, reflecting people's own changing definitions of difference, and not simply the structured differentiation of the society at large' (ibid.: 209). She concludes by suggesting that Titmuss's classic statement could be rephrased thus: 'perhaps the real challenge resides in the question how can government at local, national and international levels facilitate the universal articulation and provision for diverse welfare needs' (ibid.: 209).

In a world freed from the depressing reality of scarce resources Williams's liberating notions of self-articulated need would present no problems, but whatever else postmodernist theory might have achieved it has not abolished scarcity: choices still have to be made and the notion of opportunity cost is still relevant.

We are still no nearer to a resolution of these problems. The thoughts of Titmuss and Pinker are echoed in the work done by and for the Commission on Social Justice, work which, essentially, addresses the philosophical and political issues involved by defining them away. The Commission's staff have accused politicians and commentators of frequently posing a choice between 'universalist' and 'targeted' (selective) benefits, and has suggested, perhaps anachronistically given the comments made above, that 'those on the right [favoured] a shift towards targeting and those on the left usually defend[ed] universality' (Commission on Social Justice, 1993). However, for the Commission this 'simple dualism' was inappropriate both in describing the existing complex system and in developing new proposals. The solution was easy because both terms had been abused so much they should be abandoned completely and replaced by a different classification system. In future, benefits should be categorized as 'contributory' (based on National Insurance contributions); 'means tested' (based on a test of income and savings); or 'categorical' (awarded to a particular group of people without a test of either contributions or means). The Commission's concluding thoughts on the matter are worth noting. 'This is not simply a matter of terminology: the choice before us is not a crude one between means-tested and non-means-tested benefits, but a complex one between a wide variety of different kinds of provision' (1993: 6).

The line of descent from Titmuss is obvious but whether it provides any more of an answer must remain conjectural.

Activity 11.4

In what ways, if any, does targeting overcome the problems associated with the universal/selective debate?

Summary and Conclusions

In this chapter we have considered the most important non-market approaches to the allocation of a number of services, access to which is generally agreed to be vital in determining quality of life in an urban-industrial society. Universalism, selectivism and, to a much more limited extent, positive discrimination have been defined as concepts, had their respective strengths and weaknesses examined in theory and practice, been located in the intellectual and political context of Britain since 1945, and been analysed in the setting of a society whose economic and social structure has been changing at an increasingly rapid and bewildering rate. What general conclusions can be drawn from this exercise?

First, this is a significant debate which should not be reduced to a barren shouting match between the competing claims of 'social justice and cohesion' on the one hand and 'giving most help to those whose needs are greatest' on the other. Simple and beguiling though each of these positions might be, they are of little use in helping us unravel what in reality is a complex problem of public policy. Each of the approaches is reflective of different theoretical models of welfare, possessing conflicting views about what are the most relevant and valid mechanisms for the allocation of a vital range of resources. Is it to be the state or the market? In this sense the universality–selectivity debate can also be seen as one dimension of a perennial, profound fault line in western political thought: the relationship between state and civil society, between the market and the state.

Second, it is a mistake to believe that there is a clear and simple political dichotomy between Conservative/selectivists and Labour/universalists. No such set of relationships exists any longer, although in the past, certainly in the immediate post-war years, left-of-centre political opinion tended to be rather more inclined to universalism and right-of-centre towards selectivism.

Third, both philosophies, and the delivery systems associated with them, have important weaknesses. Whereas universal benefits might encourage work incentives and be more successful in reaching relevant target populations, there is no denying the fact that they do demand a huge commitment of public expenditure and, as Titmuss admitted, by their nature they are wasteful.

In contrast, although selective benefits are more economical in the demands they place on scarce resources, there are very real problems of take-up, stigma, disincentives and costs of administration. It may well be that these problems are intractable no matter how ingenious and subtle policy instruments might become in future.

Fourth, is a 'perfect' solution possible at all, or will we have to recognize that something like the present admixture of fudge and compromise will continue into the foreseeable future – a compromise, moreover, which will accord with no theoretical ideal type and therefore be continuously vilified by ideologues of all persuasions?

Fifth and finally, a point not directly concerned with the substance of the debate at all, but rather more with questions of general intellectual procedure. It can be argued that the issues dealt with in this chapter, which in the first instance appear to be simple and non-problematic, soon reveal themselves as difficult and controversial in nature. As such they can stand as a powerful encouragement to students always to go beyond superficial certainties and to explore the stimulating reality of context.

12

Poverty and the 'Underclass'

Tony Novak

This chapter sets out to consider how sections of the poor have come to be identified as an 'underclass'. It argues that this is not a neutral concept, but contains assumptions about supposed causes of poverty which can legitimate harsher policies and treatment. There is a need to think about the causes of poverty and the different ways that 'the problem' of poverty is defined. The social construction of poverty reflects who is defining it – their 'race', gender and class – and ultimately whose interests different definitions of poverty are seen to serve.

Poverty in Britain in the closing two decades of the twentieth century has not so much changed as taken a more savage turn. The numbers of people affected by the stresses and struggles of poverty have increased dramatically, while the poor, in material terms, have got poorer (Oppenheim, 1993). For many of those in work, wages have fallen behind the growth in economic progress, as more jobs have become casualized, part-time and lower paid. For those out of work, since 1980, social security payments and other welfare benefits have been subject to progressive and substantial reductions, falling most heavily on the poorest, and rules of eligibility and the attitudes of officialdom have become tighter and harsher (Andrews and Jacobs, 1990). As inequalities – both in and out of work – have expanded, Britain has become a more polarized society. The most recent research suggests that between 1979 and 1993 the poorest quarter of the population saw their incomes absolutely frozen, while the richest tenth saw their incomes increase by 60 per cent (*The Guardian*, 8 December 1994).

In the midst of this, since the late 1980s, there has been a growing – and concerted – move to characterize sections of the poor as a separate and identifiable 'underclass'. This move has focused most directly on the young, on single-parent mothers, on the increasingly long-term unemployed, and on those of the poor identified as breaking the law. It has, by implication if not by design, frequently been used to identify and target a much larger group, to identify poverty as the result of individual lifestyles and attitudes, and to construct an image of this so-called 'underclass' as a threat to social well-being that justifies their curtailment and punishment.

The idea of and evidence for the existence of 'an underclass' are theoretically weak and empirically unproven, yet their use by social scientists, governments and opinion-formers serve to focus attention away from the processes that have created a more divided and impoverished society and onto the behaviour and supposed culpability of the poor themselves. It is a construction of a way of looking at poverty that has immense implications. As Neil Ascherson argued in the *Independent on Sunday* in 1993, following the Prime Minister's statement that social breakdown indicated the need 'to condemn a little more and understand a little less':

> We are going through a period of monstrously artificial media uproars – stories which are exaggerated and inflated into 'issues' supposed to reveal this or that sickness of our society . . . The trick in such spasms of provoked anxiety is to look in the opposite direction. Who exactly wants the British public to understand less and condemn more? Who is encouraging us to demonize sections of our society as if they had been infiltrated by aliens? . . . What is this spectacle really about? It is about the grand British engineering project of the 1990s – the construction of the Underclass. Much of the preparatory work has already been done. Unemployment has passed three million . . . welfare payments have been reduced, inequality has been drastically increased, and an imaginative programme for poverty creation is on the way to completion. What remains, in the second phase, is to shift the whole bottom third of British society to these new foundations, by establishing that poverty, combined with idleness and savagery, is its natural and incurable condition.

The Growth of Poverty

Over the past two decades, British society has changed in a number of very fundamental ways (see, for example, Ball et al., 1989; Hudson and Williams, 1989). Many of these changes have been brought about by a style of government and a series of policies that from 1979 onwards championed individualism and self-interest, the supremacy of the market economy over collective responsibility and action, and that saw a widening of inequalities as the necessary incentive to economic growth. Other changes lay less directly within government control, although they often worked to a similar purpose. Economic change signalled by the growth of an increasingly international world economy has seen the economies of countries like Britain radically transformed, and in particular has put an end to the pattern of full-time, regular male employment and growing working-class standards of living that characterized the 35 years of boom that followed the Second World War. Finding a job is no longer a guarantee of an escape from poverty; indeed, in 1989 almost one-third of the poorest households had at least one member in full- or part-time work. Taken together with other growing causes of poverty this meant that by then 16.5 million people, or 29 per cent of the population, lived beneath or on the margins of a narrowly defined poverty line (Oppenheim, 1993: 47).

Social changes too have been allied to these economic changes. For many households, having two wage-earners has become the only means of financial solvency; at the same time women have come to challenge their traditionally ascribed role as dependent home-makers. Later, and shorter, marriages, increased cohabitation, separation and divorce, and the growth of

analysis; rather, it is included in the FACTOR procedure as a method of factor extraction. The steps of computation as well as the results with large numbers of variables are very much the same. Yet it is easy to get confused in understanding.

The FACTOR procedure will first produce a correlation or intercorrelation matrix, containing the correlation coefficients for all pairs of variables. From this correlation matrix, which is convertible to a covariance matrix, some components or factors will be extracted that form an initial component/factor matrix. SPSS will then rotate this matrix to simplify the distribution of the factor loadings of the original variables. Finally, SPSS will calculate component/factor scores, which can be used in place of the values of the original variables for further analysis with reduced complexity.

The method of extraction determines the meaning of the FACTOR procedure. The techniques of "real factoring" based on various common factor models intend to obtain a reduced yet accurate "latent variable" structure of the data. This involves some stringent assumptions about the pattern of the covariance such as a multinormal distribution. To explain the maximum amount covariance, common factor analysis will have to start from estimating the commonality of the variables by using the squared multiple correlation coefficient of each variable. The diagonals of the correlation matrix using such estimates are usually smaller than 1, which is the most obvious operational difference from the principal components model.

The method of principal component analysis, on the other hand, is the only means by which exact factor scores can be obtained without imposing the causal and multinormal models which are oftentimes questionable. Principal components analysis, therefore, is a method most frequently used in applied behavioral and social science research. The objective of principal components analysis is a simple summary of information contained in the raw data. The first step in extraction is to select a linear combination of the variables that will explain the greatest amount of the total variance. In a space determined by these standardized variables, the results are represented by a straight line whose direction is that representing the maximum variance of the data set. This is called the first component. The second component will be extracted by repeating the procedure. Yet the second combination will explain the greatest amount of the variance that remains and need be orthogonal to the first line represented by the first component. This procedure may continue, until as many components have been extracted as there are variables. The number of acceptable components is a matter of the decision of the researcher, though common rules of thumb are available

single and other types of household have radically transformed the nature of domestic as well as public life. These changes have brought a number of opportunities, as well as a large number of problems; neither of these are distributed equally among the population.

Unemployment

In economic terms, one of the most dramatic contributors to the rise in poverty has been the return of mass unemployment as a feature of the British economy. Mass unemployment has not only drastically reduced the income of those who have lost their jobs, and of those dependent on them, but it has also had a powerful effect in decreasing the bargaining power, and therefore the wages, of many of those in work, especially the lower-paid. This was something that was well understood for most of the first half of the twentieth century, and it was the political consequences of unemployment that led successive governments after the Second World War to proclaim a commitment to 'full employment'.

For the duration of the long post-war boom, unemployment never rose above a few hundred thousand. Having reached, and remaining at just over one million by the time of the first major check to this boom in the middle of 1975, it increased rapidly during the economic slump in Britain brought about by the monetarist policies of the Thatcher administration during the early 1980s. For the whole of that decade registered unemployment never fell below 2.5 million, while in seven of the ten years it averaged over 3 million.

With the exception of a relatively short and largely speculative boom in the mid-1980s that benefited very largely the already well-off, mass unemployment has persisted as a chronic feature of the British industrial and economic landscape. Geographically it has hit the older industrial areas the hardest as primary industries such as coalmining or shipbuilding and large sectors of manufacturing have been closed down, either permanently or to be relocated in other parts of the world. It has forced many workers, often with dependants, to move in search of work, increasing the competition for any new jobs that become available, while those who remain behind equally face prolonged periods of idleness punctuated by often doomed attempts at self-employment or temporary work in short-lived jobs that increasingly characterize the economically depressed areas. So, with mass unemployment, has grown long-term unemployment, with over one million of those unemployed in the mid-1990s having been out of work for over a year, and often much longer.

Unemployment is not random, and this concentrates its effects on the living standards of the poor. The chances of losing, or of never finding, a job are concentrated, repeatedly, upon manual workers, minority ethnic groups (who are disproportionately relegated to manual jobs) and the young. In 1985, for example, when unemployment on average stood at 10 per cent of the total workforce, 23 per cent of manual workers, 29 per cent of minority ethnic workers and 35 per cent of those aged 18–24 had experienced unemployment at least once during the year (Central Statistical Office, 1985). The young too bear a heavy burden of long-term unemployment: in 1993 one-fifth were under the age of 25, and one-half under the age of 34.

For the vast majority of people in Britain, reliance upon paid work is the major means of achieving economic security and escaping the worst effects of poverty, although (as we shall see) for an increasing number even a full-time job does not provide any escape. For the unemployed, the only alternative is reliance on the state and its system of benefits. In Britain this system takes two forms: Unemployment Benefit (now renamed Jobseeker's Allowance), which is paid to those who qualify by establishing a record of contributions, and a more conditional system called Income Support which is paid to those unemployed and others not in full-time work whose income falls below a minimal level of subsistence. As unemployment has increased since the late 1970s, the value of Unemployment Benefit has been cut. In 1980 the government announced that in future it would raise all benefits only in line with prices, and not in line with the general increase in wages and living standards. Together with the abolition in 1982 of earnings-related supplements to Unemployment Benefit and in 1984 of payments for dependent children, this meant that the value of Unemployment Benefit fell from 47 per cent of net average earnings for a single person in 1978 to 18 per cent by 1988, and for a married person with two children from 66 per cent to 34 per cent (Deakin and Wilkinson, 1989: 13).

As unemployment has come to be experienced more regularly, and for longer periods, so increasing numbers of the unemployed fail to qualify for or exhaust their entitlements to Unemployment Benefit: in 1961 less than a quarter of a much smaller number of unemployed people had to rely upon means-tested benefits alone; by 1981 this had grown to nearly one-half, and by 1992 almost two-thirds of the unemployed were only eligible to receive Income Support (Central Statistical Office, 1994). Similar reductions in the relative value of and eligibility for Income Support have further increased the poverty of those out of work. In 1986, for example, the fall-back of means-tested Income Support for unemployed 16- and 17-year-olds was removed altogether, while unemployed people aged 18–25 were relegated to a lower rate of Income Support than other adult claimants (for fuller details see Andrews and Jacobs, 1990). The result has been an increasing concentration of poverty among the unemployed: in 1979 unemployed people counted for 1 in 6 of the poorest of the population; by 1989 they counted for nearly 1 in 3, while almost 70 per cent of the unemployed had an income less than half of the national average (Oppenheim, 1993: 47).

Low pay

Unemployment, however, is not the only factor in the increased levels and severity of poverty. As competition for work has increased – especially for the less skilled, lower-paid and more insecure jobs that the vast majority of the unemployed invariably have to seek – so the wages and working conditions of a large minority of the labour force have deteriorated. Employers too, both large and small, have responded to the changing economic and political climate by restructuring their demand for labour. Full-time and permanent jobs have been cut back, and replaced by increasing numbers of part-time, temporary and casual workers (Ball et al., 1989). By the 1990s fully one-third of workers were employed on this basis. Such changes of course also had their racialized and gendered effects: full-time permanent jobs for men were often substituted by temporary or part-time work for women; and effects on employment – by 1991 88 per cent of all part-time workers and 55 per cent of all temporary workers were women, with consequent effects in terms of lower wages and poorer working conditions. Similarly, average full-time wages for black workers were only 82 per cent of those of their white counterparts, while they also faced added burdens of shift work and unsocial hours (Oppenheim, 1993: 60).

During the 1980s a succession of government policies, including the repeal of parts of the Employment Protection Act, the weakening and abolition of minimum Wages Councils, the introduction of competitive tendering and the abandonment of the Fair Wages Resolution sought to encourage this trend on the argument that lower wages would increase levels of employment. The result has been an increase in the number of low-paid workers and a growing polarization between the highest- and lowest-paid. By the end of the 1980s, nearly 6 million full-time workers (37 per cent of all full-time adult workers) in Britain were earning less than the Council of Europe's 'decency threshold', while the position of the lowest-paid relative to average earnings was worse than the position of the lowest-paid had been 100 years earlier (Low Pay Unit, 1990).

Changing Families

Whether in or out of work, the experience of the poor from the late 1970s onwards was that of growing numbers and increasing poverty. This situation has been further compounded by social and cultural changes that have placed particular groups in positions of vulnerability. Of these one of the most important has been the growing number of single-parent households. Change in household formation and structure has been one of the most significant of social developments that have taken place in Britain during the closing decades of the twentieth century. The once dominant pattern of lifelong marriage, based on a breadwinning husband and father with a dependent wife and mother bringing up children and looking after the home, has given way to a much more fluid and varied pattern of work, household and family relationships. Beneath this change lie a great many factors, among the most significant of which must be counted the increased participation of women in the paid labour market, so that by 1994 for the first time in history women outnumbered men as paid employees (though still not even equalling men in terms of pay or conditions), and the growth of a feminist consciousness that challenged arbitrary male authority and violence and the supposed inevitability of women's dependency. This was to be reflected in increasing levels of divorce (the majority initiated by women), which between 1971 and 1991 increased twofold, and a decline in the popularity of marriage, which over the same period fell by 16 per cent (Central Statistical Office, 1994). This is not to say that marriage was rejected altogether: rather, that for many it ceased to be a lifelong and unquestionable commitment, a phenomenon reflected in the fact that by the early 1990s over one-third of marriages occurred among people who had previously been married to someone else, compared with 10 per cent 30 years earlier (Central Statistical Office, 1994). One consequence of these changes was that more parents – the vast majority of them women – were left to bring up children on their own.

'The family' has always been a central concern of social policy, used as a means of buttressing the wage system and reproducing the labour force, and as an institution for exercising male authority. In this role 'the family' has always meant a supposed ideal of breadwinner husband, with dependent wife and children, and social policies have in general been constructed around this assumption, despite the fact that increasingly this particular family form has come to represent only a tiny minority of households. The growth of single-parent households very clearly challenges this assumption, yet social policies in general have failed to make provision to match this development. For the majority of single parents, single parenthood means poverty. Even where single mothers can find work, the varied patterns of discrimination facing women in the labour market mean that many cannot earn enough for an adequate standard of living; more commonly, the lack of child-care arrangements and the lack of a partner to support them means that the majority of single parents must rely on benefits provided by the state. Here they and their children too have faced declining living standards as levels of support have been cut back.

Activity 12.1

- In what ways do state policies favour the 'traditional' nuclear family?
- Who benefits from this?

The Construction of an 'Underclass'

How a society thinks about poverty and about the poor is crucial, both in terms of understanding and explanation, and in terms of appropriate government responses. The widening gulf between rich and poor in Britain during the 1980s and 1990s poses this issue in a particularly acute form. Taken as a whole, Britain is one of the richest societies in the world. The fact that one-third of its population live in intolerable conditions of deprivation, neglect and poverty – and that as others get wealthier they get relatively poorer – challenges notions of fairness, progress and justice. Such inequalities can only be maintained and the potentially explosive consequences of poverty minimized so long as the real causes of poverty are obscured and a different construction of poverty is put in their place.

Activity 12.2

- What image does the concept of an 'underclass' conjure up?
- How might these images affect the way people see and understand poverty?

It is important to remember that the poor have always been marginalized and stigmatized. It is also true that the range of images, fears and preoccupations generated about the poor – by politicians, government officials or the media – has moved over the past 100 years and more within a narrow range of circles that depict the poor as work-shy and promiscuous, as lacking in independence and verging on criminality (Macnicol, 1987; Novak, 1988; Dean, 1991). What is true, however, is that the force and severity of this assault, and of the state policies towards the poor that have accompanied it, have been subject to fluctuation. Dependent upon the state of the economy, the numbers in poverty and the state of political struggle, the poor have been treated perhaps at best with condescension and pity and at worst with savage vindictiveness and brutality.

Since the 1970s the faint tide of benevolence that was reflected in the expanding welfare state of the post-war era has turned sharply and decisively against the poor, and as the number of the poor has risen, so has the intensity of the attack upon them. Beginning with an assault on benefits, wages and job security it has deepened its assault with an ideological campaign that portrays the poor (or at least significant sections of the poor) as a so-called 'underclass'. In this construction the 'underclass' is seen as qualitatively different from other poor people and from the rest of society. Charles Murray, a right-wing American social scientist, put this at the core of his analysis. In common with the right's demonology of the 1960s as the time when the rot of advanced capitalist societies first set in, he identified this period as marking an 'intellectual reformation' in the way people viewed poverty, during which

> the poor were to be homogenized. The only difference between poor people and everyone else, we were told, was that the poor had less money. More importantly, the poor were all alike. Poor people, *all* poor people, were equally victims. (Murray, 1990: 2)

It is against this notion that the poor are like everyone else – that all that separates them is a lack of money – that the notion of the 'underclass' is directed. From the point of view of an 'underclass' they are to be seen as qualitatively different and distinct.

Activity 12.3

The use of the word 'underclass' is a relatively recent intro-duction, but the labelling of the poor as different from the rest of the population has a long history.
  In what ways, and by whom, are the poor labelled?
  How does the negative labelling of the poor legitimate the *status quo*?

Murray was one of the first to popularize the use of the term in Britain. Drawing upon images first developed in the United States where, since the 1960s, the notion of an 'underclass' has increasingly been used to character-ize – and explain – the situation facing in particular the black American poor, he was paid by the *Sunday Times* to visit Britain and produce a report on 'The emerging British underclass', which was published in that news-paper in November 1989. As he recounted, 'I arrived in Britain earlier this year, a visitor from a plague area come to see whether the disease is spreading' (Murray, 1990: 3). His conclusion, if not his evidence, was strikingly clear:

> Britain has a growing population of working-aged, healthy people who live in a different world from other Britons, who are raising their children to live in it, and whose values are now contaminating the life of entire neighbourhoods'. (Murray, 1990: 4)

Since then the notion of an 'underclass' has gained increasing credence – among a number of social scientists, with politicians, in newspaper, radio and television reports – both as a description of and explanation for the conditions of poverty in Britain and for what has been taken to be the associated rise in welfare dependency, the breakdown of 'the family', unemployment, lawlessness, riot and social unrest. What these accounts all have in common is an argument that something new is happening among the poor in Britain, and that in the emergence of a so-called 'underclass' which is qualitatively different from the rest of the population we have the appearance of a new social problem that will not disappear with rising prosperity or the return of full employment. As the Labour MP Frank Field has argued:

> We've got a number of young people who are now outside the labour market, who've created their own world, partly through drugs, partly through crime, partly through drawing welfare, and who are not prepared to join Great Britain Ltd again on the terms that we offer . . . That group is different from the vast majority of the unemployed, most of whom are anxious to return to work, almost on any terms'. (BBC Radio 4, 'Analysis', 3 December 1992)

Similarly, according to Charles Murray, such long-term unemployment is 'the definite proof that an underclass has arrived . . . large numbers of young, healthy, low-income males choose not to take jobs' (Murray, 1990: 17). In equal terms, rising levels of theft and burglary, especially the much-publicized appearance of 'joy-riding' in poor working-class communities in the 1980s where young males would steal and openly display fast expensive cars, together with more profound outbursts of social and urban unrest, has led to an increasing demonization of the activities of the poor as constituting a new and threatening phenomenon. According to Charles Pollard, the Chief Constable of Thames Valley Police:

> [They] are disconnected from society in a variety of ways, certainly they are totally indifferent to the sensitivities and needs of others . . . the amount of crime they're committing is on a totally different scale from the past, and their determination to take on the system is also very different from the past. . . . They are prepared to take on the whole of the criminal justice system with total impunity; they have absolutely no respect for anyone or anything to do with the criminal justice system; to them it's just an absolute joke'. (BBC Radio 4, 'Analysis', 3 December 1992)

As early as 1983 the Metropolitan Police Commissioner spoke of 'what many commentators refer to as "the underclass" – a class that is beneath the working class' that was to be found in places 'where unemployed youths – often black youths – congregate. . . . They equate closely with the criminal rookeries of Dickensian London' (cited in Campbell, 1993: 108). With such a perspective, the policing of 'the underclass', and in particular of those black communities identified with it, could not, he believed, have 'an over-regard for individual liberties' (ibid.). On the contrary, the demonization of the 'underclass' as a class apart – as outside the framework of 'normal' rules and values – necessitated a suspension of the normal rules of policing, and in particular of policing by consent. In its place came 'swamp operations', riot gear and a militarization of the police force designed to keep the so-called 'underclass' in its place.

Activity 12.4

In the United States the 'underclass' has been most commonly used to identify the position of poor black people. In what ways can the 'underclass' be seen as a racialized phenomenon in Britain?

The creation of a moral panic over a criminal 'underclass' was to be overshadowed only by an extraordinary outburst of moral condemnation during the early 1990s – at Conservative Party conferences, by government ministers, and within significant sections of the media – of the growing phenomenon of single parenthood. For many proponents of the 'underclass' thesis, single parenthood – and in particular the increase in the number of single unmarried women (rather than divorced or separated women) becoming mothers – is the key to this supposed new phenomenon. According to

Murray, the increase in illegitimate births is 'the best predictor of an underclass in the making' (1990: 4), and from this lack of male authority within single-parent households stems many of those other features – the failure to respect authority, law-breaking, the rejection of the work ethic – that are held to characterize 'underclass' behaviour. As a *Sunday Times* editorial intoned in the aftermath of the murder of the baby James Bulger by two 10-year-old children – an event taken by the media to symbolize the decline of British 'morality':

> the past two decades have witnessed the growth of whole communities in which the dominant family structure is the single-parent on welfare, whose male offspring are already immersed in a criminal culture by the time they are teenagers and whose daughters are destined to follow in the family tradition of unmarried teenage mothers. It is not just a question of a few families without fathers; it is a matter of whole communities with barely a single worthwhile male role-model. No wonder the youths of the underclass are uncontrollable by the time (sometimes before) they are teenagers. . . . In communities without fathers the overwhelming evidence is that youngsters begin by running wild and end up running foul of the law. (*The Sunday Times*, 28 February 1993)

The 'overwhelming evidence' that is called upon on such occasions is, however, simply not available. That poor single parents or the long-term unemployed have a different set of values and live by a different set of standards than the rest of the population, that they are unable to control their children or provide a stable and loving environment, or that they have rejected the work ethic and prefer a life on benefits is not supported by research (see Brown, 1990; Smith, 1992; Gallie, 1994; Payne and Payne, 1994). Not only is it empirically unproven but the very concept of an 'underclass' is itself theoretically unsound. Even as a descriptive concept the 'underclass' is, as Hartley Dean has argued, hopelessly imprecise. It lumps together a diverse group of people and situations – including, in both its 'academic' and popularized accounts, young unmarried mothers, old age pensioners, alienated black communities, divorced and separated mothers, the long-term unemployed, drug dealers, petty and organized criminals – as if they shared a common position and could be covered by the same explanation. This lack of precision makes the 'underclass' a very elastic term, and it is this elasticity that makes it both a powerful, if simplistic, means of explaining away social problems and allows it to be used to label and stigmatize ever-larger groups of the population.

In this sense it is never clear what makes a particular individual a member of the 'underclass'. According to Murray, 'Underclass does not refer to degree of poverty, but to a type of poverty . . . [they are] defined by their behaviour' (1990: 1), yet the behaviour, for example, of poor unmarried mothers is in this sense no different from the behaviour of a great many other unmarried mothers in the population. In 1976 single parents had made up 10 per cent of all families with children; by 1991 this had risen to 19 per cent. This is still nevertheless a far cry from the image of hordes of unmarried teenage mothers conjured up by proponents of a so-called 'underclass'; 80 per cent of single parents are aged 25 and over, and three-quarters have previously been married but are now widowed, separated or divorced. While there has been a remarkable increase in the number of births outside marriage, it is hard to conclude that this is the product of a growing 'underclass'. During the first half of the twentieth century, the number of illegitimate births averaged approximately five per cent of all births, in 1971 it was eight per cent, in 1981 14 per cent, and by 1992 it had reached 32 per cent (Central Statistical Office, 1994). That one-third of all births now take place outside marriage reflects a change in social and cultural values and norms that extends across the whole population. To see this as something confined to the very poor, still less as the contagious product of the abnormal values of an 'underclass', is to twist social reality beyond recognition.

The concept of an 'underclass' is untenable even in the literal sense. It cannot be got hold of. It has no boundaries to it. If single parents constitute, at least in part, the 'underclass', then large numbers of the middle class – not to mention British royalty – must be numbered among its members. Similarly, if criminality, or even dependence on the state, is taken as the touchstone, there are many thousands of wealthy people who would have equal claim to be included. If the characteristics most frequently identified with it – single parenthood, criminality, long-term unemployment, dependency on the state – were taken to define it, the 'underclass' would likely encompass a majority of the population.

What this reveals is that throughout such discussions of 'the problem of the underclass' runs a distinct and pervasive class bias. It is not criminal activity *per se* which defines someone as part of the so-called 'underclass', but criminal activity among the poor. It is true that such activity is likely to be more visible and to take its toll more directly on the neighbourhoods in which the poor live, but the crimes of the rich receive very different attention, although both in scale and in terms of cost to the community corporate fraud and other crimes committed by the economically and politically powerful far outweigh the activities of petty burglars or those who cheat the social security system. Equally, the view that long-term unemployment demoralizes – or more frequently is caused by the demoralization of – the so-called 'underclass' fails to find equal concern for or condemnation of the idle rich.

It is of course poverty which makes unemployment or single parenthood a problem, not the other way round, and it is the dependence of the poor on the system of social security that constitutes a major part of the agenda behind the construction of the 'underclass'. It is again worth stressing that it is not dependence in itself that is seen as 'the problem': should single mothers move to a dependence on a husband, or the young unemployed on their families, as government policy has urged, the problem disappears. Nor is it a simple problem of dependence on the state: many thousands of former MPs, civil servants, high court judges and others continue to receive handsome state pensions without any fears of their demoralizing effects. As is often the case, it is the poor – and only the poor – who are seen as at greatest danger from the supposed demoralizing effects of dependence on state benefits. Their demonization as part of a swelling and incorrigible 'underclass' thus becomes a thinly veiled disguise to erode their social support yet further.

The Wider Agenda

At the same time as attention is focused on single mothers, crime or the unemployed, the agenda that lies behind the construction of the 'underclass' draws upon wider fears and preoccupations identified by the political right. As Hartley Dean (1991) has argued, vague and generalized definitions of an 'underclass' can perhaps best be understood not by who the 'underclass' are supposed to be, but by the values and institutions which they are seen to threaten. The power of the concept thus stems not from its ability to define with any precision or accuracy who does or does not belong – far from it – but from its ability to evoke a somewhat formless and unquantifiable threat to the values of marriage and 'the family', to law and order, and to the value and disciplines of the labour market.

The simple notion that 'the family' is breaking down, however, disguises a number of other assumptions and values. For what is referred to is not the changing forms that family life is taking in the late twentieth century, but rather the decline of the male-headed, two-parent household. As the *Sunday Times* has argued (in terms almost directly lifted from Murray's earlier writing)[1]: 'Illegitimacy produces an underclass for a compelling practical reason which has nothing to do with morality or the sanctity of marriage: for communities to function successfully they need families with fathers' (*The Sunday Times*, 28 February 1993).

Patriarchy is under threat, challenged on the one hand by the growing independence of women and on the other by the dramatic shifts in the labour market that have removed for many young men the traditional route of paid work that characterized the passage to a masculine identity. As one threatened neo-conservative writer put it:

> Man has the sinking feeling that his role as provider, the definitive male activity from the primal days of the hunt, through the industrial revolution and on into modern life, has been largely seized from him. (George Gilder, cited in Levitas, 1986: 153)

Growing recognition of the problem of male violence, whether on the streets and football terraces, or more particularly within the supposed cosy confines of 'the family', reveals a deep crisis which questions the 'normality' of family life and the legitimacy of male authority. Faced with such a situation, the dominant response has been to deny what is happening and instead to fix the blame for the situation on single mothers themselves.

This crisis of patriarchy is equally mirrored in a crisis of a capitalist economy which since at least the mid-1970s has been unable to deliver secure and adequately paid employment for all. The government's response

such as the requirement for eigenvalues to be greater than 1. The smaller the number of accepted components, the higher the degree of simplification but the more information that will be lost. SPSS will give the variance explained by each component as well as the cumulative variance explained by all the components. On the other hand, SPSS will also calculate the commonality of each variable that indicates its contribution to selected components. In scale development, this will be an indication of the usefulness of each individual item.

After the components/factors have been extracted, SPSS will rotate them to redistribute the component/factor loadings so that the selected components or factors will represent the maximum amount of variance in a way that best serves a particular research purpose. Different rotation methods will have different effects. Oblique rotation may result in the maximum fit of the component/factor model with the data, whereas orthogonal rotation may help to gain the maximum convenience in treatment. Orthogonal rotation has two forms: varimax solution and quartimax solution. Varimax rotation is the most frequently employed method since it is simple and good for clarifying a multiple component/factor structure where the loadings on different component/factor are concentrated on different groups of variables. Quartimax solution, on the other hand, is good for identifying a single factor structure, and the loadings of all variables are focused on the first component/factor. This solution is sometimes needed for scale development purposes. A compromise of the two models is called an equimax solution. With this, one tries to accomplish both purposes but may not meet either of the research needs.

A component or factor score is a linear combination or weighted sum of the variables. Since the process of standardization will turn the initial weights for all variables to 1, their component/factor loadings reflect their relative importance in determining the variance along a specific dimension. Component/factor scores have important use in multidimensional scaling. The utility of the principal component/factor analysis techniques depends on the plan by which we handle the extracted components/factors as well as the way in which we score and weight the various subscales. Even if we decide to use multiple measures, we still have a choice as to whether to adopt component/factor scores or to construct separate summated subscales. We also have a chance to pursue ultimate uni-dimensionalization (at the most general level). We will further discuss this in the next chapter.

Generally speaking, the results of intercorrelation analysis will also help to develop theoretical understanding. The resulting clusters, components, and

to this has been to encourage – largely through punitive measures against those out of work – the growth of insecure part-time and low-paid work in a downward spiral that requires ever more punitive measures against the unemployed in order to succeed. When faced with the consequences of such a policy in the form of rising crime, the alienation of young unemployed men and social disorder, the response has been to portray such disorder as the mindless activities of a criminalized 'underclass'.

The fear of the breakdown of mechanisms of social control, however, while it centres on the so-called underclass, is most acute in the fears that their supposed behaviour and attitudes will spread to and infect others. The belief that once one person is allowed to get away with it, then all the rest will follow is a belief that has long dominated social policy provision, and which has on specific occasions been used to justify punitive treatment of the unemployed and other groups of the poor as an example to others. The 'underclass' thus becomes in Murray's own words a 'disease' and is created as the whipping post by which the poor in general are to be kept in line.

Conclusion

Whether the 'underclass' is empirically viable or theoretically coherent is not really the point. The concept of the 'underclass' is not about a lived social reality, but is a social construction: an attempt to portray the poor – or at least certain groups of the poor – in certain ways. It is about the construction of a set of assumptions and a way of looking at the poor that above all else sets them apart from everyone else, and constitutes them as a new and distinct 'social problem'.

The most immediate consequence of this is of course a continuing erosion of welfare provision, and a continuing justification for doing so. Cuts in benefit are justified as a means of eroding the 'dependency culture' in which the 'underclass' are supposed to live and which is taken as the cause of their poverty. Demonstrating the way in which the elasticity of the concept is used to affect larger groups of the poor, the rights of the homeless and other groups to priority in rehousing have since 1994 been abolished, on the grounds that teenage girls were deliberately getting pregnant in order to jump the housing queue. In the wake of comments such as that from the then Home Secretary Kenneth Clarke that 'it is not good permanently finding excuses for a section of the population who are essentially nasty pieces of work' (*The Independent*, 28 February 1993), penal policy has been shifted yet further from a rehabilitative to a controlling and containing role.

This shift in penal policy exemplifies ways in which images of an 'underclass' are used to justify and legitimate the abandonment of the social democratic form of the welfare state that dominated social policy provision in Britain (and elsewhere) for the three decades that followed the Second World War. This social democratic form stressed the need to incorporate the poor within the mainstream structures and institutions of society; it rested on a belief that those deemed deviant and anti-social could be rehabilitated, that the causes of their behaviour could be understood, and that policies could be developed that would at least ameliorate, if not prevent, the problem. The portrayal of the poor as an 'underclass' rejects this approach. Once certain groups are seen as essentially evil, as holding abnormal values out of line with the rest of society, the way is opened, to reiterate the words of the Prime Minister in 1993, 'to condemn a little more and understand a little less'. The construction of an 'underclass' as an explanation for Britain's growing poverty thus serves the two purposes of shifting attention away from other explanations for deep-rooted social problems by blaming the poor themselves, and provides legitimation for a harder, more coercive and much reduced welfare state.

Notes

1 Murray himself wrote: 'In this concentration of illegitimate births lies a generational catastrophe. Illegitimacy produces an underclass for one compelling practical reason having nothing to do with morality or the sanctity of marriage. Namely, communities need families. Communities need fathers' (1990: 2).

13

Quasi-markets and the Mixed Economy of Welfare

Gerry Mooney

The state's role in welfare provision has been a central political issue throughout the 1980s and 1990s. Successive Conservative governments have been concerned to reconstruct the welfare state during this period, and while we can identify a number of policies and proposals – for example, in the provision of health and community care – these are themselves open to very different interpretations. As in many other areas of social policy analysis there is a problem distinguishing between political rhetoric and the reality of policy intervention. However problematic such difficulties are, they do not preclude analysis. For Cochrane it is possible to identify important aspects of Conservative rhetoric during the period in question and consider changes in welfare polices which are associated with them (Cochrane, 1993). More important is that these problems should be recognized as stemming in part from the wide range of theoretical analyses which attempt to provide an explanation of the developments which have taken place in relation to the welfare state. Such issues are therefore highly politicized and contentious.

This chapter will focus on the government's strategies in two of the main areas of the welfare state: the NHS and the personal social services. It examines the key policies, particularly in relation to its strategy of 'rolling back' the state and its attempts to promote non-statutory forms of health and care provision. The chapter begins by examining the background to the government's approach to welfare provision. There is no one single 'policy' which can be identified. Instead, it is possible to discern particular views which the government has about state responsibilities in relation to the role of the family, voluntary and commercial sectors. In this respect the Conservatives' approach to social policy has never been simply about rolling back the state. Welfare policies and the promotion of the market have been tools to realize more specific political and ideological objectives, particularly in relation to the family. The backdrop is the interpretation of a 'crisis' in the welfare state in the 1970s which draws on New Right theories. The chapter then considers the Conservative approach to the welfare state. Here the idea of an internal market will be explored. One area of interest is the central role that management plays in the government's strategy for reform. The next section reviews the Government's policies and considers the competing claims that welfare pluralism has increased choice or, alternatively, that the major effect of reforms has been to residualize state welfare provision.

Background

The period from 1948 through to the 1970s was characterized by a relative consensus on the need for a welfare state (Lowe, 1993). For some, such as Pimlott (1988), however, this consensus was more 'myth' than reality, the notion disguising the extent of political conflict over post-war welfare reforms. By the 1970s, however, this 'consensus' was shaken by both economic crisis and ideological attacks on the welfare state itself. The emergence of mass unemployment and a declining economy eroded one of the main 'pillars' of support for the welfare state (Clarke and Langan, 1993), one consequence of which was a widespread reassessment of the role of the state in welfare provision (see Deakin, 1994, and Sullivan, 1994). Moreover, it was becoming increasingly difficult to finance the costs of maintaining welfare provision. This was exacerbated by a growing demand for welfare services as a consequence of demographic trends, with a significant increase in the proportion of the elderly in the population and, more importantly, as a result of rising unemployment.

Arguments for a reduction in state welfare expenditure came from across the political spectrum, but many of those who were to the fore behind such calls were on the political right. One influential argument was that state expenditure itself was inefficient and unproductive, undermining private enterprise through 'squeezing out' profitable sectors and utilizing resources which would have been better used by the private sector (Bacon and Eltis, 1976). These arguments increasingly turned the spotlight on levels of welfare expenditure and these rapidly became a target for those seeking a reduction in the level of state welfare activity. The main point to emerge from this is the idea that public expenditure, especially that used to fuel the welfare state, was a burden, and a burden that a declining British economy could no longer afford. Other arguments were more ideological in character, though not unconnected to the issue of public expenditure (see Chapter 3 for a fuller discussion of these issues).

One of the major claims made by supporters of the New Right at this time was that a large welfare state had a detrimental impact on the ability of people to take responsibility for their own lives. The effect was to 'demoralize' people, leading them to believe that the state would always provide (Clarke and Langan, 1993) Thus the welfare state was a 'nanny state', undermining initiative and enterprise, creating in its wake a 'dependency culture' (Dean and Taylor-Gooby, 1992).

Such claims were eagerly taken up by those on the right in Britain who were seeking ammunition with which to attack the welfare state (see, for example Boyson, 1971, and Joseph, 1976). The following argument from

Boyson was by no means out of step with much of radical Conservative thought at this time:

> A [welfare] state which does for its citizens what they can do for themselves is an evil state: and a state which removes all choice and responsibility from its people and makes them like broiler hens will create the irresponsible society. In such an irresponsible society no one cares, no one saves, no one bothers – why should they when the state spends all its energies taking money from the energetic, successful and thrifty to give it to the idle, the failures and the feckless? (Boyson, 1971: 9)

These ideas continue to occupy the minds of many New Right theorists. Thus Barnett writes: 'It was the welfare state that turned the mass of British people into a subliterate, unskilled, unhealthy and institutionalized proletariat hanging on the nipple of state maternalism' (1986: 304).

It is possible to identify here many of the central arguments used by Conservatives in their arguments for reorganizing the welfare state. Clearly evident are claims that state provision is bureaucratic, paternalistic and stifles choice. Together with arguments about levels of expenditure we have the seeds of the government's approach to the welfare state in the late 1980s and 1990s. The key theme emerging here is *anti-statism*. The source of such ideas is not difficult to locate. While American New Right theorists clearly exercised some influence, much of Conservative thinking in this area derives from liberal political thought (see Chapter 3). Much of the Conservatives' approach to social policy since the mid-1980s is in tune with Hayek's arguments. Neo-liberal political thought provides the ideological justification for many of the government's policies, as we will see below. It regards 'the market as a means of financing the provision of goods and services as infinitely superior to taxation, that in the absence of competition there is inefficiency, and that the proper role of government is a minimal one' (Dunsire, 1990: 39).

Activity 13.1

What were the main elements of the New Right attack on state welfare provision during the 1970s?

Restructuring the Welfare State

Many of the New Right arguments used to promote changes in the welfare state were to come to the fore after the Conservatives' general election victory in 1979. By the late 1970s and early 1980s critiques of the 'monolithic and restrictive' nature of state welfare were common currency in government circles. The solution was seen increasingly in terms of generating greater *welfare pluralism*, where more choice and responsiveness would be created. Such a view clearly related to the strategy of constraining welfare state growth and promoting the role of the private sector. But the concern to reform the welfare state was also a product of increasing fiscal pressures on state expenditure and the growing dislocation between the demand for services and the resources available to meet this.

For Norman Johnson, Conservative social policy during the first two terms of the Thatcher government (1979–87) had three main objectives (Johnson, 1990):

1 To increase the role of the private sector through various 'privatization' schemes.
2 To attack the power of local authorities.
3 To promote inequality.

There was also an important political objective, with the Conservatives attempting, through policies such as the privatization of local authority housing stock, to widen their electoral base.

Johnson's argument is that during this period the aim of the government was not to dismantle the welfare state, but to transform it. But as Sullivan has pointed out, the distinction between the two is a very fine one (Sullivan, 1994). Privatization in all its guises basically involved reducing the activities of the state, the vast majority of which were said to be inefficient and bureaucratic.

Despite the rhetoric Tory plans for social policy, as contained in their 1979 Election Manifesto, did not represent a radical change of direction (Sullivan, 1994). During their first period of office, the evolution of policy was more pragmatic and moved rather slowly. Indeed, while it is important not to attribute too much significance to trends in expenditure, particularly in respect of welfare outcomes, it is noteworthy that during the period 1973–74 to 1987–88, overall welfare spending increased by 37 per cent (Le Grand, 1990b: 340). Indeed, over the period patterns of welfare expenditure had been relatively stable. For Le Grand, this serves to highlight the 'robustness' of the welfare state and he identifies three important factors to explain this. First, that the welfare state was characterized by a degree of professional and bureaucratic inertia and hence the 'system' was itself slow to change. Second, changing demographic trends were creating more demand for welfare services. In part this was accounted for by the growing number of elderly in the population but demand was also stimulated by the rapid growth in unemployment during the first half of the 1980s and by an increase in levels of poverty. Finally, he argues that those services which were more extensively utilized by the middle classes fared better over the period (Le Grand, 1990b). According to Le Grand then, the Conservatives were relatively cautious in their initial approach to social and welfare policy reforms; there was no overarching vision directing this. His conclusion is that 'one of the striking features of the first eight years of Mrs Thatcher's government was how little it affected the welfare state' (1990b: 351).

Despite this claim it is evident that the Conservatives were starting to put together the basis for a major reorganization of the welfare state. During the first two terms of Conservative government, the ideological onslaught on the welfare state continued, and from the early 1980s arguments were being advanced for a fundamental reduction in the role of the state. One year after Thatcher's first general election success, the newly founded Social Affairs Unit published its first study. Entitled 'Breaking the Spell of the Welfare State', its authors, Anderson, Lait and Marsland (1981), claimed that welfare states were damaging to society and undermined potential sources of welfare such as the family. In addition, some Conservative politicians and strategists were proposing an 'enabling' role for the state rather than one of large-scale provision. This idea was clearly expressed by the then Secretary of State for Health and Social Services, Norman Fowler, in 1984. The role of the state, he claimed, was 'to back-up and develop the assistance which is given by private and voluntary support' (Fowler, 1984: 13).

The following section examines the ways in which these arguments were utilized by the government in its approach to social policy after its third successive general election victory, in 1987.

1988: a Watershed for Social Policy?

For Le Grand, the welfare state in 1987 was much the same as that inherited by the Tories from Labour in 1979 (Le Grand, 1990b). But after the general election success that year it became clear that the Conservatives were prepared to adopt a much more aggressive ideological stance against state welfare provision in its existing form (Sullivan, 1996). From 1988 the government began to look for 'market reforms' in the 'heartland' areas of social policy: education, health and the personal social services, promoting and encouraging greater use of the private sector. In January Mrs Thatcher announced a long-awaited review of the NHS, which eventually was to conclude by recommending the introduction of internal markets. The 1988 Education Act also allowed schools to 'opt out' of local authority control, and in the same year reforms of the welfare benefits system came into force. Health and welfare services were targeted by the government to adopt the '3 Es' – economy, efficiency and effectiveness – and in general the goal was that these services should be provided in a more 'business-like' way (Clarke and Langan, 1993: 63).

We turn now to consider the impact of such thinking on the government's proposals for reforming the NHS and personal social services. First we examine the arguments put forward for 'marketization'.

The Case for Reform

Previously we discussed some aspects of the ideological attack on the welfare state from sections of the New Right. A strong moral argument was integral to this, claiming that too much welfare provision by the state simply reinforced problems of 'dependency' and 'social irresponsibility' (Murray, 1990, 1994). But the idea that the welfare state 'damages society' (Segalman and Marsland, 1989) was only one element of the case for welfare reform advanced by the government and its supporters in the mid-1980s. This section will focus on the other arguments made for reform.

A basic principle of the neo-liberal tradition is that the state's role should be a minimal one. This is reflected in arguments that state provision was necessarily inefficient, unproductive and failed to address individual needs. Conservative arguments that the welfare state was inefficient appeared to tap into discontent that the recipients of state services were being poorly provided for. Media reports about long NHS waiting lists, the declining standards of much of local authority housing stock and the bureaucratic inefficiencies of both the benefits system and personal social services, were seized upon by proponents of reform as a key rationale for change. But underlying these populist issues were the key arguments of the New Right: that the welfare state was not inefficient because of lack of funding but rather because state provision itself failed to ensure that services would be supplied at minimum cost. The concern to emphasize the inefficiency of state provision of welfare was directly linked to other claims: that value for money was not being achieved and that the existing system was ineffective in meeting the needs of those who utilized its services. This relates closely to the neo-liberal argument that the main beneficiaries of welfare state programmes were the professionals and bureaucrats themselves. Attacking the 'despotic' welfare state then was to be a central plank of government policy. But the most forceful argument advocated by supporters of reform was the lack of 'choice' in existing forms of welfare provision. Arguments about the need to enhance choice served to provide popular legitimation for government proposals.

For those supporters of reform among the Conservatives monopoly state provision was regarded as a barrier to the goals of increasing choice, efficiency, effectiveness, innovation and consumer influence on the delivery of services. Increased competition and the marketization of welfare provision were promoted as the means by which these could be achieved (see Chapter 3). The task for the government was to facilitate the introduction of the market into those spheres of welfare provision which were largely undertaken by the state. Therefore there would be a greater role for the private and voluntary sectors in the 'new' welfare arrangements.

At this stage it is important to introduce the concept of *welfare pluralism* (sometimes referred to as the *mixed economy of welfare*). This notion refers to the different forms and sources of welfare provision. Provision comes from four sources:

1 the state;
2 non-statutory for-profit organizations;
3 non-statutory voluntary organizations;
4 the informal sector.

Thus a call for greater welfare pluralism involves redrawing the relations and boundaries between the state, the market and the family. This should be understood as reorganizing or restructuring *existing* patterns of provision. What is being laid down is the basis of a *new* mixed economy of welfare. Pinker has argued that welfare pluralism/mixed economy of welfare has had a long history (1992). Since the creation of the infrastructure of the welfare state, welfare services have been provided by a range of public and private organizations. Therefore the idea of welfare pluralism operates in two ways: first as a *description* of the sources of welfare provision and, second, as an *ideological* theme to release the power of markets and make voluntary effort more effective. What this highlights is that public and private provision are closely interrelated:

> the distinction between the two sectors of formal services is rarely a simple one of private versus public, market versus non-market principles. Market mechanisms and assumptions are a common feature of public services. Rather than a simple dichotomous framework of public and private institutions, social services consist of a wide range of sometimes overlapping provisions. (Walker, 1984: 23)

The mixed economy of welfare then has been in existence for some considerable time. But the balance between the public and private sectors, which comprise a significant segment of the *welfare mix* (Rose, 1985), is one that is changing in favour of the non-statutory sector. (Another section of the welfare mix, the household, has always been integral whatever the balance between other sources.) The mix itself will vary over time and between the types of service being provided. Thus the mixed economy of welfare was built into the very fabric of the post-war welfare state, especially in the field of personal social services. The idea that welfare pluralism represents some kind of 'radical break' with the past is misleading, as it exaggerates the extent to which post-war welfare provision was the responsibility of the state alone, thus allowing little recognition of the contribution of other forms (Pinker, 1992: 272).

Support for greater welfare pluralism and competition is primarily founded upon arguments that it would enhance choice and efficiency, as well as *empowering* the customer or consumer. The welfare state was regarded as particularly deficient in this respect (Klein and O'Higgins, 1985; Day and Klein, 1987). Greater welfare pluralism is viewed as the means by which a more user-sensitive and accountable welfare system can be developed. Clearly, such arguments have to be evaluated. In order to do this the discussion shifts to consider the government's welfare policies in practice. Two case studies are introduced at this stage: the 1989 plans for reforming the NHS and the reorganization of the personal social services in 1990. There are very similar themes and issues, as will become evident. The discussion focuses primarily on the changing role of the state through the introduction of internal markets.

Activity 13.2

What do you understand by the term 'welfare pluralism'?

The 1989 NHS Reforms

Wistow has identified three phases in Conservative government policy towards the NHS (Wistow, 1992):

1 1979–82 Decentralization and the attempt to eradicate bureaucracy.
2 1982–89 Centralization and the strategic role of management.
3 1989–   The introduction of internal markets and the creation of a mixed economy of provision.

Throughout the 1980s the market made inroads into the NHS through various forms of privatization. The competitive tendering and contracting-out of in-house services such as cleaning, catering and portering also led to the steady expansion of managerialism. The major consequence of these developments was to drive down the wages and employment conditions of workers who were already among some of the most poorly paid in the country. While it is possible to identify the origins of the 1989 reforms during this period, the focus here is on the third phase identified by Wistow. The background to this was the comprehensive review of the NHS announced by Mrs Thatcher in 1988. The central focus of this review, which was conducted by a small group of Cabinet ministers, was on the efficient delivery of health care. In 1987–88 there was growing public and professional concern about NHS funding, but the review neatly side-stepped issues of resources and the emphasis was on the wasteful and inefficient use of existing funds (Paton, 1990: 120). The review was published in 1989 in the White Paper *Working for Patients* (DOH, 1989b). Competition was at its heart, and the main proposal to emerge was the introduction of an internal market in the NHS, necessitating fundamental internal reorganization (Sullivan, 1996).

An internal market

> mimics the market form of coordination. Within the organization there are sub-units which act as buyers and sellers, exchanging goods and services with each other. Competition is promoted by ensuring that the buying and selling units have alternative parties with whom they can exchange and so trade with external agents is usually encouraged. (Levacic, 1993: 179)

The essence of this internal market was that health-care services would be purchased from a variety of competing providers on behalf of patients. The purchasers, health authorities and fund-holding GPs, would act as the patient's agent in the market. But both purchasers and providers would remain within the NHS.

Le Grand has suggested that the term *quasi-market* may be more appropriate in capturing the essence of the internal market in large public-sector organizations:

> The proposed reforms in primary and secondary education, health and housing and social services all involve the introduction of what might be termed 'quasi-markets': the separation of state finance from state provision and the introduction of competition and provision from independent agencies. If these reforms are

factors may suggest some important directions for deeper-going analysis, which has been evidenced by the recent development of the hypothetical latent structure of a data set. Intercorrelation analysis may also be used to explore the relationships between independent and dependent variables. An analytic model will be more pertinent if independent and dependent variables are all selected from one group. Combined with careful selection, data reduction by grouping will make an analytic model more concise and efficient.

The above intercorrelation models are suitable for analyzing the relationships among a set of interval or continuous variables. Lower level measures may also be analyzed by a technique called smallest space analysis. The relationships among such variables may be measured by Lambda or Gamma coefficients.

Longitudinal data analysis

Probably you have noticed something missing in all the above discussions, that is, a time dimension. If your research adopts a longitudinal design, then you will have longitudinal rather than cross-sectional data to deal with. Usually you can still treat your data cross-sectionally at one point in time, or at more than one point in time for a comparison. To cover the entire time horizon and gain the most clear and efficient description of the process of change, however, there are certain ways and special techniques that you should know in analyzing the kind of data. We will leave these for a brief discussion in chapter thirteen, as the following chapter is concerned with some important issues generally associated with the use of path analysis, factor analysis, etc.

carried through to their logical conclusion, the welfare state in the 1990s will be one where local authorities will not own and operate schools, houses or residential homes, and where health authorities will not own and operate hospitals. Instead local authorities and, increasingly, central government will be financing a growing number of private and voluntary institutions, all competing for custom. . . . This shift from the state as funder and provider to the state primarily as funder with perhaps only a residual role as provider will undoubtedly create enormous changes in the way services are delivered and employees treated. (Le Grand, 1990b: 351)

In the quasi-market, relationships are established which attempt to 'mimic' the market, but these remain regulated and managed by the state. The provider organizations are not necessarily private or out to maximize profits (Le Grand, 1990a; Le Grand and Bartlett, 1993; Bartlett et al., 1994).

In the 1989 NHS reforms, the internal market was based upon a divide between *purchaser* and *provider* functions. District Health Authorities or Health Boards were to commission health-care services from whichever hospital or unit was regarded as providing the best quality and most efficient service. The purchasers, DHAs and certain GP practices, were thus entrusted to choose on the basis of these criteria. Provider units were expected in turn to increase efficiency and the quality of service in order to attract orders from purchasers who in turn would 'shop around' for the best priced product or service. Providers now had to compete in terms of costs and outcomes. *Working for Patients* envisaged that three types of provider hospitals would begin to compete against one another: those under the direct control of DHAs/Health Boards, independent hospitals and self-governing NHS Hospital Trusts, primarily the large general hospitals providing a variety of health services. These Trusts were no longer under DHA control and could buy and sell goods and services and compete for both private and NHS patients. Revenue would derive solely from the sale of services.

Such 'managed competition' was at the heart of the White Paper. The role of DHAs was completely transformed, at least in appearance. Instead of providing and managing all health-care services in one locality, they were now simply the purchasers of such services. These proposals were to be enacted under the 1990 National Health Service and Community Care Act, with the internal market operational by April 1991. Both purchasers and providers were to become trading entities within the NHS, the relationship between them being a contractual one. Such a proposal could be interpreted as implying a reduced role for the state. But as Sullivan (1994) indicates, the reforms are not as revolutionary as they might first appear. The relationship between hospitals and DHAs remains largely unaltered, while NHS hospitals still provide the overwhelming majority of health care in this country. Thus there are strong continuities with previous administrative and structural arrangements. However, notwithstanding these continuities, it is clear that the government aimed to make the NHS function more like a business. The waste and inefficiency, which were regarded as hallmarks of the old NHS monopoly, would thus be overcome. Therefore, although the NHS has not been privatized, it is important that the significance of these reforms is not underestimated. The separation of the provision of health care from the commissioning of care has meant that the NHS monopoly has been effectively broken. Further, for Sullivan, the introduction of a quasi-market in health has made privatization of the NHS a much more straightforward task in the future, establishing as it does that the market has a major role to play (Sullivan, 1994, 1996).

The NHS reforms signalled the increasing penetration of the market into the welfare state. One important consequence has been a change in the nature of the relationship between the providers and recipients of services. In the new internal market, patients, claimants and clients have been replaced by customers, contractors and users. One major issue was the extent to which the market would be allowed to operate unfettered within the NHS.

What is also clear is that the development of the purchaser–provider division has thrown issues of rationing into centre stage. Prior to the 1989 reforms decisions about rationing were largely informal, subsumed under the general ideology of clinical freedom. With the introduction of an internal market the rationing of health care becomes more visible (and increasingly politicized) as the responsibility of the purchasing agency. One other significant outcome of the internal market has been the enhanced role of management, with the creation of a more effective line of control. This is an issue which received considerable attention in the 1989 White Paper and one we will return to below.

Reforming Community Care

The community-care component of the 1990 NHS and Community Care Act has also promoted the mixed economy of care, this time in the delivery of personal social services. For long the services had been the primary responsibility of local authorities, and the Act sought to restructure their provision. Since the 1960s there had been increasing calls for more 'community care'. The ambiguity of this notion meant that it was an objective subscribed to by all the main political parties. In the 1970s, both Conservative and Labour governments were keen to promote the de-institutionalization of care, and advanced community care as 'the right way' to support those individuals who found it difficult to be self-caring and live independent lives. But by the 1980s community care became one of the most popular slogans utilized by the Conservative government to promote its reform of local welfare provision.

The Conservatives had made their intentions clear as early as 1981 with the publication of the White Paper *Care in the Community* (DHSS, 1981). One of its main recommendations was to become a central plank in future policy: 'care in the community must increasingly mean care by the community' (1981: 3). This implicitly suggested a reappraisal of the role of the public sector, an issue taken up three years later by Norman Fowler, then the

Secretary of State for Health and Social Services. For Fowler, the primary role of the state was 'to back-up and develop the assistance which is given by private and voluntary support' (Fowler, 1984). His comments came during a period when existing community care policies were coming under increased scrutiny. In its 1986 Report, *Making a Reality of Community Care*, the Audit Commission criticized existing provision as offering poor value for money. Too many people, it was claimed, were being cared for, at a huge and increasing cost, in institutions. Ways had to be found to reduce this financial burden (Audit Commission, 1986). In this Report community care was now recast and reinterpreted as the means by which public provision of services would become less significant.

In March 1986 Sir Roy Griffiths was appointed to investigate problems in the delivery of care. His recommendations matched the government's concern to replace costly institutional care with other forms of provision (Griffiths, 1988). The most fundamental justification for change then was financial, not needs-based (Walker, 1993: 218). Griffiths's proposals formed the basis of the 1989 White Paper *Caring for People* (DOH, 1989a), and it is to an examination of this that we now turn.

> The role of the public sector is essentially to ensure that care is provided. How it is provided is an important, but secondary consideration and local authorities must show that they are getting and providing real value. (DOH, 1989a: para 25)

The above statement encapsulates much of the thrust of the White Paper and the government's plans in this field. As is evident, the emphasis once again was on greater welfare pluralism, with the state's role being reduced from one of *providing* welfare to *supporting* welfare provision. In this context 'enabling' meant both promoting choice and stimulating the role of the non-statutory sector.

> The government envisages . . . that the statutory sector will continue to play an important role in backing up, developing and monitoring private and voluntary care facilities, and providing services where this remains the best way of meeting care needs. (DOH, 1989a: para 22)

The resulting Act declared an end to the role of social work/social services departments as the 'monopoly providers' of welfare services. Care services were now to be purchased from within the mixed economy of welfare in specific localities, with the informal and voluntary sectors playing a bigger part. Further, the local state as 'enabler' would also ensure that services should intervene no more than is necessary in order to foster self-help, thereby avoiding 'problems of dependency'. This should not be taken as implying that local authorities no longer had a major input into the delivery of social services. Their role was transformed. Under the Griffiths proposals and the 1990 Act, which came into force on 1 April 1993, local authority social work/social services departments were the 'lead agencies', playing a strategic role in identifying and assessing needs in their area, both at a community and individual level. They were to ensure the provision of the necessary services, purchased from a variety of agencies and organizations. In preparing community care plans, local authority welfare departments would therefore address the needs of their locality in a more flexible and sensitive way, widening consumer choice in the process. With the emphasis on the maximum utilization of services from non-statutory organizations, greater efficiency and innovation in the delivery of care would be encouraged.

What is also evident is that the role of social work and welfare professionals has been changed. Social workers were now recast as case or care 'managers'. To borrow a term used by the Audit Commission, as managers they were to become the 'bolsheviks' of the community care 'revolution' (Audit Commission, 1992). In 1986 the Audit Commission had judged local authority welfare services to be expensive, inefficient and wasteful, lacking the necessary expertise to provide services in a cost-effective way. Establishing market forces within the sphere of welfare would therefore enhance efficiency. But this was dependent on securing the appropriate quantity and quality of services at the lowest cost. Case managers would be entrepreneurial in outlook and flexible and innovative in the way they planned to meet objectives (Kelly, 1991: 187). These policies, which were to transform the role of social workers, were couched in terms of an attack on the bureaucracy of large state organizations and on 'self-interested' professionals themselves. As case managers social workers would act as 'purchasers' of care, attempting to address needs and ration resources simultaneously.

In the new mixed economy of welfare, the social work department remains the central planning and purchasing body but, in tune with the central objective of the community-care reforms, the provision of care will be largely undertaken by other agencies – and families. For Griffiths the end result would be 'needs-led' as opposed to a service/supply-led process, with the customer being provided with greater choice and better quality services.

The fragmentation of provision, as opposed to full 'privatization', is said to enhance welfare pluralism and 'empower' the individual. As with the NHS reforms, purchaser and provider functions were to be separated with the intention of ending the role of the state as the funder *and* provider of welfare, so that as the 'enabling authority' it might stimulate such provision in other ways, stressing in particular the role of family and community.

The development of the mixed economy of care represents another attempt to 'roll back' the state, thus altering the balance in the welfare mix. As we have seen, state provision was portrayed as inevitably bureaucratic and inefficient, contrasting with the apparently flexible and innovative dynamism of the non-state sectors. As in most other areas of welfare provision, however, representation and reality often diverge considerably. But it is clear that through the community care reforms, the government was also concerned to re-establish family and individual responsibility for certain types of care.

Activity 13.3

Drawing on the discussion in the previous two sections, in what ways would you say the purchaser–provider split has altered the delivery of health and care services?

The Welfare State Reforms: Critical Review

The primary objective of community-care policy is arguably one that sees a reduction in the role of the public sector as the main provider of care. This was legitimized in terms which stressed greater value for money, and effectiveness in meeting need and choice. In the 1990 community-care legislation no recommendations were made for empowering the service user, despite the widespread rhetoric of 'choice'. The 'case managers' are the people who have the power and authority to decide and to choose what services are provided, and by whom. Those who actually use the services remain largely the passive recipients of care. The title of the White Paper itself, *Caring for People* (DOH, 1989a; my emphasis), provides some indication of this. Claims that the purchaser–provider split and the development of an 'enabling' role for the state would make services more sensitive and responsive to the needs of users appear to have been ill founded. A large gap remains between needs and resources, and the providers continue to remain dominant in the new arrangements. It has also been argued that the new 'social care markets' are unable to guarantee the provision of the range of services required to fulfil designated community-care objectives (Forder et al., 1996: 201).

In the 1989 White Paper, 'choice' is defined as 'giving people a greater individual say in how they live their lives and the services they need to help them' (DOH, 1989a: 4). This was to be achieved through greater welfare pluralism and care management. But care management and the assessing of needs is directly linked to the rationing of resources. Thus the introduction of internal markets and the purchaser–provider divide may actually increase, not diminish, the power of professional groups within the mixed economy of welfare. For the Audit Commission, the introduction of care managers would be a way of removing 'vested interests' from the process of providing care services. But what has emerged is a system whereby the vast majority of 'customers' are not in a position to choose but are instead dependent on an assessment of the services they require, an assessment still conducted by a professional.

This situation emerges from the underlying principles of the quasi-market itself: consumer power is not expressed in the form of cash, nor is it exercised by the consumers of the service themselves, but by care managers who are the 'managerial proxies' acting on behalf of the consumer. But will these proxies always behave in a way suited to the best interests of the consumers and users of the services? As Walker indicates, consumerism is not the same as 'empowering' the users of services (Walker, 1993). Power then is not transferred to the customers (who can be regarded as *quasi-customers*) but to their 'agents', the managers who are assumed to be more user-sensitive than the professionals. But 'the manager' is also a gatekeeper, determining access to limited resources. Decision-making power remains in the hands of the professionals. This should not be taken as implying that the role of such professionals is unaltered. They are simultaneously deskilled (with the role of generic social worker being replaced by specialists in particular fields such as child protection), while increased professional judgement is required in the balancing of needs and resources.

Greater welfare pluralism does not necessarily mean greater choice. Some individuals and groups are clearly in a better position to exercise choice than others. Choice always involves costs, and therefore many will not be in a position to exercise what choice there is. But choice also implies the availability of alternatives, and clearly realistic choices are rarely available for the most vulnerable groups of users. What this demonstrates is that the welfare reforms discussed here involve both the reproduction of inequalities and their reinforcement. This is an issue we return to in the conclusion.

The Managerialization of Welfare Provision

The promotion of the role of management was an integral feature of the Conservative government's reforms of the welfare state. The lack of management and inadequate management were highlighted as major causes of the spiralling costs of welfare provision before the reforms were implemented. Management innovation in the 'new' welfare state was regarded as the vehicle through which greater efficiency, effectiveness and economy could be achieved. Management was at the core of the internal market, defining both the needs of the consumer and the resources required. The attractiveness of what has been termed 'new managerialism' is obvious: it appears politically neutral and treats highly political issues as objective, technical matters. Central here is the ideology of '*the right to manage*', that is, freedom from government and political 'interference'. Furthermore, Clarke and colleagues have highlighted the ways in which this new managerialism attacks the professional–client relationship which existed previously in welfare provision (Clarke et al., 1994: 6). But at times 'managerialism' as a strategy has politicized both issues of welfare delivery and welfare professionals forced to adopt new work practices, something we can detect in the opposition of the British Medical Association to many aspects of the NHS reforms. In early 1996, for example, political controversy surrounded the publication by the Labour Party of staffing changes in the NHS. Between 1989 and 1994 the number of NHS managers in Scotland alone multiplied by five, while there was a 29 per cent decrease in the number of nurses employed (*The Herald*, 18 January 1996). This is a pattern reproduced across Britain.

The enhanced role of management then, is reflected in the redefinition of relationships not only between purchasers, providers and users but also within the labour market of the welfare state itself. In the rush to achieve a 'competitive edge', the result has been a continual drive for cost-cutting, demoralization for many welfare workers and an explosion in the role of 'consultants'. The restructuring of the mixed economy of welfare has meant a fundamental shift in control, both in the internal market of the mixed economy of welfare and between providers/purchasers and users.

Summary and Conclusion

The nature of the welfare regime to emerge from the government's reforms has been the subject of much controversy and debate. Hills, for example, has stressed the continuing stability in levels of provision for welfare services (1990), while Le Grand has argued that the welfare state has been resistant to the most radical plans of the Conservative reformers (1990b). Krieger, on the other hand, has claimed that welfare provision has been fundamentally altered and that 'roll-back' has led to the end of the welfare state itself (1987). But for Clarke and Langan, no simple picture of 'roll-back' has emerged from the reforms which have been introduced (Clarke and Langan, 1993: 69). The welfare state has not emerged from the period unchanged, however. For Michael Sullivan, some of the changes have been significant in that the welfare state now more fully resembles market organizations than at any time throughout the post-war period (Sullivan, 1996: 119).

The welfare state reforms took place against a background of deepening economic and social inequalities. Poverty, unemployment and homelessness in particular were much higher during this period than for much of the 1970s. This has meant that pressure on services has increased. Pressures to cut costs have been felt most acutely by many of the users and those in the front line of provision. Cost-cutting and greater efficiency have been achieved at the expense of a major deterioration in the wages and conditions of employment of many social care staff and created major divisions between core and casual or subcontracted staff. Caring has become increasingly the task of part-time workers in day-care units, home-care workers and the families of relatives. Greater inequalities in pay are emerging within the NHS and care sectors. But inequalities are also emerging in other ways.

Arguably the NHS and community care reforms have led to the creation of a two-tier welfare state. Walker in particular has argued that the main objective of the community care legislation was to *residualize* the role of public sector provision, under the 'guise' of welfare pluralism (Walker, 1993: 204). The fragmentation of state provision has served to encourage the development of cheaper sources of care, both formal and informal. Le Grand has highlighted the ways in which the private sector has tended to concentrate on areas where expectations of profitability are highest (Le Grand, 1990b). In addition, there is also a tendency for private providers to 'cream off' the less costly users, leaving the most needy and dependent to be catered for by poorer-quality public provision. Already fears have risen that fund-holding GPs will seek to prevent potential patients (deemed to be most needy) from registering with their practice. The result is that a growing number of people may find themselves in temporary 'transit' between GPs, seeking registration where possible. What emerges is a situation where providers are able to select consumers (a form of adverse selection), not one in which the consumer or user is sovereign. Those services which are aimed at the poorest and most vulnerable groups within society will remain, for the time being at least, the responsibility of state provision. Underlying this are the social relations of class. Choice and diversity of provision will clearly be greater at the top of the class hierarchy. The middle classes, as with the 'old' welfare state, will be the most likely beneficiaries of the new arrangements. But there is also another source of inequality here: one that is premised on the gendered division of labour in contemporary British society. In this respect the public–private distinction refers not to the division between state and for-profit forms of care provision, but to a more fundamental socio-economic division.

The community-care legislation in particular involved the largely hidden transfer of care responsibility from the public realm to the private sphere of the family, redrawing in the process the boundaries between the two. Community caring thus was to be resourced largely by women's unpaid domestic labour, consequently entrapping many women even further and reinforcing their economic dependency on men (Graham, 1993). The welfare reforms then have had the effect of reinforcing 'private' forms of care in the home. The welfare state was built upon a particular understanding of the relationship between public and private spheres, and a large amount of unpaid domestic caring by women in particular has always been an integral part of the mixed economy of welfare. Thus, while the boundaries between public and private are drawn and redrawn by the state, the two spheres are not, and have never been, separate but are crucially interlocked. Welfare outcomes then are the product of a mix of provision, central to which has been care in families and households.

This discussion highlights the political and contested nature of the welfare reforms. 'Political' here refers to power relations and social divisions within society. Yet much of the debate has taken place in a rather 'depoliticized' way, focusing often on which particular variant of welfare reforms is most efficient or effective. The result is that the debate has tended to become preoccupied with technocratic investigation, critical analysis being accorded at best a secondary status (Page, 1995). For Page this 'drift to neutrality' has a specific party political aspect. Arguably, much of the Labour Party's recent policy discussions on welfare provision have embraced large elements of the Conservative government's reforms. The Labour Party-sponsored Commission on Social Justice, for example, effectively retreated from some central aspects of post-1945 welfarism, particularly in relation to collectivism and the pursuit of equality (Page, 1995). Under Tony Blair 'New Labour' has tended to stress social responsibility, not social rights, in the language of 'communitarianism' and the 'stakeholder' society. The Party's strategy for 'modernizing' or 'reconstructing' the welfare state emphasizes the importance of private forms of provision and this is reflected in its plans for the NHS, where the purchaser–provider split has effectively been accepted (Labour Party, 1995). For the Labour MP Frank Field the key thrust of Labour's plans for welfare reform must be to control welfare expenditure (Field, 1995). Much of this appears to accept some of the key tenets of Conservative policy in recent years. This raises an important issue: the extent to which we are witnessing the emergence of a new 'welfare consensus', in which issues of service delivery, efficiency and effectiveness take centre place, and in which 'managerialism' and 'marketization' are accorded a pivotal role. The signs are already in place that the Labour Party has taken on board many of these ideas. But while a narrow party political consensus *may* emerge to some extent, this does not detract from the central thrust of this chapter, that the reforms discussed and the general debate about welfare provision is highly political in the broader sense of the notion.

Thus the welfare state and the mixed economy of welfare are not separate from wider patterns of social relations. The welfare state emerged from a society in which inequalities of class, gender and ethnicity were/are integral features. Although it has undergone major changes during the 1980s and 1990s, it is questionable whether these changes have led to the creation of a *new welfare regime*. But what is clear is that the introduction of quasi- and internal markets and the other reforms explored here must be understood in relation to prevailing patterns of power and to the multi-dimensional nature of inequality in modern Britain.

Activity 13.4

What signs are there that a new political consensus has emerged about the direction and shape of welfare provision in contemporary British society?

Glossary

Anti-statism

New Right view of the state as an inefficient, bureaucratic and ineffective provider of goods and services. By contrast, the market is seen as most efficient method of distributing and allocating goods and services.

Biological determinism

This concept claims that biological differences between women and men and the psychological characteristics of each sex determine their social roles, so that social relations are reduced to biological features which cannot therefore be altered by social practices. The concept has often been used to restrict women's activities and has been associated with traditional constraints; for example, discriminatory legislation which prevents women from participating fully in social and political life.

Biopolitics

A concept developed by Michel Foucault used to describe the intervention of the state into the private arena of the home from the eighteenth century onwards in Europe. From this period the body became the target of state regulation and intervention. Jacques Donzelot applies this concept to the 'policing of families', where the state has intervened, for example, to regulate child-rearing practices and to produce a discourse of 'the good mother'. Such a concept is useful to feminists in exploring how women have been the target of state intervention.

Corporatism

Term used to describe a number of modern societies, or trends within modern societies, which stress their 'corporate' nature. Usually based on 'tri-partism', agreements between the state, capital and labour, with the state playing the leading role in establishing national social and economic policy direction.

Dependency culture

Disparaging term used to refer to the supposed attitudes prevalent among sections of modern societies who choose to become reliant on welfare services and 'welfarism' (as opposed to work) to provide their living requirements and, as a result, have their autonomy, independence and self-respect destroyed or undermined.

CHAPTER TWELVE

Measurement and Analysis Issues in Psychosocial Research

The term path analysis has been used to refer to the analysis of causal models when single indicators are employed for each of the variables in the model (Pedhazur & Schmelkin, 1991). When multi-item measures or composite variables are involved, issues of scaling will complicate your data analysis. You will have to deal with both scale development and substantive model construction. Conventionally, researchers would first conduct needed dimensional analysis, specifically factor or principal component analysis, for each composite measure that represents a given theoretical construct, and then test their substantive hypotheses and models using selected factor- or component-based scales. Recent developments in analytic technology, however, have emphasized the simultaneous treatment of scaling and hypothesis testing based on the theoretical idea of a "latent structure" for a data set. This approach has resulted in a conspicuous new model combining path analysis with (confirmatory) factor analysis in the same procedure.

An integral and optimal model

Generally speaking, scale development and substantive model testing should be viewed as two inseparable aspects of a research process. Substantive findings will depend on the measures used. The best substantive results must be the best measurement results. On the other hand, the development of measurement tools must be tested by substantive results and ultimately serve specific substantive purposes.

Difference Principle	The principle that social and economic inequalities are to be arranged so that they are of greatest benefit to the least advantaged.
Entitlement conception of justice	This is the name Robert Nozick gives to his own conception of justice, which is both unpatterned and historical.
Essentialism	This concept is based on biological assumptions about sex/gender, claiming that there is a unique female nature. This has been linked to feminist positions which seek to revalue and celebrate that essential female nature.
Historical materialism	Marx's method of analysis which locates the production of material goods at the centre of his analysis. Production is an activity which entails (usually unequal) social relations between people and groups. Historically, production has been organized in a number of different ways.
Historical principles of distributive justice	This is Robert Nozick's term for principles of distribution of goods and services in which whether the distribution is just depends on how it came about.
Ideology	Can be used in two ways. First, the 'positive' usage which refers to a set of beliefs or a value system which binds groups, classes or political parties together. Second, the 'negative' usage refers to a set of beliefs about the world which can be characterized by their overall falsity. Nevertheless, in this second form, the ideas must have the capacity to offer a partial explanation of the social world and partly match people's lived experiences of life in complex societies. In Chapter 4 ideology is used in this second sense.
Individualism	The belief that the individual ought to be the focus of economic and social policy and that all phenomena are reducible to individual behaviour; the individual, not the state, knows best.
Institutional: racism/sexism/ heterosexism	This refers to the way(s) that government policies, state activities and institutional practices discriminate, consciously or unconsciously, against minority ethnic communities/women/gays and lesbians.
Internal markets	Term used to describe the organization of service provision within state organizations through institutional arrangements which resemble the workings of the market. A key component of this is the division between purchaser and provider functions.
Less eligibility	The idea, originally articulated most clearly in the 1834 Poor Law Report, that the level of living of those

	people in receipt of relief (or today, benefits) should be worse than (i.e., less eligible) the lowest-paid independent member of the labour force.
Liberal	The political tradition which, in different ways, contends that the individual (with her or his rights) is the most significant economic, political and social actor and that 'liberty' is the prime political value.
Mixed economy of welfare/welfare pluralism	Can be used in two ways: as a description of the multiple sources of welfare provision; and as an ideology promoting the greater use of non-state provision in the delivery of health and welfare services.
Neo-liberal	Literally, those intellectuals who have resurrected the economic and philosophical beliefs of classical liberalism with its emphasis on free markets and individual choice.
Paradigm	In the social sciences, a self-contained theoretical model which offers both explanation and policy prescriptions.
Patriarchy	This is a system of male authority where men have power over women through the operation of economic, political and social institutions. Patriarchal societies have taken different economic and political forms historically, but in each the distribution of power is based on a sex/gender division where men have access to and control over resources which enable them to oppress women both inside the private arena of the home and within the public sphere of politics, culture and paid work/production.
Patterned principles of distributive justice	This is Robert Nozick's term for distribution of goods and services in accordance with the formula 'to each according to his/her X' where X may be 'need' or 'merit'. (An unpatterned principle of distribution would be one where this does not apply.)
Quasi-markets	Term used to distinguish internal markets within the public sector from conventional markets.
Selectivism	The principle of allocating welfare resources ostensibly to the most 'needy' through an income or means test.
Social construction	Refers to the way in which apparently 'real' phenomena (such as gender roles or 'race' classifications) have actually been created and established as a consequence of the historical interaction of social, political and economic forces.
Social democracy	A political movement whose aims are to reform capitalism, removing its worst excesses and gradually move towards a socialist socio-economic system. Its aim is to utilize the legislative framework of society to

	spread the political democracy of modern societies gradually to the economic and social spheres.
Social totality	Phrase used to refer to the interaction of economic, political, social and cultural phenomena that occur within societies, the difficulty of splitting these into discrete entities and, hence, the necessity to treat societies as complex wholes.
Stakeholder society	A concept associated with the work of Will Hutton and which has been adopted by the 'New' Labour Party. It speaks of the need to spread ownership and opportunities more diffusely within a co-operative version of capitalism.
Underclass	A problematic and contested concept used to refer to a group in modern Britain who, it is claimed, have fallen below the 'normal' class structure and are, as a result, living outside the boundaries of society and its moral code.
Undeserving/ deserving poor	Belief, replicated within social policies from the Elizabethan Poor Law onwards, that among the poor or recipients of welfare are two groups: one deserving of community support because they are worthy or find themselves in difficulties due to circumstances beyond their own control (e.g., widows, orphans, war wounded); the other in a position of dependency as a consequence of their own (inappropriate) behaviour or action, and are thus undeserving of community support. These groups are often disparagingly referred to as 'the work-shy, the malingerers, the idlers', etc.
Universalism	The principle of allocating welfare resources on the basis of contingency experience without the application of secondary criteria such as an income or means test.
Well-ordered society	This is John Rawls's term for a society which advances the interests of all its members and is regulated by a public conception of justice, i.e., a conception of justice about which there is consensual agreement between all the society's socio-economic groups.

Bibliography

1 Introduction

Gil, D. (1973) *Unravelling Social Policy*. New York: Schenkman.
Hutton, W. (1995) *The State We're In*. London: Cape.
Myrdal, G. (1972) 'The place of values in social policy', *Journal of Social Policy*, 1 (1).
Ringen, S. (1986) *The Possibility of Politics*. Oxford: Oxford University Press.
Titmuss, R.M. (1962) *Income Distribution and Social Change*. London: Allen and Unwin.
Titmuss, R.M. (1974) *Social Policy*. London: Allen and Unwin.
Titmuss, R.M. (1976) *Commitment to Welfare*, London: Allen and Unwin.

2 Social Democratic Perspectives on the Welfare State

Commission on Social Justice (1994) *Social Justice: Strategies for National Renewal*. London: Vintage.
Crosland, C.A.R. (1956) *The Future of Socialism*. London: Constable.
Dahrendorf, R., Field, F., Hayman, C., Hutchenson, I., Hutton, W., Marquand, D., Sentance, A. and Wrigglesworth, I. (1995) *Report on Wealth Creation and Social Cohesion in a Free Society*. London: Commission on Wealth Creation and Social Cohesion.
Gray, J. (1996) *Beyond Social Democracy*. London: Demos.
Hall, S. (1984) 'The rise of the representative/interventionist state', in G. McLennan, D. Held and S. Hall (eds), *State and Society in Contemporary Britain: A Critical Introduction*. London: Pluto Press.
Hutton, W. (1995) *The State We're In*. London: Jonathan Cape.
Marquand, D. (1987) *The Unprincipled Society*. London: Fontana.
Mill, J.S. (1972) *On Liberty*. London: Dent.
Minford, P. (1987) 'The role of the social services: a view from the New Right', in M. Loney, R. Bocock, J. Clarke, A. Cochrane, P. Graham and M. Wilson (eds), *The State or the Market: Politics and Welfare in Contemporary Britain*. London: Sage.
Novak, T. (1988) *Poverty and the State*. London: Open University Press.
Tawney, R.H. (1931/1951) *Equality*. London: Unwin Books.

3 Neo-liberalism and the Growth of the 'New Right'

Bacon, R.W. and Eltis, W.A. (1976) *Britain's Economic Problem: Too Few Producers*. London: Macmillan.
Bosanquet, N. (1983) *After the New Right*. London: Heinemann.
Downs, A. (1957) *An Economic Theory of Democracy*. New York: Harper and Row.
Esping-Anderson, G. (1990) *The Three Worlds of Welfare Capitalism*. Oxford: Polity Press.
Gamble, A. (1987) 'The weakening of social democracy', in M. Loney, R. Bocock, J. Clarke, A. Cochrane, P. Graham and M. Wilson (eds), *The State or the Market: Politics and Welfare in Contemporary Britain*. London: Sage.
Geiger, T. (1979) *Welfare and Efficiency*. London: Macmillan.
Gray, J. (1993) *Beyond the New Right*. London: Routledge.
Gray, J. (1994) 'On the edge of the abyss', *The Guardian*, 18 July.

Hall, S. (1984) 'The rise of the representative/interventionist state', in G. McLennan, D. Held and S. Hall (eds), *State and Society in Contemporary Britain*. Oxford: Polity Press.

Hayek, F.A. (1944) *The Road to Serfdom*. London: Routledge and Kegan Paul.

Hutton, W. (1995) *The State We're In*. London: Cape.

Joseph, K. and Sumption, J. (1979) *Equality*. London: John Murray.

Kavanagh, D. (1990) *Thatcherism and British Politics: the End of Consensus?* (2nd edn). Oxford: Oxford University Press.

Keynes, J. M. (1936). *The Central Theory of Employment, Interest and Money*. London: Macmillan.

King, D.S. (1987) *The New Right: Politics, Markets and Citizenship*. London: Macmillan.

Lowe, R. (1990) 'The Second World War, consensus and the foundation of the welfare state', in *Twentieth Century British History*, 1 (2): 152–82.

Lowe, R. (1993) *The Welfare State in Britain since 1945*. London: Macmillan.

Marquand, D. (1987) *The Unprincipled Society*. London: Fontana.

Marshall, T.H. (1950) *Citizenship and Social Class*. Cambridge: Cambridge University Press.

Minford, P. (1987) 'The role of the social services: a view from the New Right', in M. Loney, R. Bocock, J. Clarke, A. Cochrane, P. Graham and M. Wilson (eds), *The State of the Market: Politics and Welfare in Contemporary Britain*. London: Sage.

Nozick, R. (1974) *Anarchy, State and Utopia*. New York: Basic Books.

Plant, R. (1985) *Equality, Markets and the State*. Fabian Trust 495, London: Fabian Society.

Plant, R. (1990) 'The New Right and social policy: a critique', in N. Manning and C. Ungerson (eds), *Social Policy Review 1989/90*. Harlow: Longman.

Pope, R., Pratt, A. and Hoyle, B. (1986) *Social Welfare in Britain, 1885–1985*. Beckenham: Croom Helm.

Seldon, A. (1977) *Charge*. London: Temple Smith.

Self, P. (1993) *Government by the Market? The Politics of Public Choice*. London: Macmillan.

Tawney, R. (1931) *Equality*. London: Unwin Books.

4 Marx and the Marxist Critique of Welfare

Barrett, M. and McIntosh, M. (1980) 'The "family wage": some problems for socialists and feminists', *Capital and Class*, 11.

Birchill, I. (1986) *Baling Out the System*. London: Bookmarks.

Branson, N. (1979) *Poplarism 1919–1925*. London: Lawrence and Wishart.

Bryson, L. (1992) *Welfare and the State*. Basingstoke: Macmillan.

Callinicos, A. (1983) *The Revolutionary Ideas of Karl Marx*. London: Bookmarks.

Callinicos, A. (1987a) *Making History*. Oxford: Polity.

Callinicos, A. (1987b) 'The "new middle class" and socialist politics', in A. Callinicos and C. Harman, *The Changing Working Class*. London: Bookmarks.

Callinicos, A. (1990) *Trotskyism*. Milton Keynes: Open University Press.

Callinicos, A. (1993) *Race and Class*. London: Bookmarks.

Creighton, C. (1980) 'Family, property and relations of production in Western Europe', *Economy and Society*, 9.

Creighton, C. (1985) 'The family and capitalism in Marxist theory', in M. Shaw (ed.), *Marxist Sociology Revisited*. Basingstoke: Macmillan.

Croucher, R. (1987) *We Refuse to Starve in Silence*. London: Lawrence and Wishart.

Cunningham, H. (1990) 'The employment and unemployment of children in England, c.1680–1851', *Past and Present*, 126.

de Ste Croix, G.E.M. (1981) *The Class Struggle in the Ancient Greek World*. London: Duckworth.

Department of Social Security (1995) *Social Security Statistics 1994*. London: HMSO.

Edgell, S. (1993) *Class*. London: Routledge.

Engels, F. (1845) *The Condition of the Working Class in England*. London: Lawrence and Wishart.

Frow, E. and Frow, R. (1970) *The Half-time System in Education*. Manchester: E.J. Moxton.

George, V. and Wilding, P. (1994) *Welfare and Ideology*. London: Harvester Wheatsheaf.

Geras, N. (1983) *Marx and Human Nature*. London: Verso.

German, L. (1989) *Sex, Class and Socialism*. London: Bookmarks.

Gough, I. (1979) *The Political Economy of the Welfare State*. Basingstoke: Macmillan.

Harloe, M. (1981) 'The recommodification of housing', in M. Harloe and E. Lebas (eds), *City, Class and Capital*. London: Arnold.

Harman, C. (1984) *Explaining the Crisis*. London: Bookmarks.

Harman, C. (1991) 'The state and capitalism today', *International Socialism*, 2: 51.

Harman, C. (1993) *How Marxism Works* (4th edn). London: Bookmarks.

Harris, N. (1983) *Of Bread and Guns: the World Economy in Crisis*. Harmondsworth: Penguin.

Hay, J.R. (1975) *The Origins of the Liberal Welfare Reforms 1906–1914*. Basingstoke: Macmillan.

Humphries, S. (1981) *Hooligans or Rebels?* Oxford: Blackwell.

Johnson, N. (1990) *Reconstructing the Welfare State*. London: Harvester Wheatsheaf.

Jones, C. and Novak, T. (1980) 'The state and social policy', in P. Corrigan (ed.), *Capitalism, State Formation and Marxist Theory*. London: Quartet.

Klein, R. (1993) 'O'Goffe's tale', in C. Jones (ed.), *New Perspectives on the Welfare State in Europe*. London: Routledge.

Lavalette, M. (1994) *Child Employment in the Capitalist Labour Market*. Aldershot: Avebury.

Mann, K. (1992) *The Making of an Eglish Underclass?* Milton Keynes: Open University Press.

Marx, K. (1976 [1867]) *Capital*, vol. 1. Harmondsworth: Penguin.

Marx, K. and Engels, F. (1846) *The German Ideology* in *Collected Works*, vol. 5, London: Lawrence and Wishart (1976).

Marx, K. and Engels, F. (1848) *The Manifesto of the Communist Party* (Communist Manifesto), in *Collected Works*, vol. 6, London: Lawrence and Wishart (1976).

Mayer, T. (1994) *Analytical Marxism*. London: Sage.

Melling, J. (1983) *Rent Strikes*. London: Polygon.

Miles, R. (1984) *Racism and Migrant Labour*. London: Routledge.

Mishra, R. (1977) *Society and Social Policy*. London: Macmillan.

Mishra, R. (1984) *The Welfare State in Crisis*. London: Harvester Wheatsheaf.

O'Connor, J. (1973) *The Fiscal Crisis of the State*. New York: St Martin's Press.

Offe, C. (1984) *Contradictions of the Welfare State*. Cambridge, MA: MIT Press.

Rogers, A. (1993) 'Back to the workhouse?', *International Socialism*, 59.

Simon, B. (1960) *Studies in the History of Education*. London: Lawrence and Wishart.

Simon, B. (1968) *Education and the Labour Movement 1870–1920*. London: Lawrence and Wishart.

Squires, P. (1990) *Anti Social Policy*. London: Harvester Wheatsheaf.

Waddington, K. (1974) *Outlines of Marxist Philosophy*. London: Lawrence and Wishart.

Wright, E.O. (1979) *Class Crisis and the State*. London: Verso.

5 Feminist Critiques of Social Policy

Aziz, R. (1992) 'Feminism and the challenge of racism: deviance or difference?', in H. Crowley and S. Himmelweit (eds), *Knowing Women*. Oxford: Polity.

Barrett, M. and McIntosh, M. (1980) 'The "family wage": some problems for socialists and feminists, *Capital and Class*, (Summer): 51–72.

Barrett, M. and McIntosh, M. (1985) *The Anti-Social Family*. London: Verso.

Bart, P. (1971) 'Depression in middle-aged women', in V. Gornick and B. Moran (eds), *Women in Sexist Society*. New York: Basic Books.

Beechey, V. (1985) 'Familial ideology', in V. Beechey and J. Donald (eds), *Subjectivity and Social Relations*. Milton Keynes: Open University Press.

Bernard, J. (1973) *The Future of Marriage*. New York: Souvenir Press.

Beveridge, W. (1942) *Social Insurance and Allied Services*. Cmnd 6404. London: HMSO.

Black, M. and Coward, R. (1981) 'Linguistic, social and sexual relations', *Screen Education*, 39 (Summer).

Campbell, B. (1984) *Wigan Pier Revisited: Poverty and Politics in the 80s*. London: Virago.

Campbell, B. (1987) *The Iron Ladies: Why Do Women Vote Tory?* London: Virago.

Chodorow, N. (1978) *The Reproduction of Mothering*. London: University of California Press.

Crowley, H. and Himmelweit, S. (eds) (1992) *Knowing Women*. Oxford: Polity.

Dalley, G. (1988) *Ideologies of Caring*. London: Macmillan.

Daly, M. (1978) *Gyn/Ecology: the Metaethics of Radical Feminism*. Boston: Beacon Press.

Daly, M. (1994) 'A matter of dependency: gender in British income maintenance provision', *Sociology*, 28 (3), Exeter, British Sociological Association Publications.

Davis, A. (1991) 'Hazardous lives – social work in the 1980s: a view from the Left', in M. Loney, B. Bocock, J. Clarke, A. Cochrane, P. Graham and M. Wilson (eds), *The State or the Market: Politics and Welfare in Contemporary Britain*. London: Sage.

Dinnerstein, D. (1976) *The Rocking of the Cradle and the Ruling of the World*. London: Souvenir Press.

Donzelot, J. (1980) *The Policing of Families*. London: Hutchinson.

Doyal, L. (1985) 'Women and the National Health Service: the carers and the careless', in E. Lewin and V. Olesen (eds), *Women Health and Healing*. London: Tavistock.

Eichenbaum, L. and Orbach, S. (1982) *Outside In, Inside Out*. Harmondsworth: Penguin.

Eisenstein, H. (1984) *Contemporary Feminist Thought*. London: Unwin.

Feminist Review (1988) 'Family secrets: child sex abuse', special issue, 28.

Finch, J. (1988) 'Whose responsibility? Women and the future of family care', in I. Allen, M. Wicks, J. Finch and D. Leat (eds), *Informal Care Tomorrow*. London: Policy Studies Institute.

Finch, J. and Groves, D. (1983) *A Labour of Love: Women, Work and Caring*. London: Routledge and Kegan Paul.

Finkelhor, D. (1983) 'Common features of family abuse', in D. Finkelhor, R.J. Gelles, G.T. Hotaling and M. Straus (eds), (1983) *The Dark Side of Families*. London: Sage.

Firestone, S. (1970) *The Dialectic of Sex: the Case for Feminist Revolution*. New York: Bantam Books.

Foucault, M. (1987) *The History of Sexuality: Volume 1, an Introduction*. Harmondsworth: Penguin.

Friedan, B. (1963) *The Feminine Mystique*. Harmondsworth: Penguin.

Gavron, H. (1966) *The Captive Wife: Conflicts of Housebound Wives*. Harmondsworth: Penguin.

Gilbert, B.B. (1970) *British Social Policy 1914–1939*. London: Batsford.

Gilligan, C. (1982) *In a Different Voice: Psychological Theory and Women's Development*. London: Harvard University Press.

Gittins, D. (1985) *The Family in Question*. London: Macmillan.

Graham, H. (1987) 'Being poor: perceptions and coping strategies of lone mothers', in J. Brannen and G. Wilson (eds), *Give and Take in Families*. London: Allen and Unwin.

Hartmann, H. (1979) 'The unhappy marriage of marxism and feminism: towards a more progressive union', in L. Sergent (ed.), *Women and Revolution*. London: Pluto.

Holdsworth, A. (1988) *Out of the Doll's House*. London: BBC Publications.

hooks, b. (1984) *Feminist Theory: from Margin to Center*. Boston, MA: South End Press.

Jeffreys, S. (1986) *The Spinster and Her Enemies*. London: Pandora Press.

Kelly, E. (1988) *Surviving Sexual Violence*. Cambridge: Polity Press.

Lerner, G. (1979) *The Majority Finds its Past: Placing Women in History*. New York: Oxford University Press.

Lister, R. (1990) 'Women, economic dependency and citizenship', *Journal of Social Policy*, 19 (4) 445–68.

Loney, M., Bocock, R., Clarke, J., Cochrane, A., Graham, P. and Wilson, M. (eds) (1991) *The State or the Market: Politics and Welfare in Contemporary Britain*. London: Sage.

Lewis, J. (1992) *Women in Britain since 1945*. Oxford: Blackwell.

Lewis, J. (1993) *Women and Social Policies in Europe, Work, Family and the State*. London: Edward Elgar Publishing.

Lorde, A. (1984) *Sister Outsider: Essays and Speeches*. New York: Crossing Press.

MacLeod, H. and Saraga, E. (1988) 'Challenging the orthodoxy: towards a feminist theory and practice', *Feminist Review*, 28: 16–25.

Mann, M. (1987) 'Ruling class strategies and citizenship', *Sociology*, 21 (3): 339–54.

Marshall, T.H. (1950) *Citizenship and Social Class*. Cambridge: Cambridge University Press.

Marshall, T.H. (1975) *Social Policy in the Twentieth Century*. London: Hutchinson.

Marshall, T.H. (1981) *The Right to Welfare*. London: Heinemann.

Millar, J. and Gendinning, C. (1987) *Women and Poverty in Britain*. Brighton: Wheatsheaf.

Millett, K. (1971) *Sexual Politics*. New York: Avon Books.

Oakley, A. (1974) *The Sociology of Housework*. London: Martin Robertson.

Pahl, J. (1985) *Private Violence and Public Policy*. London: Routledge and Kegan Paul.

Pateman, C. (1988) *The Sexual Contract*. Cambridge: Polity.

Pateman, C. (1992) 'The patriarchal welfare state', in L. McDowell and R. Pringle (eds), *Defining Women: Social Institutions and Gender Divisions*. Oxford: Polity.

Payne, S. (1991) *Women, Health and Poverty: an Introduction*. Hemel Hempstead: Harvester Wheatsheaf.

Rapp, R. (1979) 'Household and family', in R. Rapp, R. Ross and R. Bridenthal, 'Examining Family History', *Feminist Studies*, 181 (Spring).

Rendall, J. (1985) *The Origins of Modern Feminism: Women in Britain France and the United States, 1780–1860*. London and Basingstoke: Macmillan.

Rich, A. (1977) *Of Woman Born: Motherhood as Experience and Institution*. London: Virago.

Rich, A. (1980) 'Compulsory heterosexuality and the lesbian existence', in *Signs* 5 (4) (Summer 1980): 389–417.

Richardson, D. (1993) *Women, Motherhood and Childhood*. London: Macmillan.

Roll, J. (1992) *Lone Parents in the European Community*. London: Family Policy Studies.

Rowbotham, S. (1969) *Women's Liberation and the New Politics*. Pamphlet.

Rowbotham, S. (1974) *Hidden from History: Three Hundred Years of Women's Oppression and the Fight against It*. London: Pluto Press.

Rowbotham, S. (1989) *The Past is Before Us: Feminism in Action since the 1960s*. Harmondsworth: Penguin.

Ruddick, S. (1980) 'Maternal thinking', *Feminist Studies*, 6 (2) (Summer): 342–67.

Sapsford, R. and Abbott, P. (1988) 'The body politic, health, family and society', in *Family, Gender and Welfare*. Milton Keynes: Open University.

Saraga, E. (1993) 'The abuse of children', in R. Dallos and E. McLaughlin (eds), *Social Problems and the Family*. London: Sage.

Segal, L. (1987) *Is the Future Female? Troubled Thoughts on Contemporary Feminism*. London: Virago.

Segal, L. (1993) 'A feminist looks at the family', in M. Wetherell, R. Dallos and D. Miell (eds), *Interactions and Identities*. Milton Keynes: The Open University.

Social Trends (1994) No. 24, London: HMSO.

Turner, B. (1990) 'Outline of a theory of citizenship', *Sociology*, 24 (2): 189–217.

Walby, S. (1988) 'Gender politics and social theory', *Sociology*, 22 (2): 215–32.

Walby, S. (1994) 'Is citizenship gendered?', *Sociology*, 28 (2): 379–95.

Walkowitz, J. (1980) *Prostitution in Victorian Society: Women, Class and the State*. Cambridge: Cambridge University Press.

Webster Gardiner, G. (1986) 'Putting father back at the head of the table', Press Conference Speech, 14 March.

Weeks, J. (1977) *Coming Out: Homosexual Politics in Britain from the Nineteenth Century to the Present*. London: Quartet.

Wicks, M. (1991) 'Family matters and public policy', in M. Loney, R. Bocock, J. Clarke, A. Cochrane, P. Graham and M. Wilson (eds), *The State or the Market: Politics and Welfare in Contemporary Britain*. London: Sage.

Wilson, E. (1989) 'In a different way', in K. Gieve (ed.), *Balancing Acts: On Being a Mother*. London: Virago.

Yllo, K. and Bograd, M. (eds) (1988) *Feminist Perspectives on Wife Abuse*. London: Sage.

6 Racism and Social Welfare

Ali, Y. (1991) 'Echoes of empire: towards a politics of representation', in J. Corner and S. Harvey (eds), *Enterprise and Heritage: Crosscurrents of National Culture*. London: Routledge.

Benyon, J. and Solomos, J. (eds) (1987) *The Roots of Urban Unrest*. Oxford: Pergamon Press.

Bridges, L. (1994) 'Tory education: exclusion and the black child', *Race and Class*, 35 (1).

CCETSW (1991) *One Small Step Towards Racial Justice*. London: CCETSW.

Cohen, P. (1987) *Racism and Popular Culture: a Cultural Studies Approach*. Working Paper No. 9, Centre for Multicultural Education, University of London.

Department of Education and Science (DES) (1981) *West Indian Children in our Schools* (the Rampton Report). London: HMSO.

Department of Education and Science (DES) (1985) *Education for All: the Report of the Committee of Inquiry into the Education of Children from Ethnic Minority Groups* (the Swann Report). Cmnd 9453. London: HMSO.

Department of Education and Science (DES) (1988) *Education for All*. London: HMSO.

Eggleston, J., Dunn, D., Anjali, M. and Wright, C. (1986) *Education for Some*. Stoke-on-Trent: Trentham Books.

Elton, Lord (1989) *Discipline in Schools: a Report of the Committee of Enquiry*. London: HMSO.

Gill, D., Mayor, B. and Blair, M. (1992) *Racism and Education: Structures and Strategies*. London: Sage.

Gilroy, P. (1987) *There Ain't No Black in the Union Jack*. London: Hutchinson.

Hall, S., Critcher, C., Jefferson, T., Clarke, J. and Roberts, B. (1978) *Policing the Crisis: Mugging, the State and Law and Order*. London: Macmillan.

Institute of Race Relations (1980) *Equal Opportunities: a Report by the ILEA Inspectorate*. London: ILEA.

John, G. (1990) 'Taking sides: objectives and strategies in the development of anti-racist work in Britain', in *London 2000*. London, Equal Opportunities Unit, pp. 68–71.

MacDonald, I., Bhavnani, T., Khan, L. and John, G. (1989) *Murder in the Playground: the Report of the MacDonald Inquiry into Racism and Racial Violence in Manchester Schools* (the Burnage Report). London: Longsight Press.

Oppenheim, C. (1990) *Poverty, the Facts*, London: CPAG.

Palmer, F. (ed.) (1986) *Anti-racism: an Assault on Education and Value*. London: Sherwood Press.

Ranger, C. (1988) *Ethnic Minority School Teachers (a Survey in 8 Local Authorities)*. London: CRE.

Sarup, M. (1991) *Education and the Ideologies of Racism*. Stoke-on-Trent: Trentham Books.

Sivanandan, A. (1991) 'Black struggles against racism', in CCETSW, *Setting the Context for Change*. London: CCETSW.

Skellington, R. (ed.) (1992) *'Race' in Britain Today*. London: Sage.

Solomos, J. (1988) *Black Youth, Racism and the State: the Politics of Ideology and Policy*. Cambridge: Cambridge University Press.

Troyna, B. (1992) 'Multi-cultural and anti-racist educational policies' in D. Gill, B. Mayor and M. Blair, *Racism and Education: Structures and Strategies*. London: Sage.

Wright, C. (1992) 'Multi-racial primary school classrooms', in D. Gill, B. Mayor and M. Blair, *Racism and Education: Structures and Strategies*. London: Sage.

7 Social Policy and Sexuality

Abelove, H., Barale, M.A. and Halperin, D.M. (eds) (1993) *The Lesbian and Gay Studies Reader*. London: Routledge.

Blumenfeld, W.J. and Raymond, D. (eds) (1993) *Looking at Gay and Lesbian Life*. Boston: Beacon Press.

Bristow, J. and Wilson, A.R. (eds) (1993) *Activating Theory: Lesbian, Gay, Bisexual Politics*. London: Lawrence and Wishart.

Cooper, D. (1994) *Sexing the City: Lesbian and Gay Politics within the Activist State*. London: Rivers Oram Press.

Cruikshank, M. (1992) *The Gay and Lesbian Liberation Movement*. London: Routledge.

Evans, D. (1993) *Sexual Citizenship: the Material Construction of Sexualities*. London: Routledge.

Foucault, M. (1978) *The History of Sexuality, Volume 1, an Introduction*. Trans., R. Hurley. Harmondsworth: Penguin.

George, S. (1993) *Women and Bisexuality*. London: Scarlet Press.

Grey, A. (1992) *Quest for Justice: Towards Homosexual Emancipation*. London: Sinclair-Stevenson.

Herman, D. (1994) *Rights of Passage: Struggles for Lesbian and Gay Legal Equality*. Toronto: University of Toronto Press.

Hyde, M. (1970) *The Love that Dared Not Speak its Name: a Candid History of Homosexuality in Britain*. Boston: Little, Brown.

Jeffery-Poulter, S. (1991) *Peers, Queers and Commons: the Struggle for Gay Law Reform from 1950 to the Present*. London: Routledge.

Jeffreys, S. (1990) *Anti-climax*. London: The Women's Press.

Levay, S. (1993) *The Sexual Brain*. Cambridge, MA: MIT Publishing.

Lewin, E. (1981) in Rights of Women Lesbian Custody Group (1984) *Lesbian Mothers' Legal Handbook*.

Logan, J., et al. (1996) *Confronting Prejudice*. Aldershot: Arena.

McIntosh, M. (1975) 'The homosexual role', in K. Plummer (ed.), *The Making of the Modern Homosexual*. London: Hutchinson.

Mason, A. (1994) 'A case for change', London: Stonewall.

Plummer, K. (ed.) (1975) *The Making of the Modern Homosexual*. London: Hutchinson.

Rich, A. (1981) *Compulsory Heterosexuality and Lesbian Existence*. London: Onlywoman.

Rights of Women Lesbian Custody Group (1984) *Lesbian Mothers' Legal Handbook*. London: The Women's Press.

Stonewall (1993) *Less Equal than Others*. London: Stonewall.

Tatchell, P. (1992) *Europe in the Pink: Lesbian and Gay Equality in the New Europe*. London: GMP.

Thomson, R. (1993) 'Unholy alliances: the recent politics of sex education', in J. Bristow and A.R. Wilson, *Activating Theory: Lesbian, Gay, Bisexual Politics*. London: Lawrence and Wishart.

Waaldijk, K. and Clapham, A. (eds) (1993) *Homosexuality: a European Community Issue*. Dordrecht, Netherlands: Martinus Nijhoff.

Weeks, J. (1977) *Coming Out: Homosexual Politics in Britain from the Nineteenth Century to the Present*. London: Quartet.

CHAPTER TWO

When to Start Planning Your Work

For many folks in the research community, the thesis or dissertation for an academic degree is their most important starting point for publication. The students pursuing an academic or professional degree in the United States, however, usually have a heavy load of coursework before they can formally engage in the thesis or dissertation process. In the years of undergraduate studies, the honors students are used to being driven by numerous course assignments, tests, and exams. For the graduate students, their first year of study of the required courses could be even more stressful. For example, the students in a doctoral program should anticipate a qualifying examination, usually at the end of the first year, which will determine their fate in the program. It seems unrealistic to ask the students to talk about their thesis or dissertation before they have secured some good course grades and passed all the exams. In reality, it is not hard to meet students who have been around for quite a while but still have no idea about what they are going to do for their thesis or dissertation.

The British educational system, in contrast, would require the prospective "research students," as so labeled, to submit a proposal for their thesis or dissertation as part of the admission procedures. The required course load for such students, if any, is substantially less than those who will meet their degree requirements mainly by coursework. It seems that those research degree pursuers would be in a better position to get an early start with their project. This is, however, not necessarily the case. On occasion you can find some students who have been in a program for a couple of months or even a few years but are still shopping around and struggling for a "researchable" topic.

Due to the difference in previous experience and level of preparation, some

In a single piece of study, social investigators used to concentrate on either scaling issues or substantive model testing using existing or developed measures. The two modes of research can now be combined into an integral approach to data analysis. Particularly, the simultaneous analysis of measurement and statistical (substantive) models has been a new optimal scaling strategy. Jacoby (1991) describes such an approach, named "Alternating Least Squares, Optimal Scaling (ALSOS)," to data analysis. It is based upon the idea that the measurement characteristics of the data can be regarded as parameters to be estimated during the course of an analysis. As Jacoby (ibid.) writes, this approach "holds that empirical statistical analyses involve two different models of the observations. The first represents the structural relationships between the variables. The second involves the measurement characteristics of the variables" (p.74).

From the point of view of substantive analysis, the study of the relationship between two composite measures may represent different steps beyond canonical analysis on two groups of individual items or "manifest" variables. The immediate step is the introduction of factor analysis, either in its traditional form of exploratory factor analysis (EFA) or in a new structural form of confirmatory factor analysis (CFA). This leads to the exploration or confirmation of the so-called "latent structure" of a data set as opposed to its manifest structure represented by those elementary measurement items or individual variables. Factor analysis has a two-fold function in conceptualization and measurement. When used with path analysis, it leads to the study of the ties that link various latent and manifest variables, which is a detail-oriented and deep-going approach to the study of the relationships among multidimensional constructs. We have talked about data reduction and analysis separately, but here the two tasks are combined together in a simultaneous manner. This kind of method, generally called Factor Analytic Simultaneous Equation Model (FASEM) (Bentler, 1986), has been developing rapidly in recent years. The major idea underlying such methods is to take confirmatory factor analysis "as a submodel of the more general Structural Equation Modeling (SEM) approach" (Pedhazur & Schmelkin, 1991, p.632). Obviously, a causal model based on components or factors ("latent variables") would present a clearer structure of the data than the models solely based on individual indicators (manifest variables). There are now advanced statistical packages capable of integrating path analysis with factor analysis, such as the LISREL program (Jöreskog & Sörbom, 1989) and the EQS program (Bentler, 1985).

Weeks, J. (1981) *Sex, Politics and Society: the Regulation of Sexuality since 1800*. London: Longman.

Weeks, J. (1985) *Sexuality and its Discontents: Meanings, Myths and Modern Sexualities*. London: Routledge and Kegan Paul.

Weeks, J. (1986) *Sexuality*. Chichester: Ellis Horwood.

Weeks, J. (1991) *Against Nature: Essays on History, Sexuality and Identity*. London: Rivers Oram Press.

Wilson, A.R. (1994) *A Simple Matter of Justice? Theorizing Gay and Lesbian Activism*. London: Cassell.

8   'New' Social Movements and Social Policy: a Case Study of the Disability Movement

Abel-Smith, B. and Townsend, P. (1965) *The Poor and the Poorest*. London: G. Bell.

Allen, V.L. (1971) *The Sociology of Industrial Relations*. London: Longman.

Bagguley, P. (1992) 'Social change, the middle class and the emergence of "New Social Movements": a critical analysis'. *The Sociological Review*, 40 (1): 26–48.

Barbelet, J.M. (1988) *Citizenship*. Milton Keynes: Open University Press.

Barnes, C. (1991) *Disabled People in Britain and Discrimination: a Case for Anti-discrimination Legislation*. London: Hurst.

Barnes, C. (1992) 'Institutional discrimination against disabled people and the campaign for anti-discrimination legislation', *Critical Social Policy*, 34 (12: 1) (Summer).

Barnes, C. and Oliver, M. (1995) 'Disability rights: rhetoric and reality in the UK', *Disability and Society*, 10 (1): 111–16.

Barrett, M. and McIntosh, M. (1980) 'The "family wage": some problems for feminists and socialists', *Capital and Class*, 3 (Autumn): 45–66.

Barton, L. (1993) 'The struggle for citizenship: the case of disabled people', *Disability, Handicap and Society*, 8 (3): 235–48.

Berger, P., Berger, B. and Kellner, H. (1974) *The Homeless Mind: Modernisation and Consciousness*. Harmondsworth: Penguin.

Boggs, C. (1986) *Social Movements and Political Power*. Philadelphia: Temple University Press.

Borsay, A. (1986) *Disabled People in the Community*. London: Bedford Square Press.

Brisenden, S. (1986) 'Independent living and the medical model of disability', *Disability, Handicap and Society*, 1 (2): 173–8.

Burrows, R. and Loader, B. (eds) (1994) *Towards a Post-Fordist Welfare State?* London: Routledge.

Bynoe, I., Oliver, M. and Barnes, C. (1991) *Equal Rights for Disabled People*. London: Institute for Public Policy Research.

Cawson, A. (1982) *Corporatism and Welfare: Social Policy and State Intervention in Britain*. London: Heinemann.

Clarke, J. (1992) *New Times, Old Enemies*. London: HarperCollins.

Clarke, J. and Langan, M. (1993) 'The British welfare state: foundation and modernisation', in A. Cochrane and J. Clarke (eds), *Comparing Welfare States: Britain in an International Context*. Milton Keynes/London: Open University/Sage.

Cockburn, C. (1983) *Brothers: Male Dominance and Technological Change*. London: Pluto Press.

Croft, S. and Beresford, P. (1992) 'The politics of participation', *Critical Social Policy*, 35 (12: 2): 20–44.

Dally, G. (1988) *Ideologies of Caring – Rethinking Community and Collectivisn*. London: Macmillan.

Dalton, R.J. and Kuechler, M. (eds) (1990) *Challenging the Political Order: New Social and Political Movements in Western Democracies*. Cambridge: Polity Press.

Diani, M. (1992) 'The concept of a social movement', *The Sociological Review*, 40 (1): 1–25.

Disabled People's International (DPI) (1986) 'DPI-Calling', *European Regional Newsletter*, 1 (March): 21.

Driedger, D. (1989) *The Last Civil Rights Movement: Disabled People's International*. London: Hurst.

Duke, V. and Edgell, S. (1984) 'Public expenditure cuts in Britain and consumption sector cleavages', *International Journal of Urban and Regional Research*, 8: 177–201.

Dunleavy, P. and O'Leary, B. (1987) *Theories of the State*. Basingstoke: Macmillan.

Finch, J. (1984) 'Community care: developing non-sexist alternatives', *Critical Social Policy*, 9 (3: 3): 6–18.

Finkelstein, V. (1993) *Being Disabled*, Workbook One. Open University K665, *The Disabling Society*. Milton Keynes: Open University Press.

Fry, E. (1987) *Disabled People and the 1987 General Election*. London: Spastics Society.

Gamble, A. (1985) *Britain in Decline*. Basingstoke: Macmillan.

Garner, R. and Zald, M. (1985) 'The political economy of social movement sectors', in G. Suttles and M. Zald (eds) *The Challenge of Social Control*. Norwood: Ablex.

Gibson, T. (1979) *People Power: Community and Work Groups in Action*. Harmondsworth: Penguin.

Gilroy, P. (1987) *There Ain't No Black in the Union Jack*. London: Hutchinson.

Ginsburg, N. (1992) *Divisions of Welfare: a Critical Introduction to Comparative Social Policy*. London: Sage.

Gough, I. (1979) *The Political Economy of the Welfare State*. Basingstoke: Macmillan.

Hall, S. and Jacques, M. (1989) *New Times: the Changing Face of Politics in the 1990s*. London: Lawrence and Wishart.

Harrison, M. (1993/94) 'The black voluntary housing movement: pioneering pluralistic social policy in a difficult climate', *Critical Social Policy*, 39 (13: 3): 21–35.

Held, D. (1989) *Political Theory and the Modern State*. Cambridge: Polity/Blackwell.

Hewitt, M. (1993) 'Social movements and social need: problems with postmodern political theory', *Critical Social Policy*, 37 (13: 1): 52–74.

Hildebrandt, K. and Dalton, R.J. (1978) 'The new politics: political change or sunshine politics?', in M. Kaase (ed.), *Election and Parties*. Beverly Hills and London: Sage.

Holmes, C. (1979) *Anti-Semitism in British Society 1876–1939*. London: Edward Arnold.

Laclau, E. and Mouffe, C. (1985) *Hegemony and Socialist Strategy: Towards a Radical Democratic Politics*. London: Verso.

Lash, S. and Urry, J. (1987) *The End of Organised Capitalism*. Cambridge: Polity Press.

Lee, P. and Raban, C. (1988) *Welfare Theory and Social Policy – Reform or Revolution?* London: Sage.

Lustiger-Thaler, H. and Shragge, E. (1993) 'Social movements and social welfare', in G. Drover and P. Kerans (eds), *New Approaches to Welfare Theory*. Aldershot: Edward Elgar.

Marshall, T.H. and Bottomore, T. (1992) *Citizenship and Social Class*. London: Pluto.

McCarthy, J. and Zald, M. (1977) 'Resource mobilisation and social movements: a partial theory', *American Journal of Sociology*, 82: 1212–41.

McIntosh, M. (1981) 'Feminism and social policy', *Critical Social Policy*, 1 (1: 1): 32–42.

Melluci, A. (1980) 'The new social movements: a theoretical approach', *Social Science Information*, 19: 199–226.

Morris, J. (1991/92) ' "Us" and "them"? Feminist research, community care and disability', *Critical Social Policy*, 33 (11: 3): 22–9.

Morris, J. (1992) 'Tyrannies of perfection', *New Internationalist* (theme for July – disability).

Morris, J. (1993) *Independent Lives: Community Care and Disabled People*. Basingstoke: Macmillan.

National Consumer Council (1991) *The Citizen's Charter: Getting it Right for the Consumer*. London: NCC.

Offe, C. (1985) 'New social movements: challenging the boundaries of institutional politics', *Social Research*, 52 (4): 817–68.

Oliver, M. (1990) *The Politics of Disablement*. Basingstoke: Macmillan.

Oliver, M. and Zarb, G. (1989) 'The politics of disability: a new approach', *Disability, Handicap and Society*, 4 (3): 221–39.

Pagel, M. (1988) *On Our Own Behalf: an Introduction to the Self-organisation of Disabled People*. Manchester: Greater Manchester Coalition for Disabled People Publications.

Pfeiffer, D. (1993) 'Overview of the disability movement: history, legislative record, and political implications', *Policy Studies Journal*, 21 (4): 724–34.

Piven, F.F. (1995) 'Globalising capitalism and the rise of identity politics', in L. Panitch (ed.), *Why Not Capitalism: Socialist Register 1995*. London: Merlin.

Piven, F.F. and Cloward, R.A. (1977) *Poor People's Movements: Why They Succeed, How They Fail*. New York: Pantheon.

Plant, R. (1988) *Citizenship Rights and Socialism*. Fabian Tract 531, London: Fabian Society.

Roche, M. (1992) *Rethinking Citizenship: Welfare, Ideology and Change in Modern Society*. Cambridge: Polity.

Rowbotham, S., Segal, L. and Wainwright, H. (1979) *Beyond the Fragments: Feminism and the Making of Socialism*. London: Merlin Press.

Scott, A. (1990) *Ideology and New Social Movements*. London: Unwin Hyman.

Sedgewick, P. (1982) *Psycho Politics*. London: Pluto Press.

Shakespeare, T. (1993) 'Disabled people's self-organisation: a new social movement?', *Disability, Handicap and Society*, 8 (3): 249–64.

Smith, M. (1990) *British Politics, Society and the State*. Basingstoke: Macmillan.

Solomos, J. (1989) *Race and Racism in Contemporary Britain*. Basingstoke: Macmillan.

Spicker, P. (1993/94) 'Understanding particularism', *Critical Social Policy*, 39 (13: 3): 5–20.

Taylor, G. (1993) 'Challenges from the margins', in J. Clarke (ed.), *A Crisis in Care*. Milton Keynes/London: Open University/Sage.

Taylor-Gooby, P. (1994) 'Postmodernism and social policy: a great leap backwards?', *Journal of Social Policy*, 23 (3): 385–404.

Taylor-Gooby, P. (1995) 'In defence of second-best theory: state, capital and class in social policy', Plenary Session Paper, *Social Policy Association Annual Conference*, Sheffield, Sheffield Hallam University (18 July).

Taylor-Gooby, P. and Dale, J. (1981) *Social Theory and Social Welfare*. London: Arnold.

Thompson, S. and Hoggett, P. (1996) 'Universalism, selectivism and particularism: towards postmodern social policy', *Critical Social Policy*, 46 (16: 1): 21–43.

Tilly, C. (1978) *From Mobilisation to Revolution*. Reading: Addison-Wesley.

Tilly, C. (1984) 'Social movements and national politics', in C. Bright and S. Harding (eds), *State-Making and Social Movements: Essays in History and Theory*. Ann Arbor: University of Michigan Press.

Touraine, A. (1977) *The Self-production of Society*. Chicago: University of Chicago Press.

Touraine, A. (1981) *The Voice and the Eye: an Analysis of Social Movements*. Cambridge: Cambridge University Press.

Touraine, A. (1985) 'An introduction to the study of social movements', *Social Research*, 52: 749–88.

Townsend, P. (1986) 'Democracy for the poor', in M. McCarthy (ed.), *Campaigning for the Poor: CPAG and the Politics of Welfare*. Beckenham: Croom Helm.

Turner, B.S. (1986) *Citizenship and Capitalism: the Debate over Reformism*. London: Allen and Unwin.

Turner, R. and Killian, L. (1987) *Collective Behaviour*. Englewood Cliffs, NJ: Prentice-Hall.

Ungerson, C. (1987) *Policy is Personal*. London: Tavistock.

Williams, F. (1992) 'Somewhere over the rainbow: universality and diversity in social policy', in N. Manning and R. Page, *Social Policy Review no. 4*. Canterbury: Social Policy Association.

9   Social Justice and Social Policy

Barry, B. (1972) *The Liberal Theory of Justice*. Oxford: Clarendon Press.
Daniels, N. (ed.) (1975) *Reading Rawls*. Oxford: Basil Blackwell.
Hayek, F.A. von (1960) *The Constitution of Liberty*. London: Routledge and Kegan Paul.
Nozick, R. (1974) *Anarchy, State and Utopia*. Oxford: Basil Blackwell.
Paul, J. (ed.) (1982) *Reading Nozick*. Oxford: Basil Blackwell.
Plant, R. (1984) 'Equality, markets and the state', Fabian Society Pamphlet No. 494.
Pogge, T.W. (1989) *Realizing Rawls*. Ithaca, NY: Cornell University Press.
Rawls, J. (1972) *A Theory of Justice*. Oxford: Oxford University Press.
Sandel, M. (1982) *Liberalism and the Limits of Justice*. Cambridge: Cambridge University Press.
Wolff, R.P. (1977) *Understanding Rawls*. Princeton, NJ: Princeton University Press.

10   Citizenship and Welfare

Adriaansens, H. (1994) 'Citizenship, work and welfare', in B. van Steenbergen (ed.), *The Condition of Citizenship*. London: Sage.
Alcock, P. (1993) *Understanding Poverty*. Basingstoke: Macmillan.
Barbalet, J.M. (1988) *Citizenship*. Milton Keynes: Open University Press.
Barton, A. (1994) 'DIY politics', *The Guardian* (7 October).
Blair, T. (1994) 'Socialism', Fabian Pamphlet No. 565.
Boddy, M. and Fudge, C. (1984) *Local Socialism?* Basingstoke: Macmillan.
Bottomore, T. (1992) 'Citizenship and social class, forty years on', in T.H. Marshall and T. Bottomore, *Citizenship and Social Class*. London: Pluto Press.
Cannan, C., Berry, L. and Lyons, K. (1992) *Social Work and Europe*. Basingstoke: Macmillan.
Cochrane, A. and Anderson, J. (eds) (1989) *Politics in Transition*. London: Sage.
Commission on Citizenship (1990) *Encouraging Citizenship*. London: HMSO.
Cram, L.T. and Richardson, J. (1992) *Citizenship and Local Democracy: a European Perspective*. Luton: Local Government Management Board.
Ditch, J. (1992) 'The undeserving poor: unemployed people, then and now', in M. Loney, R. Bocock, J. Clarke, A. Cochrane, P. Graham and M. Wilson (eds), *The State or the Market Politics and Welfare in Contemporary Britain* (2nd edn). London: Sage.
Field, F. (1981) *Inequality in Britain*. London: Fontana.
Fraser, N. and Gordon, L. (1994) 'Civil citizenship against social citizenship', in B. van Steenbergen (ed.), *The Condition of Citizenship*. London: Sage.
George, V. and Wilding, P. (1984) *The Impact of Social Policy*. London: Routledge and Kegan Paul.
George, V. and Wilding, P. (1985) *Ideology and Social Welfare*. London: Routledge and Kegan Paul.
Ginburg, N. (1979) *Class, Capital and Social Policy*. London: Macmillan.
Ginsburg, N. (1992) *Divisions of Welfare*. London: Sage.
Golding, P. (1986) *Excluding the Poor*. London: Child Poverty Action Group.
Golding, P. and Middleton, S. (1982) *Images of Welfare: Press and Public Attitudes to Welfare*. Oxford: Basil Blackwell and Martin Robertson.
Gough, I. (1979) *The Political Economy of the Welfare State*. London: Macmillan.
Groves, D. (1992) 'Occupational pension provision and women's poverty in old age', in C. Glendinning and J. Millar (eds), *Women and Poverty in Britain: the 1990s*. London: Harvester Wheatsheaf.
Harrison, P. (1983) *Inside the Inner City: Life under the Cutting Edge*. Harmondsworth: Penguin.
Henwood, M. (1992) 'The demographic context', in *Who Owns Welfare?* London: National Institute for Social Work.

Hill, D. (1995) 'Unlevel fields', *The Guardian* (21 March).

Hill, D.M. (1994) *Citizens and Cities*. London: Harvester Wheatsheaf.

Hill, M. (1993) *The Welfare State in Britain: A Political History since 1945*. Aldershot: Edward Elgar.

Hodge, M. (1991) 'Quality, equality, democracy: improving public services', Fabian Pamphlet No. 549.

Howe, D. (1995) as quoted in G. Younge, 'Black in Britain', *The Guardian* (20 March).

Hutton. W. (1994) 'Written constitution would fortify unions', *The Guardian* (5 September).

Ignatieff, M. (1991) 'Citizenship and moral narcissism', in G. Andrews (ed.), *Citizenship*. Chichester: Lawrence and Wishart.

Johnson, R.W. (1985) *The Politics of Recession*. Basingstoke: Macmillan.

Jones, J. (1992) 'Health care costs eroding old people's wealth', *The Independent* (6 October).

Joseph, K. and Sumption, J. (1979) *Equality*. London: John Murray.

Jowell, R. and Airey, C. (1985) *British Social Attitudes: the 1985 Report*. Aldershot: Gower.

Judge, K. (1982) 'The growth and decline of social expenditure', in A. Walker (ed.), *Public Expenditure and Social Policy*. London: Heinemann.

Labour Party (1989) 'Quality Street: Labour's quality programme for Local Government', London: Labour Party.

Lansley, S. Goss, S and Wolmar, C. (1991) *Councils in Conflict: the Rise and Fall of the Municipal Left*. Basingstoke: Macmillan.

Lawrence, R. (1983) 'Voluntary action: a stalking horse for the right?', *Critical Social Policy*, 2 (3).

Le Grand, J. (1982) *The Strategy of Equality*. London: Allen and Unwin.

Lipsey, D. (1992) 'The name of the rose', Fabian Pamphlet No. 554.

Lister, R. (1990) *The Exclusive Society: Citizenship and the Poor*. London: Child Poverty Action Group.

Low Pay Unit (1992) 'Poor Britain – poverty, inequality and low pay in the nineties', LPU Pamphlet No. 56.

Mack, J. and Lansley, S. (1985) *Poor Britain*. London: George Allen and Unwin.

MacQueen, J. (1993) 'Old seek a future with a caring face', *Grey Power* (April).

Marquand, D. (1992) *The Progressive Dilemma*. London: Heinemann.

Marshall, T.H. (1992) *Citizenship and Social Class*. London: Pluto Press.

Mayo, M. (1994) *Communities and Caring*. Basingstoke: Macmillan.

Midwinter, E. (1992) 'Feedback on empowering older people?', *Community Development Journal*, 27 (3) (July).

Modood, T. (1994) *Racial Equality, Colour, Culture and Justice*. London: Institute for Public Policy Research.

Murray, C. (1994) *Underclass: the Crisis Deepens*. London: Institute of Economic Affairs.

Oppenheim, C. (1990) *Poverty: the Facts*. London: Child Poverty Action Group.

Pampel, F.C. and Williamson, J.B. (1989) *Age, Class, Politics and the Welfare State*. Cambridge: Cambridge University Press.

Panorama (1994) 'The age of fear', BBC 1 (10 October).

Phillips, K. (1977) 'The nature of Powellism', in N. Nugent and R. King (eds), *The British Right*. London: Saxon House.

Phillips, T. (1995) as quoted in G. Younge, 'Black in Britain', *The Guardian* (20 March).

Plant, R. (1984) 'Equality, markets and the state', Fabian Tract No. 494, Fabian Society.

Plant, R. (1988) 'Citizenship, rights and socialism', Fabian Pamphlet No. 531.

Roche, M. (1992) *Rethinking Citizenship*. Cambridge: Polity Press.

Smith, J. (1992) 'Opening statement', in J. Smith, B. Gould, M. Beckett and J. Prescott, 'Labour's choice : the Fabian debates', Fabian Pamphlet No. 553.

Steenbergen, B. van (ed.) (1994) *The Condition of Citizenship*. London: Sage.

Townsend, P. (1979) *Poverty in the United Kingdom: a Survey of Household Resources and Standards of Living*. Harmondsworth: Penguin.

Turner, B.S. (1993) *Citizenship and Social Theory*. London: Sage.

Vidal, J. (1994) 'DIY politics', *The Guardian* (7 October).

Walker, A. (1993) 'Poverty and inequality in old age', in J. Bond, P. Coleman and S. Peace (eds), *Ageing in Society* (2nd edn). London: Sage.

Williams, F. (1992) 'The welfare state as part of a racially structured and patriarchal capitalism', in M. Loney, R. Bocock, J. Clarke, A. Cochrane, P. Graham and M. Wilson (eds), *The State or the Market: Politics and Welfare in Contemporary Britain* (2nd edn). London: Sage.

Younge, G. (1994) 'Talkin' 'bout my generation', *The Guardian* (7 October).

Younge, G. (1995) 'Black in Britain', *The Guardian* (20 March).

11   Universalism or Selectivism?

Abel-Smith, B. and Townsend, P. (1965) *The Poor and the Poorest*. London: George Bell.

Bennett, F. (1993) 'Social insurance: reform or abolition', Commission on Social Justice, vol. 1, London: Institute for Public Policy Research.

Boulding, K.E. (1967) 'The boundaries of social policy', *Social Work*, 12 (1): 3–11.

Bradshaw, J. and Wakeman, I. (1972) 'The poverty trap up-dated', in *The Political Quarterly*, 43: 459–69.

Bull, D. (ed.) (1971) *Family Poverty*. London: Duckworth.

Collard, D. (1971) 'The case for universal benefits', in D. Bull (ed.), *Family Poverty*. London: Duckworth.

Commission on Social Justice (1993) 'Making sense of benefits', Commission on Social Justice, staff paper, vol. 2, London: Institute for Public Policy Research.

Commission on Social Justice (1994) 'Social justice: strategies for national renewal', London: Institute for Public Policy Research.

Conservative Political Centre (1950) 'One nation', London: CPR.

Davies, B., with Reddin, M. (1978) *Universality, Selectivity and Effectiveness in Social Policy*. London: Heinemann.

Department of Health and Social Security (1985a) 'Reform of social security', vol. 1, Cmnd 9517; vol. 2, 'Programme for change', Cmnd 9518; vol. 3, 'Background papers', Cmnd 9519 (June), London: HMSO.

Department of Health and Social Security (1985b) 'Programme for action', Cmnd 9691 (December), London: HMSO.

Field, F. and Piachaud, D. (1982) 'The poverty trap', in F. Field, *Poverty and Politics: the Inside Story of the Child Poverty Action Group's Campaigns in the 1970s*. London: Heinemann. (First published in the *New Statesman*, 1971.)

Gunter, R. (1967) *The Sunday Times* (19 August).

Harris, R. with Seldon, A. *Choice in Welfare, 1963, 1965*. London: Institute of Economic Affairs.

Houghton, D. (1967) 'Paying for the social services', Occasional Paper 16, London: Institute of Economic Affairs.

Hutton, W. (1995) *The State We're In*. London: Jonathan Cape.

Lees, D. (1967) 'Poor families and fiscal reform', in *Lloyds Bank Review* (October).

Lowe, R. (1990) 'The Second World War, consensus, and the foundation of the welfare state', *Twentieth Century British History*, 1 (2): 152–82.

Lowe, R. (1993) *The Welfare State in Britain since 1945*. London: Macmillan.

McLaughlin, E. (1994) 'Flexibility in work and benefits', Commission on Social Justice, vol. II, London: Institute for Public Policy Research.

Macleod, I. and Powell, E. (1952) 'The social services: needs and means', Conservative Political Centre, London (updated by Powell, 1954).

Marquand, D. (1967) 'Change gear', *Socialist Commentary* (October).

Meacher, M. (1972) 'The malaise of the low-paid worker', in J. Hughes and R. Moore, *A Special Case: Social Justice and the Miners*. London: Penguin. pp. 92–103.

Owen, D. (1967) 'Change gear', in *Socialist Commentary* (October).

Page, R. (1984) *Stigma*. London: Routledge and Kegan Paul.

Piachaud, D. (1971) 'Poverty and Taxation', *The Political Quarterly*, (January–March), pp. 31–44.

Pinker, R. (1971) *Social Theory and Social Policy*. London: Heinemann.

Pratt, A. (1976) 'The Family Income Supplement: origins and issues', unpublished Master's thesis, University of Salford.

Pratt, A. (1988) 'The Labour Party, Family Income Support policy, and the labour market, 1940–79', unpublished PhD thesis, University of Bradford.

Reisman, D. (1977) *Richard Titmuss: Welfare and Society*. London: Heinemann.

Seldon, A. (1967) 'Taxation and welfare', Research Monograph 14, London: Institute of Economic Affairs.

Seldon, A. and Gray, H. (1967) 'Universal or selective social benefits', Research Monograph 8, Institute of Economic Affairs, London.

Social Security Consortium (1986) 'Of little benefit, a critical guide to the Social Security Act', London: SSC.

Sullivan, M. (1992) *The Politics of Social Policy*. Hemel Hempstead: Harvester Wheatsheaf.

Titmuss, R.M. (1950) *Problems of Social Policy*. London: HMSO.

Titmuss, R.M. (1962) *Income Distribution and Social Change*. London: George Allen and Unwin.

Titmuss, R. M. (1976[1968]) *Commitment to Welfare*. George Allen and Unwin.

Townsend, P. (1972) 'Selectivity: a nation divided', in *Sociology and Social Policy*. London: Penguin. pp. 122–3.

Williams, F. (1992) 'Somewhere over the rainbow: universality and diversity in social policy', in N. Manning and R. Page (eds), *Social Policy Review*, 4, London: Longman.

12 Poverty and the 'Underclass'

Andrews, K. and Jacobs, J. (1990) *Punishing the Poor: Poverty under Thatcher*. London: Macmillan.

Ball, M., Gray, F. and McDowell, L. (1989) *The Transformation of Britain*. London: Fontana.

Brown, C. (1990) 'The focus on single mothers', in C. Murray (ed.), *The Emerging British Underclass*. London: Institute of Economic Affairs.

Campbell, B. (1993) *Goliath: Britain's Dangerous Places*. London: Methuen.

Central Statistical Office (1985) *Social Trends 1985*. London: HMSO.

Central Statistical Office (1994) *Social Trends 1994*. London: HMSO.

Deakin, S. and Wilkinson, F. (1989) 'A new Poor Law? Wages and social security', *Low Pay Review*, 38.

Dean, H. (1991) 'In search of the underclass', in P. Brown and R. Scase (eds), *Poor Work: Disadvantage and the Division of Labour*. Milton Keynes: Open University Press.

Field, F. (1989) *Losing Out: the Emergence of Britain's Underclass*. London: Blackwell.

Gallie, D. (1994) 'Are the unemployed an underclass? Some evidence from the social change and economic life initiative', *Sociology*, 28 (3): 737–57.

Hudson, R. and Williams, A. (1989) *Divided Britain*. London: Belhaven.

Levitas, R. (1986) *The Ideology of the New Right*. Cambridge: Polity Press.

Low Pay Unit (1990) *Low Pay Review*. London: Low Pay Unit.

Macnicol, J. (1987) 'In pursuit of the underclass', *Journal of Social Policy*, 16 (2).

Morris, L. (1994) *Dangerous Classes: the Underclass and Social Citizenship*. London: Routledge.

Murray, C. (1990) *The Emerging British Underclass*. London: Institute of Economic Affairs.

Novak, T. (1988) *Poverty and the State: an Historical Sociology*. Milton Keynes: Open University Press.

Oppenheim, C. (1993) *Poverty: the Facts*. London: Child Poverty Action Group.

Payne, J. and Payne, C. (1994) 'Recession, restructuring and the fate of the unemployed: evidence in the underclass debate', *Sociology*, 28 (1): 1–19.

Pilkington, A. (1992) 'Is there a British underclass?', *Sociology Review* (February): 29–32.
Robinson, F. and Gregson, N. (1992) 'The "underclass": a class apart?', *Critical Social Policy*, 34: 38–51.
Rodger, J. (1992) 'The welfare state and social closure: social division and the 'underclass', *Critical Social Policy*, 35: 45–63.
Smith, D. (ed.) (1992) *Understanding the Underclass*. London: Policy Studies Institute.

13 Quasi Markets and the Mixed Economy of Welfare

Anderson, D.C., Lait, J. and Marsland, D. (1981) *Breaking the Spell of the Welfare State*. London: Social Affairs Unit.
Audit Commission (1986) *Making a Reality of Community Care*. London: HMSO.
Audit Commission (1992) *The Community Revolution: the Personal Social Services and Community Care*. London: HMSO.
Bacon, R. and Eltis, W.A. (1976) *Britain's Economic Problems: Too Few Producers*. London: Macmillan.
Barnett, C. (1986) *The Audit of War*. London: Macmillan.
Bartlett, W., Propper, C., Wilson, D. and Le Grand, J. (eds) (1994) *Quasi-Markets in the Welfare State: the Emerging Findings*. Bristol: School for Advanced Urban Studies.
Bornat, J., Pereira, C., Pilgrim, D. and Williams, F. (eds) (1993) *Community Care: a Reader*. London: Macmillan.
Boyson, R. (ed.) (1971) *Down with the Poor*. London: Churchill Press.
Bradshaw, J. (1992) 'Social security', in D. Marsh and R.A.W. Rhodes (eds), *Implementing Thatcherite Policies*. Buckingham: Open University Press.
Burrows, R. and Loader, B. (eds) (1994) *Towards a Post-Fordist Welfare State?* London: Routledge.
Chamberlayne, P. (1991/2) 'New directions in welfare? France, West Germany, Italy and Britain in the 1980s', *Critical Social Policy*, 33: 5–21.
Clarke, J. and Langan, M. (1993) 'Restructuring welfare: the British welfare regime in the 1980s', in A. Cochrane and J. Clarke (eds), *Comparing Welfare States*. London: Sage.
Clarke, J., Cochrane, A. and McLaughlin, E. (1994) 'Why management matters', in J. Clarke, A. Cochrane and E. McLaughlin (eds), *Managing Social Policy*. London: Sage.
Cochrane, A. (1993) 'Challenges from the centre', in J. Clarke (ed.), *A Crisis in Care? Challenges to Social Work*. London: Sage.
Cochrane, A. and Clarke, J. (eds) (1993) *Comparing Welfare States*. London: Sage.
Commission on Social Justice (1994) *Social Justice: Strategies for National Renewal*. London: Vintage/Institute for Public Policy Research.
Day, P. and Klein, R. (1987) 'The business of welfare', *New Society*, 19 June.
Deakin, N. (1994) *The Politics of Welfare*. London: Harvester Wheatsheaf.
Dean, H. and Taylor-Gooby, P. (1992) *Dependency Culture*. Hemel Hempstead: Harvester.
Department of Health (1989a) *Caring for People: Community Care in the Next Decade and Beyond*. Cmnd 849. London: HMSO.
Department of Health (1989b) *Working for Patients*. Cmnd 555. London: HMSO.
Department of Health and Social Security (1981) *Care in the Community*. London: HMSO.
Dunsire, A. (1990) 'The public–private debate: some U.K. evidence', *International Review of Administrative Sciences*, 56, 1.
Esping-Anderson, G. (1990) *The Three Worlds of Welfare Capitalism*. Cambridge: Polity.
Evandrou, M., Falkingham, J. and Glennerster, H. (1990) 'The personal social services: everyone's poor relation, but nobody's baby', in J. Hills (ed.), *The State of Welfare*. Oxford: Clarendon Press.
Field, F. (1995) *Making Welfare Work*. London: Institute of Community Studies.
Finch, J. and Mason, J. (1993) 'Filial obligations and kin support for elderly people', in J. Bornat, C. Pereira, D. Pilgrim and F. Williams (eds), *Community Care: a Reader*. London: Macmillan.

Forder, J., Knapp, M. and Wistow, G. (1996) 'Competition in the mixed economy of care', *Journal of Social Policy*, 25, 2.

Fowler, N. (1984) *Speech to the Joint Social Services Annual Conference*, 27 September, London: DHSS.

George, V. and Miller, S. (eds) (1994) *Social Policy towards 2000*. London: Routledge.

George, V. and Page, R. (eds) (1995) *Modern Thinkers on Welfare*. London: Harvester Wheatsheaf.

George, V. and Wilding, P. (1994) *Welfare and Ideology*. London: Harvester Wheatsheaf.

Ginsburg, N. (1992) *Divisions of Welfare: a Critical Introduction to Comparative Social Policy*. London: Sage.

Glennerster, H. (1992) *Paying for Welfare: the 1990s*. London: Harvester Wheatsheaf.

Glennerster, H. and Midgely, J. (eds) (1991) *The Radical Right and the Welfare State*. London: Harvester Wheatsheaf.

Gough, I. (1979) *The Political Economy of the Welfare State*. London: Macmillan.

Graham, H. (1993) 'Feminist perspectives on caring', in J. Bornat, C. Pereira, D. Pilgrim and F. Williams (eds), *Community Care: a Reader*. London: Macmillan.

Griffiths, Sir R. (1988) *Community Care: Agenda for Action*. London: HMSO.

Hill, M. (1993) *The Welfare State in Britain*. Aldershot: Edward Elgar.

Hills, J. (ed.) (1990) *The State of Welfare*. Oxford: Clarendon Press.

Hoyes, L. and Means, R. (1993) 'Markets, contracts and social care services: prospects and problems', in J. Bornat, C. Pereira, D. Pilgrim and F. Williams (eds), *Community Care: a Reader*. London: Macmillan.

Johnson, N. (1987) *The Welfare State in Transition*. London: Harvester Wheatsheaf.

Johnson, N. (1990) *Reconstructing the Welfare State*. London: Harvester Wheatsheaf.

Jordan, B. (1987) *Rethinking Welfare*. Oxford: Blackwell.

Joseph, Sir K. (1976) *Stranded on the Middle Ground*. London: Centre for Policy Studies.

Kelly, A. (1991) 'The "new" managerialism in the social services', in P. Carter, T. Jeffs and M.K. Smith (eds), *Social Work and Social Welfare Yearbook 2*. Buckingham: Open University Press.

Klein, R. (1993) 'O'Goffe's tale', in C. Jones (ed.), *New Perspectives on the Welfare State in Europe*. London: Routledge.

Klein, R. and O'Higgins, M. (eds) (1985) *The Future of Welfare*. Oxford: Blackwell.

Krieger, J. (1987) 'Social policy in the age of Reagan and Thatcher', in R. Miliband, L. Panitch and J. Saville (eds), *Socialist Register 1987*. London: Merlin.

Labour Party (1995) *A Policy for Health*. London: The Labour Party.

Langan, M. (1993) 'New directions in social work', in J. Clarke (ed.), *A Crisis in Care? Challenges to Social Work*. London: Sage.

Land, H. (1991) 'Time to care', in M. MacLean and D. Groves (eds), *Women's Issues in Social Policy*. London: Routledge.

Le Grand, J. (1990a) *Quasi-Markets and Social Policy*. Bristol: School for Advanced Urban Studies.

Le Grand, J. (1990b) 'The state of welfare', in J. Hills (ed.), *The State of Welfare*. Oxford: Clarendon Press.

Le Grand, J. and Bartlett, W. (eds) (1993) *Quasi-Markets and Social Policy*. London: Macmillan.

Le Grand, J. and Robinson, R. (eds) (1984) *Privatisation and the Welfare State*. London: Unwin Hyman.

Levacic, R. (1993) 'The coordination of the school system', in R. Maidment and G. Thompson (eds), *Managing the United Kingdom*. London: Sage.

Lewis, J. (ed.) (1993) *Women and Social Policies in Europe*. Aldershot: Elgar.

Light, D. (1991) 'Observations on the NHS reforms: an American perspective', *British Medical Journal*, 303.

London Edinburgh Weekend Return Group (1980) *In and against the State*. London: Pluto.

Lowe, R. (1993) *The Welfare State in Britain since 1945*. London: Macmillan.

Maidment, R. and Thompson, G. (eds) (1993) *Managing the United Kingdom*. London: Sage.

Marsh, D. and Rhodes, R.A.W. (eds) (1992) *Implementing Thatcherite Policies*. Buckingham: Open University Press.

Mayo, M. (1994) *Communities and Caring: the Mixed Economy of Welfare*. London: Macmillan.

Midwinter, E. (1994) *The Development of Social Policy in Britain*. Buckingham: Open University Press.

Mishra, R. (1990) *The Welfare State in Capitalist Society*. Hemel Hempstead: Harvester.

Murray, C. (1984) *Losing Ground: American Social Policy, 1950–1980*. New York: Basic Books.

Murray, C. (1990) *The Emerging British Underclass*. London: Institute of Economic Affairs.

Murray, C. (1994) *Underclass: the Crisis Deepens*. London: Institute of Economic Affairs.

Newman, J. and Clarke, J. (1994) 'Managerialisation of public services', in J. Clarke, A. Cochrane and E. McLaughlin (eds), *Managing Social Policy*. London: Sage.

NHS Management Executive (1992) *The NHS Reforms: the First Six Months*. London: HMSO.

Page, R. (1995) 'The attack on the British welfare state – more real than imagined? A Leveller's tale', *Critical Social Policy*, 44/45: 220–8.

Paton, C. (1990) 'The Prime Minister's review of the National Health Service and the 1989 White Paper Working for Patients', in N. Manning and C. Ungerson (eds), *Social Policy Review 1989–90*. London: Longman/SPA.

Pierson, C. (1991) *Beyond the Welfare State*. Cambridge: Polity.

Pimlott, B. (1988) 'The myth of consensus', in L. Smith (ed.) *The Making of Britain*. London: Macmillan.

Pinker, R. (1992) 'Making sense of the mixed economy of welfare', *Social Policy and Administration*, 26, 4.

Ridley, N. (1988) *The Local Right: Enabling not Providing*. London: Centre For Policy Studies.

Rogers, A. (1993) 'Back to the workhouse?', *International Socialism*, 59.

Rose, R. (1985) *The State's Contribution to the Welfare Mix*, Studies in Public Policy No. 140, Glasgow, University of Strathclyde.

Segalman, R. and Marsland, D. (1989) *Cradle to Grave*. London: Macmillan/Social Affairs Unit.

Sullivan, M. (1992) *The Politics of Social Policy*. London: Harvester Wheatsheaf.

Sullivan, M. (1994) *Modern Social Policy*. London: Harvester Wheatsheaf.

Sullivan, M. (1996) *The Development of the British State*. London: Harvester Wheatsheaf.

Titmuss, R.M. (1963) *Essays on the Welfare State* (2nd edn). London: Allen and Unwin.

Tomlinson, J. (1995) 'Hayek', in V. George and R. Page (eds), *Modern Thinkers on Welfare*. London: Harvester Wheatsheaf.

Walker, A. (1984) 'The political economy of privatisation', in J. LeGrand and R. Robinson (eds), *Privatisation and the Welfare State*. London: Unwin Hyman.

Walker, A. (1989) 'Community care', in M. McCarthy (ed.), *The New Politics of Welfare*. London: Macmillan.

Walker, A. (1993) 'Community care policy: from consensus to conflict', in J. Bornat, C. Pereira, D. Pilgrim and F. Williams (eds), *Community Care: a Reader*. London: Macmillan.

Williams, F. (1989) *Social Policy: a Critical Introduction*. Cambridge: Polity.

Wistow, G. (1992) 'The National Health Service', in D. Marsh and R.A.W. Rhodes (eds), *Implementing Thatcherite Policies*. Buckingham: Open University Press.

Wistow, G. and Henwood, M. (1991) 'Caring for people: elegant model or flawed design?', in N. Manning (ed.), *Social Policy Review 1990–91*. London: Longman/SPA.

The methods mentioned above represent a truly integral and optimal approach to data analysis, with the simultaneous handling of measurement and substantive analysis issues. Taking LISREL, for example, "it is a very versatile approach that may be used for the analysis of causal models with multiple indicators of latent variables, reciprocal causation, measurement errors, correlated errors, and correlated residuals to name but a few" (Pedhazur, 1982, pp.637-38). Nonetheless, as a model of relations of indicators (manifest variables) to interrelated principal components or factors (latent variables), the FASEM approach is too complex for many research applications. Unless the particular purpose is to establish an alleged or hypothetical latent structure of the data set, researchers will gain little either in scale development or in theoretical generalization.

The key fact is that confirmatory factor analysis does not promise any breakthrough in scaling multidimensional constructs. Rather, it seems to demonstrate that a broad concept is actually unscalable in terms of a general measure when more than one component/factor is identified. As Chen (1997) points out, staying at the component/factor level with an obsession in hypothesized latent structures may lead to the denial of the significance or feasibility of any kind of general theoretical constructs. Consequently, a theorist will be disappointed to see her relatively simple ideas always be broken and bogged down in a complicated research model represented by, for example, a FASEM diagram. Indeed, the theorist would be confused because what she expects is but some simple quantitative indication of the actual relationship between her theoretical constructs. Yet almost for certain she will be told by senior research fellows that they cannot help with the apparently too broad or general concepts unless she is going to be fooled by some dull treatments. The hopeless theorist, however, has a cause to appeal to more relevant research. After all, scientific tenets instruct that pertinence, accuracy, and simplicity are the essence of good research approaches.

In real terms, analysis would be of little use if it could not lead to synthesis. If a theoretical construct makes real sense, then it should be scalable since operationalization is nothing but moving back to specific observations. When the interrelationship between and among (rather than within) composite measures is the focal research interest, we need to find a way to generalize not only individual items but also components/factors to overall or comprehensive scales. This will help to maintain the integrity of theoretical constructs, especially in light of uncorrelated components or factors. Chen (ibid.) shows that when structural

Name Index

Subject Index

equations modeling techniques are used for simple path analysis using good global measures of the psychosocial constructs, they would contribute more directly to the development of behavioral and social theories. Specifying only one latent variable in the FASEM model, however, does not necessarily mean a good or the best measure. Chen (ibid.) tries to accomplish this in a general and systematic manner without resorting to the idea of factoring at higher levels. This will help bridge over the gap between the theoretical psychometricians and the practical scale developers.

The Chen Approaches to Unidimensionalized Scaling (CAUS)

In many research situations, the pursuit of the hypothetical latent structure of a data set is not the purpose. Oftentimes, this is treated like a "black box" (no matter what is inside) so that the relationships between and among the composite measures (multidimensional constructs) can be simplified and highlighted.

The significance of dimensional analysis, however, is also recognized. And for some "pure" purpose of research, investigators from all fields may well be satisfied with the results of component/factor analysis, which involves both the clarification and the reduction of dimensionality among a pool of individual measurement items. They can stay with a few dimensions, proceed with the development of some subscales, and look at the targeted substantive relationships based on such measures. A common approach to measurement and analysis is to select a component- or factor-based subscale to represent each construct. In practice, a set of subscales may be used in a single study. The result is a currently mainstream approach using multiple subscale measures (component/factor scores or other component/factor-based subscales). From the findings of such research, recommendations for intervention in various aspects can be generated.

In professional practices and theoretical studies where a clear-cut diagnosis or an overall assessment of the domain is needed, however, these are not enough. Scores on various dimensions or subscales being simply pooled together could give just the same messy presentation as scores on individual measurement items. The selected dimensions as represented by the extracted factors/components may still be too many, though statistically reduced to "the minimum." And more importantly, they vary both in number and in direction (structure) from one particular items pool to another, from case to case and from population to population, which leaves their comparison with each other and with other studies